Little Big Year

Little Big Year

Chasing Acadia's Birds

Richard Wayne MacDonald

Cover photo: Snowy Owl atop Sargent Mountain, Acadia National Park, Maine. Photographed 02 December 2010 by the author.

Back cover author inset: Self-portrait atop Sargent Mountain, 29 August 2020.

Copyright © 2020 Richard Wayne MacDonald

ISBN 978-0-578-82009-5

FIRST EDITION

To Jerry Farrell and J.M.C. "Mike" Peterson,
my birding mentors

My Little Big Year

Probably since at least the time of the Neanderthals, when Ug challenged Magog—"Good sir, I wager ten Saber-toothed Tiger tusks that I am a better hunter than you"—people have been competing. The Olympics, the World Cup, the Tour de France, the Kentucky Derby, the Super Bowl. All are ultimate expressions of human achievement in their respective sports. Heck, even birding, that so-called passive recreational activity of grandmas, grandpas, asthmatic geeks (by the way, that would be me), and home-schooled children, has its own crowning jewel: The World Series of Birding.

What is the World Series of Birding, you may ask?

Each spring since 1984, on a mid-May day, teams of the nation's best birders[i] gather in New Jersey to spend twenty-four hours combing the state, looking for as many species of birds as possible. This singular event may well have done more to inch birding closer to the national limelight than any other single activity. We now know birding (or bird-watching, as some call it) is not just a lifetime hobby. For some, it can be intensely competitive.

In the World Series of Birding, the rules are few and all are bound to the honor system. But, to have an actual crack at being competitive takes incredible knowledge and skills acquired through years of concerted effort. You must be able to identify hundreds of birds by sight—often you only get the merest glimmer of a fraction of a bird—and sound, being able to recognize every single song, call note, flight note, alarm note, chip note. You not only need to know count-less dozens of habitat types, but also be able to quickly identify and locate them. You need to know the time of day a given species is most active, when it is most likely to be singing on territory, when it may be foraging, where it might roost. And you need to link all of these disparate sets of knowledge into a whole in order to strategize your plan of attack so that in twenty-four hours, you and your team can identify over 200 species of birds.

Is there a better way to prove your birding mettle than competing in a twenty-four-hour birdathon? How about a year-long effort to identify as many species of birds as possible?

That would make it a "Big Year"!

According to Wikipedia, that venerable source of knowledge on everything, a big year is "a personal challenge or an informal com-petition among birders who attempt to identify as many species as possible by sight or sound, within a single calendar year and within a specific geographic area."

Birders can choose to report the numbers of birds they have seen across North America, and these numbers are then published annu-ally by the American Birding Association. In 1998, three men—Sandy Komito, Al Levantin, and Greg Miller—unbeknownst to each other, at least at first, set out to set the record for identifying the most species of birds in one year in North America, north of Mexico. Although they were far from the first to do a big year, their effort was immortalized in the 2004 book, *The Big Year*, written by Mark Obmascik. *The Big Year* was later turned into a humorous, if not largely fictionalized[ii], screen adaptation starring Jack Black, Steve Martin, and Owen Wilson. The film not only made the three birders famous, but elevated birding to a more visible level. For a birder, it is practically required watching, being arguably the first movie exclu-sively about birding. Besides, it is really just good, clean fun!

Undertaking a continental "big year" may be many birders' dream, but it is prohibitively expensive! The moment a rare bird shows up, you drop everything and drive or hop on a plane to go see it. To get pelagic seabirds on your list requires going on chartered boats well offshore of both the Atlantic and Pacific coasts. For the significant number of Eurasian birds you'll want to rack up, a trip to Attu Island (the last in the Aleutian chain) is practically mandatory and costs many thousands of dollars. By the end of the year, the best birders will have ticked well in excess of 700[iii] species of birds for their North American list and have spent hundreds of thousands of dollars traveling more than 100,000 miles by air, many tens of thousands of miles by car, hundreds (if not thousands) of miles by boat, and certainly hundreds of miles on foot. And, to top it all off, undertaking a big year leaves a significant carbon footprint.

For those of us goal-driven/data-oriented birders on a budget, surely there must be another way to pursue a big year. Some people restrict their big year to their state. In 2011, Maine Audubon's Doug Hitchcox took the year as a post-college holiday of sorts, crisscrossing the State of Maine, raising the local bar considerably by tallying an impressive 314 species!

But why stop at the state level? Why not tighten the scope even more? Most birders are intimately familiar with their local environs. Enterprising birders can do a big year while never straying far from home, setting some logical boundary that is easily manageable, and offers birding challenges for the whole year. This could mean birding a county, town, local park, or even your yard.

Now, I have never been one to do things "just because." Instead, I am driven by purpose or meaning.

During childhood, when my mother gave an answer any reasonable child could deem unsatisfactory, I would wheedle, "Why? Why, why, why?" The standard reply: "Because I said so." I vowed, if ever fatherhood was in my future, to always explain my reasons when faced with the question, "Why?"

The pursuit of purpose and meaning has permeated my life. For instance, the world of mountaineering has long intrigued me. My brothers—Rob and Ramsey—and I would scale the icy hillside next to our Water Street home, screwdrivers and clawhammers serving as makeshift ice tools, recreating our version of Sir Edmund Hillary's and Tenzing Norgay's fabled exploits on the world's highest mountain. It would seem the mountaineering bug bit early on. Later, living in the Adirondack Mountains of northern New York State, I was surrounded by a community of mountain adventurers. Lecturers routinely came to town. However, one, when asked why he climbed 8,000-meter mountains, gave the answer-without-an-answer: because it was there. He wasn't the first to say this. A year before he perished on Mount Everest in 1924, George Mallory, during an interview with *The New York Times*, replied, "Because it's there," to the question of why did he want to climb the world's highest peak.

"Because it was there" has never been good enough for me.

Maybe it was my childhood self, promising to give my future progeny complete answers, but it has always been important for me to find purpose in the things I do. As a young man, just out of university, I found purpose in my work studying acid rain and climate change. And birds. The next step in my professional path, working for The Nature Conservancy, was filled with purpose working toward preservation of intact landscapes. And birds.

Birds have been a unifying theme throughout my life. At the impressionable age of about ten, I started banding ducks. In college, I could always be found with binoculars at the top of my bookbag. Overlapping with my mountaintop work in the atmospheric sciences, I began working with High Peaks Audubon, monitoring and studying the waterbirds of Lake Champlain. On the side, I began leading bird tours, participating in Christmas Bird Counts, and generally spending all of my time outdoors. No matter what I was doing, you could count on the fact that I would always be listening and looking for birds.

So, when the woman who was quickly becoming my best friend and future wife first told me her dream of pulling together a five-month sea kayak adventure—the Gulf of Maine Expedition—and that it would have an educational mission as its purpose, I was ready to sign up. On that five-month journey I documented birds along the route, tallying 199 species.

Yes, having purpose has always been important to me. And so it was. With 2017 winding down, it dawned on me that the next year was significant for the birds. The year would mark the 100th anniversary of ratification, by the United States of America, of the Migratory Bird Treaty Act. This land-mark legislation, the most significant legislative protection our country ever afforded birds, finally gave federal protection to those hundreds of species of birds that undertake twice-annual north-south peregrinations. Some, such as the American Robin, who do not migrate great distances, can be found during the winter in each and every of the lower forty-eight states. Others, such as the Arctic Tern, work their way clear south to Antarctica. (What joy when I saw some Arctic Terns on the Antarctic Peninsula during my first trip to The Ice in 2013!)

Thanks to the Migratory Bird Treaty Act, it is unlawful, shy an appropriate waiver from the U.S. Fish & Wildlife Service, to pursue, hunt, take, capture, kill, sell, or harass migratory birds, living or dead, in whole or in part, including feathers, eggs, and nests. This protected status applies to more than 800 species of birds.

Alas, with the political climate since 2016, the Migratory Bird Treaty Act (along with the Endangered Species Act, as well as any other legislation designed to offer protections to the natural world) has been under attack. As 2018 wound down, shortsighted appointed leaders within the U.S. Department of the Interior were trying to change one of the key tenets of the legislation: incidental take (which, essentially, means the accidental harming or killing of protected birds). Specifically, they wanted to eliminate any mitigation efforts designed to reduce incidental take. Instead, they turn a blind eye to any and all incidental take peddling it as unfettering business from allegedly stifling regulations.

This could mean corporate owners of open pits of toxic residue, byproducts of some mining and oil extraction techniques, would not be held accountable for the death of waterfowl in their poisonous pools. Nor would owners of wind turbines that kill Golden Eagles and other protected species be held accountable. And energy companies, with millions of miles of transmission wires that kill up to sixty million birds annually, will conduct business as usual.

Instead, all these violators would have to do is say, "Oops, I'm sorry," and hence, no harm no foul.

Despite the current administration's efforts to undermine the Migratory Bird Treaty Act, most consider its centenary worth celebrating. National Geographic, National Audubon, Cornell Lab of Ornithology, and Birdlife International partnered with dozens of other organizations to declare 2018 the "Year of the Bird." Each of these environmental leaders has gone beyond their norm, all in the name of birds. For instance, National Geographic kicked off the year with the January issue of their magazine dedicated to birds.

Closer to home, the State of Maine embarked on a five-year bird atlas, an effort to document the distribution of both its breeding and wintering birds. The Maine Bird Atlas took on particular importance to me as I am one of the regional coordinators.

Breeding bird atlases are citizen science projects designed to engage people in documenting the distribution of breeding birds across large geo-graphic areas. The first breeding bird atlas was completed in 1970 in England[iv] while in the U.S., Vermont was the first state breeding bird atlas[v], con-ducting theirs from 1976—1981. Here in Maine, we were not far behind, completing our first atlas in 1983[vi].

With these events denoting 2018 as a significant year in the world of birds, I felt compelled to do something of my own to celebrate: I embarked on my own big year, albeit on a small scale—a "Little Big Year." My goal was to identify as many species of birds as I could within the confines of Hancock County, Maine.

Hancock County, at 2,345 square miles and with its western boundary nearly marking the centerline of the coast of Maine, extends from the Penobscot River east forty miles to Gouldsboro, Beddington, and Sysladobsis Lake. To the south, Hancock County reaches out into the Gulf of Maine to Mount Desert Rock, twenty-five miles off the coast of Mount Desert Island and Acadia National Park. And the county extends north eighty-five miles, reaching its terminus northeast of Bangor in Passamaquoddy Tribal Trust Lands and logging country.

The county is heavily forested with patches of prime boreal habitat. The coast is stippled with islands. Acadia National Park falls almost entirely within Hancock County. Peninsular features, jutting south into the Gulf of Maine, serve as migrant traps[vii], especially during autumnal migration.

And, finally, this is the county in which I live.

My Little Big Year was not a competition, other, perhaps, than with myself. It was not about seeing the most birds in a year or having the biggest life-list. Instead, it was about learning, setting personal goals, and following them through to completion. It was about heralding in the Maine Bird Atlas. It was about honoring the anniversary of the Migratory Bird Treaty Act. It was about celebrating the Year of the Bird. It was a personal challenge to see as many species of birds as possible within a limited geographic area. It was a reason to explore the northernmost portions of Hancock County, an area virtually unknown to me (especially compared to my grasp of the coastal regions). Most importantly, it was about wholly immersing myself in an ecology that makes me immensely happy and drives my natural history passion.

eBird

Right around Y2K[i], Tim Barnett, my boss and then executive director of the Adirondack Chapter of The Nature Conservancy, received a request from Cornell Lab of Ornithology looking for people to beta test a new citizen science portal for entering bird observations. Being the office bird nerd, it fell to me. And so, over several months, at the end of each workday, I logged my bird sightings into this new electronic portal, transcribing from my field notebook to a desktop computer, and offered feedback to the developers.

It is worth observing that this was in the era before cell-phones and high-speed internet. Today, we are accustomed to 4G networks with download speeds approaching 50 megabits per second. Contrast that to my turn-of-the-century computer with its 28 kilobits per second data transfer rate. That old computer was 1,700 times slower!

After I had been trying eBird for some time, I remember a conversation with Tim that went something like this:

Tim: "So, you have been using eBird for a while now. Do you have a feel for it?"

Me: "Yes."

Tim: "What do you think? Might it be a tool for us to use?"

Me: "This is not going to go anywhere. It's not user
               friendly and adds the extra step of having to tran-
               scribe records from your field notebook to the
               computer. It is particularly difficult to extract infor-
               mation. It will never catch on. Nobody is going to
               want to spend time in front of a computer to enter
               their observations."

Well, I have never been so glad to be so wrong! Today, eBird is
the world's largest citizen science project. According to "Year in Review"[ii], 2017 marks eBird's fifteenth year. In that time, "More than
360,000 eBirders have submitted 472 million bird sightings, repre-
senting 10,364 species across every country in the world."

eBird's purpose is to "document bird distribution, abundance,
habitat use, and trends through checklist data collected within a simple, scientific framework."[iii] In practice, what this means is that you
set up a free account, then enter your observations.

For the average user, the benefits are that eBird allows you to
keep a list of all the birds you see anywhere in the world. There are
robust quality control mechanisms built into eBird to reduce the like-
lihood of egregious mistakes.

If I report one Snowy Owl in Acadia National Park in January,
eBird accepts it without question. However, if seven Snowy Owls
were reported (and I have observed seven at one time!), eBird flags
it as an unusually high number. Likewise, a Snowy Owl reported in
July would be flagged as a date when it does not normally occur. In
both cases, you can either correct your mistake or submit further
information supporting your observation.

As our scientific knowledge of birds and their evolutionary relationships grows, so too does our naming—both common and scientific—of bird species. These changes are automatically reflected in
eBird.

Birders can also use eBird to plan trips or see what birds are in your neighborhood. It engages a new generation of younger naturalists who are seamlessly connected to the digital world.

Furthermore, by reporting your observations to eBird, you are contributing to a better global understanding of many aspects of avian ecology. Everyone has access to this database. Scientists can use it, accessing large pools of data they might otherwise not have the budget to gather for their own research projects. Land managers can use eBird for conservation planning. The potential uses are nearly as vast as our imagination.

Despite my less-than-flattering review of eBird before it was debuted to the public in 2002, I have come around to its value and been a steadfast user ever since. With the power and utility of eBird in mind, I will be using it to document all of my bird observations throughout my Little Big Year.

In the end, eBird is a robust tool that birders of all levels can use to increase their knowledge and skill. Today, it is an intuitive app that works on any smart-phone (and for any luddites out there, it works on desktop computers, too). You should try it; it might just be fun.

Monday, 01 January

New Year's Day.

8:00 a.m.   I hit the snooze button one too many times. Man, do I need more sleep. The friggin' Schoodic Christmas Bird Count is ALWAYS 01 January, the very first day of the new year. For me, New Year's Eve is a time for celebration. A group of my friends drink a few drinks, play a few games (this year, we were introduced to a dice game called Fargo), and solve the nation's problems—hmmm, sounds like a typical night at the Thirsty Whale—and stay up well past midnight. I'm supposed to meet Don Lima and his twenty-year-old son, Kyle, at Winter Harbor in an hour. I need a shower to clear the cobwebs from my head, have to gather binoculars and camera and spotting scope, put together a day's worth of food, and drive forty minutes to the Winter Harbor IGA, our previously-agreed-upon meeting place. The thermometer outside my home office window reads a bitter -14° Fahrenheit. This is going to be a cold one.

Cold on the coast of Maine is not like cold in the Adirondack Mountains of northern New York, where I spent twenty years. There, on a six million-acre outcrop of the Canadian Shield, temperatures can plunge to -20° Fahrenheit during the winter. Cold? Yes, but surprisingly not as biting when it lacks the humidity to sap your heat. Here in Maine, we can rely on Arctic north winds traveling unhindered over long fetches of open saltwater. All this water guarantees high relative humidity, a dampness that further saps heat from any exposed flesh or areas not covered by enough clothing, some-times even seeming as though it will suck out your soul.

Still, it is the first day of my Little Big Year. If I am going to reach my goal of 225 species—a worthy, and better yet, achievable tar-get—intimately getting to know every back road, mountain, and trail in pursuit of seeing as many species of birds as possible, I had to get cracking.

If you are a birder, you likely have the basic tools of the trade: a pair of binoculars and a field guide. You also probably know about, or may have even participated in, a Christmas Bird Count.

The first Christmas Bird Count was held in 1900. Frank Chap-man, author of books on birds, founder and editor of *Bird-Lore*, the official publication of the Audubon Societies, and ornithologist with the American Museum of Natural History in New York City, was appalled with a longstanding tradition known as the "Christmas Side Hunt," where men and boys set forth to blast as many birds and mammals as they could on Christmas day. Whoever had the largest pile of dead animals was declared the winner.

Chapman wanted to offer an alternative to this gruesome event, so he came up with the idea of censusing living birds. His first count, on Christmas day, 1900, had twenty-seven men and women identi-fying and counting birds across thirteen American states and two Canadian provinces, tallying over 8,000 birds of at least eighty-seven species[i].

Now, well over 100 years later, Christmas Bird Counts are annual events that have contributed greatly to our understanding of winter bird populations and distributions. They have also engaged tens of thousands of people across the Western Hemisphere. For instance, during the 117th Christmas Bird Count around Christmas 2016 (the year with the most recent data as of this writing), 73,153 people participated in 2,536 Counts, tallying 56,139,812 individual birds from 2,636 species. WOW!

Today, Christmas Bird Counts are conducted each year between 14 December and 05 January. Each Count is a fixed circle of fifteen miles diameter. And best of all, not only can anyone participate, it's free. Don't worry if you feel inexperienced: Count coordinators try to match teams so that they include veteran and novice birders alike.

9:15 a.m. By the time I pulled into the Winter Harbor IGA, the display on the dash of my new Toyota Sienna minivan read -2° Fahrenheit. Being a northern boy, dressed in layers of L.L. Bean, Patagonia, and Woolrich, I embrace the relatively balmy temperature (all day it will never rise above 4° Fahrenheit). No sign of Don and Kyle yet, so I sling my Canon 7D Mark II camera with the 300 mm prime lens and Opticron DBA 10x42 binoculars over my shoulder, grab my Opticron MM3 60 ED spotting scope, extend the carbon fiber legs of the tripod, and walk across the street.

A Black-capped Chickadee, the state bird of Maine, announces its presence with its onomatopoeic intonation: *chick-a-dee-dee-dee*. My first bird of 2018!

At the water's edge, the temperature differential between water and air has resulted in dense sea-smoke over the frig-id-but-unfrozen water. As beautiful as it is, this fog-like fea-ture of the coastal landscape greatly limits visibility over the open water, limiting the number of birds I might be able to see.

Several hundred feet out, at the edge of the ice, a group of gulls is hunkered down against the cold and wind. They all appear to be the same size with white heads and gray mantles. A careful count reveals ninety-seven Herring Gulls.

Looking through the spotting scope, I carefully scan the roosting gulls in hopes of a "white-winged" gull or two amidst the Herring Gulls. Herring Gulls, the ubiquitous "seagull" of the New England coast, have black wingtips, as do the almost equally common Ring-billed Gulls. In their current aspect, wings folded over their back, the black wing-tips appear as black tails, so birds lacking any black would be either Iceland or Glaucous Gulls, both birds of the High Arctic who come south to places like the relative tropics of Maine for the winter. Alas, no "white-winged" gulls here.

In the meantime, Don and Kyle arrived.

I first met this father/son duo on a Schoodic Peninsula winter field trip I led for the Downeast Chapter of Maine Audubon a number of years before. I instantly bonded with Don. We both have a similar sense of humor, what I call "dad humor," where oft-repeated juvenile jokes never lose their ability to incite mirth (even if we are the only ones laughing). We both have an easygoing manner that is accepting of people at face value. And we both have a love of nature, especially birds. Most importantly, we quickly established I am the elder…by exactly two weeks.

Kyle is now an undergraduate student at UMO—the University of Maine, Orono campus. During the summer of 2015, Kyle worked for me at The Natural History Center. When he first inquired about work, I knew I was going to hire him, but I put him through the entire application process—application, interview, calling references—thinking that it would be an invaluable learning experience for him. Kyle's passion for birds has made him into an incredible birder. The fact that he is just a really nice young man makes it all the better.

The three of us scanned the harbor of Winter Harbor, adding two Bufflehead. A nearby Common Loon dwarfed the Buffleheads. Don turned to look behind us as a lone White-breasted Nuthatch furtively flew into a maple. Two Common Grackle flew overhead, their black bodies highlighted with an iridescent purple sheen about their heads. Four Mourning Doves, fluffed up against the cold, making them look plumper than usual, quickly winged overhead. And a roost of fourteen Rock Pigeons brought my Little Big Year total to six.

Twice a year I am actually pleased to see Rock Pigeon, European Starling, and House Sparrow: at the beginning of the year when I begin my annual count of birds (hey, they all add a tick to the year-list) and again toward the end of May when I conduct a birdathon in efforts to raise money to help the Downeast Chapter of Maine Audubon provide scholarships for local youths to attend summer nature camp. But that is it.

These three species—Rock Pigeon, European Starling, and House Sparrow—in particular, are "non-native, invasive species." This is a phrase that routinely makes the news. According to the U.S. Forest Service, "A species is invasive when it is **both** nonnative to the ecosystem in which it is found and capable of causing environmental, economic, or human harm. Invasive species often compete so successfully in new ecosystems that they displace native species and disrupt important ecosystem processes."[ii] Ecologists further refine the nonnative adjective to relate to those species introduced by humans, whether intentionally or not. Each of these three species have their own unique story of intro-duction to North America.

A.W. Schorger offers an excellent history on the intro-duction of Rock Pigeons[iii] (formerly known as Rock Doves) to North America by early French colonists in Nova Scotia. Schorger quotes historian Marc Lescarbot as writing that in 1606, the only domestic animals in Port Royale, Nova Scotia, were hens and pigeons. Bald Eagles, on the other hand, were plentiful. Lescarbot writes that "[T]here are such a quantity of them [eagles] in those parts that often they ate our pigeons, and we had to keep a sharp look-out for them."

The story of the introduction of the European Starling to North America is a bit muddier[iv] and more recent. What is known is that in 1890, New York pharmacist Eugene Schieffelin orchestrated the release of sixty starlings in New York City's Central Park, followed by an additional forty in 1891. At the time, Schieffelin was chairman of the American Acclimatization Society, a group that wanted to introduce "such foreign varieties of the animal and vegetal kingdom as may be useful or interesting."[v] Many sources consider that Schieffelin was motivated by his ardor for the works of William Shakespeare and wanted to introduce all of the species mentioned by the Bard. For instance, starlings appear in *Henry IV, Part 1*, when Hotspur is in conversation with Northumberland and the Earl of Worcester:

> *I'll have a starling shall be taught to speak*
> *Nothing but 'Mortimer,' and give it him*
> *To keep his anger still in motion.*

(Starlings are noted as something of a mimic and training one to constantly utter "Mortimer" in the ear of King Henry IV would be penance for the king's slander of Hotspur's brother.)

Anyway, from that initial release of 100 birds, the population today of the European Starling is estimated at 200 million birds and they can be found coast to coast and from Hudson Bay to the north, down south into Mexico.

As with the starling, there are various stories concerning the introduction of House Sparrows to North America. Just sixteen House Sparrows from Europe were first introduced in 1852, the first of numerous introductions. Acclimatization societies were a thing during the 1800s and in this case, it was the Cincinnati Acclimatization Society that introduced the House Sparrow, both to eradicate nuisance in-sects and to make immigrants feel more at home through the presence of familiar species.[vi]

This discussion of non-native, invasive species is an important one when considering our impact on the landscape around us. To determine whether a species is native or not depends on your time reference. During the Wisconsin glaciation, when there was a mile and more of ice over Han-cock County, there were no plants or animals, certainly no birds. During the intervening 15,000 years, as the ice re-treated, species returned. And they have been returning ever since.

Species such as House Finch, Turkey Vulture, Northern Cardinal, and Tufted Titmouse have appeared just within the past 100 years, and most of those since the 1960s. But these species have expanded their range under their own power, whereas Rock Pigeons, European Starlings, and House Sparrows arrived with the intentional assistance of people.

It is difficult to assess whether one means of introduction is better than another, but all-too-often, species we intentionally introduce cause irreparable ecological harm.

9:30 a.m.   Once upon a time, there was a sardine cannery in Prospect Harbor, Maine. Workers in this Downeast com-munity made a good living—not a bad thing in an area otherwise known for high unemployment and poverty. Given their location, it was inevitable, if not intentional, that some of the fishy waste ended up in the harbor. For us birders, that was a good thing as it drew in white-winged gulls; namely, Iceland Gulls and Glaucous Gulls. Seeing dozens of these birds in the winter was a sure thing.

But on 18 April 2010, after more than 100 years of processing fish, the clanking machinery ground to a halt, resulting in the closure of the plant. This was the sad result of steadily declining herring stocks, as well as the parent company deciding it was no longer economical to run this, the last cannery in the United States. No more fish processing meant no more food for the white-winged gulls. Still, more out of habit, or perhaps tradition, we stopped in hopes of finding those elusive birds.

No white-winged gulls but we did score American Black Duck, Common Eider, Long-tailed Duck, Red-breasted Merganser, Horned Grebe, American Crow, Golden-crowned Kinglet, Downy Woodpecker, European Starling, Dark-eyed Junco, and American Goldfinch. A highlight of this stop was a Brown Creeper creeping up the trunk of a wind-blasted spruce.

10:07 a.m. Moving further down east we reached the village of Corea, nestled on a secluded, rocky coastline, with waves crashing ashore. This is a place we can reliably find Harlequin Ducks during the winter. Just drive out Cranberry Point Road, park in the big, vacant, paved lot on the landward side, cross the road, walk out the narrow social trail to the rocky ledges, and scan the water, especially where there is surf.

Harlequin Ducks are stunningly beautiful, with a variegated pattern of distinct white patches on a background of slate blue and ruddy brown. They are also amazingly hardy, as they are the daredevils of North American Anatidae, the family of geese, ducks, and swans. Harlequin Ducks breed alongside fast flowing streams of the far north with the majority of the eastern portion of their population wintering along Maine's rocky coast where they show a predilection for diving in crashing surf to feed on marine invertebrates such as mussels and urchins.

Even though the ocean was about as calm as it gets, with no crashing surf for a change, Harlequin Ducks were the first species we found at this locale; fourteen, to be exact. Don, Kyle, and I watched these magnificent birds for easily twenty minutes, looking through our binoculars and taking turns with Don's and my spotting scopes.

Harlequin Ducks were not the only species we added to our list from this vantage; we also saw Common Eider, Common

Goldeneye, two Red-necked Grebe, two Bald Eagles (one adult and one immature lacking the white head and tail), Common Raven, Blue Jay, Mallard, and Ring-billed Gull. Two White-winged Scoter flying past were identified through the heat shimmer coming off the water by their distinct white scapulars (trailing edge wing feathers closest to the body).

Leaving Corea, we saw a Sharp-shinned Hawk, one of our tiniest local raptors, fly across the road with its typical manner of constant-flapping flight.

During the course of the day, as we continued to bird the Schoodic Peninsula, we visited places with names such as Paul Bunyon Road, Grindstone Neck (where we picked up Wild Turkey in the exact same driveway as the year previous), and, of course, the Schoodic Section of Acadia National Park.

At Schoodic Point, the southernmost tip of the Schoodic Peninsula and part of Acadia National Park, the sea-smoke was dense with tendrils blown like armies of wraiths marching across the sea's surface ahead of the stiff northeasterly breeze. As I scanned the limits of my vision, a stocky seabird with an oversized bill flew through the haze, beating its wings like one of those whirligig birds you find in people's dooryards. Razorbill! I was able to get both Don and Kyle on this bird for quick confirmation. Two Black-legged Kittiwakes, wingtips black as though dipped in ink, were flying parallel to the shoreline. The first of the day's Black Guillemots, which could just as easily be called White Guillemots to favor their winter plumage, were constantly diving for sandlance.

Continuing around the Schoodic Loop Road, our penultimate stop was at Blueberry Hill. In all the years of visiting the Schoodic Section of Acadia National Park, with every single visit to Blueberry Hill, I just have to make some crack about finding my thrill[vii]. In terms of birds, the elevated parking lot at Blueberry Hill offers a good vantage of Schoodic Island, nearly half a mile to the east-southeast. For some reason—perhaps it's the remoteness or the windswept barrenness or the availability of just the right foods or some combination of these—Rough-legged Hawks are reliably observed on Schoodic Island every winter. Even at this distance, they are readily identifiable by the dihedral "V" of their wings in flight and the white underwings with the black "wrists." This day we found both light phase and dark phase Rough-legged Hawks working the exposed spine of the island.

Continuing our scan of the area, perched on green can number one, was the day's only Great Cormorant. Four Great Black-backed Gulls were scattered about, one perched on the seabird nesting island sign on Schoodic Island. Black Scoter, ol' butterbill, greatly outnumbered the lone Surf Scoter.

As we made our way to the Park's exit, one last bunch of birds caught our eye. Of course, that meant we had to stop. A duck with its head tucked under a wing was slowly swimming lazy circles. The bird had a dark chest, head (well, at least what we could see of it), and hindquarters with nearly white sides and a slightly less white back. Getting our scopes on it, we realized the head had a bluish cast to it. Lesser Scaup, an unexpected bird this time of year, which brought my year-list to forty.

After parting ways with Don and Kyle, and with less than an hour of daylight remaining, I decided to detour to Marlboro Beach to look for the Dunlin rumored to be there. One day away from the first of January's two "super moons,"[viii] tide was particularly low. With the exposed mud flats liberally strewn with Blue Mussels, it was virtually impossible to find the Dunlin. A group of seventy Herring Gull hunkered down, facing into the cold blow, were just close enough to warrant closer attention. Scanning the birds through my spotting scope, one creamier colored gull got my blood boiling. I watched and watched, waiting for it to move in some way to reveal whether it was a Glaucous Gull or not.

Clammers have to be among the toughest people working the Maine coast (along with every other breed of commercial fishermen).

Fortunately for me, a clammer walked near the gulls, sending them aloft. VOILÀ! The creamy colored gull, which I had already ascertained to be similarly sized to the Herring Gulls, lacked black in the wingtips. It was a Glaucous Gull!

As the day wound down, I reflected on the birds we had observed. In my book, any day when you find Harlequin Ducks, Rough-legged Hawks, Razorbills, or Glaucous Gulls is a good day. And this day, I was privileged to see all four!

One day into my Little Big Year and you may be wondering more about me. Who am I? How did I become so keen on birds? Do I have other interests besides birds? You know, the usual biographical portrait.

I grew up in Lewiston, New York, on the lower Niagara River[ix], that portion of the Niagara below the actual falls and Lake Ontario. As an asthmatic kid, I did not participate in extracurricular sports. Instead, I developed a passion for self-paced pursuits which were immersed in the natural world.

At about ten years of age, local duck biologist, Gerry Farrell, invited me and my brother, Rob, to help band[x] ducks during migration. There is nothing like putting a wild animal in a kid's hands to hook them on appreciating the "ologies" (biology, ecology, ornithology, zoology, dendrology, limnology, and so on). While birds have been a recur-ring theme throughout my personal and professional life, other passions include skiing, paddling canoes and kayaks, photography, and traveling.

Winter was a time when my allergies were virtually nonexistent. Given that allergies were one of many triggers for my asthma, I quickly became more active in the winter: downhill skiing and cross-country skiing. In college, through the outing club, I learned that the two could be combined into telemark skiing. I soon shed my alpine gear in favor of telemark skis, enabling me to explore further into the backcountry, as well as go up and down snow-covered mountains.

I lived in the Adirondack Mountains of northern New York State during college and for nearly twenty years after. My first post-college professional job was with the Atmospheric Sciences Research Center, which enabled me to ski at Whiteface Mountain nearly every day of the season. (If you have ever been to 4,867-foot Whiteface Mountain, you likely saw a four-story silo at the top: that was my office, laboratory, and research site for most of my tenure.)

One of my first purchases upon graduating college was a Fingerling, Mad River Canoe's solo, downriver, Kevlar racing canoe. This sixteen-foot boat opened up all of the Adirondack's waterways to me. It was a short stretch to go from a canoe to whitewater kayaking and then sea kayaking.

It was sea kayaking that brought my wife and me together. She lived in Bar Harbor, Maine; I lived 400 miles away in Keene Valley, New York. In July 2000, during our second date, she shared a dream of paddling sea kayaks around the perimeter of the Gulf of Maine. I told her I was in!

I can imagine Natalie thinking, "Yeah, right." Imagine being on a second date and committing to a five-month, 1,500-mile sea kayak expedition. Well, we did it! Neither of us wanted to do it just "because it's there." Instead, we craft-ed a mission to raise awareness about the ecology of this vast, international watershed and the issues facing coastal communities, as well as to promote kayak safety. It took nearly two years of planning, but we did it, calling ourselves the Gulf of Maine Expedition. And what a success!

Toward the end of the expedition, while sitting on Owls Head Island, east of the Tusket Islands and south of Yarmouth, Nova Scotia, watching the sun set, I proposed to Natalie...and she said yes!

Today, I live in Bar Harbor. Natalie and I have a daughter, Anouk. As of this writing, Anouk is ten. When I talk about birds, she, without exception, chimes in, "Birds, schmirds," or "Birds are boring." Of course, there is a twinkle in her eye, a look which says, "Gotcha, Daddy!"

Since 2010, I have run a nature tour company, The Natural History Center. The Natural History Center leads birding and nature tours from Maine to Newfoundland. I also have the pleasure of working annually as a naturalist on ships going to the Antarctic (including the Falkland Islands and South Georgia Island). For twelve years running, beginning in 2005, Natalie and I coordinated the educational programming on cruise-ships chartered by Garrison Keillor and his radio show, A Prairie Home Companion.

Today's birds of the year:

1. Black-capped Chickadee
2. Herring Gull
3. Bufflehead
4. Common Loon
5. White-breasted Nuthatch
6. Common Grackle
7. Mourning Dove
8. Rock Pigeon
9. American Black Duck
10. Common Eider
11. Long-tailed Duck
12. Red-breasted Merganser
13. Horned Grebe
14. American Crow
15. Golden-crowned Kinglet
16. Downy Woodpecker
17. European Starling
18. Dark-eyed Junco
19. American Goldfinch
20. Brown Creeper
21. Harlequin Duck
22. Common Goldeneye
23. Red-necked Grebe
24. Bald Eagle
25. Common Raven
26. Blue Jay
27. Mallard
28. White-winged Scoter
29. Ring-billed Gull
30. Sharp-shinned Hawk
31. Wild Turkey
32. Razorbill
33. Black-legged Kittiwake
34. Black Guillemot
35. Rough-legged Hawk

36. Great Cormorant	39. Surf Scoter
37. Great Black-backed Gull	40. Lesser Scaup
38. Black Scoter	41. Glaucous Gull

Why are the birds in my list ordered as they are? I have eschewed my usual predilection for taxonomic[xi] order in favor of the order in which the species were first observed this day. This is a pattern I will follow throughout my Little Big Year.

Tuesday, 02 January

I love the beginning of a new year! As someone who keeps track of the birds…

As an aside, on a fairly regular basis I emphatically decry to my wife, I am NOT a "lister." In the birding world, listers are often portrayed in a negative light (especially by non-listers). Driven by nothing but the almighty life-list, they have to see every rare bird, going to great lengths (and expense) to see new birds. When a rare bird turns up, they drop everything to see it. They will travel almost anywhere to see specific birds to add to their life-list.

I, on the other hand, love birds and birding as an activity. In the grand scheme of all things bird, my life-list is not that impressive. I rarely travel beyond an hour's drive from my house with the sole purpose of birding (let me qualify that, I rarely travel beyond an hour's drive from my house with the sole purpose of birding for personal pleasure; I some-what regularly do so as a bird guide, but that is a different beast). I do keep a life-list, but I generally do not chase rare birds when they are reported.

... the beginning of the year is always exciting as you can find new year-birds with virtually every outing. And some of those outings are as easy as going to a friend's house to see a few feeder birds!

Ed and Deb Hawkes have the biggest yard-list of anyone I know. Certainly, this is true for Maine, all of New England, and even New York State. Located near the head of Mount Desert Island, their thirty-eight-acre property fronts Western Bay and includes a significant salt-water wetland. There is a mixed upland forest heavy with White Pine and Red Oak. Their mown yard is landscaped with a variety of shrubby vegetation, including *Rosa rugosa*, or Seaside Rose. The fruit, which they leave on the few heritage apple trees, often lasts until late winter, providing food for members of the finch family. And they feed birds, sprinkling cracked corn on the ground, filling tube and platform feeders with black-oil sunflower seeds or thistle seed, and hang home-crafted suet feeders for the woodpeckers.

Ed bought this property back in the 1970s and has been keeping track of the birds ever since. Ed and Deb's yard-list is a very respectable 150 species of birds.

Ed and I use a similar metric for determining our yard-lists: any bird seen in or directly over your yard can be counted. We also count any bird that we see while standing in our yards. In Ed's case, he counts that Red-throated Loon swimming a quarter mile offshore yet observed clearly through a spotting scope set up in his porch.

To further illustrate how good Ed's yard is for birds, over the years, he has observed Glossy Ibis, White-winged Dove, White-eyed Vireo, Varied Thrush, and Green-tailed Towhee, all actually in his yard. I routinely make birding pilgrimages there. I even bring people who are on my birding tours to see his yard. Of course, Ed always invites them in for tea!

8:27 a.m.   I made a quick perusal of Ed's yard. Nothing too exciting, but ticks for my Hancock County Little Big Year list include some birds I expected: Hairy Woodpecker, Red-breasted Nuthatch (how the heck did we NOT see one the previous day, I'll never know), White-throated Sparrow, and Northern Cardinal.

Next up, Marlboro Beach, to look for some previously reported Dunlin.

9:12 a.m.   Marlboro Beach, in the town of Lamoine, is on the mainland, across Mount Desert Narrows from Mount Desert Island. This glacial outwash plain affords the opportunity to drive right down to the water's edge and bird from the comfort of your car. With a stiff northeasterly breeze making it feel much colder than the already cold 1° Fahrenheit, that is a good way to bird.

After parking, we eventually decided it was time to brave the elements and so Ed and I walked for about five minutes, scanning the high tide shoreline for any sign of Dunlin. I was wishing I had followed Ed's lead and put hand-warmers in my gloves. We were just about to turn around when he spotted movement in the wrack line (wrack being that line of desiccated seaweed pushed up to the high tide line—in this case, it was way, way up, indicating the height of the highest of the high tides, those tides caused by the super moons, like we had overnight). Horned Lark!

Horned Lark have an extensive range across much of North America[i], extending from coast to coast and from Mexico up to the High Arctic. Horned Lark can be found within the continental United States and Mexico year-round. While in the Arctic, they only breed. Here in Maine, Horned Lark is a bird you find in winter in open habitat such as beaches, meadows, farmlands, and alpine summits.

We observed this beautiful bird with the bright yellow facial markings for a while, then walked back to the heated comfort of my minivan....

Minivan, ugh! I still hear the riotous laughter of Tom and Ray Magliozzi, from National Public Radio's weekend show, Car Talk, when they used to mock minivans as the "wussification of the American male." That may be, but minivans are an incredibly practical vehicle, not to mention darn comfortable. And for me, my 2017 Toyota Sienna offers the amenities people expect on my birding and nature tours.

… Next, I grabbed my camera and walked back to snap some photos. I enjoy photography and the technology of my Canon 7D Mark II helps with the quality of my efforts. As I was photographing the bird, a second Horned Lark seemed to materialize out of nowhere. It is truly amazing how well birds can be camouflaged, even when you are looking directly at them.

After twenty minutes of looking, we gave up on the Dunlin. There is always tomorrow, right? We started driving out when Ed shouted, "STOP! I have the Dunlin!"

Not ten feet away, hunkered down at the water's edge, were three Dunlin, seemingly unconcerned by our presence. We observed the birds for several minutes when again, like the Horned Lark, two more seemed to materialize out of nowhere. In the fifteen minutes we watched them, we noticed one had icicles dripping off its rear end. That had to be one cold Dunlin!

Dunlin are a shorebird, a medium-sized sandpiper, who, despite a drab winter plumage, are readily identifiable by their long and slightly decurved (curving downward) bill. These birds breed in the High Arctic, along the very northernmost reaches of North America, then migrate across much of the continent to winter on small stretches of both coasts.

10:46 a.m. One more stop for the day. Several King Eider had been reported frequenting the shoreline of Acadia National Park's Ocean Drive over the past several weeks with the most recent report coming yesterday from local birder, Craig Kesselheim, on New Year's Day!

Ed and I birded the two-mile Ocean Drive[ii]. We stopped several times to set up our spotting scopes and carefully scan the water, looking at every single Common Eider we could find, but with no sign of the King. We did tally an impressive nineteen species, but mostly those you would expect to see on the ocean this time of year. The one notable exception was a Razorbill. Even though I had one at Schoodic Point the day before, I never tire of seeing these wonderful alcids.

Near the end of Ocean Drive, shortly before we were to turn off onto Otter Cliffs Road, we drove through a stand of Black Spruce bracketing the road. At first glance, we took a small, chunky bird feeding on grit[iii] in the road to be a Dark-eyed Junco. In birding, there is one important mantra to always keep in mind: you have to look at every bird. And so we did. Look at the bird. Fox Sparrow!

This is a large sparrow (as sparrows go) with a reddish hue. And it should have been considerably further south by now. Craig did report seeing it yesterday but somehow it had slipped under our radar as a target for today.

Well, there it was! Another bird for the year-list, which now stood at forty-eight, almost halfway to another benchmark: try to identify 100 species before finding my first warbler in the spring.

Today's birds of the year:

42. Hairy Woodpecker
43. Red-breasted Nuthatch

44. White-throated Sparrow
45. Northern Cardinal

46. Horned Lark
47. Dunlin

48. Fox Sparrow

Wednesday, 03 January

This morning, after a minor outpatient medical procedure at the MDI Hospital, Natalie picked me up. Knowing she is always game to see King Eiders, I suggested a detour on our way home to go in search of the bird.

10:42 a.m.   We arrived at the parking lot for Acadia National Park's Sand Beach. Normally, I am quite sure-footed, but being under doctor's orders to take it easy (what with the lingering effects of anesthesia), coupled with the cement steps to the beach in-filled with packed snow, I clung to the handrail with a death-grip. I was determined to stay upright...and I did. Searching from the beach we found the usual suspects—Common Eider, Common Loon, Horned Grebe, Black Guillemot, Herring Gull, and American Crow. We continued. Drive. Stop. Bird (as in the verb).

Along Ocean Path (the walking trail paralleling Ocean Drive), there is a new pullout with a wooden railing to keep you from falling off this elevated lookout. It did not take long scanning through the spotting scope, looking at each and every Common Eider, to finally find one that had a blue-gray head, black back, and a very different bill.

The male King Eider is a magnificent seaduck! It has a black back (whereas the male Common Eider's is white), which makes it easily discernable at a distance. But it is the head that is particularly striking: jutting from the pearl blue head is a red bill with a yellow-orange knob that looks regal, if nothing else, likely the source of its royal name.

These birds nest on the tundra and range to both coasts for the winter[i]. In Maine, they are relatively uncommon but during the winter, a few can always be found somewhere along our 350-mile-long coast.

While scoping the King Eider, a stocky bird with rapidly whirring wings flew by. It was clearly smaller than the King Eider. Meanwhile, its counter-shading marked it as an alcid, in the puffin family. And that is exactly what it was: an Atlantic Puffin! While puffins nest on the coast of Maine, they are quite rare in the winter....

The story of the Atlantic Puffin is a good one. By 1900, puffins were extirpated from Maine, pushed away by a combination of egg collection and harvesting, hunting, habitat change, and introduction of grazing sheep to nesting islands. In 1977, a young scientist named Steven Kress hatched the idea of using a combination of puffin decoys and broadcasting sound recordings of existing colonies, coupled with the physical relocation of some puffins from Newfoundland to Eastern Egg Rock, an offshore island in Maine's Muscongus Bay[ii].

And it worked! But it took a few years to start seeing puffins return on their own. Which is to be expected as puffins usually don't start breeding until their fifth year after hatching.

Today, puffins now nest on at least six[iii] of Maine's 4,600 or so coastal islands. You might wonder where do they go the other eight months of the year when they are not on the nesting islands? Ornithologists are only just beginning to figure this out!

In recent years, scientists attached geolocators to the legs of several puffins. These are tiny devices that allow them to download spatial data revealing the movements of the device, and hence, the bird. Of course, this means that you have to recapture the bird with the geolocator in order to collect the data. Fortunately, puffins return to the same islands, if not the same nesting burrow. Still, some of these tags may fall off, while others could be lost when a puffin succumbs to predation.

The first year of geolocator returns revealed a small number of puffins far offshore from New York and New Jersey, but one was found to have gone to the Bahamas (smart puffin, right?).[iv]

Now, a few more years' worth of data has been collected and scientists are seeing a pattern: puffins seem to migrate to an area hundreds of miles off the New York/New Jersey coast. This area has a bathymetry of deep canyons and seamounts that deflect deep ocean currents into areas of upwelling, bringing nutrients to the surface. With the nutrients comes an explosion of food.

One further intriguing fact is that puffins are able to drink seawater directly. Then they employ a natural salt regulation system, using both their kidneys and a specially evolved salt gland, to filter out the sodium and keep just the water to satisfy their metabolic needs.[v]

This fact enables young puffins to stay at sea for several years, that is, until they reach breeding maturity. Then they make their own brief visit to a nesting colony and attempt to attract a mate and raise their own family.

... As we finished looking at the King Eider and turned back to the car, a female Pileated Woodpecker very cooperatively flew into a nearby tree for some exploratory excavations. These birds look more prehistoric than most. With a decades-old physical scar from one boring into my hand when I pulled it out of a net prior to banding it, I have been up close and personal enough to have a well-formed opinion on the matter.

All-in-all, not a bad morning for an hour's outing.

Today's birds of the year:

49. King Eider
50. Atlantic Puffin

51. Pileated Woodpecker

Thursday, 04 January

James Bond's Birthday!

Another day, another bird. Today, I decided to do a little town-based birding. And what birds do I anticipate finding in Bar Harbor to add to my Little Big Year list? House Finch and House Sparrow. Not that these are difficult to find, but hey, it is fun to front-load the year-list. With a serious winter storm forecast to start precipitating what may be a foot of snow, I thought I had better get birding while the birding is good.

9:24 a.m.   I parked at the end of Albert Meadow, intent on walking a loop through town and back along the Shore Path[i]. The breeze quickly freshened. And when coupled with single-digit temperatures, it was downright chilly. (Silly me, why didn't I wear any long underwear?)

Up Albert Meadow I strolled, dipping on the Gray Catbird reported the day before. No worries, this is a common bird in the summer, so I will eventually find one. Down Main Street with nary a House Sparrow in sight—now that is downright unheard of—but seventy-some Rock Pigeons hunkered on a rooftop at least were a diversion. I could always hope for a marauding Peregrine Falcon to stir things up.

The Town Pier was deserted. When the harbormaster looked out his window and saw this stranger with binoculars and a long-lensed camera rig slung off his shoulder, he must have wondered who would be so bold as to brave the conditions. That, or he knew it was just a birder.

At the end of the pier, I realized it was not as deserted as I had thought: five Common Loons in winter plumage were parading, periodically diving and coming up with Green Crabs and unidentifiable fish. A variety of ducks and gulls rounded out the avian menagerie.

As I began my walk down the Shore Path, the Bar Harbor Inn on my right, the Town Beach on my left, a mother and her young son, perhaps three years old, playing, was a heartening sight. It was almost a page out of the Norwegian playbook that has children outside every day regardless of the weather. (In Norway, everyone is raised with the adage, "There is no bad weather, just bad clothing.")

Rounding the corner, the glacial erratic known locally as Balanced Rock is a striking landmark. It was also offering a bit of shelter to a group of seven Purple Sandpipers sitting out the frigid northeasterly[ii] wind.

Purple Sandpipers are circumpolar High Arctic nesters, nesting further north than any other species of shorebird. The entire North American population nests on those large Arctic islands north of the mainland—islands such as Ellesmere Island and Baffin Island, all names integral to the history of Arctic exploration—and they regularly winter on rocky shorelines, stone jetties, and groins, from Atlantic Canada to South Carolina. Although I have seen Purple Sandpipers at this location before, I'm most accustomed to seeing them on more exposed rocky shorelines such as Acadia National Park's Ocean Drive and Schoodic Point.

Continuing along the Shore Path, at Grant Park, one last scan of Frenchman Bay revealed a more delicate-looking loon holding its bill at a thirty-degree angle. Red-throated Loon! If you overlap breeding range maps of both Red-throated and Common Loons, it is almost as if fitting two pieces in a puzzle, with the Red-throated Loon's range fringing the northern margins of the continent and the Common Loon's largely filling in the rest of Canada and some of the northern states. Curiously, Red-throated Loons defy two loon stereotypes: they don't carry their young on their backs and they can take flight from land, not needing an aquatic runway.

I was ready to get out of the cold for a bit but not quite ready to call it quits. I just had to find at least one House Sparrow. I mean, they are an ever-present part of the village of Bar Harbor's avian landscape. I had tapped my usual haunts—the banks, the Post Office, Hannaford Supermarket—all to no avail. Well, there is one nearby yard and feeder worth checking on Elbow Lane.

So, I drove just around the corner from the feeder and parked. As soon as I opened my door, the familiar scolding call of a Song Sparrow took me by surprise—not the hoped-for House Sparrow, but a bird for my Little Big Year check-list all the same. And then there was a second Song Sparrow. But they were not scolding me; rather, they were scolding a skulking cat. Song Sparrows are abundantly common during the warmer months, but it is not entirely unusual to see one or two of these hardy birds in the winter.

Finally, at the yard with the feeders I was pleased[iii] to see a passel of House Sparrows, thirty-five to be precise. And in amongst them were six House Finches. Check and check.

Any similarity between these two species ends with their love of birdseed and being a species out of place. House Sparrows, members of the Old World Sparrows, were introduced to North America in 1851. These beautiful-but-pesky sparrows are aggressive to other bird species and have been known to evict Eastern Bluebirds, Purple Martins, and Tree Swallows from their nest cavities. Meanwhile, the House Finch is a bird of the Southwest that was introduced to Long Island, New York, in 1940. Ever since, its population has been expanding, reaching Hancock County probably by the 1960s.

We love our pet cats. Unfortunately, any domestic cat that is let outside kills birds. And domestic cats can yield feral cats, which kill more birds. There have been a number of reputable studies[iv] estimating the impact of domestic cats on birds. Researchers Scott Loss, Tom Will, and Peter Marra estimated the number of birds killed annually by cats at between 1.3 and 4 billion! Furthermore, they estimated the number of mammals killed annually by cats at between 6.3 and 22.3 billion!

There are several takeaways from this, and other, research: cats should be kept indoors. Or, do as my friend Lynn Havsäll does, walk your cat on a leash. Feral cats need to be better managed. Scientific studies have shown that feral cat colonies serve as magnets for more cats, often growing in size, and that maintaining them does not help native species.

None of this is to suggest we should get rid of cats, only that we have a responsibility to be kind stewards of all our native wildlife.

10:51 a.m.   Driving home from Bar Harbor, just over an hour from high tide, I passed over Northeast Creek. At 13.3 feet, this tide will be the second highest of the month (the high tide over night was 0.2 feet higher[v]). For Northeast Creek, this meant that as I drove by, the water level was already as high as a normal tide. There was a small lead of open water, perhaps a few hundred square feet, where the constriction of the culvert under Route 3 creates a current exacerbated by the tides, thus preventing freezing.

My eye is always drawn to this spot to look for birds and this time, six Hooded Mergansers—three each males and females—were my reward. Look forward: no cars; look in the rearview mirror: no cars. So, I pulled over, did a quick U-turn, and went back to watch these beautiful birds for several minutes. They were actively feeding, diving constantly and coming up with small fish.

If Red-breasted Mergansers, with their spiky feather crests, are the punk rockers of the bird world, then the male Hooded Merganser is Marie Antoinette or Jacky Kennedy, all sharing a bouffant headdress. There are so many facets of the Hooded Merganser that makes it a particularly intriguing species. Females can lay up to thirteen eggs, but sometimes they will lay their eggs in the nest of another Hoodie. That could explain why nests have been reported with as many as forty-four eggs!

For anyone that has ever watched a nature documentary, chances are you have seen day-old precocial Hooded Merganser chicks climb up the inside of their next cavity or box, then freefall to the ground (sometimes up to fifty feet below, their thick downy covering cushioning the impact), where momma merg will queue them up and march them to the nearest body of water.

Anytime you drive by a small body of water, take a look. That small, seemingly nondescript duck you see out there might just be a Hooded Merganser.

Today's birds of the year:

52. Purple Sandpiper
53. Red-throated Loon
54. Song Sparrow
55. House Sparrow
56. House Finch
57. Hooded Merganser

Saturday, 06 January

When a dog is part of your family, it needs to go out several times a day. When it is 8:00 in the morning, the sun has been up for just under an hour, and the thermometer reads a grizzly -21° Fahrenheit, someone has to volunteer for doggy duty. This morning, I offered to be the day's martyr. Fortunately, we have three acres of mostly forested land with a network of trails for Fogo to stretch his legs. So, while he is doing his thing in the woods, I am birding. More often than not, this means enjoying chickadees, nuthatches, and kinglets.

8:01 a.m.   This morning, no Black-capped Chickadees were garrulously *chickadee*ing away. No Red-breasted Nuthatches were creeping down the trunks of trees looking for hidden morsels. No Golden-crowned Kinglets were doing whatever it is they do to survive the bitter cold.

So much of bird-watching could more aptly be labeled bird-listening. Walking in the woods, or anywhere for that matter, I always have at least one ear attuned to the infinitely varied sounds of our feathered friends. Was that *spring's here* call more wheezy than usual: it could be a Boreal Chickadee rather than its tamer Black-capped cousin? Did I hear a faint peep just the other side of the rocks? In the winter, it is very likely a Purple Sandpiper. How about the soft tapping on wood? In their pursuit of food, Black-backed Woodpeckers do more flaking of bark than the boring of holes. As a result, the sound of their bill on wood is more quiet than any of our other local woodpeckers.

So, when a series of quick, harsh *jips* suddenly interrupted the quiet, I knew it was a flock of Red Crossbills flying overhead. While I never saw anything more than a few small silhouettes against the bright sky, the call was diagnostic. Check, another bird for my Little Big Year list.

Every species of bird is intriguing in its own right. Here in Maine, the crossbills may just take the cake. Both the Red Crossbill and the White-winged Crossbill have evolved bills with tips that actually cross, akin to crossing your fingers. This unique evolutionary adaptation is specifically designed to enable them to prise open their primary food: cones of conifers, especially spruce and pine.

Crossbills' numbers are tied to the cone crop. When cone yields are high, crossbill populations go up. An abundant cone crop means less time is required to find enough food to survive and more time can be spent in the care of young. In such a situation, crossbills will extend their breeding season, even into the depths of winter.

We do not think of birds as farmers, but crossbills are! They are known to prune conifers with the clear intent of planning ahead for even more food. Using their powerful bills, they will clip the bud at the end of a branch, biting it cleanly off. The following year, where they clipped the bud, new growth forks, creating multiple buds. And, by extension, there will be multiple cones.

Crossbills are so dependent on conifer cone crops that they tend to be highly mobile, moving to where food is abundant. For us, it means that we might see either of the crossbill species year-round, for a number of years, and suddenly, they seem to be gone. If that happens, check out your nearest conifer forest. Chances are there are no cones.

Today's bird of the year:

58. Red Crossbill

Monday, 08 January

For the first time in nearly three weeks, the thermometer climbed out of the single digits and well into the 20s Fahrenheit—simply balmy. It was lightly snowing, a wonderful powder that surprisingly added up to about four inches. School was on a two-hour delay because of slippery roads. What to do? Why, go birding (after skate-skiing around the 3.3-mile Witch Hole Pond Carriage Road loop with Fogo), of course.

In recent days, Fred Yost, U.S. Fish & Wildlife Service fisheries biologist, had reported a Northern Pintail at Green Lake National Fish Hatchery. As this is an uncommon species in Hancock County, it is possible to miss it during a year of birding, so I thought it worthy of the chase.

12:55 p.m. Northwest of Ellsworth, turning north off Route 1A onto Route 180, the road conditions had deteriorated. No worries, just drive slowly. The Fish Hatchery is four miles down a very snowy road with snowbanks several feet high. Green Lake was clearly frozen. All ducks need open water, so this did not bode well for finding the Northern Pintail.

Turning into the Fish Hatchery, I could see a bunch of dabbling ducks huddled in a small lead of open water. Without getting out of the minivan, a quick scan of the ducks revealed one with a long, thin neck. Bingo! Northern Pintail, readily identified by both the thin neck and the white stripe winding part way up the back of the brown head.

I stayed and watched for a good fifteen minutes, observing their feeding and social behavior. Pintails feed by dabbling, tilting their body, head down, tail up, to browse on aquatic plants, crustaceans, worms, and snails. This pintail was sometimes amiably paddling along with the Mallards and American Black Ducks, other times aggressively chasing them. Meanwhile, as I was looking around, four Wild Turkeys, their backs sprinkled with the fresh snow, were settled in the upper third of a maple, seemingly too big to be supported by branches of such thin diameter. All of a sudden, I heard the wing noise from eight Mallards, twelve American Black Ducks, one Northern Pintail, and four Wild Turkeys all taking flight. This could only mean one thing: eagle! Sure enough, a Bald Eagle swept through. Fortunately for the ducks (and turkeys), this eagle did not make a meal of them this time.

Since I was already out birding, I decided to drive to Penobscot to look for Harold Shaw's Red-bellied Woodpecker.

1:15 p.m.   On my way to Penobscot, a municipal snowplow turning around in the middle of the road briefly caused traffic to stop in both directions on Route 1 at the Christian Ridge Road stop sign. This interruption turned out to be a good thing: my first American Robin of the year flew across the road, not ten feet in front of my windshield, landing in a shrubby Winterberry.

1:49 p.m.   My friend, Harold Shaw, had been reporting a Red-bellied Woodpecker at his Penobscot feeders for several weeks (Harold is relatively new to birding but has really taken to it, regularly reporting his observations to eBird). This woodpecker normally is found year-round in an area bounded by the mighty Mississippi River, the Gulf of Mexico, the Atlantic Ocean, and southern New England. For reasons ornithologists have not discerned, we can almost always find some Red-bellied Woodpeckers scattered around Hancock County (as well as the rest of Maine) throughout the winter and into early spring. This is well north of their usual range. Perhaps this un-explained behavior has to do with young birds being evicted by their parents and other adult birds from their natal territories and the only area left is beyond their known breeding range.

While I am fairly certain to find one before the year is out, an old adage comes to mind: "A bird in the hand is worth two in the bush." Somehow, though, I don't think it quite means observing a bird to-day versus tomorrow, but there is a corollary there.

Harold was not at home but his wife Sue (whose efforts in the fifteen or so years I have known her have made her quite the birder, especially when it comes to identifying them by sound) invited me in to their 1820 farmhouse to sit at the comfort of their dining room table which was set up against a large bay window looking out on their network of feeders. There were the usual winter suspects, at first: chickadees and nuthatches and juncos and goldfinch. Both Downy and Hairy Woodpeckers came to the suet feeder. When they are side-by-side as they were, it is easy to see their differences: Down-ies are substantially smaller with a much smaller bill proportional to their body size.

Four American Tree Sparrows feeding on the ground below the feeders were another first-of-the-year (or FOY) for my year-list. A lone European Starling came to the heated water bath. Three Tufted Titmice were another FOY. Several White-breasted Nuthatch were intoning their raucous and nasal *ank, ank, ank*. Blue Jays were trying their best to be the bully....

Blue Jays have a habit of bombing into a feeding station, flaring their wings, scattering the other songbirds. I have long thought of them as bullies, but I was to learn that, like all bullies, all you have to do is stand up to them. Mike Peterson did that (stand up to Blue Jays, that is).

In 1989, I started working as a part-time warden for the Four Brothers Islands Preserve, in the "broad lake" of Lake Champlain, between Willsboro, New York, and Burlington, Vermont. My supervisor, Mike Peterson[i], who also became one of my most significant mentors, was a master bander. I regularly helped him band countless thousands of birds over a span of nearly twenty years, whether at The Four Brothers, at his house, or at the Crown Point State Historic Site spring migration bird banding station.

Whenever he caught a Blue Jay, he liked to show it who was boss. After extracting the bird from the mist net and slapping on a size 2 band, he would flip it over onto its back and stroke its belly, calming the bird. The Blue Jay would go limp, as if to say, "I'm sorry, I'll behave." Then, Mike would pull a pencil out from behind his ear, hold it parallel to the ground, and lower it into the relaxed toes of the humbled jay. Perhaps as reflex, the ignoble jay would quickly close its feet, firmly grasping the pencil in a death-grip. Mike would slowly raise the pencil with the jay hanging from it, immobile, then begin to whistle *The Daring Young Man on the Flying Trapeze* while swinging the bird back and forth. As he wound down the song, he would give the pencil a gentle flourish, sending the bird flying for the nearest cover.

… In ones and twos, a flock of thirty-one Mourning Doves quickly showed up, taking over much of the available feeding area on the deck, at the water bath, and on the platform feeder.

And then the Red-bellied Woodpecker made an appearance. Normally, when I see these guys, they are in trees or at suet feeders. Previously, I had never observed a Red-bellied Woodpecker drinking at a water bath but, in fact, that was what this one chose to do. When you think about it, it makes sense: they need a source of water. I had just assumed they satisfied their water requirements from their primary diet of insects, spiders, and arthropods.

After a long while of watching the host of birds, they all took off like the proverbial bat out of hell. I looked and looked, knowing that this behavior was most certainly caused by some predator. Sure enough, a Cooper's Hawk performed its flap-flap-glide routine through the wide-open back yard, landed briefly in an old apple tree, then, realizing all the prey had vacated the premises, took off for parts unknown. (By the way, the Coop was my sixty-fourth species for my year-list.)

Not a bad day, picking up six species for the year.

Today's birds of the year
:

59. Northern Pintail
60. American Robin
61. American Tree Sparrow

62. Tufted Titmouse
63. Red-bellied Woodpecker
64. Cooper's Hawk

Wednesday, 10 January

Throughout the off-season (that is, November through April), my nature tour business—The Natural History Center—offers a Weekly Birding Tour most Wednesday mornings. After a weeks-long cold spell, it was good to get out in more moderate temperatures (18° Fahrenheit); certainly a more moderate temperature than the single digits we had been experiencing.

To enhance my Little Big Year bird count, I use some of my Weekly Bird Tours to target specific species of birds while still offering participants a (hopefully) great birding experience[i]. The focus of this day's outing was Black-backed Woodpeckers, which are occasionally found at The Nature Conservancy's Blagden Preserve on Indian Point, here on Mount Desert Island.

8:22 a.m.   Carol & Wally Muth, Jane Potter, and I arrived at the Blagden Preserve trailhead. Blagden Preserve offers a wonderful alternative to the better-known and more popular trails of Acadia National Park. Very few people visit, so we almost always have the trails to ourselves, especially this time of year.

The 1.2-mile Big Wood Trail traverses the preserve's 110-acre forest, made up mostly of mature Black Spruce which is representative of how the forests on the eastern half of MDI[ii] would have been had they escaped the ravages of the Great Fire of 1947[iii]. The northwestern edge of the preserve fronts Western Bay for over 1,000 feet. At the far western edge of the waterfront, a series of ledges are visible at almost all tides (a pair of binoculars helps in scanning them). Every single time I have perused them, I have always observed Harbor Seals hauled out. Very cool! The return trip is up the private Higgins Farm Road back to the parking lot.

This was a productive outing. From the get-go, we were finding Red-breasted Nuthatches and Black-capped Chickadees.

Tramping through the snowy woods, trying to keep our footfalls in the old snowshoe tracks to save us from sinking in up to our knees, the dusting of fresh powder yielded a treasure trove of animal signs. Lines of White-tailed Deer tracks stippled the forested landscape. Red Squirrel tracks stitched the arboreal interstices. Snowshoe Hare tracks occasionally followed the same snowshoe tracks we were treading. And below a few of the spruce, the snow was sprinkled with shredded cones and twig tips, likely the work of a hungry horde of crossbills.

Closer to the ocean, the forest transitions from one comprised almost exclusively of spruce to a mixture of conifers and hardwoods. This change in habitat greatly increased the diversity of birds, adding Downy and Pileated Woodpeckers, Blue Jays, American Crows, and American Goldfinch to the mix. Some of us even had a brief look at a lone Brown Creeper[iv] skulking up the trunk of a large White Pine.

At the sea's edge, even before we saw them, large numbers of Long-tailed Duck were audible, continuously squabbling their repetitive call, *ararat, mount ararat*. Carol called out, "There are two seals!" We all immediately found her "seals," except that one of them spy-hopped, poking its head up and out of the water to get a better view of us funny-looking bipeds. These were no seals: they were two River Otter!

While I was in the process of pulling my spotting scope out of my backpack, five American Black Ducks flew by, seeming to be in more of a hurry than usual. The ducks had barely passed when Carol once again called out, "Hawk!" We all looked up just in time to see a large, long-tailed raptor powerfully winging by.

It was all gray above, heavily barred below, with a bold, white supercilium (the technical term for the white stripe above the eye). All of these features readily identified this bird as a Northern Goshawk. According to the All About Birds website entry for goshawk[v], the name derives from the "Old English word for 'goose hawk,' a reference to this raptor's habit of preying on birds." Usually I find goshawks during the breeding season as I inadvertently walk into their territory: they are aggressively territorial and make a vigorous defense.

Whether the bird was hunting the ducks or just happened to fly by at that very moment, finding an otherwise secretive Northern Goshawk certainly capped an already good day, even if we went away sans Black-backed Woodpecker.

Today's bird of the year:

65. Northern Goshawk

Saturday, 13 January

A low pressure system had been building, raising temperatures well above freezing, maxing out in the 50s Fahrenheit. Overnight, this system brought extremely high winds accompanied with rain. A LOT of rain! The foot of heavy, packed snow on the ground was completely wiped out. The rain and melting snow combined caused flooding in low-lying areas . . . including our basement. ACK!

So, my family's plan to get out for a hike became the race to drain four inches of water from our basement and then dry everything before winter returned. This was NOT the way I had hoped to spend a three-day weekend.

Soaked carpet remnants were dragged outside, water mopped, and metal shelving propped so that our six fans could move air around to speed the drying process. With the dehumidifier working overtime, I finally decided to make the short, four-mile jaunt to Hancock County-Bar Harbor Airport to see if I might find something interesting in the grassy meadows surrounding the runways.

12:33 p.m. If you were a bird from the Arctic tundra and came south in search of food, you would likely look for familiar terrain: flat open areas covered in short vegetation. Sounds like an airport to me.

13 January

From past experience, I knew that heading down Caruso Drive offered a few perks, such as good views of the area within the fence encompassing the airport, easy parking along the shoulder of the road, and very little traffic.

There is one swale, in particular, that seems to routinely produce birds. And so it was that when I turned off the car, I could almost immediately hear the high-pitched music of a flock of foraging Snow Buntings. These guys are skittish. Or maybe it is just that they are frenetic, perhaps the avian equivalent of hyperactive, driven by the need to constantly move, find food, and eat. With a little patience, I found the small flock, watched as it took wing, flew a short distance, and settled, disappearing in the grass. The next time they moved, a Horned Lark was the first bird I saw. Then there were the flashes of white of all the Snow Buntings.

Back in the late 1980s, not long out of college, I worked for the Atmospheric Sciences Research Center. We had a field station atop 4,867-foot Whiteface Mountain, the fifth tallest peak in New York State's Adirondack Park. During the summer months, it was an easy, six-mile drive from our offices and laboratories at the old Marble Mountain ski lodge (Marble Lodge, the original Whiteface Mountain ski lodge), up the Whiteface Veteran's Memorial Highway, to the four-story summit research silo. In the winter, the road was closed and our regular transportation was a Snowcat.

One of my colleagues (who I'll refer to as "Mark" to avoid embarrassment for those involved) and I routinely made the drive up the mountain together. In my mind, I likened the two of us to Abbott and Costello: he was the strait-laced, articulate, intelligent Boston boy to my inveterate rural New York State small-town, sheltered kid. After several years of working together, Mark started to become curious about my obsession with birds. (It should be noted that Mark was quite a skilled climber, on both rock and ice, with all of the requisite gear, including technical clothing, such as Patagonia bunting jackets. Do you see where this is going?)

I began giving him bite-sized birding lessons, little things he could focus on and retain. What was the relative size of the bird? Small like a chickadee? Medium sized like a robin? Big like hawk? Really big and it is likely an eagle. Where was it? On the ground? In a tree? Lower on the mountain? Nearer the summit? What was the shape of the bill? Thick, powerful, seed-crunching like a finch? Even thicker and more powerful? It may be a grosbeak (remember, this was back in the days when Evening Grosbeaks were commonplace).

Over some period of weeks, all the while sharing my knowledge of bird identification and behavior—Mark took to calling our time together Birding 101 with Rich. One day, as we were rounding the Wilmington Turn at an elevation of about 4,000 feet, he called out that there were some birds in the road. "What are they?"

"You tell me," replied me the teacher.

As he pulled up his binoculars, Mark said, "Let's see, they are small, but bigger than a chickadee. A LOT of white on the body but the back is more brownish. Looks like a finch-like beak. What could it be?"

I handed over my trusty *Peterson Guide to Eastern Birds* (the pocket-sized version, back in the days when they still made their book in the smaller format) and told him to look through it and find his bird....

While contemporary interest in natural history goes back hundreds of years to the great gentlemen, and gentlewomen, naturalists of the eighteenth century, field guides lagged. The first popular field guides designed for the masses were not developed until the early 1890s. Each author tried to develop their own style, something that would make their guide stand out, but their vision was limited, perhaps constrained by the times.

Finally, in 1934, a young man named Roger Tory Peterson published a revolutionary field guide to the birds. A talented artist, Peterson raised the bar, portraying birds clearly, employing arrows to point out key identifying field marks. With his first guide, he almost single-handedly made birding approachable for everyone. For the next seventy years, having the Peterson imprimatur on a field guide was a guarantee for success.

For me, as a young birder, my key requirement for a field guide was that it fit in my back pocket. Peterson field guides did that handily. Plus, I really, REALLY liked the arrows.

Toward the end of the 1990s, Houghton Mifflin, publisher of the Peterson guides, made a decision I have never understood: they increased the size of their guides to the point they no longer fit in one's back pocket. When the convenience of size went out the door, so too did my brand loyalty, liberating me to be more objective in my choice. After careful deliberation, I felt National Geographic published the best bird guide at that time.

In 2000, the next real leap in birding (at least, to my way of thinking) came with the release of David Allen Sibley's first guide to birds. Sibley was a modern Peterson, a talented artist and a gifted observer of the natural world. His guide offered a fresh take on the art of birds. His timing didn't hurt either, what with the popularity of birdwatching taking off, and with it, a surging demand for a diverse offering of field guides in an attempt to quench our thirst for knowledge.

Today, there are seemingly countless different field guides available, many with big names associated—Audubon, Crossley, Kaufman, Peterson, Sibley, and Stokes, to name a few. The reality is that they are all good. Now, when people ask me which field guide to get,

I suggest going to your local bookstore and flip through several. If one has illustrations you prefer, consider that as your guide of choice.

... Eventually, Mark hesitantly asked, "Is it a Snow Bunting?"

BINGO!

Now, this is the part where Rich the practical joker couldn't resist....

"This is an amazing find! Snow Buntings are incredibly rare outside the Arctic. They have evolved special hollow feathers which retain their body heat with incredible effectiveness; so much so that they can comfortably withstand the frigid temperatures of the polar night. They also have amazing powers of propagation, sort of like lemmings: one pair breeding in the early summer will lay up to eighteen eggs. Most of those young survive to also have a clutch of eighteen eggs that season. Meanwhile, the original parents will lay a second, and often a third clutch of eggs, most all of which survive through the summer. And each of those young can produce a clutch or two. By the end of the Arctic summer, one pair of Snow Buntings can turn into more than 5,000 birds! This incredible fecundity is important as so very few survive the winter."

"Knowing all this," I continued, "Yvon Chouinard [of Patagonia clothing fame] pays Inuit hunters a bounty to collect these birds and send him the skins so that he can process their feathers, turning them into bunting jackets."

Well, Mark was beside himself with this newfound knowledge. He kept looking at his Patagonia bunting jacket with particular interest. After our day's work, we returned to Marble Lodge.

As was our collective habit, the research staff stayed long after the regular 9-5 staff had left. We were sitting around on the couches in the great room, looking out the picture windows across the Wilmington Valley and toward the Sentinel Range, sipping Saranac beers. Mark couldn't wait to tell everyone about our exciting find up on the mountain.

"You guys won't believe what we saw today! We saw Snow Buntings! You know, like Yvon Chouinard uses to make bunting jackets. Did you know how fecund these birds are, with a logarithmic reproductive success. Why, one pair of birds can lead to over 5,000 birds a season! And then the Inuit go and harvest them to sell to..."

And then he stopped talking.

Everyone was looking at him as if he had grown a second head. It was at that moment Mark realized it. He looked at me, sitting there, head down, trying to hide my ear-to-ear grin. He had been had.

Yeah, I got him good.

By the time I returned home from the airport, the temperature was dropping. From a high of nearly 50° Fahrenheit in the morning, it would dip back into the single digits overnight.

1:53 p.m.   It was a relatively balmy 29° Fahrenheit. Fogo, our Goldendoodle, begged to go outside, so I took him for a lap around the path in our woods. A particular eighty-foot White Pine dominates our property and it is adorned with a healthy cone crop. A chorus of *jip jip jip*s sang out from the top of the pine. Crossbills!

Wait, these sounded a bit more musical than the typical *jip jip jip*s to which I am accustomed. Good thing I always carry my binoculars when I take Fogo out. Scanning the treetop, I eventually discerned a bunch of red finches with crossed bills. And there it was: the bold, white, double wingbar of the White-winged Crossbill. Another first of the year.

Today's birds of the year:

66. Snow Bunting   67. White-winged Crossbill

Monday, 15 January

Reverend Dr. Martin Luther King, Jr., Day.

"Free at last! Free at last! Thank God Almighty, we are free at last!"

Few words from our American history are as instantly recognizable as this final line from Martin Luther King, Jr.'s, famous "I have a dream..." speech[i]. And few are as important. King had an oratory eloquence to which most of us can only aspire. Every year, on this day, I listen to his inspiring speech, and each time, I am both moved and motivated by this great American hero. Thank you, Martin Luther King, Jr., for your leadership and the sacrifices you made.

Being Martin Luther King, Jr., Day meant no school for Anouk. Previously, Mary Lyman (who runs an after-school art program in which Anouk participates) had polled her students' parents about whether she should run the program this day. The kids LOVE Mary and learn so much about art from her, so a resounding yes was a ringing endorsement. With a 3:30 p.m. drop-off and a 5:00 pick-up, Natalie and I suddenly had a window of time to ourselves. What to do? Why, go birding, of course!

3:42 p.m.   Maine Coast Heritage Trust is one of our local land trusts. They have a wonderful network of preserves sprinkled around

Mount Desert Island. Their Blue Horizons Preserve, not far from where we dropped off Anouk for her art class, offers a peaceful walk through a mixed coniferous/deciduous forest with trails meandering down to Clark Cove. The recent rain entirely eliminated our snow, so we had an easy walk to the shoreline cottages, then continued on the northern loop trail.

During our two-mile walk, the birds were relatively quiet, save for a few that are familiar to us. The gentle staccato tapping of a lone Downy Woodpecker greeted us at the trailhead. Two American Crows could be heard cawing in the distance. Not far down the trail, a Mourning Dove was plaintively *hoo-hoo*ing. We encountered a total of four Black-capped Chickadees during our entire walk. As we approached the cottages, the distinctive *ararat, mount ararat* of two Long-tailed Ducks were audible. At another point, after the sun had set, two Red-breasted Nuthatches and two Golden-crowned Kinglets, along with a solo Dark-eyed Junco, made up a mixed foraging flock gleaning unseen (to us) food from the crevices in the tree bark and amongst the needles at the end of the branches of some spruce.

Making our way back, Natalie suggested a detour down the side trail that heads west to Clark Cove. I had never been down this trail, so I was game. When we reached the water, I scanned the stillness of the cove in the fading light. Six ducks feeding a few hundred feet away against the other shore were distinguishable.

What I could make out of the three males was a dark chest, head, and rear with the middle third of the bird much lighter in color. The bright white flanks stood out. The back was not jet black, so that ruled out Bufflehead and Ring-necked Duck. The lack of white cheek patches meant it could not be one of the goldeneyes. That left one of the scaups.

There are two scaups: Lesser Scaup and Greater Scaup. As a crude rule of thumb, Lesser Scaup tend to be found more regularly—when it is found at all—on freshwater, while Greater Scaup tend to frequent more saline waters.

The "gizz" of the bird, or the general impression of size and shape[ii], spoke Greater Scaup to me. Going through the mental checklist of field marks, it may be easiest to describe this bird with a side-by-side comparison:

Greater Scaup	Lesser Scaup
In profile, head stockier, more rounded	In profile, head taller and narrower
Viewed from front or back, head much wider with a sharply defined angle between wide cheek and narrower upper head	Viewed from front or back, cheeks and upper head are both narrower, so the angle between them is much closer to a straight line
Forehead appears slightly peaked	Back of head seems to have a slight peak
May have a greenish sheen to head	Head may have dark blue or purple sheen

Finally, according to eBird, of the two scaups, Greater is the one we are more likely to find in these parts this time of year. While range eBird frequency of occurrence is not definitive, it is a good guideline.

All that said, we had confirmed Greater Scaup.

Today's bird of the year:

68. Greater Scaup

Saturday, 20 January

S aturday morning, the one-year anniversary of the famous Women's March in Washington, D.C. This time last year, untold thousands of women, men, and children gathered around the country (in Washington, D.C., the epicenter of the national demonstration, over 200,000 people marched) to continue their laudable efforts to protest the inhumanity of our current administration. I had planned to head to Miramichi, New Brunswick, to lead a "Guided Mistle Thrush" trip, but departure was postponed for a day. Natalie was off to this year's Women's March in Augusta; Anouk had a triple play-date lined up. Oh no, what ever will I do with myself?

Why, go birding, of course! This was an easy decision. For me, nature is paramount. During my five-plus decades, it has been central to both my vocation and avocation. I feel at peace with the world when out in nature.

Birding is more than looking at little feathered creatures. It is also a time and a means to connect with some of the people important in my life. While birding, we talk about life, the universe, and everything.

Today, I reached out to my friend Don Lima. Don is "essential personnel" with the U.S. Fish & Wildlife Service. With a Federal government shutdown looming, that means he needed to work until such time as our elected officials miraculously get their act together and wrangle the votes for a continuing budget resolution. However, Don said his son Kyle, an excellent birding companion in his own right, had the weekend free before heading back to school at UMO[i].

And so it was, on this important day, I took to observing the natural world with a college age fellow bird nerd, looking for birds, watching their behavior and interactions, taking in their beauty.

We hatched a plan to visit Winter Harbor for white-winged gulls, drive the Loop Road on the Schoodic Peninsula to look for all manner of winter seaducks and alcids, head over to Prospect Harbor in hopes of seeing a Harlequin Duck, explore the Tunk Lake area, the blueberry barrens around Franklin for upland species, and finally return back to Ellsworth. Our goal was to add birds to our day-list, as well as finding a few for my Little Big Year.

8:15 a.m.   The day started off a balmy (balmy when you consider all the cold weather that started the year) 37° Fahrenheit, with a high, overcast ceiling.

A quick visit to Gordon's Wharf in Sullivan did not turn up anything new. Although there is a house with feeders on Wharf Road which, when coupled with the surrounding dense, shrubby vegetation lining the road, often yields interesting birds, we came up empty and so moved on.

Sullivan Harbor always looks like it should be an amazing place for shorebirds, especially at low tide when the mudflats are exposed, but it rarely has more than a few Greater Yellowlegs in season (alas, this was not the season). Today, three beautiful colonial houses, each with feeders, offered the usual assortment of American Tree Sparrows, Dark-eyed Juncos, and a couple of Song Sparrows.

Winter Harbor was quiet with few birds. In fact, other than the six Common Grackles, which were probably the very same ones we saw during the Christmas Bird Count three weeks earlier, there was nothing we had not already seen this day.

Now, I should say that I like seeing the usual suspects. Actually, I LOVE seeing the usual suspects! Taking time to observe common birds can be very rewarding. You may study their feeding behavior, perhaps divining their dietary preferences, or their method for selecting specific food items. You can observe how much they eat and whether they eat where they find their food or take it to a safer perch.

Observing familiar species affords opportunity to closely study plumage. There is more to this, though, than simply learning key field marks for identification. Are there any feathers missing? Often, missing feathers are most evident in the primary and secondary flight feathers of the wings or in the rectrices, the tail feathers. Can you see signs of wear? Does it look "fresher," less worn, more brilliantly colored than those surrounding it? Most birds of North America have two molts every year—spring and fall. They don't entirely drop their feathers all at once. Look to see if a feather is noticeably shorter than its neighbors. If yes to either, or both, of these questions, this may be a new feather molting in.

With common birds, you begin to learn the intricacies of avian hierarchy. This could be the manner in which one species interacts with another or the intraspecies pecking order, the manner in which individuals within a given species interact with one another.

I never tire of watching the local chickadees and sparrows and finches; or Mallards cruising along in the shelter of the shore; even Rock Pigeons cruising about in formation. All provide endless sources of entertainment, if not contemplation. Common birds are so interesting that when I teach ornithology at College of the Atlantic, the very first paper I assign is an observational piece on either Mallards, Black-capped Chickadees, or American Robins.

We next made our way through the Schoodic Section of Acadia National Park, finding a variety of seaducks and loons along the way.

10:55 a.m.   We finally arrived at Schoodic Point, the southernmost terminus of the Schoodic Peninsula and the Schoodic section of Acadia National Park. It may have been 38° Fahrenheit, but with the stiff southerly breeze, it felt a lot colder. From the warmth of the parked car, facing south, looking out over the open Gulf of Maine, we observed three Black-legged Kittiwakes as they flew past before we even had a chance to get out.

Black-legged Kittiwakes are true "sea gulls," only needing to come ashore to breed on the cliffs of coastal islands; otherwise, they are content to remain at sea.

Outside, we had not yet set up our spotting scopes, when an Iceland Gull flew through our field of view, following the contours of the shoreline. Like its Glaucous Gull cousin, the Iceland Gull is a "white-winged" gull, lacking the distinctive black wingtips of birds such as Ring-billed and Herring Gulls. The "white-winged" gulls are "ice" gulls, spending most of the lives around the frozen far northern margins of the continent where pack ice meets open water.

11:34 a.m.   Continuing our way around the Schoodic Loop Road, we came to Blueberry Hill, the place where I hoped to find my thrill, this time in the form of a Snowy Owl. Or three (my friend Seth Benz had reported seeing three just two days prior). I have always parked at the small *cul-de-sac*, but seeing as it was not plowed and the snow depth was just at that point where we might get bogged down, I opted to park at the pullout 100 feet up the road. This was a fortuitous move as the extra bit of elevation enhanced our perspective of the island.

Spotting scopes set up, Kyle and I got to work, carefully scrutinizing the length of Schoodic Island. The island is nearly a ½-mile distant, so with our scopes zoomed way in, we looked. And looked. And looked some more.

Right off the bat: four Harlequin Ducks. Common Eider, Long-tailed Ducks, Bufflehead, Red-breasted Merganser. We also spotted two Red-throated Loons, heads out, legs trailing, in flight. Horned and Red-necked Grebes. A lone Great Cormorant. A Black Guillemot in pale winter plumage. Four species of gulls—in addition to the Black-legged Kittiwake, there were Ring-billed, Herring, and Great Black-backed Gulls. Even a lone Dark-eyed Junco performing what I consider its "bell" call. But no Snowy Owl.

After half an hour snooping for Snowies with no success, Kyle suggested it may be time to move to the next spot on our day's itinerary. Before hopping in the car, I had to give the island just one more scan. Starting on the north end (or left as you face the island), I slowly worked my way south, looking on every rock, every point of elevation offering a vantage for a Snowy Owl. I looked in the lee of every surface, hoping to find a Snowy Owl sheltering from the wind's onslaught. I scanned through the copse of Black Spruce. At the southern end, I scanned the barren rocks that gradually descend into the water, creating a reef that extends far enough to warrant a U.S. Coast Guard bell buoy.

Voilà! There, on a pile of bedrock, stood a young male Snowy Owl, heavily barred with black over its white background. Was this bird there the whole time I repeatedly scanned the island? Or did it suddenly materialize? (Yes, I know, it probably flew up there between my scans, but that is not as mysterious.)

I love Snowy Owls! This is Hedwig, Harry Potter's owl. It is the owl you may see in the winter sitting on a farm field fencepost. Or along the side of a runway at an airport: John F. Kennedy International Airport in New York City and Boston Logan International Airport are two that are particularly well-known for their Snowy Owls.

In Maine, they are regularly found around Biddeford Pool and at the Portland International Jetport. The more ambitious among us ofttimes hike or snowshoe or ski the mountains of Acadia National Park to look for them.

That's where I try to find them every winter.

Since January 2001, not all that long after I first met Natalie, the woman that would become my wife, I have been hiking the mountains of Acadia during the winter. When we were first dating, my work schedule back in the Adirondack Mountains of northern New York allowed me to come to Maine for regular and longer visits. Therefore, on weekdays, while Natalie was at work, I hiked.

Early on, perhaps even during my very first winter hike up Sargent Mountain, I encountered Charlie Jacobi, Acadia National Park's (now recently retired) resource specialist. He told me that he has been hiking up Sargent since 1994 and has seen Snowy Owls in the alpine zone every winter, if not every hike. This has long been nagging at me because back in my college days, I was taught that Snowy Owls were an irruptive species: if food was scarce, they would fly south; otherwise, they did not wander far beyond their Arctic ecoregion. And yet, according to Charlie, and based on my own observations, at least some Snowies come south every single winter, at least to Acadia National Park.

Some winters are particularly fruitful (wouldn't it be more appropriate to write "owlful") for Snowy Owl sightings. For instance, during the winter of 2013—2014, a major Snowy Owl incursion occurred. Where I learned that they were irruptive, I think incursion is the better technical term for this mass movement from the far north toward the south. That winter, numbers of these birds were found in every province and in EVERY state! Yes, Hawaii, too! One was even found in Bermuda!

To me, this question of how to characterize the seasonal movement of Snowy Owls is intriguing. During the 1990s, when Charlie was regularly seeing Snowy Owls during the winter on the mountaintop alpine zones of Acadia National Park, I was back-country skiing in the Adirondack Mountains of northern New York, summiting countless times every winter. And when I wasn't skiing, I was out birding, visiting such seemingly suitable habitats as patterned peatland bogs, frozen wetlands, and snow-covered farmland. Not once did I see a Snowy Owl! Yet, during the past five or so years, they have been starting to be reported from across the Adirondacks. Seems like a good topic for a graduate research project, if anyone is looking.

Snowy Owls breed in the High Arctic, from Alaska to Labrador, and across northernmost Eurasia. You expect to find them during the winter in those states bordering Canada. But states bordering the Gulf of Mexico? And some Caribbean islands? You would NEVER foresee finding them in such warm climes.

Snowy Owls are the definition of charismatic megafauna. People are entranced by these beautiful Arctic denizens with their piercing yellow eyes. So, when a Snowy Owl showed up at the Honolulu International Airport, birders were elated. Alas, it was shot.

Shooting birds at airports is an issue of safety. Birds and planes don't mix. Great lengths are normally taken to catch and relocate larger species such as Snowy Owls, but sometimes they just cannot, or will not, be captured.

In the Arctic, Snowy Owl populations reflect that of the Bog Lemming, smallish Arctic rodents related to voles, muskrats, and beavers. When lemming populations are high, Snowy Owls feast, lay more eggs, and fledge more young. Come winter, this increased number of birds disperses, looking for food. Quite often it is the adults who stay north, on or near territory, and force younger birds away as there is limited food available during the winter, a time when the ground is frozen and covered in snow and ice.

Young Snowy Owls can be distinguished by their plumage with bold and heavy dark barring. When they come south, they are looking for tundra-like habitat. Hence, they frequent beaches, farmlands, open mountain summits, and airports.

If you are fortunate enough to see a Snowy Owl, please enjoy it from a distance so as not to disturb it and cause it unnecessary stress. Thank you.

2:30 p.m.   After exploring the old Stinson Seafood plant in Prospect Harbor for seabirds, the blueberry barrens on the way to Tunk Lake for open habitat birds such as Snow Bunting and Horned Lark, the Green Lake Fish Hatchery for any unusual ducks that might be congregating in the open water by the outfall pipe, and several other prospective birdy spots, we found ourselves back in Ellsworth. Kyle mentioned Common Merganser being down by the boat launch all winter; so, off we went for one last species for our day-list. And for my year-list.

Sure enough, one of the first species we saw at the boat launch was Common Merganser, the last of the three Maine merganser species I needed for the year. These were all females, readily identified by the distinct demarcation between the ruddy head and the white chest.

Several of my guy friends wanted a "boys' night out." For us, "boys' night out" typically means a night at the movies. John Carpenter's 1982 incarnation of *The Thing* showing at The Criterion, the 1932 art deco theater in Bar Harbor, seemed just the ticket.

During the movie, my phone vibrated (yes, it was in silent mode). I glanced at the screen to make sure it wasn't my daughter, who would only call it was an emergency, and saw it was Rob Packie. I always enjoy talking to him, but that was not the time.

After the movie, I checked my messages. Rob had been calling to report a Northern Saw-whet Owl tooting near his Hulls Cove home. He said the bird was sitting in a small spruce immediately at the end of the road. So, on the eight-mile drive home, making a ¼-mile detour put that spruce within earshot.

9:03 p.m.   Car turned off, I stepped outside and walked away to get a better audio environment. Nothing. DRAT! I walked up the old Breakneck Road slowly, stopping frequently to listen. About a tenth of a mile up, *toot-toot-toot-toot-toot-toot-toot-toot-toot-toot-toot-toot-toot-toot-toot-toot-toot.* Yes! The back-up beeper call of a Northern Saw-whet Owl....

The Northern Saw-whet Owl is a diminutive owl, indigenous to North America, found coast to coast and from mid-latitude Canada to the Mexican border. Its name—"saw-whet"—comes from the sound of one of its many vocalizations that is reminiscent of the sound of an old-style, steel cross-cut saw being sharpened. The owl preys on small rodents, especially Deer Mice (I really need to erect my Northern Saw-whet Owl box to encourage one to take up residence near my house to help with my mouse problem).

The mated Northern Saw-whet Owl pair split the early natal responsibilities with the female doing most of the incubation and brooding and the male providing food. When young are eighteen days old, the female leaves the nest. Meanwhile, the male will continue to feed the young until they fledge.

You can increase your chance of a pair of Northern Saw-whet Owls taking up residence near your home if you are adjacent to a significant wooded area and put up a suitable nest-box[ii] no later than March, before the nesting season begins in early April.

... I have seen Northern Saw-whet Owls in the past. I have banded them. I have seen them in educational programs put on by both Ann Rivers of Acadia Wildlife Foundation[iii] and Grayson Richmond of Birdsacre[iv]. I have even held an injured Northern Saw-whet Owl[v]. Rather than track the bird down the bird I could hear happily tooting away and shine a light on it so that I could actually see it, I felt no need to further intrude on this tiny owl, so I slowly retraced my way back to my car and headed home.

Today's birds of the year:

69. Iceland Gull
70. Snowy Owl
71. Common Merganser

72. Northern Saw-whet Owl

Wednesday, 24 January

7:07 a.m.   Up and at 'em! This morning, my routine was no different than usual: wake before sunrise (it is a LOT easier to do this in the winter when sunrise is nearly 7:00), eat breakfast, shower, and while dressing, look out the window, cracking it to feel the temperature. Except this time, as I looked out the window, a large bird flew overhead.

The gizz of the bird, the general impression of size and shape, instantly said raptor, a large raptor.

When gauging the size of raptors, I ask myself a series of questions: How big is it? Is it really big, so big that it almost seems unreal? Then it is an eagle. Is it really big, but not quite unreal big? Then it is most likely a Red-tailed Hawk.

This bird was that "really big, but not quite unreal big." Add in whitish underparts with a distinct dark belly-band (which is all I could see in my brief encounter) and that clinched the identification as a Red-tailed Hawk. I would have liked to see the red tail, but in the early morning light, conditions did not facilitate seeing that level of detail.

Red-tailed Hawks are not overly common on Mount Desert Island, but they are occasionally seen, even in the winter. In Maine, this is a bird we tend to see along the highway during the day, sitting in trees or perched on fenceposts. Of course, I cannot see a Red-

tailed Hawk without singing one of the more famous songs by Richard Rodgers and Oscar Hammerstein II in my head:

> *Oklahoma, where the wind comes sweepin' down the plain,*
> *And the wavin' wheat*
> *can sure smell sweet*
> *When the wind comes right behind the rain.*

> *Oklahoma, ev'ry night my honey lamb and I*
> *Sit alone and talk*
> *and watch yon hawk*
> *makin' lazy circles in the sky.*

Today's bird of the year:

73. Red-tailed Hawk

Saturday, 27 January

I t was the weekend; Natalie was off to Maryland to visit her ninety-one-year-old father and Anouk had her friend, Cecelia, over. Ten-year-old energy times two, throw in a seventy-pound Goldendoodle who desperately wants to run, equals a recipe for outdoor activity.

One of my favorite birds is the Black-backed Woodpecker. I don't know if it is because of its relative scarcity, its elusiveness, it being a denizen of my favorite forest type (the boreal forest of northern latitudes), or the striking contrast of the male's glossy black back and yellow topknot. Actually, I think it is a combination of all these factors.

Here on Mount Desert Island, Black-backed Woodpeckers, always uncommon, have become increasingly rare in recent decades. This species is illustrative of a mantra I regularly preach: "You have to spend time outdoors if you want to see interesting things." Clearly, I spend plenty of time outdoors because invariably I see one or two Black-backed Woodpeckers each year. And when I do see one, generally it is at one of two places: The Nature Conservancy's Indian Point Blagden Preserve or working the Tamaracks (my favorite species of tree) along the west side of the Mount Desert Island High School's settling ponds.

11:46 a.m.   Four of us—Anouk, Cecelia, Fogo, and me—parked on Pine Heath Road to walk the Kittredge Brook Trail.

Situated between Pine Heath Road to the west and the high school's ponds to the east lies the 523-acre Kittredge Brook Preserve[i]. Kittredge Brook bisects a lovely, mature mixed forest, heavy with White Pine and other conifers. Immediately surrounding the brook, the riparian zone, partially impounded by the industrious work of North American Beaver, is largely fen (a fen is essentially a bog but with a stream flowing through it). The trail itself is a bit over one mile long with minimal elevational change.

Recently, I have noticed the stand of dead spruce along the north side of the fen exhibiting the ongoing work of Black-backed Woodpecker. The bark on many of the trees has clearly been flaked away, leaving unweathered wood freshly exposed, clear signs of the unique manner of this woodpecker's foraging technique.

Walking in from Pine Heath Road, the trail is laid out on something of a shallow ridgeline, perhaps a relic glacial esker. With the attendant noise and energy of my hiking posse, I did not expect to see or hear much more than a few chickadees, nuthatches, and kinglets working the canopy in their mixed foraging flocks or, perhaps, a few over-flying goldfinch repetitively intoning *per-chick-o-ree, per-chick-o-ree....*

Over the past 100 or so years, scientists have learned a lot about birds by banding, the affixing of a uniquely numbered metal band to the leg of a bird. Bird in hand, we make measurements such as wing chord—the length from the tip of the wing to the first joint (think elbow)—which, for many species, can also be used to separate male or female birds. In songbirds, the wing chord in males tend to be longer than the females while in raptors, the reverse is true (that is because female raptors tend to be larger than the males). Looking at the shape and patterning of the tips of wing- or tail-feathers can often be used to determine age.

It is also possible to estimate the amount of fat. Birds metabolize fat differently than people. For instance, during migration, they can add 50% to their mass in a day's foraging and then burn it all in a night's flight. Their translucent skin enables bird banders to estimate energy reserves by ruffling the feathers on their head or belly to see the white patches of fat.

All the millions of birds banded have helped generate comprehensive assessments of bird populations continent-wide.

Finding a bird with a band and reporting it[ii] continues to provide crucial data about the distribution and longevity of birds.

In North America, banding's roots trace to John James Audubon (1785—1851). Audubon is best known for his painting of life-size, double-elephant folio lithographs of U.S. and Canadian birds. He took the traditionally staid manner of portraying wildlife and stood it on its head, painting birds in poses showing multiple angles and key field marks, all in a single image. In about 1803, Audubon observed a nest of Eastern Phoebes on the banks of Perkiomen Creek, near Philadelphia. "When they were about to leave the nest, I fixed a light silver thread to the leg of each, loose enough not to hurt the part, and so fastened that no exertions of their own could remove it. … At the next year's season when the Pewee[iii] returns to Pennsylvania I had the satisfaction to observe those in the cave and about it. Having caught several of these birds on the nest, I had the pleasure of finding two of them had the little ring on their leg."

While living in the Adirondack Mountains of northern New York, whenever I was banding, I welcomed people to come and learn, especially children. My friends Steve and Nan would bring their young daughter, Anika. The first bird I caught during her first visit was an American Goldfinch. After affixing the band, taking my various measurements, and explaining what I was doing, I asked

Anika if she would like to release the bird. "Yes!" she enthusiastically, if not more than a little cautiously, replied. I showed her how to hold the bird without hurting it and then put it in her hands. She whispered to the bird, then opened her hands. As the bird flew away, it said, "*Per-chick-o-ree, per-chick-o-ree!*" I told Anika that that was the bird's name for her. For years, whenever I would see Anika, I would lean toward her, quietly saying, "*Per-chick-o-ree,*" and she would smile.

… Not long into our walk, we came to a bench offering a vantage of Kittredge Brook. While the girls played, I bushwhacked to the riparian edge. A thin veneer of ice marked the high-water line from a recent major rainstorm, which had been immediately followed by a deep freeze, made crossing the brook challenging, at best.

Standing at the foot of a dead spruce, I looked around. A small flake of bark landed at my feet. Literally! It landed right at my feet, one foot away! I looked up. There it was! A female Black-backed Woodpecker! Being a female, it lacked the yellow cap of the male, but she was every bit as spectacular!

Bird found, we continued on our way. Shortly, we came to an intersection. Going right would take you back to the car the way we came; going left takes you up a short, steep bank, then out on to the end of Pine Heath Road. The girls wanted to race back, with them going right, me going left. The race was on!

Not too far up my trail, head down to watch my footing on the ice, moving quickly so that I might be the first to the car, and still on a high from seeing the Black-backed Woodpecker, I had a form of tunnel-vision. A BURST of motion, seemingly from right under my feet, nearly gave me a heart attack.

Ruffed Grouse have a habit of doing that to you. Their camouflage keeps them so well hidden that you rarely see them when they are still. But if you walk too close, they take to the air in a flurry of feathers, wings beating furiously, all a commotion of blurry brown.

I did not get a very satisfying look at the bird but a positive identification, nonetheless.

Oh, and as for the race, I came in third.

Today's birds of the year:

74. Black-backed Wood-
    pecker

75. Ruffed Grouse

Monday, 29 January

What a crazy winter we are having: cold, wonderful packed powder snow, making for perfect cross-country skiing on Acadia National Park's Carriage Roads. Cold, and more cold. Then, BLECH! Rain. GGGRRRrrr!!! Repeat: more cold, a little more snow, okay skiing. Then, BLECH! Rain again. GGGRRRrrr!!! Cold again, no snow. But with the ground frozen yet again, the hiking is actually pretty darned good.

Fogo and I needed some exercise, and with trail-running being an activity we both enjoy, Great Head seemed the solution to our problem. This has long been a favorite hike of mine and one that my daughter, Anouk, has been calling the "greatest hike in the universe" since she was at least four.

9:05 a.m.   Fogo, on a leash attached to a harness designed to discourage pulling, and I, binoculars slung over my shoulder, set off down the steps to Sand Beach, making for Great Head. We had the usual assortment of winter waterfowl in Newport Cove: American Black Duck, Common Eider, Bufflehead, Red-breasted Merganser. A Red-throated Loon was a nice find; not unexpected, but more often than not it is missed as it is far less common than the Common Loon....

A note about loons and loon identification.

Within their range and in the right habitat, Common Loons are, indeed, common. We think of them as the iconic symbol of Maine's pure freshwater lakes and larger ponds. In reality, they are only there for an extended breeding season, beginning not long after ice-out and present straight through until autumn, departing well before ice sets in.

All Common Loons have their legs set so far back that they physically cannot walk on land. If you have ever seen an illustration or taxidermied mount with a loon standing erect on land, this is one of those rare times in the universe of natural history that I can categorically state IT IS WRONG! That said, they do come ashore to nest, and that is it. Their nests will be right at the water's edge so that they can scoot out of the water on their belly to lay and then incubate eggs. When danger arises, they can quickly slide back into the water without needing to walk.

Their chicks are born precocial, meaning that from nearly the moment they are hatched, they take to the water and swim. With the impressive swimming abilities shared by all loons, they are much safer in an aqueous environment than on land where they have neither maneuverability nor defenses.

Outside of the season for raising young, loons are, arguably, a saltwater bird. Here in Maine, a loon spends its first four years of life on the ocean. Visit most any shoreline access year-round, scan the ocean with a pair of binoculars or a spotting scope, and chances are good you will find a loon. Or two. Or twenty (my personal high count of loons from one vantage is twenty-three!).

I routinely hear from people that either they see no loons on the ocean or that they are only there a short time. We need to remember that the iconic breeding plumage of the Common Loon, the one immortalized by Katherine Hepburn and Henry Fonda in the 1981 movie, *On Golden Pond*, is not retained all year long. The basic, or winter, plumage is much drabber, being washes of gray and brown and dingy white, so they might just be less noticed rather than less present.

Still, on the ocean, Common Loons are readily identifiable by their size and profile. They are a large bird, ranging from twenty-six to nearly thirty-six inches in length. That size range is important to keep in mind (more on that shortly). They have a robust bill—next time you look at a Common Loon, take careful note of the bill size and shape, especially in relationship to the size of its head—almost always held parallel to the surface of the water. Their head can be rather blocky, sometimes with pronounced rounded peaks fore and aft (some people refer to this as being "squared"). And their winter plumage exhibits a faint "necklace" that is best viewed with the aid of optics.

Meanwhile, in order to avoid confusion, there are other loons to consider.

The Red-throated Loon is far less abundant in Maine waters than its larger cousin, but it is still common enough in winter to merit consideration. There are a few important cues to aid in its identification.

First: size. Red-throated Loons range from twenty-one to twenty-seven inches in length. This slightly overlaps the smaller end of the Common Loon size range, so pay careful attention to all the other field marks. That said, they are a noticeably more petite bird, as loons go.

Red-throated Loons may be seen most any time throughout the year, but the bulk of their sightings are between October and May. During the short Arctic breeding season, they inhabit ponded waters of the tundra.

We rarely see Red-throated Loons in their rich breeding plumage here on the coast of Maine. Instead, their drab basic plumage is quite similar to that of the Common Loon, albeit they tend to be paler.

For that matter, all loons look relatively similar in their winter plumages.

The real clue to identifying a Red-throated Loon on our shores is the bill. Their bill is substantially smaller—both shorter and less robust—than a Common Loon's. And Red-throated Loons almost always hold their bill at an angle of thirty degrees or so. Finally, they also show much more pronounced white on their throat and up the side of their head.

Then, to throw a little mud in the water, there are Pacific Loons and Yellow-billed Loons to consider. The former is rare, small like a Red-throated Loon, but darker, with only a few individuals reported most winters from the entire coast of Maine; the latter is so rare in Maine as to barely be worth mentioning. And if you are really lucky and want to make the record books of the Maine Bird Records Committee, maybe, just maybe, you'll be the one to find the Pine Tree State's first Arctic Loon.

... At the end of Sand Beach, our way was blocked by a flooded stream. Normally, it is shallow enough to pick your way across, but this day, as a result of the recent rain, it was a foot deeper. Fogo, ever impervious to cold water, happily splashed his way across, tail pinwheeling with excitement. Using my powers of prognostication, I could vividly see a leap across ending badly for me, so we retraced our route in favor of the longer loop around Great Head.

As we made our way through the forest, there was a paucity of songbirds. A few Black-capped Chickadees, a Red-breasted Nuthatch, and a Dark-eyed Junco started off the day's tally. The Downy Woodpecker I saw, part of the mixed foraging flock of chickadees, nuthatch, and junco, is not actually a songbird but a near-passerine, or a near-songbird.

At the southernmost tip of Great Head, I stood perhaps 100 feet above the water with a view toward Old Soaker, the rocky islet guarding the approach to Newport Cove and Sand Beach. Four Great Cormorants standing on the northeast end served as sentinels. My ears caught a distinctive and repetitive screech. While the sound alone was enough for a tick of the ol' year-list, I still wanted to see the marauding Peregrine Falcon. Training my ears on the next series of screeches, I realized it was coming from below me. A male Red-breasted Merganser was repeatedly ducking its head as the Peregrine made dive after dive on it. Once known as Duck Hawks, this falcon was not having much success with this potential meal and eventually flew off, screeching its seeming frustration....

Peregrine Falcons are one of the success stories of the Endangered Species Act. However, the fact that they ended up on the endangered species list in the first place is a sad story.

Raptors have long been given a bum rap. People would steal their eggs and chicks to sell to falconers. Some people take potshots at raptors out of fear they are a threat to livestock.

I witnessed this lack of regard toward Peregrine Falcons back in the late 1980s in the Champlain Valley of northern New York at the Coot Hill Hawk Watch. My birding mentor, Mike Peterson, spotted a Peregrine flying toward us. So did a group of locals partying nearby. One man went to his four-wheel-drive pick-up truck, took a rifle out of the rear window rack, and, as the bird flew closer, raised his gun and shot. BAM! The bird tumbled out of the sky. I was aghast! At first glance, Mike, wearing a long-sleeved tan button-down-the-front shirt adorned with patches from various environmental organizations, looked much like a forest ranger. Walking up to the shooter from behind, he said, "Nice shot." "Thanks." When the man turned and took in Mike's "uniform," thinking him law enforcement, he ran for his truck and sped down the mountain track. Mike, ever fast on his mental feet, wrote down the license plate number. The man was eventually caught and arrested for killing an endangered species.

The population of Peregrine Falcons took a real hit after World War II. During the war, dichlorodiphenyltrichloroethane, better known as DDT, was used extensively by the military to control insects carrying diseases such as typhus in Europe and malaria and dengue fever in the Pacific Theater. After the war, there was widespread application of DDT in the U.S. to control mosquitos. (I vividly remember being a little kid, running behind the spray truck as it drove down our dead-end street, plying its poison, the other kids in the neighborhood right alongside me, all of us bathing in the mist.) As we now know, DDT's lethal effects were not limited to insects.

It took us a long time to understand that DDT is not only a toxin, but that it bio-accumulates in the environment. Insects poisoned by DDT would be eaten by rodents or songbirds, building up toxic levels in their system. They, in turn, would be eaten by a larger predator. As this moves up the food-chain, the levels of DDT get more and more concentrated. At the highest trophic levels in birds—this included cormorants, pelicans, ospreys, eagles, and falcons—elevated levels of DDT and its by-products inhibited the uptake of calcium, which is essential to egg formation. The immediate manifestation of this problem was that eggs were laid with too-thin shells and were often were crushed during incubation, resulting in the collapse of entire populations. Birds affected by this included Osprey, Bald Eagles, American White Pelicans, Double-crested Cormorants, and, of course, Peregrine Falcons.

With the publication of Rachel Carson's book, *Silent Spring*,[i] in 1962, the public started to become aware of the scope of this tragedy. Alas, it took another decade before the Environmental Protection Agency finally banned DDT in 1972.

Peregrine Falcons were extirpated from the eastern U.S. The last known Peregrine nesting in Acadia National Park was 1956. A reintroduction program was launched in 1984. It took until 1991 before this program finally saw a successful nesting attempt. Today, Peregrine Falcons once again nest in Maine. In Hancock County, I know of at least six active nesting sites. With its population restored, the Peregrine Falcon was removed from the endangered species list—a true success story of the Endangered Species Act.

… Continuing along the trail around Great Head, I made my way to a pile of rubble, clearly manmade as many of the stones retain remnants of mortar[ii]. For me, this particular site, this very spot, is the confluence of human ecology, blending the natural world—coastal scrub pine forest with rocky shoreline and spectacular views across the water south and east—and the social world.

In this case, the social world includes a bit of human history, which I discovered unexpectedly while working on a project about the history of birds, birding, and bird study on Mount Desert Island[iii].

One day, I was sitting on the floor in the stacks of the Raymond H. Fogler Library at the University of Maine in Orono, sequentially pulling out old bird journals, volume by volume, to peruse the table of contents and read intriguing articles. Some of these old journals have yet to be digitized and made available online, so this was the analog version of browsing the internet. A 1937 article on the longevity of birds[iv] piqued my interest. Reading through it, imagine my surprise when I read the following:

"Chickadee. *Penthestes atricapillus*. . . . C21641, banded at Great Head, Bar Harbor, Maine, on October 16, 1929, by Mrs. E. Anthony, was retrapped at the same place April 23, 1934, March 15, 1935, and December 4, 1935."

Great Head! Each and every time I walk by this place, knowing this little bit of arcane history, further reinforces that this is, indeed, "the greatest hike in the universe."

So, after paying homage, I scanned the horizon for signs of life. A distant glint of bright white, so white as to almost hurt the eyes in direct sunlight, effortlessly soaring 100 feet above sea level, shaped like a cross, was no UFO but a Northern Gannet. There are few birds in this part of the world so immediately identifiable at such great distance.

Gannets are one of my favorite birds. I say this about a lot of birds, but in this case, it is true! The image of the bird silhouette is in the logo for my business, The Natural History Center. The word is also on the license plate of my car. When I go to Cape St. Mary's, on the Avalon Peninsula in Newfoundland, I spend hours sitting and watching the workings of the gannetry. Gannets have this amazing ability to soar, wings locked in a relaxed attitude of flight, head down looking for delectable piscine treats. When they see food, they fold their wings back to plunge-dive, spearing the water with a small splash, sometimes diving to depths of 180 feet.

When I see a Northern Gannet, my day is complete. And this particular gannet enabled me to fill another check on my year-list.

Today's birds of the year:

76. Peregrine Falcon   77. Northern Gannet

Saturday, 03 February

For many years, perhaps decades, the Downeast Chapter of Maine Audubon has been offering a winter birding field trip of the Schoodic Peninsula. When I first participated on the trip in 2003, it was co-led by Clark "Chip" Moseley and Ed Hawkes.

Getting to know these two through birding set me on a path to friendship, not just with them both, but also with many other members of the Downeast Chapter of Maine Audubon community. (It also led to my serving on the board of directors Downeast Audubon for ten years.) Ed and Chip have each, separately and together, provided me with many hours of shared discovery of birds and taught me many life lessons.

Take Chip, for instance. On these tours, he always wore well-loved denim overalls, reminiscent of those worn by my grandfather, Wayne Bolyard, when he was working in the garage at our family's former business, MacDonald's White House Dairy, which was located in my childhood hometown of Lewiston, New York. Chip knew his birds better than most and loved to talk about them. Drawing on his years as a veterinarian, he could talk at great length about the anatomy, physiology, and biology of birds. In later years, as his hearing diminished with age, Chip would ask me to tell him which birds I was hearing. "Yup, I can picture it in my mind, but I can't hear it," would be a typical Chip response.

For his part, Ed has become my most regular birding buddy; however, my path to birding with Ed was initially via bird carving.

Ever since I was a young boy attending scout camp, I wanted to carve. Except I didn't know that's what it was. The concept of carving wasn't in the lexicon of my friends, nor the camp leaders. No, we whittled. We regularly took sticks and whittled them into lengthy pointed spears. Some of us graduated to lengths of 2"x2" dimensional lumber which we whittled into chain links. Shortly after moving to Maine in the fall of 2002, I saw an ad for a bird carving continuing education class. This was exactly what I was looking for!

Turned out Ed was the instructor and that we were, by Maine standards, neighbors, as we lived only two miles apart. After the first class, Ed and I began carpooling. I would show up early at his house to help load the requisite tools and supplies. When I expressed interest in signing up for the next birding class, Ed refused me. Instead, he asked me to be his assistant! Over the years, he has become a mentor, maybe something of a father-figure, certainly a friend. Today, there are few things I enjoy more than a birding outing with Ed, puzzling through bird i.d.s, his friendly teasing when I make a mistake, and just talking about most anything under the sun.

Over time, I became one of the group leaders for the Schoodic trip. These last few years, as Chip and Ed have not gotten any younger, I have become the sole leader, taking on their mantle.

7:45 a.m.   For this year's Downeast Audubon Schoodic field trip, I shared the ride with some of my regular birding buddies. Rob Packie and Jane Potter met at my house to carpool to the Schoodic Peninsula. On our way, we picked up Ed and his wife Deb. With five dedicated birders in the minivan, we didn't talk about much other than birds. Ahhh, life was good. At one point, I could just imagine my daughter Anouk's response, were she there, "Birds, schmirds; birds are boring," followed by a quick glance to see if I was rising to her bait.

Rob and I have a fun, teasing, brother-like banter. Now, I may have birded longer and spend more time doing (perhaps I should have written "obsessing") this activity, but Rob grew up on Mount Desert Island. Being the outdoorsman and sportsman that he is, Rob has seen more of the island's nooks and crannies than have most. While he has shown me many of those "secret" nooks and crannies, I have shown him many birds. We routinely call each other, sharing our most recent bird sightings. This day, Rob said he wanted me to find him a life-bird. The reality is that I have found him more birds than he has found me, but he claims this should be the case. According to Rob's logic, for every bird he finds me, I need to find him six. (I'm not so sure about this....)

Jane, on the other hand, wanted to find a Snowy Owl. Although she has seen them in the past, she has to see it with me to count toward her MDI Bird Club statistics.

Ed and Deb were talking about going to New Brunswick in the coming week to chase a Mistle Thrush, this particular European species' first appearance in North America. And as a bonus, they were going to look for a reported Harris's Sparrow, a bird of the middle longitudes of North America. Neither of these birds had any business being in New Brunswick.

Meanwhile, I said that I would like to see either a Thick-billed Murre or a Dovekie for my year-list.

9:00 a.m.   Our birding officially began at Frazer Point, in the Schoodic section of Acadia National Park. It was below zero in Bar Harbor at sunrise. By 9:00, the temperature had at least crept above zero to a whopping 3° Fahrenheit, offering the barest modicum of psychological comfort. Slowly, the rest of our group trickled in: Sue and Harold Shaw, then Ellen Lehto, followed by Brendan White, Joanne Kilton, Sherry Downing, and Laurie Yntema. A stiff northerly breeze sucked any heat out of us as we scanned the harbor of Winter Harbor turning up exactly one Surf Scoter, six Long-tailed Ducks, and three Common Loons, a far cry from what we normally see at this locale. Perhaps the birds are smarter than us and had holed up behind a lee shore.

We slowly drove, making our way around the Schoodic Loop Road, stopping to look for birds at all the usual vantages, focusing especially on every cove. Along the way, we continued to see sea-ducks and gulls.

Being a group leader, there is one very important fact to always keep in mind: Never, ever pass up a chance for a pit stop! Fortunately, Schoodic Institute keeps a heated restroom open near the entrance to their campus, just off Arey Cove.

9:51 a.m.   While some of our group lined up to use the facilities, the rest of us walked the fifty yards to Arey Cove. The first bird we saw was a beautiful male Red-breasted Merganser. Just behind it was small alcid. It was small, very small, with a tiny bill, and lacked any discernable sign of white wing patch. DOVEKIE! I have not seen many of them, but they are unmistakable....

Dovekies are the smallest of the Alcidae, the family of seabirds that includes puffins; they are the size a small and very fat American Robin.

The first Dovekie I ever saw has indelibly burned its visage into my memory. It was during the six months Natalie, Anouk, and I were exploring Newfoundland's fisheries heritage, part of Natalie's sabbatical from the University of Maine Sea Grant Program. Driving north on the Cape Shore Road toward the tip of the Bonavista Peninsula, the winds were blowing near a gale out of the west, driving a good number of seabirds over this narrow stretch of land from the water on one side to the other.

HEY! "There goes a Dovekie! It just flew across the road!" I distinctly remember excitedly saying to Natalie. And then there was another. And another. A veritable stream of Dovekies flying across the road (okay, maybe five or six). One flew too close to the car driving ahead of us. Sadly, it was hit, tumbled through the air, landing on the shoulder of the road.

We pulled over to check on this poor bird. Unfortunately, it had suffered a compound fracture of both the radius and ulna (the equivalent of the two bones in our forearm), broken bones piercing through the skin. With no nearby wildlife rescue to take in this broken little bird, it was doomed. I was so sad for this pitiful wretch, feeling helpless as there was nothing we could for it. Well, almost nothing. I decided to dispatch it and then return its lifeless body to the sea to continue the cycle of life, hoping it would feed new life.

… Our Arey Cove Dovekie was actively feeding, spending no more than a few seconds on the surface, then diving. It took some doing to eventually direct everyone in our group of twelve to the bird. Someone would get on it, "OH, I see it!" and then it would dive yet again.

Meanwhile, those that saw it were now busy looking for other birds. "Rich, what's that bird over there?" "Over where?" I would look to whoever shouted the question, observe where they were looking, then take a quick scan, shout out the identification, and get right back to the Dovekie.

I could have stayed there all day to watch this bird. Normally, they are found in the furthest north reaches of the Atlantic, breeding in the largest seaside colonies of all the auks (for example, the breeding population in northwestern Greenland has been estimated at 30 million). Maybe I will get to see more Dovekies when I take a College of the Atlantic class to Newfoundland in June. Considering how abundant they are in the northernmost stretches of the Atlantic Ocean, they are infrequently seen along the U.S. east coast.

10:57 a.m. We arrived at Blueberry Hill. If you are birding at Schoodic, this should be a required stop. To fully appreciate the diversity of birds this stop can offer, it really helps to have a spotting scope to scan Schoodic Island, a ½-mile distant.

Almost as soon as our battery of spotting scopes was set up, I found myself shouting, "Snowy Owl!" Seriously, who doesn't like Snowy Owls? Looking across the stretch of water to Schoodic Island, my eyes were drawn to the huge sign alerting boaters to the fact of it being a seabird nesting island. Perched on the top edge was a magnificent Snowy Owl. Jane was first in line to see the bird. This also earned her, and, for that matter, everyone else in the group, a checkmark in the MDI Bird Club. Although I found no birds here to count toward my Little Big Year list, we made Jane happy....

Among my goals when I created The Natural History Center was to find ways to further engage people in birding. I believe that birding can be a gateway to the greater good of environmental conservation; my thinking being that if people enjoy the birds, they will want to see more of them. To see more of them means proactively taking action to enhance their populations. This could be as simple as feeding birds or planting native plants in your yard. Better yet, this could be putting your back woods under a conservation easement or contributing to your local land trust[i] or to national conservation organizations[ii] doing work in the latitudes that take in birds' wintering grounds.

As a modest incentive to encourage people to go birding, I created the MDI Bird Club[iii]. When people participate in one of the programs offered by The Natural History Center, we keep track of the birds they observe. When they reach certain thresholds—specifically, when they have observed 100, and then 200 species—they receive a certificate and a two-inch embroidered patch and The Natural History Center contributes $10 to Frenchman Bay Conservancy[iv].

... I continued scanning Schoodic Island. Two more Snowy Owls were sitting close together in the saddle of the island. As a bonus, flying high above, a pair of Rough-legged Hawks were riding the sea breeze, hunting for small mammals.

By noon, our frigid birding day was wrapping up. On the drive back to Bar Harbor, Rob, Jane, Ed, Deb, and I rehashed our morning's sightings. While I did not find Rob a life-bird (sorry, Rob), Jane got her Snowy Owl (and then some) and I found a Dovekie. (Ed and Deb did eventually go to New Brunswick and enjoyed the Mistle Thrush. Alas, they dipped on the Harris' Sparrow.) We tallied thirty-three species of birds, as well as a few Gray Seals and Harbor Porpoises. Certainly, the Dovekie was the bird of the day as it was a life-bird for many in the group, but we had seen other intriguing birds as well: Harlequin Duck, Razorbill, Black-legged Kittiwake, Rough-legged Hawk, and Snowy Owl would be at the top of my list.

Good friends, birding, time outdoors, good birds. This was a good day.

Today's bird of the year:

78. Dovekie

Monday, 05 February

My 2017 Toyota Sienna minivan recently hit 5,000 miles, so it was time for its first servicing at the dealer located in Brewer, nearly forty miles north of my Bar Harbor home. Afterward, heading home, I decided to take a slight detour down the Branch Pond Road to look for waxwings and finches in the apple orchard. Alas, no birds at all; not a one. Chuck Whitney, another friend I enjoy birding with, lives down this road, so I decided to pay him a visit.

Chuck's whole persona breathes passion for life, nature, music, and, of course, birds. His keen eye takes in the minutiae of avian activity. And having lived and taught in the Ellsworth area since 1979, he knows more than a thing or two.

11:22 a.m. Chuck and I walked behind his house to watch his feeders. At first, our presence surely flushed the birds as there was no activity. Soon, the Black-capped Chickadees began filtering in. One. Two. Six. Ten. Fifteen was the maximum we could confirm seeing at one time....

Back in the day, when I lived in the northern New York town of Keene Valley, home of the Adirondack Mountains' High Peaks, I banded birds, a LOT of birds. At The Four Brothers Preserve, four islands totaling seventeen acres in the middle of Lake Champlain, I banded gulls and herons and egrets and ibises and cormorants[i]. I also ramped up my banding of songbirds, often banding at my home, in order to contribute to the greater knowledge of songbird populations and distributions.

One winter morning, while sitting at my kitchen table eating breakfast, staring out the window at the feeders and the dearth of snowpack (no skiing this day), I saw a Black-capped Chickadee come in, get a black-oil sunflower seed out of the feeder, and fly off. I never tire of watching these valiant little birds and their friendly antics. When they come to a feeder, I always think of them as Norm from the television show *Cheers*. I can imagine, if not almost hear, the other birds chirp, "NORM!" every time a chickadee comes in.

But just how many "Norms" were there? When watching my feeders, chickadees are always coming and going, making it difficult to truly gauge their numbers. I can usually get to a dozen or so, but was that a realistic number? I set up a few mist nets around the feeders and commenced banding in order to capture chickadees with hopes of getting a better picture of just how many were coming in.

I love chickadees; I loathe banding them. If you have ever had a chance to hold a chickadee, you know what I mean. Extracting them from the mist net can be its own form of torture. They twist and they turn, more than any other bird I have ever banded, wrapping themselves in the net, making it incredibly difficult to unravel the sewing-thread-fine netting from around their legs and necks and wings and unsnagging it from their miniscule barbed tongues. All the while you are doing this, their tiny feet are tightly balled, holding on for dear life to whatever netting they can grab.

And then there is the beak. They may be omnivores, but their beak is particularly good at crunching seeds. Which means it is powerful and exceptionally good at pinching little bits of skin. Or jamming it under fingernails and cuticles.

It always seemed that just as you were on the verge of fully extracting the bird, it would twist just so and be fully ensnared once
again. @#$%!!!

When I was a kid, the novelty of banding was such that I overlooked the unpleasantness of handling chickadees. But as I got older,
in college and beyond, I realized that, as I was often the youngest
bander in the group, inevitably, I was designated the one to remove
far more chickadees from the mist nets than my older colleagues.
Clearly, there was some form of ornithological hazing going on. I
still have the emotional scars from handling and banding Black-
capped Chickadees!

Back to that morning, in my Keene Valley backyard. I began
banding. I quickly caught six, ten, fifteen, twenty. Alright, this was in
the range of what I expected. Thirty. Not too far out of range. Forty.
Fifty! Sixty, seventy, eighty! Eight-six!!! Eight-six was the magical
number: in one day, I banded eighty-six Black-capped Chickadees at
my feeders! WOW!

My studies, as well as those of many other ornithologists, have
found that chickadees have a feeding circuit, sometimes quite a size-
able one. They come in, take a seed or two, and zip off to feed or
even cache it for a later meal. Then they fly on to the next food site
and repeat the process. Again and again and again, each time a different site. It might be hours before the same chickadee comes back.
In the meantime, numerous other chickadees are in the midst of their
feeding circuit doing the same thing. Now, when I look at a feeder
and count chickadees, I know there are likely far more than the four
or six or eight I tally. So, when you see a few chickadees at your
feeder, ask yourself just how many there really are.

… Oh, look, a pair of Tufted Titmice. These birds do look a little
mousey, except for the little crest on their heads. A lone Red-
breasted Nuthatch. Dark-eyed Juncos on the ground, catching the

bird seed castoffs from the feeders. Eventually, a large flock of American Goldfinch came in, roosting in the uppermost branches of a Eurasian poplar and darting down to the Nyjer, or thistle seed, feeder.

All of this was wonderful—watching the birds, swapping stories with Chuck—but no new birds for the year-list. Half an hour later, we walked around the house and back to my car.

When Chuck and I get together, we talk. And talk. And talk. Our conversation revolves around exchanging stories. And so, extricating ourselves is a challenge because there is always one more story to tell.

As we were talking, I suddenly heard a buzzy, *zreeeeet*. Pine Siskin! One, lonely, Pine Siskin. The first I have seen or heard in months! Usually they are in good numbers, often foraging with their American Goldfinch cousins. Where have they all gone? All I know is that this vocalization—for I never actually saw the bird—counts toward the year-list.

Pine Siskins are the more boreal cousin of the American Goldfinch, looking and sounding similar, the way a cousin should, and yet, not quite the same; in this case, being less yellow and more brown and streaky (although there are yellow accents in the wings). During the first half of 1997, while living in Keene Valley, we saw a major incursion of these northern finches. Although they can usually be found year-round, that winter, the numbers were off the charts. Just how many there were became apparent as I ran the banding station at my home.

Normally, Pine Siskins breed from Alaska to Newfoundland & Labrador. They may be found year-round along much of the U.S./Canadian border region and winter throughout most of the United States, even stretching down into Mexico. In the

Adirondacks, it was not uncommon to hear their distinctive, ascending *zreeeeet* as they forage in the tops of pines and other conifers.

I often set up my mist nets at sunrise to band for an hour or so as I was getting ready for work at The Nature Conservancy. One still March day, a Thursday, to be exact, with about eighteen inches of snow on the ground, the banding was slow. When banding during the winter, I keep a close eye on the nets, never letting more than ten minutes elapse without removing birds, so this slump in activity meant there was time for a quick shower.

The way my house was laid out, the living room, dining area, and kitchen were all part of an open floor plan. The south wall was all picture windows and sliding glass doors, looking south toward the mountains of the twelve-mile-long Great Range of the Adirondacks—Lower Wolfjaw, Upper Wolfjaw, Armstrong, Gothics, Saddleback, Basin, and Haystack[ii]. The sliding glass door opened onto a wrap-around deck. And by that door, I kept a pair of Sorel pac boots.

After my shower, I came out of the bathroom, towel wrapped tightly around my waist. I glanced out the window, toward the nets. All empty. Suddenly, out of nowhere, there was a burst of feathered activity. Previously unseen birds were scattering in every direction. There must be an avian predator. Several of the birds flew into the net. Pine Siskins are generally quite passive in the net, but these guys were squirming as though their life depended on it—maybe because it did. Mere seconds later, a larger bird, the size of a robin, light gray in color, with black wings and a matching bold eyestripe, flew into the net as it targeted one of the siskins. Northern Shrike!

There was no way I was going to lose this bird as it would be the first shrike I ever banded. I ran to the sliding glass doors, grabbing my bird bags (used for safely and securely holding the birds prior to banding), practically jumped into my pac boots, and flew through the door. Only, as I ran out the door, my towel caught on the latch. We'll just say that I was not entirely naked—I had my boots on. But I got both the Northern Shrike and the Pine Siskins.

After this, the number of Pine Siskins really exploded. During the rest of the winter, I banded nearly 400 of them. Of those, one merits further mention. Not six months later, one was found dead, impaled on barbed wire in Montana near the gates of Yellowstone National Park. The fact of being impaled is typical of the manner in which Northern Shrikes store food—impaling it on something like buckthorn or barbed wire to save for a later meal.

As for the Pine Siskin, I was extremely surprised by this extreme western movement. Upon further investigation, I learned that Pine Siskins are, indeed, known to occasionally undertake great east-west peregrinations.

Today's bird of the year:

79. Pine Siskin

Wednesday, 07 February

Wednesdays are The Natural History Center's Weekly Birding Tour. I can usually count on a good group of folks keen on natural history turning out for this event. However, with a storm in the offing for today, the only soul who dared brave the impending weather was Jane Potter. Jane has been seriously bit by the birding bug and joins in nearly every week. As of this writing, she has seen 131 species on our tours.

The original plan for today was to explore the "Quiet Side" of Mount Desert Island, walking some easy trails in pursuit of winter finches. With just the two of us, Jane casually raised an idea, "Did you know Kyle Lima reported a Barrow's Goldeneye at Schoodic yesterday. Wouldn't it be great if we found it?"

Wouldn't it, indeed.

Barrow's Goldeneye—named in honor of Sir John Barrow, who, in his capacity as Second Secretary of the Admiralty, was an advocate for Arctic exploration—have two distinct populations in North America. The vast majority of them range from Alaska to northern California. Meanwhile, the eastern population is relatively small, nesting along the north shore of the Gulf of St. Lawrence and wintering from there, through the Northumberland Strait, to Cape Breton Island; in other words, along the northern edge of Maritime Canada. What that means for us here in Maine is that they are an uncommon occurrence, one about which we local birders tend to get excited.

Given that the Schoodic section of Acadia National Park is a good hour drive, that coupled with a weather forecast of sloppy snow leading to local schools calling for early release, meant I needed to be home by noon to meet Anouk when the bus dropped her off at the end of our driveway. We could do this amended tour, but we would have to stick to a whirlwind schedule. Jane was all in!

10:38 a.m.   We still hadn't found the Barrow's Goldeneye and the clock was ticking as Anouk was fully expecting to meet me when she got off the bus. In our hurried tour, we had tallied over twenty species to this point, with highlights including Harlequin Ducks, a Ruffed Grouse posing like a statue beside the road, three raptors—Bald Eagle, Red-tailed Hawk, and Rough-legged Hawk—and Black-legged Kittiwake. We had visited most all of the usual sea-birding hotspots, including Frazer Point, Arey Cove, Schoodic Point, and Blueberry Hill (where we scanned Schoodic Island for Snowy Owls—alas, no Snowies for us this day—and Rough-legged Hawks—two of these), but we had not quite reached Buck Cove, the final cove along the Schoodic Loop Road, and the place where the Barrow's Goldeneye had been reported.

Apparently, this hen Barrow's Goldeneye had been frequenting Buck Cove, by itself, staying apart from the much more abundant Common Goldeneyes. It's funny, in hindsight now knowing this, I am quite certain we saw it on Saturday's tour. I distinctly recall seeing a lone hen goldeneye in Buck Cove; a bird that, with not much more than a cursory glance, I called a Common, even though a vague, niggling feeling said that I should have looked at it further.

As we approached Buck Cove, my mind distracted by the ticking clock, there was a lone hen goldeneye visible through the trees. We quickly parked, bushwhacked the short distance to the water's edge, and waited for the bird to surface from a foraging dive. When it did, we saw a female goldeneye with a steeply inclined forehead with a short and stubby yellow bill. Bingo! Barrow's Goldeneye! Another tick for the year-list.

Barrow's Goldeneye look quite similar to Common Goldeneye. With a little more attention to detail, it is possible to discern which is which. The males are easy: the white cheek patch on the male Barrow's is obviously crescent shaped, whereas that on the Common is much more circular. In the case of the hens, the easiest field make is the bill: female Barrow's have a mostly yellow bill; that of the Common is mostly dark gray, or even black.

The fact of the two separate populations mentioned above does not appear in the genetics. Perhaps an industrious graduate student will investigate emigration and immigration between birds of these two regions on opposite sides of the continent.

Oh, as for my noon bus deadline, I made it with about fifteen minutes to spare.

Today's bird of the year:

80. Barrow's Goldeneye

Friday, 09 February

I would hazard to say that most people, especially non-birders, consider birding something you do "out in nature." That is to say that you have to go out in the woods, meadow, mountain, lakeshore, or seashore, in a place that at least feels wild, if not being outright wilderness. The reality is somewhat less well defined. In large metropolitan areas, as well as small towns, parks can serve as oases for birds. *Birders: The Central Park Effect*, a 2012 movie, nicely illustrates the fact of this phenomenon in New York City.

On this particular gray day, Fogo needed a walk. For that matter, so did I. So, I opted for birding in town for a change, walking around Bar Harbor, its neighborhoods and side streets, in my pursuit of birds.

12:30 p.m.   Parking at Grant Park, which is often filled with tourists during the summer but was devoid of activity on this winter's day, Fogo ran unencumbered while I birded. Separating the park and the Bar Harbor Inn immediately to the north is a fence grown over into a dense tangle of bittersweet forming a hedgerow that our urban birds seem to love.

Almost immediately, I found four House Finches, the male a wonderfully rich wash of raspberry red. When I need House Finch for a day-list, Grant Park is my go-to spot. Black-capped Chickadees were busily scavenging bits of difficult-to-see food. A Downy Woodpecker was quietly pecking a hole that threatened to topple a skinny tree. A Dark-eyed Junco was shuffling through the leaf litter in that very sparrow sort of way (yes, juncos are sparrows).

There were numbers of Common Eider, Long-tailed Duck, and Bufflehead down at the water's edge. Foreshadowing spring, the males of this last were already starting to corral the females in the age-old dance of courtship. Single White-winged Scoter and Black Scoter hens were readily identified. Red-breasted Mergansers, Common Loons (eleven!), Horned Grebes, Black Guillemots, and Herring Gulls rounded out my list for the day's seabirds.

I walked the length of the Shore Path, coming out on Wayman Lane. Up Wayman and down Hancock Street. Then over to Atlantic Avenue, crossing Elbow Lane to Derby Lane. There are numerous feeders throughout; all, surprisingly, filled with feed (all-too-often I get excited to see a bird feeder and then notice it is empty and may have been for some time).

The ecology, as well as the psychology, of feeding birds is complex. While the majority of studies show feeding has a spectrum of influences on birds, most all seem to be in the positive. Furthermore, it seems very few native birds actually rely on feeders; instead, they have an intricate foraging network with any given feeder only figuring in as a stop on a circuit of potential food sources.

This time of year, birds are more widely dispersed as they seek wild foods that require more effort to glean. Meanwhile, feeders concentrate activity and can make for grand entertainment watching the interspecies dynamics.

At the Elbow Lane feeders, there is an abundance of shrubby vegetation that particularly attracts the birds for its relative security. More Black-capped Chickadees and Dark-eyed Juncos, along with Northern Cardinals and House Sparrows, were making a racket that could be heard half a block away. As I was standing in the street, binoculars scanning for anything different or unusual, Fogo sitting, both of us intently watching the birds, I'm sure we made quite a sight.

The buzzy calls of a flock of American Goldfinch announced their arrival. First, they came into the treetops, then they descended upon the lone Nyjer seed feeder. Every year at this time, I am always struck by the fact that some of the males are already beginning to molt into their brilliant yellow breeding plumage. And every year I have to remind myself that this is not inordinately early.

Wait! That's not a goldfinch! Although the size and shape were right, it was too pale and had a distinct red topknot. A Common Redpoll! My experience with redpolls has always been where there is one there is a flock, so I looked and looked and looked some more. Alas, this guy was, indeed, solo (well, along with his twenty goldfinch cousins; they are in the same subfamily—Carduelinae—after all).

Continuing my walking tour of Bar Harbor, I slowly rack up a respectable day-list. At twenty-three species, I pondered what else I might possibly find. Perhaps a Northern Mockingbird.

Northern Mockingbirds have never been a common bird on Mount Desert Island. They were rare enough that Maurice Sullivan, chief naturalist for Acadia National Park in the 1930s and 1940s, chose to make note of one in 1940 in the same report in which he detailed Maine's first Ivory Gull[i]. Another mockingbird was noted in Southwest Harbor in 1946[ii]. James Bond (the ornithologist, not Her Royal Majesty's secret agent)[iii] wrote, "Mockingbirds have been reported a number of times from Mt. Desert, but I believe all have been vagrants from the south. The species has extended its range northward in recent years and has been found nesting in Nova Scotia and even in Newfoundland. During some forty seasons on the island I have seen but one, a bedraggled individual that spent several weeks at the Goose Cove cemetery."[iv] Ralph Long, a former teacher of science at Mount Desert Island High School, wrote, "They have been reported many times on the island during the breeding season. I have often seen them in Southwest Harbor in early June, but none has stayed more than a few days."[v]

For my part, I manage to see one or two a year in Bar Harbor. And Bridge Street is where most of those sightings have taken place, including today's. Heading down Bridge Street, just before you reach the low-tide bar (at low tide, you can walk across the bottom of the ocean to Bar Island), there is a dense hedgerow. This is the place. And it was the place this day! Sure enough, a Northern Mockingbird responded to my pishing, popping up, fixing me with the steely-eyed glare in a way that only mockingbirds can do.

By the time I finished my morning tour of Bar Harbor, I had spent two hours walking nearly five miles, taking in many of our residential streets and neighborhoods. During that time, I walked the ½-mile Shore Path, from the Town Pier to Wayman Lane, tallying seven species of ducks, Red-necked Grebe, and Common Loon. Our several town parks yielded nine species. Hedgerows of bittersweet and buckthorn, homes with feeders (some elaborate displays, some single feeders) all were sources of birds. My efforts resulted in twenty-four species. Not bad for a winter's day birding in downtown Bar Harbor.

Today's birds of the year:

81. Common Redpoll   82. Northern Mockingbird

Sunday, 11 February

It has been a weekend of gloomy, dreary, rainy weather. So, what did Natalie, Anouk, Fogo, and I do today? Why, go hike around Little Moose Island in the Schoodic section of Acadia National Park. We firmly believe that a little inclement weather should not inhibit your enjoyment of the great outdoors. As part of that conviction, we rely on good outdoor clothing and footwear so that we can stay dry. Well, if not dry, at least warm. (And, for a ten-year-old, a bit of chocolate is a great motivational inducement, too.)

This was my fourth trip in two weeks to the Schoodic Peninsula as I try to fill in a few of the winter seabird gaps in my year-list. Specifically, Thick-billed Murre. If I don't find one in the next month or two, chances were slim I would see one in any other season this year.

On our way to Moose Island, we made two brief stops—Arey Cove and Schoodic Point—both in hopes of increasing the odds of finding the elusive bird. Arey Cove, ever a glorious landscape of rocky shorelines, crashing waves, and musical, bowling-ball-sized cobbles, is also a good birding site. Today, a pair of Harlequin Ducks close to shore gave us memorable views. Even Anouk, who perpetually has a mischievously derisive bird remark, was impressed. But no Thick-billed Murre.

Schoodic Point was quiet, at least in terms of birds. Across the rocks, I saw a fellow birder with a spotting scope set up, so I approached him and introduced myself by way of asking what he was seeing. Turns out he was a freshman College of the Atlantic student I had corresponded with via email. He had just seen a Thick-billed Murre flying across the water. What?! Not fair! So, I looked, scanning the waters for anything that might resemble a murre. The closest I got was a string of lobster trap buoys.

12:51 p.m.   With tide ebbing, we parked along the Schoodic Loop Road and walked across the bottom of the ocean to Little Moose Island. There is not much in the way of trails, certainly nothing formal, circumnavigating the island. Wearing our foul weather gear and Wellies (tall, rubber Wellington-style boots are *de rigueur* in Maine), we tromped through the exposed intertidal zone and then scrambled on the rocky perimeter of the island.

At our first vantage of the ½-mile distant Schoodic Island, our binoculars enabled us to find a Snowy Owl fittingly perched on the large, blue sign denoting the island's status as a seabird nesting site. While we watched the Snowy sitting there, a second flew by! Seeing a Snowy Owl is always a good way to start an outing; seeing two is doubly so.

Some of the usual sea-ducks—Common Eider, Black Scoter, Bufflehead, Common Goldeneye, Red-breasted Merganser—were present in small numbers. A lone Great Cormorant flew by at breakneck speed, ushered by the wind. A pair of distant Razorbill were sitting on the water (with the Razorbill, I could have gone home and been happy with the day). A black-backed gull showing notable contrast between its mantle and wingtips had me trying to turn it into a Lesser Black-backed Gull, but no luck: pink legs confirmed it as a Greater Black-backed Gull (the Lesser Black-backed would have had yellow legs).

Every time a seabird winged past, I peered through rain-flecked eyeglasses and rain-stippled binoculars. Common Eider. Common Merganser. Common Loon. Red-necked Grebe. Each and every one got my heart-rate up in hopes that it might just be a Thick-billed Murre.

As we reached the southern tip of the island, another seabird blew by. Just like all the others, it was beating its wings rapidly, flying before the wind. This one, though, had the stockier, counter-shaded body of an alcid. Fingers crossed! A rather stout and pointed bill. Good! Blacker back and head with only minimal white under the bill. Yes! A Thick-billed Murre! PHEW! As much as I love going to the Schoodic Peninsula, this had proved to be a lot of work for one bird, especially one that a number of other birders had been seeing.

What is it that makes this bird both so elusive to find and so intriguing? Murres are in the family Alcidae, the same family that includes Atlantic Puffins and Razorbills. All alcids are found in the cold northern latitude waters, the northern counterpart of penguins in the Southern Hemisphere. They tend to nest on remote cliffs or remote cliffs on offshore islands. In the northwest Atlantic, Thick-billed Murres nest from Labrador north to the pack-ice while their winter range can extend as far south as Cape Cod. That said, when not on nesting territory, they do tend to concentrate offshore.

As for me, I, too, am drawn to northern latitudes, and this species is yet another representative of a landscape that speaks to me.

Today's bird of the year:

83. Thick-billed Murre

Thursday, 15 February

I'm sure it's a bit of a game played among island residents every-where—it certainly is a regular topic of conversation among Mount Desert Island residents: "How long has it been since you left the island?" For years, I prided myself on how infrequently I left the island, sometimes going months, literally, without crossing the causeway onto the mainland. Somehow, it seemed there was nothing for me off-island. You know what? I was wrong. There are a LOT of wonderful places to explore off-island!

So it was that on this day, when Natalie and I had business in Ellsworth, we decided to head out early for a walk at the Frenchman Bay Conservancy's Indian Point Preserve. A mere mile from down-town Ellsworth, this wonderful little preserve on the former Tinker Farm offers a ¾-mile wooded path through an Eastern Hemlock forest taking you down to the tidal waters of the Union River.

8:31 a.m.   It was chilly, with the woods seeming to hold the cold in its forested embrace. With all the freezes and thaws, the ground was icy, making for treacherous walking.

Right at the trailhead, I heard the sweet-sounding trill of Cedar Waxwings! Most years, I find waxwings—either Bohemian or Ce-dar—all winter long. For some reason, this winter, they have been largely absent. This absence is almost certainly tied to food, either a lack of it here or a surfeit of it elsewhere.

Cedar Waxwings are so named for the waxy, red tips of the secondary wing feathers. That red, coupled with an overall khaki color scheme, black bandit mask, and brilliant yellow tail-band, make this an attractive bird.

Cedar Waxwings eat fruit almost exclusively. In the spring, the hanging fruit that has ripened, frozen, and thawed, repeatedly, sometimes ferments. Waxwings that eat this fermented fruit can actually get drunk from the alcoholic content. It is rather amusing to watch a Cedar Waxwing that has consumed too much fermented fruit. They will stagger, fall over, and crash into branches when they fly, a veritable drunken aviator.

The trail took us down to the edge of the Union River. There were informative interpretive panels, some sharing the working waterfront history, others offering natural history lessons, but our eyes were more trained on the water. We took our time, watching the Mallards and Common Mergansers. Male Common Goldeneyes were strutting their stuff, posturing, throwing their heads back, all in attempts to prove to the lone female who was the most worthy.

As I was scanning the water, looking at the gulls and waterfowl, the distinctive rattling call of a Belted Kingfisher burst out. Another first-of-the-year!

Kingfishers are wonderful birds. The casual observer can mistake them for Blue Jays, but these birds are unrelated; well, other than being in the Class Aves. Kingfishers are a bird of riparian corridors, feeding exclusively on aquatic and marine critters, and those being mostly small fish. Either along a sandy riverbank, or in a sandy cut within a short distance of water, they excavate a nesting tunnel which can be up to four feet deep. At feeding time, they seek a perch offering a water vantage. Lacking a suitable perch, they will fly, hovering thirty to fifty feet above the water, head facing down, scanning with their keen eyes. When piscine food is espied, down they plunge-dive to spear their food.

Here in Maine, we are near the very southern edge of the population of migratory kingfishers. For us, that means that while they do migrate south most years, we can sometimes find them in the winter.

Today's birds of the year:

84. Cedar Waxwing

85. Belted Kingfisher

Friday, 16 February

We were a bit late getting Fogo out for the first of his thrice-daily walks in our woods. An advantage to escorting him is that I am regularly in the woods around our house and so am attuned to the daily, as well as seasonal, goings on in the microcosm that is our woodlot. I see the latest overnight White-tailed Deer bedding spot under a Northern Red Cedar. The copse of standing dead Red Spruce is thinner as more trees came down after the latest windstorm. And the birds keep me company.

8:31 a.m.   This morning, there was a lot of bird activity out and about. Jays and crows, chickadees and nuthatches. A Downy Woodpecker was calling out its loud "whinny" call. Dark-eyed Juncos were working the exposed leaf litter on the forest floor, foraging for food. A Brown Creeper was creeping up a tree.

Wait, the jays and crows. They were not just doing their typical jay and crow things, jaying and crowing, they were agitated. Highly agitated. And, by the sound of things, there were a LOT of them. That can only mean one thing: raptor!

Fogo and I tromped deeper into the woods, toward the raucous noise of the corvids. It did not take long to see them in the treetops, swooping and diving at some unseen menace…well, unseen by me. We crept closer. Paused. Closer. Paused again. Closer yet. And there it was: a large, brown and gray feathered creature staring right at us with its intense yellow gaze, "ear" tufts erect. A Great Horned Owl!

Found across the continent, except in the furthest north stretches where the forests give way to tundra, Great Horned Owls are a large and powerful bird, even known to take down prey larger than themselves. Crows know that this is a fearsome predator and so they seem to be particularly aggressive toward it in response, occasionally gathering in immense flocks, harassing Great Horned Owls, sometimes for hours.

As for those "ears," well, they are neither ears nor are they associated with hearing. Ear tufts generally occur in woodland owls. With that in mind, current thinking is that they serve dual purposes: a form of communication and camouflage. In terms of communication, it could be a silent way to communicate with young; positioning the ear tufts in various ways may have different meanings. It could also serve as a warning to enemies, perhaps making the owl appear larger. As for camouflage, when erected, ear tufts break the rounded contour of an owls' head, perhaps allowing it to better blend in with its surroundings.

While Fogo and I stood there, watching the dynamic between the crows and the seemingly nonplussed owl, I appreciated this year-bird all-the-more for the fact that I found it in my favorite patch: my back woods. You really don't have to go far to find birds.

Today's bird of the year:

86. Great Horned Owl

Sunday, 18 February

Natalie, her sister Myriam, Myriam's adult son Tristan, Anouk, and I embarked on a three-hour drive to western Maine for a four-day cross-country skiing trip to Maine Huts & Trails[i]. This is a wonderful non-profit operation currently featuring four full-service huts and sixty miles of trails groomed for cross-country skiing. This is our idea of an idyllic retreat and each year we travel to one or more of the huts for a cross-country skiing adventure. The hut system is far removed from my Little Big Year turf, but our brief drive through Hancock County proved fortuitous.

The morning of our departure, we awoke to a blanket of fresh snow five inches deep. And it was still snowing. Hard. By the time we left our home at 8:15 a.m. (only fifteen minutes later than we had planned; not bad, not bad at all), there was at least three inches more of the fluffy white stuff.

Driving north to Bangor, the roads were sloppy, almost white-knuckle conditions. Snow was coming down sideways on the windshield, reducing visibility. Road salt was struggling to do its job of melting snow, which also meant that wet and dirty road grime was being kicked up by the vehicles ahead of us, making the windshield wipers work overtime.

8:57 a.m.   The road conditions continued to deteriorate. Snow landing on the road turned to slush, and worse, ice. Instead of driving the posted fifty-five miles per hour, we were reduced to a thirty-five miles per hour creep (and this from a guy who grew up in the Northeast and is perfectly comfortable driving in wintry conditions). Just a few miles north of Ellsworth, but still within the town and Hancock County limits, a bird flew across the road.

I couldn't divert much attention to it, but that little voice in the back of my mind—that voice that I often try to ignore but when I listen, am almost always rewarded—whispered, "Take another quick look." I did. Jay. The flight was unmistakably that of a jay. But which jay?

Maybe it was the size. Maybe it was the paler cast. Maybe it was the seeming lack of a head shaped by a flight-flattened crest. Something about the bird begged a second oh-so-brief look.

Gray Jay?

There was most definitely a pale, almost white, forehead. And the underwing linings were a very light gray.

Gray Jay! Yes!

Gobie. Camp-robber. Whiskey-jack (which is derivative of *Wisakedjak*, who was a benevolent trickster and hero in Algonquin and Cree lore). Canada Jay[ii]. Whatever moniker you choose, they can be quite tame. If there are Gray Jays around and you have food out, don't turn your back or any delectable morsels will be gone in an instant.

Look for this gregarious bird in boreal and sub-boreal forests. That makes sense: the vicinity of where it flew across the road seemed just the right mix of various age classes of conifer to be home to Gray Jays. Brief as this sighting was, it would be my last Hancock County bird for four days.

On a previous hut-to-hut cross-country ski trip, this one to Gaspésie National Park in Québec, I was reminded just how tame they are. After a ten-mile day, we finally made it to our hut, *La Mésange* (or the Chickadee)[iii]. Once we were settled—that meant the woodstove finally heating the cabin, the eighty-quart pot filled with snow and perched atop the woodstove to melt for drinking water, bunks claimed, ski boots removed, appetizers and beverages set out—I went outside to see what birds I could see.

Nothing like a day of cross-country skiing in bitter cold (it was well below 0° Fahrenheit) to work up an appetite. So, while I was looking and listening, I tore into a Nature Valley Oats 'n Honey granola bar. YUM! My favorite!

I could swear that the sound of me ripping open the thin foil wrapper was enough to call in every Gray Jay within a ½-mile radius. It seemed as if almost instantaneously, four of the gray ghosts came hawking in (or should that by "jaying in"?), lighting on the cardinal points with me as the center of the compass rose.

Being an ever-curious naturalist, I crumpled up some granola into my palm, held my hand aloft, and the Gray Jay buffet was open. The birds took turns, one by one, gliding in, taking a bit of granola, and retreating. They certainly did not weigh much in my hand.

Of course, whichever ones were not feeding at any given moment were squawking up a ruckus, enough so that my skiing buddies came out to see what the noise was all about.

And that was the very moment I had closed my fingers around the toes of one as it lit upon my hand, effectively capturing it so that I could read the band on its leg (I would later learn it had been caught and banded the previous year in Gaspésie National Park). Natalie, a Leave No Trace maven, gave me grief about disturbing the wildlife. But, I claimed, this was the workings of an ornithologist practicing his craft!

Today's bird of the year:

87. Gray Jay

Thursday, 22 February

I like to change up the Weekly Birding Tour destinations to increase the array of birds we might find over the course of the winter. This week, we were to meet at the Bar Harbor Village Green at 8:00. As I was up and raring to go, I arrived early for a little solo birding.

7:35 a.m.   I parked on Firefly Lane, adjacent to the Village Green, my shoreline blue Toyota minivan sporting "GANNET" on the license plate plainly visible to any early arriving guests. From there, I walked down Albert Meadow Lane. This short stretch of road, coupled with the Shore Path, typically yields good looks at Common Eider, Bufflehead, Common Loons, Black-capped Chickadees, Northern Cardinals, House Finch, American Goldfinch, and House Sparrow. And this day did not disappoint. There is value in observing the commoner birds over and over, learning their behaviors, discovering what they eat, observing their inter- and intra-species interactions, figuring out their seasonality—some species are common in one season but not another.

Take Gray Catbird, for instance. In a typical year, they don't begin to show up until the very end of April or the beginning of May, haunting shrubby, disturbed, edge habitat where they can be quite common. This makes sense: their genus name, *Dumetella*, is Latin for "small thicket."

Catbirds, along with mockingbirds and thrashers, are mimics. While catbirds do not have anywhere near the aptitude for mimicry of their cousins, who parrot every conceivable sound in their environment (this is especially true of mockingbirds), they do an incredibly good impression of a household cat—*meow*, hence their eponymous name—and have songs that can stretch to ten minutes!

They can also be quite bold, which makes them good study subjects. You can watch them chase away food competitors or raise the alarm when potential predators appear (we humans generally do not merit their concern but try pishing and all Hades may break loose).

This year, a number of them have already been reported around Mount Desert Island, including on Albert Meadow Lane. In my recent visits, I kept hoping to see one—there is certainly plenty of fine Gray Catbird habitat—but no such luck. Until today.

Standing on the road, scanning the ornamental vegetation for birds, it took me a moment to place the russet patch of feathers I could just barely make out through all the dense branches: I was looking at the undertail coverts (that is, the rump below the tail) of a Gray Catbird!

12:09 p.m.   My Weekly Birding tour over (this time of year, it runs from 8:00–noon), it was time to head home. As I drove down Cottage Street, one of Bar Harbor's primary business drags, a large bird, eagle-sized but lacking the heft, dark in hue, wings held in a dihedral, or upward angle, could only be a Turkey Vulture!

Turkey Vultures are a much-maligned species that have evolved to fill the important niche of scavenger. In fact, they provide valuable ecological services, removing, by eating, dead animals from the landscape. They are unique in having gut bacteria which enables them to eat rotten food that would otherwise sicken (or worse) the heartiest vertebrates among us. Their bare head, red skinned like that of a Wild Turkey, is an evolutionary adaptation allowing them to reach into rotting carcasses and pull out all manner of slimy bits without the nuisance of feathers which might retain all those nasty, slimy bits. Same with their legs and feet.

When I lead children's programs, I enjoy sharing with them how not only do Turkey Vultures eat disgusting foods, but they squirt liquid guano down their legs, whitewashing them clean of blood and guts. Sounds disgusting, but the guano is sterile, and thus, a handy form of sanitation.

Another story I sometimes tell is that, contrary to the work of John James Audubon, Turkey Vultures do, indeed, have a very keen sense of smell. The short of it is that in 1826, a then forty-year-old Audubon was of the mind that Turkey Vultures did not zero in on food as a result of smell; rather, they used keen vision. To "prove" this, he set out two pieces of meat: a fresh piece lain on the ground in plain sight and a rotten piece covered with cheesecloth. Audubon's assertion: if Turkey Vultures, with their known predilection for carrion, had an acute sense of smell, they would opt for the stench of rotten flesh under the cheesecloth rather than the visible and virtually odorless fresh meet. Well, Turkey Vultures are no dummies. Yes, they are perfectly capable of eating rotten meat, but given a choice, they would much rather food that is fresh.

As a result of Audubon's flawed experiment, we spent the better part of the next 150 years believing not just Turkey Vultures, but birds generally, did not rely on olfaction to find food.

My introduction to Turkey Vultures came when I was young, a year or two before I got serious about birding. Certain facets can make for a story that will forever stick with a youngster. Sprinkle in various doses of historical intrigue and gross facts and you can almost be guaranteed to have a prize-winner.

My family was on vacation, making our way to visit my father's youngest sister and her husband, Connie and Bill, in the greater

Washington, D.C., area. In those days, the four of us kids were piled in the back of our family's 1965 blue Ford Country Squire station wagon with the faux wood paneling on the sides. No seatbelts, no airbags. The rear seats were folded flat with suitcases and sleeping bags arranged to make a queen-sized play area.

We stopped at Gettysburg National Military Park to learn about the 1863 battle fought there during this pivotal time in our American history. What stuck in my young mind, though, was less the history and more the story told by one interpretive ranger while we were on his walking tour. In talking about the battlefield and the Union and Confederate soldiers, pointing out the positions where various officers fell, and the number of dead, the ranger suddenly pointed to the sky, indicating the Turkey Vultures soaring effortlessly on unseen thermals. His words, as I remember them, were thus:

"See those buzzards, circling above us? They live an incredibly long time. In fact, some of them were alive during the Civil War and ate the flesh of our dead soldiers." (By the way, "buzzard" is a colloquial American term for vulture.)

WOW! What eight- or nine-year-old boy in the early 1970s wouldn't have been moved by that little intellectual tidbit?

It wasn't until many decades later that I finally challenged that "fact." Turns out that the oldest wild Turkey Vulture documented by science lived just shy of seventeen years.

Today's birds of the year:

88. Gray Catbird   89. Turkey Vulture

Friday, 23 February

Here in Maine, public schools plan their weeklong winter break to coincide with Presidents' Week. While the beginning of the week saw my family and me cross-country skiing in western Maine, the end of the week had us home with time on our hands. My bargain with Anouk was that we could head up to Ellsworth to do some shopping if we did a walk and some birding along the way. "Okay, Daddy." But first...

Sitting at my desk in my home office, my laptop is situated so that I simply have to raise my eyes to look out the window. This is a good thing as it makes me infinitely happy to see trees, spruces and firs, maples and oaks. And it is sometimes a nuisance as it causes me no end of distraction every time I see movement. What bird was that? Did I just see a butterfly? What bird was that? Oh, look, a squirrel. What bird was that? Turkeys! Hey, a coyote! What bird was that? (Do you sense a theme?)

11:57 a.m.   The "Newfoundland" Robins are back! Science tells us these dark-hooded American Robins, who happen to largely breed in Newfoundland and Labrador, merely have extra pigmentation. Here it is late February and they are back, exactly on time. Migration really is an amazing natural phenomenon. There was another robin. And another. And another. Some jays and crows. More robins. Twelve in total, all "Newfoundland" Robins, were easily observed without ever moving from my desk.

But one robin, just across the road, seemed, somehow, not quite robin-like. So, I grabbed my binoculars. It turned out the reason it seemed not quite robin-like was because it was not a robin. It was a woodpecker. A woodpecker with a white rump. Northern Flicker! Unlike the robins, this bird was early. Flickers are birds we normally begin seeing at the end of March and we continue seeing them until well into November.

Migration is, indeed, a truly amazing natural phenomenon. Most people think of bird migration as discrete spring and fall events within limited windows of time when birds arrive or depart. In reality, there is some form of bird migration going on nearly year-round.

In January and February, some of the winter finches, especially Pine Siskins and both Red and White-winged Crossbills, can be on the move in search of mast, the various seed crops of the forests. These species are less migratory and more irruptive, moving to wherever the food is. All three of these species begin nesting in late winter.

Northern Saw-whet Owls, some of which might be found throughout the winter, begin arriving in earnest mid- to late-February, while "Newfoundland" Robins begin coming through later in the month.

March begins seeing an increasing number of ducks as they stage for their final northward push. Throughout the month, Red-winged Blackbirds quickly increase their numbers, too.

The first day of April, almost like clockwork, is when the first Great Blue Herons return to Mount Desert Island.

April is also when the hardier warblers typically appear. Palm Warblers begin to arrive, increasing in numbers, occupying a wide variety of habitats as they search for food. Yellow-rumped Warblers are not far behind, feeding in all levels of the canopy. (This is a good time to look for the random Orange-crowned Warbler.) At the end of the month, you should set out your hummingbird feeders[i] so that when the first ones arrive in the coming days, they are greeted with high-energy food.

May sees most of the rest of the warblers making their appearance, as well as a number of the sparrows. By mid-month, Bobolink suddenly fill the meadows, crazily singing their bubbly song. Returning Laughing Gull numbers peak by the end of the month. Shorebirds start appearing throughout the month, especially the latter half.

Nelson's Sparrows return the end of May and beginning of June. June is also when the bulk of the Blackpoll Warbler population passes through.

Shorebirds are a family of birds who largely nest in the Arctic. Those individuals not successful in attracting a mate begin meandering south as early as the end of June and July. Shorebird numbers peak in August as they head south after the short Arctic breeding season. (To truly experience this phenomenon, visit the tidal flats at Mary's Point, New Brunswick, mid-August where you might see up to 60,000 Semipalmated Sandpipers foraging at the tide's edge.)

Warbler migration peaks through September and well into October.

October and November are when sparrows largely migrate (in fact, 01 November each year is when I try offer a sparrow field trip). Hermit Thrush are largely gone south by the second half of November.

December is fairly quiet in terms of migration, but there are still some ducks and the odd skein of Canada Geese moving south, as well as a small but steady stream of Northern Gannets offshore, winging their way to the southeastern States and the Gulf of Mexico.

12:50 p.m.   On our way to Ellsworth, a quick detour to scan the grassy margins of the Hancock County–Bar Harbor Airport for Snow Buntings yielded four. I always enjoy seeing these Arctic birds. A Lapland Longspur among them was not unexpected. And added a tick to the year-list.

In non-breeding plumage, Lapland Longspurs are rather drab, sparrow-like birds. In actuality, they are more closely related to the Snow Buntings than sparrows. The name longspur refers to the fact that the hind toe has an elongated claw, or spur. Through banding studies, we know that one of these diminutive Arctic denizens lived to be at least five years old.

2:15 p.m.   We are coming into the time of year when waterfowl can start showing up, so Anouk and I intentionally overshot Ellsworth to first visit the Green Lake National Fish Hatchery. This hatchery is dedicated to the raising of federally protected, wild strain Atlantic Salmon. Anouk, who regularly decries birding as boring (all parents out there know that anything we like just has to be uncool to our progeny), was more than a little interested in the two Northern Pintails and the male Hooded Merganser. ("Daddy, will you add these to my eBird?" Yes, birding may be boring, but she does have her own eBird list.)

At the outfall, where the hatchery disgorges the treated water from its operations, was a lone Green-winged Teal! My third year-bird of the day. These are lovely little ducks. As ducks go, they are very small, only about a foot long, a little more than half the size of a Mallard. Male Green-winged Teal have a ruddy head with a bold, iridescent green swath through the eye. Minute comb-like "teeth" around the inner edge of their bill (known as lamellae) are essential in the capturing and holding of the tiny invertebrates they filter from the water while they dabble. From banding data, we know that the oldest Green-winged Teal was at least twenty years old!

2:48 p.m.   Anouk, Fogo, and I made it to the abandoned Maine Central Railroad tracks that intersect Nicolin Road, north of Ellsworth. These long-abandoned tracks go through a bog and coniferous forest. I was curious to see if there might be any activity at the old Great Horned Owl nest (there was not). Walking on the old tracks with my ten-year-old daughter gave us plenty of opportunity to play games that centered on balancing on the rails. I could also bird by ear, hearing Mourning Dove, Common Raven, Black-capped Chickadee, and Golden-crowned Kinglet. A small flock of Red Crossbills quickly passed overhead, identified by their distinctive, harsh, *jip jip* flight calls.

As we were walking, I heard a warbling song that took a while to penetrate my consciousness. Not since last fall had I heard the garrulous, rapid warbling of the Purple Finch. As virtually none have been seen in Maine this winter, I was not even thinking of this species. That said, it finally hit me. Purple Finch! Four year-birds in a day; not bad for the end of February.

Regarding their garrulous song, Purple Finches are one of those few species for which I have no mnemonic. Partly it is because the song is long and complicated, up and down and all over the scale. But they are also known to incorporate the sounds of species such as Barn Swallow, Eastern Towhee, Brown-headed Cowbird, and American Goldfinch. So, when I hear the song-without-a-mnemonic, I know it is Purple Finch.

Back on Mount Desert Island, I have a special affinity for Purple Finch. There are historical records of them being banded back in the 1930s. A Mr. Henry P. Bailey, of Northeast Harbor, banded one in 1928 that was retrapped at the old stone teahouse on Great Head (Great Head is now part of Acadia National Park) in 1934. Two more banded by Mr. Bailey in 1930 were retrapped at Great Head in 1935. Yet another bird that Mr. Bailey banded in 1937 was recaptured 465 miles away in Ardmore, Pennsylvania, twenty months later. While these distances are by no means extraordinary, what makes them intriguing is the fact that such a tiny percentage of songbirds are every recaptured. Today, when Natalie, Anouk, and I hike the Great Head Trail, I look at the ruins of the teahouse and think on those long-gone banders.

According to banding records, the oldest known Purple Finch was over fourteen years old.

Today's birds of the year:

90. Northern Flicker
91. Lapland Longspur
92. Green-winged Teal
93. Purple Finch

Sunday, 25 February

Winter for me means skiing and this day I was off to New Hampshire to meet up with five of my best ski buddies from the Adirondacks. Heading out of Bar Harbor, but still within the confines of Hancock County, I made two birding stops in hopes of adding to the year-list (and I almost made a third).

About that third stop, the one that didn't happen but almost did: I had an email this morning from College of the Atlantic professor Bill Carpenter with the simple message, "Unexpected feeder guest this morning..." and a photo of a Varied Thrush. Varied Thrush, near cousin to the American Robin, are typically found in the Pacific Northwest. Yet for some inexplicable reason, it seems one or two turn up in Maine every couple of years.

With the nearby appearance of this rarity, my morning travel plans were suddenly modified to include swinging by Bill's house. Now, I just needed to find out where he lives. A quick email exchange and my plans were dashed: turns out he lives just across the Penobscot River and the Hancock County line in Penobscot County. Bummer!

Still, I managed to add two birds to the year-list.

Two days previous, Deb Hawkes told me that Red-winged Blackbirds had arrived at their house. My hopes for a Varied Thrush thwarted, I swung by her and Ed's house just before I left Mount Desert Island.

11:50 a.m.   I had not even closed the door on my parked car when the telltale *conk-a-ree* of Red-winged Blackbirds greeted me. That was an easy year-bird tick.

Maine is one of the few of the continental United States Red-winged Blackbirds vacate for the winter. In their typical winter range, they are known to gather in vast overnight roosts that can number into the millions. That is a lot of birds! And certainly part of the reason they are despised in many locales. In contrast, during the breeding season, their nighttime roosts are quite small and usually in wetlands where the birds nest.

If we were to anthropomorphize, it would be easy to label male Red-winged Blackbirds as major philanderers, taking up to fifteen females as mates (when the male takes multiple female mates is known as polygyny). Studies have shown that as many as half of the progeny in a given male's harem do not share his DNA.

After watching the birds for a while, I went into Ed's shop where he was working on bird carvings of various seabirds[i]— Razorbills, puffins, and a variety of gulls—for the new Schoodic Marine Center. He also had a variety of other incredibly detailed carvings kicking around, including American Woodcock, American Kestrel, and Ruby-throated Hummingbird. Ed even had a drake Labrador Duck in his painting studio! Now, if I could only count some of those birds. I'm just saying....

12:22 p.m.   This morning, an email from the eBird Maine Rare Bird Alert mentioned a Gadwall observed the previous day at the Ellsworth Harbor Park & Marina by the Lima family. So, it went without saying that this would be my next, and, as it turned out, last, stop in Hancock County for the day.

As soon as I pulled up to my preferred parking slip adjacent to the boat launch (a spot offering superb views of the water from the comfort of my car), two female Common Mergansers prepared for takeoff, wings flapping, white secondary feathers a telltale identifying feature. A few Ring-billed Gulls were kicking around, perched atop various pilings, anxiously waiting the regulars who would soon arrive and scatter breadcrumbs on the ground. A large group of ducks took flight, flushed by an adult Bald Eagle, eventually landing across the Union River, darting in and out of the exposed low-tide ledges.

The ducks were just distant enough that I needed to set up my scope to carefully scan them. I looked at them one-by-one, trying to see every single one, waiting as birds swam out from behind an obstructing ledge, only to duck behind it once again.

Mallards. A lot of Mallards. Forty-seven tallied in all. A few American Black Ducks. Even a few Mallard x American Black Duck hybrids. As I was tallying the birds for my eBird report, I finally saw a Mallard-like bird with a white patch on the side (which was really a swatch of secondary feathers, but with the wings folded over its back, it looked like it was on the side): a male Gadwall. This was an important tick for the year-list. I do see a very small handful of Gadwalls each year, but they are relatively uncommon in our part of Maine, so when one turns up, it is imperative to look for it.

Male Gadwalls are a beautiful bird, in an understated way. Their body is an intricately patterned warm gray. They have tertial wing feathers that are on the red spectrum, trending somewhere between cinnamon and brick. And the undertail and uppertail coverts, the body feathers above and below the rump, are so black as to seemingly absorb all light.

In a world with 75% of all bird species in a state of population decline, Gadwall are a success story. And that can be attributed largely to the Conservation Reserve Program[ii] and the North American Waterfowl Management Plan[iii]. Thanks to these initiatives, which protect crucial habitat (both are programs with broad support from environmentalists and hunters alike), Congress has long and consistently re-authorized their funding.

Two year-birds in less than an hour's time, not bad for a quick morning's birding before leaving town.

Today's birds of the year:

94. Red-winged Blackbird   95. Gadwall

Wednesday, 28 February

O n this last day of February, as I was driving home from my New Hampshire guys' ski trip, I decided to do a little birding. Maybe, just maybe, if I was really, REALLY lucky, maybe I just might find some year birds. And maybe, just maybe, if I was really, REALLY lucky, maybe I just might find enough year-birds to push the list to 100. Of course, that would be a longshot. It was too many species (I would need five), in too short a time, at a time of year when there is not all that many birds around. Besides, I have most of those.

As soon as I crossed the Hancock County border in Hol-den, north of Ellsworth, I began looking along the road. Nothing. Not one single bird. Not even a crow.

In Ellsworth, I followed the Shore Road. All I found were the usual suspects. About 100 Mallards, a few American Black Ducks, nine Common Mergansers, Ring-billed Gulls, and a lone Downy Woodpecker. Finally, there was my American Crow. Black-capped Chickadees, American Robins, and House Finch were all added to my day's tally.

I took a detour, taking in the hay meadows of Route 204. Mud Creek Road, Marlboro Beach, Lamoine Beach, and Jones Marsh. My Hancock County day-list inched to a mere eighteen species. But no year-birds.

Approaching home, Northeast Creek was only a quarter of a mile out of the away.

1:24 p.m.   Canada Goose! Eight of them. These guys always come back early and I thought I might just find them here. There had been a few sporadic reports of Canada Goose through the winter, but either I didn't chase them (this is a bird I will definitely find at some point during the spring) or they weren't there when I finally did.

I have been unable to confirm any Mount Desert Island breeding records prior to 2010 (there have been vague reports such as "I think they nested once, maybe twenty years ago, but I don't remember where"). That changed in 2010, when one pair of Canada Geese nested on the Frenchman Hills fire pond (Anouk has dubbed it 'Lucian's Pond' for her lifelong friend who lives next to it). The next year they were back, with a second pair nesting on nearby Babson Creek salt marsh, as well.

For the next several years, the number of Mount Desert Island nesting locations has increased, as has the number of nests. In 2017, Canada Geese nested at six locations: Frenchman Hills fire pond, Babson Creek salt marsh, Bass Harbor marsh, Northeast Creek, Mount Desert Island High School water settling ponds, and the little pond at Eden Village Motel.

Back at home, I was happy with finding Canada Geese, but I came nowhere near my dreamed goal of five species for the day's list.

Today's bird of the year:

96. Canada Goose

Friday, 02 March

This evening seemed the perfect opportunity to take a nighttime walk in Acadia National Park to look for American Woodcock and Barred Owl. Headlamp? Check. Fresh batteries? Check. iPhone with RødeVideoMic Me external microphone? Check. Røde Rec audio recording app from Røde Microphones loaded on the iPhone? Check. Dog? Check. *Allons-y!*

7:15 p.m.   With most of Acadia National Park's Loop Road closed to automobile traffic for the winter, I parked at the gate toward the end of Kebo Street. Fogo had not had a proper walk earlier in the day, so he was excited to get out. Just enough ambient light pollution was coming from the village of Bar Harbor for me to see where I was walking without using my headlamp. Down Kebo Street, left on the Park Loop Road, then a quick right onto the Jesup Trail. With all the recent warm weather, rain, and melting, I was pleasantly surprised at the firmness of the trail.

Approaching the intersection with the Hemlock Trail, I hit ice. A LOT of it! Time for the headlamp so at least I could see what I slipped on when I break my neck!

It seems winter weather anymore, at least in coastal Maine, if not globally[i], has become both highly variable and quite unpredictable, no longer following long-established trends. It wasn't that long ago that February was reliable for cold and good snow conditions, making for some of the best cross-country skiing I have had anywhere!

Back in late January, the winter's cold and a three-foot snowpack gave way to (relatively) warm weather and rain. Three inches of rain! At Sieur de Monts Spring and Great Meadow, nestled as they are between Champlain and Dorr Mountains, all of this water, flowing atop the frozen ground, had to drain through a three-foot culvert under the Park Loop Road. Early on, it seems, the culvert became blocked by ice, backing up the water, entirely flooding the low-lying area to depths ranging from three to six feet! This was more flooding than anyone could recall ever seeing at this locale. Less than twenty-four hours later, temperatures plummeted into the single digits and all that frigid meltwater froze overnight. The next day, the hiking trails, boardwalk, forests, and open meadow had been turned into a vast ice-rink, which many enjoyed for just that purpose. Now, just over a month later, the considerable amount of ice blanketing the trails made for hazardous walking, but what a unique phenomenon it was!

Taking the Hemlock Trail to the right leads to slightly higher ground, which meant I quickly left the ice behind. This higher ground passes through an old-growth stand of Eastern Hemlock. It is also where Barred Owls can often be found.

Being well past sunset, I had no expectations of seeing a Barred Owl, but I sure had high hopes of hearing their distinctive *who-cooks-for-you, who-cooks-for-you-alllll* call. Most of the world's 234 species of owls are nocturnal, and this is true of Mount Desert Island's.

Contemporary ecological thinking is that owls evolved to be night hunters as that is a time when there is less competition, as well as less danger (at least in the form of predators). Furthermore, over the eons, owls have evolved large eyes (they have the biggest eye-to-head ratio of any bird) for gathering light, which are full of rods (photoreceptor cells in the retina of the eye that function in low-light conditions), giving them good night vision.

Eyes have two primary kinds of photoreceptors: rods and cones. Rods work in low levels of light but only allow for black and white vision; cones need daylight conditions and enable vision in color. It makes sense that owls, being night hunters, have more rods than cones. And it is likely that owls see primarily in black and white and shades of gray. In addition, owls have a sort of mirror at the back of their eye. This "mirror," called the "*tapetum lucidum*," reflects light, giving the rods a second chance to catch light. If you have ever seen the eyes of an animal glowing bright in the night, that is light reflecting off the *tapetum lucidum*.

In addition to highly specialized eyes, owls have evolved facial disks that serve as something of a parabolic dish, focusing sound to their asymmetrically placed ears, helping them precisely pinpoint the location of prey.

Alas, this was not the night for my nocturnal friend—I neither saw nor heard any owls.

Near the end of the Hemlock Trail, where it once again intercepts the Jesup Trail, I encountered more ice. Gingerly making my way along the heavily ice-damaged deer fence around Wild Gardens of Acadia, a bone-dry parking lot was my reward. Rather than completing my typical figure-eight loop of Jesup and Hemlock Trails, I opted for the path of least resistance: returning to my car via the snow- and ice-free Park Loop Road.

Nearing the end of my 2½-mile walk, Kebo Golf Course to my right, I heard a distinctive *peent* calling from across the green. American Woodcock!

In an earlier discussion, I touched on the topic of migration and the fact that there is almost always some species moving north or south. American Woodcock are certainly among the earlier migrants, returning from their southeastern U.S. wintering grounds. A member of the shorebird family—the family of sandpipers and plovers—they have a unique anatomical feature: their eyes are mounted on the side of their head, affording a nearly 360-degree field of view. Being able to see all around without moving is a key to self-preservation, especially when you would make a delectable meal and have no defense from predators other than camouflage.

My most memorable experience with American Woodcocks occurred on a mid-1980s spring evening. My birding mentor and friend, the late Mike Peterson, was getting poor reception on his television. He eschewed cable in favor of a roof-top antenna. I volunteered to go up and see what I could do. This was a two-ladder job: one to the eaves and the second to the peak. His was no simple antenna; rather, it was an old ham radio style mast with three-sided sections, each side crisscrossed like a Jacob's ladder. So up I went.

Fully ten feet above the peak of the roof, this was no OSHA (Occupational Safety and Health Administration) affair. My left foot was firmly wedged on a ¼-inch diameter cross piece; my right leg was hooked around for stability, freeing my hands. Each time I adjusted the antenna a smidgeon, Mike, from inside the house, would shout out further corrections to another friend, Bob, who relayed them to me. After about thirty minutes, the sun had long since set and any residual crepuscular visibility was near its end.

Just before Mike came out to give the all-clear, something buzzed me, flying between my face and the antenna, the whoosh of unseen twittering wings riffling the hair on my brow, a loud chirping practically in my face was so startling that I lurched backward! This was one of those scenes where Hollywood would have the person's life pass before their eyes. I am more of a "do not go gentle into that good night" kind of guy. Instinctually remembering an important life lesson from my old SCUBA instructor—"don't panic"—I threw my arms out and caught the tower. PHEW! And down I climbed.

All the drama aside, what buzzed me on that tower? Why, an American Woodcock, of course.

Each spring look for a bit of open field, often at a woods' edge, and plan to be there at dusk. Listen for the plaintive and regularly repeated *peent* called from the ground, the well-camouflaged

woodcock seemingly invisible, even if it is right at your feet. Periodically, the bird lifts into flight, describing large, ascending circles into
the sky, wind whistling through its wings in a loud, twittering call
interspersed with a chirping. At the peak of its flightpath, it then
plummets to earth, pulling up at the last minute for a gentle landing,
and then the *peent*ing starts again. This is the courtship display of
curious-looking American Woodcock.

Today's bird of the year:

97. American Woodcock

Tuesday, 06 March

After several days of strong winds, I was keen to explore Ocean Drive and see the surf crashing against the rocky shores of Acadia National Park. Given that the winds had largely been easterlies, there was a better than average chance for seeing alcids. Although my year-list already included Dovekie, Thick-billed Murre, Razorbill, Black Guillemot, and Atlantic Puffin, today offered a chance, albeit a small one, for Common Murre.

Common Murre nest close to Hancock County, on Petit Manan Island (one of the more than sixty islands comprising Maine Coastal Islands National Wildlife Refuge[i]), three miles across the Washington County line. Winter is often the best time to find Common Murre close to shore, especially when we get a prolonged period of strong easterlies.

Unfortunately, of all the alcids, it is the least likely to be seen in the area, probably due to some combination of extremely small population in Maine, our usual prevailing southwesterly winds, and the fact that they tend to head out toward the open sea to feed. DRAT! But an optimistic DRAT!

To compound the problem of finding Common Murre, the winds had become northerly overnight, which very likely pushed any alcids back to sea. Still, a bad day of birding is better than a good day in the office. (And this was not a bad day of birding.)

Regardless of which birds might be found, it seemed a good day to invite Ed Hawkes, my regular birding buddy, to join me. Ocean Drive, the two-mile section of Acadia National Park's Loop Road bordering the open ocean, is a wonderful place to walk with friends, affording incredible scenic views and very little automotive traffic in the off-season.

9:57 a.m.   Our outing began with a scene right out of a nature documentary. From our vantage on the Schooner Head Lookout, sheltered in my minivan from the stiff north breeze, we both looked through our binoculars toward Egg Rock, a mere 1½ away. A cloud of gulls wheeling above the lighthouse quickly resolved to be caused by an adult Bald Eagle standing over something white on the ground—probably a freshly killed gull.

Beginning our walk, we quickly tallied the expected winter sea-ducks: Common Eider, Black Scoter, Long-tailed Duck, and Buffle-head. Eleven Common Loon, some beginning to show signs of molting into breeding plumage, was a higher number than I had observed along this route since, well, last year this time.

Thirty-seven duck-like birds had us puzzled for a few minutes. These were all sitting on the water in a loosely spaced raft west of Old Soaker[ii]—the small, emergent rocky island off Sand Beach—all with heads tucked under their wings, presenting a brown feathered blob. Not much to go on. I had puzzled over this very same phenomenon in the past and had eventually come up with Red-necked Grebe. Still, I wanted to be sure. And so, we waited until one eventually raised its head, confirming my hunch.

The year-list prize of the day, though, were our first Double-crested Cormorants of the season. In another month, these will be the most numerous cormorant on the coast of Maine as they return with the spring migration. Meanwhile, most Great Cormorants, for which coastal Maine is their southern migration, eventually head north. A few (quite literally, a few), though, nest on offshore islands along Maine's coast but are infrequently seen April through November.

Growing up in western New York, along the shores of the lower Niagara River, I saw exactly zero cormorants. I would not have my introduction to Double-crested Cormorants until June 1988. At that time, I was a young scientist, two years out of university, studying the chemistry and biology of acid deposition—colloquially known as 'acid rain'—atop 4,867-foot Whiteface Mountain in New York State's Adirondack Park. As excited as I was to be applying my schooling, birds were my passion and my part-time job as warden for the Four Brothers Islands Preserve in Lake Champlain satisfied that desire nicely.

Having a pickup truck with a trailer hitch and loads of small craft experience, the job was mine. On my first day, I parked at the Willsboro Bay Boat Launch on the New York shore of Lake Champlain to prepare to launch the twenty-three-foot Midland Marine fiberglass skiff, "Four Brothers Islands Preserve" boldly emblazoned on the sides. A sport fisherman, large belly leading his way, approached me and said in his thick North Country accent, "I hope you are going out there to kill those gawd-damned birds."

Now, I had not a clue what he was talking about, but as a twenty-three-year-old kid, I can tell you I was intimidated.

Over the years of studying the birds of The Four Brothers, this was a scene that played out over and over, almost *Groundhog Day*[iii] fashion. Nearly every time I went to launch the skiff, some fishermen would approach to express the need to eliminate all the cormorants. Once, several years into my studies, after having developed something of a relationship with some of the fishermen, one approached me in his full-size pickup truck, patted a rifle next to him on the bench seat, and said, "MacDonald, I've got a bullet in my gun for you if you don't do somethin' bout those gawd-damned birds."

I came to learn that cormorants are almost universally loathed in Western society. Fishermen hate them because it is their perception that cormorants are to blame for declining sportfish populations. Never mind that many studies, including my own, have shown again and again that cormorants have a negligible impact on fish populations: science be damned! I routinely heard that cormorants are not native. Again, never mind that the archaeological record shows cormorants extended from coast to coast, nor the fact that we have been persecuting them since the earliest European settlers first came to North America and significantly reduced their population for hundreds of years.

And, as if direct persecution of cormorants was not enough, we inadvertently dealt an additional blow to their population through chemistry. Double-crested Cormorants were among the many species of birds directly affected by the bio-accumulation of DDT (for more on the history and science of DDT, see my account for 29 January). Following the 1972 banning of DDT, it took another decade for it to largely work its way out of the ecosystem. That, coupled with stricter enforcement of the Migratory Bird Treaty Act of 1918, and we finally started seeing a slight uptick in the population of Double-crested Cormorants beginning in 1984.

The increasing population of Double-crested Cormorants steadily gained speed. Numbers from The Four Brothers are illustrative of Double-crested Cormorants across North America: from twenty-two nesting pair in 1984, their population grew to a peak of over 2,000 nests by 2002.

This increased population led to human-wildlife conflicts, and not just with fishermen. Cormorants prefer to nest in trees, but readily take to nesting on the ground. On the westernmost of the Four Brothers Islands, a mature stand of White Pine was decimated by the increasing nutrient load from the nests of hundreds of cormorants. This dense concentration of colonially nesting birds is mighty foul-smelling; a fact particularly lamented by recreational boaters.

Furthermore, waterfront landowners with views of the islands complained about the vista blight.

The science of cormorants is fairly straightforward. After centuries of persecution, their numbers were finally increasing. While the population has yet to reach what ornithologists think was pre-Columbian levels, it is far greater than at any time in living memory. As predators, cormorants are skillful at catching fish. This skill has led to public concerns about declining numbers of sportfish. In turn, countless studies on the feeding habits of cormorants have been undertaken, the majority finding that cormorants are not having negative ecological impacts on fisheries. Despite the science, since early 2000, when New York Congressman John McHugh and Minnesota Congressman Collin Peterson introduced the first legislation proposing a national hunting season on cormorants, there have been persistent efforts to decrease the population of this piscivorous bird.

As a relevant aside, it is interesting to briefly contrast our response to management actions on two species: Double-crested Cormorants and Mute Swans. When the U.S. Fish and Wildlife Service announced a national management plan in 1999 to significantly cull cormorants, there was very little public opposition; however, whenever there are calls to manage Mute Swans, animal rights groups hue and cry that this cannot be done.

One species—the cormorant—is a large black bird with a croak for a voice, nests in foul-smelling colonies, and eats a lot of fish. The other—the swan—is a beautiful, white, graceful silent bird. The former is indigenous to North America; the other is a non-native invasive species that pulls up aquatic vegetation, roots and all, opening the way for non-native and invasive aquatic plants, and tramples the nests and eggs of nearby nesters, including such sensitive species as Common Loon.

Perhaps our approach to managing these two North American species is illustrative of our collective baser instincts, a form of biological racism.

Today's bird of the year:

98. Double-crested Cormorant

Wednesday, 07 March

I am perpetually amazed how one day can be so birdy and the next so relatively quiet. Yes, any number of factors, especially the weather, plays into this, but I am fascinated, nevertheless. For instance, on this day's Weekly Birding Tour, we barely managed twenty-five species. While that is not a horrible tally for a coastal Maine late-winter day of birding, a week before we observed thirty-five species.

11:40 a.m. Four stops and nearly four hours later, our list was stalled at twenty-four species. Our group of Weekly Birding Tour regulars—Jane Potter, Ken Hutchins, and me—made it to our last stop: Hamilton Pond. This is the time of year when the ice is thawing, creating open water patches that congregate waterfowl.

During the past few days, I stopped at Hamilton Pond several times. Each time, my highlights have been three male and one female Hooded Merganser and a pair of Green-winged Teal mixed in with the dozens of Mallard and handful of American Black Duck. Upon our arrival, I set up the spotting scope expecting to see the same four species.

One's expectations can often frame what you see. When I found two small ducks feeding amongst the Mallards on the far shore, they could only be one species, right? And that is what I called out: Green-winged Teal. I knew this would be an addition to Jane's list for the MDI Bird Club, so I had her look in the scope.

"Rich, I don't see the teal."

"Here, let me get the scope back on them."

"Oh, I think I see them. Are they the ducks with the white stripe on the head?"

What? Let me rack my brain for field marks. Both are small. The female is largely shades of brown, similar to a hen Mallard. The male has a ruddy head with a bold teal green eye swoosh. Neither have white on the head. Jane must be mistaken.

"Let me have another look."

American Wigeon! Of course!

I always tell my birding companions to not hesitate to question my identifications. Even the best of us make mistakes. And this was certainly one of mine.

American Wigeon is the goose of the dabbling ducks. "What?" you ask incredulously. How can a duck be a goose?

With their short bill—some say it is shaped more like that of a goose than a duck—they are clearly plant eaters; their short bills are designed for a diet heavy on terrestrial grasses. During the summer months, that largely means foraging on tundra vegetation. During the winter, contemporary American Wigeon are likely to be found in urban areas feeding on grass in business parks and golf courses. In Hancock County, they are moderately regular vagrants, meaning that with effort, a few can usually be found each year, but we are certainly not on any of their migratory flyways.

American Wigeon are among the most northerly nesters. As a result, there are significant hurdles to studying them on their breeding grounds. The result: less is known about their summer ecology (*i.e.*, nest success and offspring survival rates) than the "big five" dabbling duck species; namely, Blue-winged Teal, Northern Shoveler, Gadwall, Mallard, and Northern Pintail.

Fun fact: Based on banding records, the oldest American Wigeon was over twenty-one years old!

Today's bird of the year:

99. American Wigeon

Friday, 09 March

When I grow up, I want to be Seth Benz. He is an amazing birder; has a life filled with incredible bird adventures, both in the name of work and in the pursuit of pleasure; has a breadth and depth of avian knowledge that, if I was prone to envy, would make me green; is the director of the Bird Ecology Lab at the Schoodic Institute; and is a genuinely nice guy. Geography often conspires against us spending much time together, but it doesn't stop either of us from finding good birds and tipping the other off to rarities and vagrants. In the last few days, Seth has had two birds of particular interest: Brant and Northern Shrike.

Seth not being available, I called up Jane Potter for a spontaneous and quick birding tour of the Schoodic Peninsula. This would be a whirlwind tour, with quick stops at the hotspots along Schoodic Loop Road, a little more time in Wonsqueak Harbor to look for the Brant, then Birch Harbor to look for the Northern Shrike.

Cruising along the Schoodic Loop Road only yielded fourteen of the usual suspects, including various seaducks, loons, grebes, cormorants, and gulls.

11:18 a.m.   We pulled into the one-car pull-off along Arey Cove, at the T-intersection with Acadia Drive (the entrance to the campus of Schoodic Institute). Doing a naked eye scan, a female Red-breasted Merganser was in close to shore. Immediately behind it, a mere foot or so away, was a Black Guillemot fully molted into its plumage of all-black with white wing patches. In the distance I could see a few birds that were either eider or scoter (when I finally got my binoculars up, turned out they were both Common Eider and Black Scoter).

A small, birdy speck across the cove seemed to be a suspiciously blocky-bodied bird with a very low profile. Intriguing. Looking through my binoculars, I was most pleased to see a Common Murre! Finally! I now had a complete run on the North Atlantic alcids....

The North Atlantic members of the family Alcidae are Dovekie, Common Murre, Thick-billed Murre, Razorbill, Black Guillemot, and Atlantic Puffin. And an extinct relative, the Great Auk[i], is emblematic of our greed: crush, kill, destroy every last one for food, feathers, and oil.

We do not know with certitude when the last Great Auk was finally killed, but a series of significant dates offers some valuable insights:

1718—A sailor wrote of Funk Island, off the northeast coast of Newfoundland, that "a man could not go ashore upon those islands without boots, for otherwise they would spoil his legs, that they were entirely covered with those fowls, so close that a man could not put his foot between them."

1775—Nova Scotia petitioned English Parliament to ban the harvesting of Great Auk from Funk Island.

1785—English explorer George Cartwright wrote of the Great Auk: "A boat came in from Funk Island laden with birds, chiefly penguins. But it has been customary of late years, for several crews of men to live all summer on that island, for the sole purpose of killing birds for the sake of their feathers, the destruction which they have made is incredible. If a stop is not soon put to that practice, the whole breed will be diminished to almost nothing."

1810—The Great Auk is extirpated from Funk Island.

1840—A lone bird, the last known one in British waters, was killed on St. Kilda, a Scottish island forty miles west of the mainland.

1844—Two birds killed on Eldey, an island off the southwest corner of Iceland, are thought to be the last of the species.

Although the Great Auk is long gone, its name carries on today, even if we don't realize it. The species' genus was *Pinguinus*. Spanish and Portuguese sailors long used a version of that colloquially. Apparently, that name stuck. Sort of. Early sailors to the Southern Ocean saw a tall, counter-shaded[ii] bird that looked remarkably like the *pinguino* of the north. And so, we had penguins.

From an evolutionary standpoint, penguins are unrelated to the alcids of the North Atlantic, even though they look so similar. For this, biologists have coined the phrase "convergent evolution," meaning that species in similar ecological niches (think cold North Atlantic and cold Southern Ocean) evolve similar traits to adapt to those conditions.

Bringing this back to the Common Murre, this, along with the Atlantic Puffin, have long been important food sources in far northern communities. Today, only the puffin is harvested and eaten in Iceland. In Newfoundland, the murre, which is locally called "turre," is still a favored dish. I have eaten many strange foods in my travels, always wanting to eat like the locals, but turre is just too fishy and oily for my taste.

… Any day when I see an alcid is a good day. And seeing the Common Murre made up for dipping on Brant and Northern Shrike.

Today's bird of the year:

100. Common Murre

Sunday, 11 March

When you are obsessed with birds the way I am, you take your birding time whenever and wherever you can get it. Sometimes it is looking out the window from my desk to see a Golden-crowned Kinglet feeding in the spruce. It might be five minutes first thing in the morning when I take Fogo out in our woods for his morning constitutional. Going for a cross-country ski, the swish-swish of polyethylene sliding on snow drowns out all but the loudest Black-capped Chickadees. I can always rely on the garrulous House Sparrows chittering away in the shrubbery in front of the old Camden National Bank in downtown Bar Harbor. Or it might be a rare bird, or at least an uncommon one, that sets you out on a wild shrike chase.

Anouk convinced Natalie into going on an outing to the Orono Trampoline Park. That meant I suddenly had the better part of a weekend day free with no serious obligations. Why not make yet another trip to the Schoodic Peninsula to look for Brant, Spruce Grouse, Northern Shrike, or whatever else I might turn up?

My target birds were guided by the fact that a single Brant had recently been reported from Bunker's Harbor and a Northern Shrike had been haunting some Birch Harbor feeders. At the same time, while Spruce Grouse are not known for moving very far in their life, they are known to breed in Schoodic's spruce forests, albeit in small numbers. Although none of these three species are common at any time of year in Hancock County, the Schoodic section of Acadia National Park is certainly one of the better options for a search.

12:29 p.m.   Driving through Winter Harbor, on my way to look for my day's three target species, I quickly scanned Henry Cove for any white-winged gulls. *Nada.* In fact, there were barely any Herring Gulls, let alone anything more interesting.

Continuing east on Main Street, past the Prospect Harbor Soap Company, I gave a quick glance to the tiny, unnamed pond, expecting to see it still completely frozen. Instead, there was a corner of open water. And in that corner swam two ducks, probably Mallards. Mallards, but ones with a dark head, front, and back; gray flank; and a hint of a white ring around the bill. Doh! They're not Mallards! As soon as I found a safe spot, I U-turned to go back and take a gander. Well, not a gander, they were a pair of Ring-necked Ducks!

Yes, male Ring-necked Ducks are named for the faintly subtle chestnut ring around their neck. Why the ornithological powers that be, in their infinite wisdom and their maddening habit of routinely changing the common names of birds, do not rename this duck Ring-billed Duck, I'll never know. The ring around its neck is virtually invisible from any more than a few feet away; meanwhile, the white ring around the end of the bill is readily discernable from a considerable distance.

12:52 p.m.   I spent the better part of the next hour bushwhacking the spruce forest along the Schoodic Loop Road in search of Spruce Grouse. They favor spruce forests with a fairly open understory and a wet forest floor (the presence of sphagnum moss is always a good indicator of wetness). Let me tell you, those woods were quiet! The sum of all the birds I found was exactly two Golden-crowned Kinglets.

After a few other stops to look for birds along the Schoodic Loop Road, spending some considerable time looking through the spotting scope, scanning the ocean, wishing for a Brant, it was time to move on.

2:43 p.m.   Third time is the charm! Northern Shrike, also known as Butcher Bird for their propensity of impaling prey on buckthorn, or even barbed wire, have been scarce this winter. And not just in Hancock County, but throughout Maine. This one was behaving just like, well, a shrike, perched atop a maple in a Birch Harbor yard clear of any other trees, surveying its environs for avian food. Shrikes are medium-sized songbirds, about the size of a robin. One noticeable difference: a hooked bill that belies their carnivorous appetite.

I could have been perfectly happy resting on my laurels with the shrike, but something told me to go back to Bunkers Harbor to scope the wetland one more time.

2:57 p.m.   The Schoodic Loop Road does not really offer any good vantage of the wetland, so I pulled off the road as best as I could, then set up my spotting scope to scan the open water. A pair of Canada Geese. Another. And a third. A wedge-tailed Common Raven flew overhead. An adult Bald Eagle glided through the field of view of my spotting scope, so I glanced up to better track it. And, almost as soon as I did, a pair of Wood Ducks flushed.

Wood Ducks might just be North America's most beautiful duck species. The male has an orange bill, red eye, and an iridescent green head with a sweptback crest, all on a body of variegated whites and tans and chestnuts. The female sports a beautiful white tear-drop eye-ring, angling back as though swept by a gale.

Wood Ducks are cavity nesters, building their twig-lined abodes in holes in trees, sometimes fifty feet up. Not long after the young are hatched, they scale up to the entrance hole, then free-fall to the great unknown below in answer to their mother's beckoning. They will follow her for weeks until they are fully fledged and able to fend for themselves.

It was a good day of birding. Thirty-six species on a late winter day is not bad, not bad at all for the Schoodic Peninsula. I had struck out during my bushwhacking tromp through a spruce forest known for the occasional Spruce Grouse. The bird, or birds, were probably there, but with the ground blanketed in crusted snow, the birds were likely perched quietly high in a tree, blending in perfectly, their plumage doing the job it evolved to do. The Brant was likely long gone, having only been reported once from Wonsqueak Harbor.

In the end, although I only found one of the day's target birds, I still picked up three year-birds. I count that a successful day.

Today's birds of the year:

101. Ring-necked Duck   103. Wood Duck
102. Northern Shrike

Friday, 23 March

5:10 p.m.   Who cooks for you, who cooks for you all?

I am continuously surprised at how many people, both kids and adults, volunteer *Who cooks for you, who cooks for you all?* when I say Barred Owl.

And that is the sound Natalie and I heard after a short distance along the closed-to-automobile-traffic Cadillac Mountain Road as we cross-country skied up this night. The road up 1,530-foot Cadillac Mountain was blanketed in nearly two feet of frozen-granular snow packed firm by the passage of countless snowmobiles[i]. This was a perfect choice for a sunset adventure with Natalie.

During the day, temperatures had reached into the upper 40s Fahrenheit. By the time we started, the snow was still softened by the day's warmth. That meant a liberal application of Swix special red kick wax on the bottom of my Fischer S-Bound telemark skis.

We parked the car at the Park Loop Road entrance off Eagle Lake Road, fine-tuned our packs full of extra layers, the evening's dinner, and camera gear, put a harness and lead on Fogo, and we were off.

From the beginning, we saw fine soot stippling the snow's surface with much denser concentrations accumulating in any depression. Except that this "soot" was jumping in mighty leaps. Snow fleas!

Snow fleas, of which two species are found in the Northeast, are not related to fleas at all; instead, they are in the springtail family. Whereas the parasitic fleas that torture our pets jump as a result of the rapid extension of their enlarged hind legs, snow fleas are called "springtails" for their "furcula," the tail-like abdomen that folds and releases like a spring, flinging this minuscule arthropod distances many times the length of their body. More importantly, though, is that fact that snow fleas are not parasitic at all. They occur year-round by the hundreds of thousands in the soil, feeding on decaying leaf litter.

It is in late winter when we notice them, their dark color contrasting against the snow as their vertical movement is triggered by warming weather and increased daylight. They migrate upward through the snowpack to munch on the organic particulates that have fallen off trees. Hopping around, as they are wont to do, they end up concentrating in any low spot—animal tracks, footprints, ski tracks. Look down and it seems the ground is moving!

Snow fleas have a glycine-rich antifreeze protein[ii] which inhibits their cells from freezing—a natural anti-freeze.

Over the first mile of skiing from our car to the intersection up Cadillac Mountain, the Park Loop Road rises gradually; whereas the road up Cadillac averages a 5% grade with a maximum of 12%. Within a ½-mile up the mountain road, we paused for me to re-wax my skis. The unmistakable call of an owl drifted up to our ears from far downslope: *Who cooks for you, who cooks for you all? Who cooks for you, who cooks for you all?* No other bird vocalization can be mistaken for a Barred Owl. The sound was coming from the general direction of Sieur de Monts Spring (a reliable place to observe Barred Owls for much of the summer), nearly one mile away, a place where they nest annually.

This time of year, Barred Owls are calling to attract a mate and stake out territory. Once paired, the female will lay eggs (between one and five with two to three being the norm) in a cavity, perhaps where a tree limb broke off, allowing rain to get in over time and erode a hole, or in a hollowed dead tree. Then, the female will incubate them for twenty-eight to thirty-three days.

The female Barred Owl develops a brood patch, an area of the belly devoid of feathers. The brood patch has an abundance of capillaries close to her skin which, when she lays directly upon her eggs, incubates them. This same function is served once the eggs hatch, warming the chicks until they are big and feathered enough to properly thermoregulate on their own. Meanwhile, the male hunts for himself and his mate who is busy incubating.

Once the eggs hatch, she will continue to tend her young for an additional twenty-eight to thirty-five days, feeding them food brought by the male. After the young have fledged (developed the ability to fly on their own), both parents continue feeding them for several more months, teaching them to tear apart meat, and, ultimately, how to hunt.

To thrive, Barred Owls need intact forests. Unfortunately, as a result of logging and encroachment of human habitation, we have seen a decline in their population across the continent, so protected places like Acadia National Park are particularly important.

One important thing we can do to help this charismatic species is to leave dead trees standing. Rather than cut down what we perceive to be unsightly snags, adopt the perspective that they provide homes and sources of food for a wide variety of wildlife, including owls. Besides, Barred Owls eat a variety of foods, including nuisance rodents.

Today's bird of the year:

104. Barred Owl

Monday, 26 March

I am one of the regional coordinators for the Maine Bird Atlas and volunteered to give an evening program introducing this massive project, the whys and hows and wherefores, for the Downeast Audubon Chapter of Maine Audubon[i] at the Blue Hill Public Library. With this good excuse to make the forty-minute drive, and sunset being a bit later each day (6:56 p.m. this evening), I decided to do a little birding beforehand.

A brief stop at the Mountain Road trailhead to Blue Hill Mountain yielded no birds. Fortunately, this was more than compensated for by a plethora of waterfowl on Blue Hill Harbor. Canada Goose, Mallard, American Black Duck, Long-tailed Duck, Bufflehead, Common Goldeneye, and Red-breasted Merganser. A Wood Duck fly-by was a short-lived treat. A lone Mallard x American Black Duck hybrid[ii] was not unexpected.

Soon it was time to drive to the library to prepare for my program. Cruising past the Blue Hill Town Hall, a crabapple tree filled with birds merited a quick stop.

6:27 p.m.   A handful of American Robins could be heard as soon as I opened the car door. Standing, binoculars slung over my shoulder, their profile was instantly evident in the tree.

Automotive traffic on the road was heavier than I would have thought (or liked). The noise of combustion engines and the sound of rubber tires rolling across the pavement added to the avian cacophony, confusing my ability to discern individual bird species. Still, some I was able to make out.

The distinctive and repetitive introductory notes followed by a trill, the song of the Song Sparrow, was plain to my ears. *Purdy purdy purdy* sang the Northern Cardinal. The thin, high-pitched sound of a flock of Cedar Waxwings, ten of them, to be precise, a sort of *zeeeee*, is a sound I am always keen to hear.

There was one other call that took me a moment to place—and it took me a moment only because I hear it so infrequently: akin to the Cedar Waxwing, but a distinctly more musical trill. That's it! Bohemian Waxwing!

A species of the northernmost coniferous woodlands of both North America and the Eurasian continent, they are larger than their Cedar cousin. The cinnamon undertail and yellow piping in the wings confirm its identification (as if I needed it once I placed the song to the bird).

I long thought waxwings were species specific, that you only found one or the other—Cedar or Bohemian—but never the two together. I was actually drafting an article to that extent back in the 1990s when I started seeing mixed flocks everywhere. Nowadays, I still see the occasional mixed flock, but my experience is that it is not a common occurrence.

Wherever there is a fruit-bearing tree in winter, look for waxwings. They seem to have an almost preternatural ability to find fruit. Carotenoid pigments in fruit such as honeysuckle give color to waxwings' red in the secondary wing feather tips and the yellow terminal band of the tail.

After finding a Bohemian Waxwing, it was time to go to the Blue Hill Public Library to give the evening's program. I always start my programs with a solicitation to share recent bird sightings. When I shared my sighting of the Bohemian Waxwing, several attendees were excited and planned to look for it first thing in the morning.

Today's bird of the year:

105. Bohemian Waxwing

Thursday, 29 March

Without even trying, today was a twenty-four-species day. A five-minute morning stop at Hamilton Pond on the way home from the dentist yielded four species of ducks, including one of my favorites: Ring-necked Duck.

Later, before supper, I decided to take Fogo out for a run. Our round-trip birding jog (remember, I am ALWAYS birding) took us from our home to Clark Cove and back and yielded six sparrow species!

4:55 p.m.   A Dark-eyed Junco in the woody shrubbery of our lilac was the first bird of the run. Approaching Red Rock Corner (the intersection of Gilbert Farm Road and Route 102 is known today for the glacial erratic that has long been painted red), the unnamed wetland nestled between the south side of Gilbert Farm Road and the KOA Campground was teeming with singing Red-winged Blackbirds (granted, blackbirds are not sparrows). Just beyond the wetland, a house with a number of feeders was bustling with activity. In fact, almost all of the rest of the birds from my outing were represented here.

Before I even stopped and pulled my binoculars up to my eyes—yes, I run with my binoculars; who doesn't, right?—hopping about the ground a mix of Passerellidae, the Latin name for the family of sparrows.

Chewink! The loud, metallic call of the Eastern Towhee greeted me before I even identified any of the sparrows. I love it when I hear a bird's vocalization and there is no worry about confusing it with some other species. Usually towhees, a species of sparrow particularly fond of foraging in understory leaf litter, arrive a few weeks later than this. Unlike my experience with towhees elsewhere, the Eastern Towhees of Mount Desert Island seem to generally prefer the high-elevation forests of Acadia National Park over the lower broad-leafed forests. So, I was excited to see one somewhere other than the upper reaches of Cadillac or Sargent Mountains.

Scanning the ground, a lone American Tree Sparrow was probably thinking about its impending migration north to the edge of the tundra. (Okay, it wasn't actually thinking about that; rather, it was my anthropomorphization.) Two large sparrows with a reddish hue, boldly streaked, could only be Fox Sparrows. These, too, will soon be heading north to the taiga and the edge of the tundra.

A lone Savannah Sparrow was the second new year-bird of the day, after the towhee. This is a thinner sparrow (at least, it is thinner when compared to Song Sparrows or Fox Sparrows), heavily streaked, it is the ubiquitous LBJ (Little Brown Job). Except it has an obvious flash of yellow through the supercilium, the bold stripe above the eye. Savannah Sparrows were my first lesson in regional dialects not being restricted to people.

I lived in Keene Valley in the Adirondack Mountains of northern New York for years. Every spring, Mary Thill, one of my colleagues at The Nature Conservancy, and I would take our lunch walks around Marcy Field Airport. This old grass airstrip along Route 73 is on the west edge of the town. Every year, there would come a day when we would hear the gentle, melodic song of the Savannah Sparrow: *see-say*.

This quickly became my favorite birdsong, embodying the plaintive cry of a species seeking a mate, and yet, being a bird of open habitats—it is not called *Savannah* Sparrow for naught—it has to temper its decibel output to minimize the chance of attracting a predator. What a conundrum: attract a mate or become dinner. When you are a 5½-inch long, seed-eating species, you are pretty low on the foodchain.

Moving to Bar Harbor, Maine, I was excited when I saw my first Savannah Sparrow of the spring foraging in the grass around the Mount Desert Island High School settling ponds. I stopped, binoculars up, waiting for the bird to throw its head back and announce its intentions with a wisp of song.

Imagine my consternation when, instead of the soothing *see-say* to which I was accustomed, there was a harsh, almost raspy, *SEE-SAY!* The same mnemonic but there was nothing musical about it (at least, not by my aesthetic). Yes indeed, birds can have regional dialects.

Today's birds of the year:

106. Eastern Towhee   107. Savannah Sparrow

Friday, 30 March

One of the many advantages to living next to a National Park such as Acadia is the ease of taking a morning walk in the woods. And one of my many favorite walking loops is from Schooner Head Overlook, down Schooner Head Road to the Great Head parking lot, around the perimeter of Great Head, crossing Sand Beach, then looping back down Schooner Head Road to the parking lot.

9:38 a.m.   Natalie and I regularly try to get out for a morning walk and this morning was one of those. Fourteen species (thirty-two individual birds) was not bad for an hour's walk. Coming off Great Head, down the trail to Sand Beach, I could just make out the emphatic *k'dee, k'dee, k'dee* of a Killdeer drifting up from the seaside over the sound of the stiff sea breeze singing through the spruce.

Temporarily leaving the forest behind, the stream draining the salt pond impounded by the dunes of Sand Beach cuts across the east side of the beach, regularly changing its course like the sinuous movements of a living organism. In the space of the past few months, winter storms have variously dammed the stream, dried it up, and broadened it, making it mere inches deep, shallow enough to wade. On this day, as a direct result of the last round of storms, the outflow had been narrowed and deepened, leaving no dry way across.

While we pondered the engineering needed to bridge over the brackish river, I spied the pair of Killdeer foraging the wrack line, that line of rockweed, kelp, and various other marine algae, interspersed with eel-grass, demarking the highest high tide. It is also a zone full of delectable marine invertebrates, including the millimeters-long, crustacean-like amphipod, *Gammarus* (locally called Scuds), which can readily be seen springing about in magnificent leaps.

Killdeer are a shorebird in the plover family.

To answer one of the age-old questions, the correct way to say plover is with a short "o" in the first syllable, as in "ton" or rhyming with the word "the". Or, you can say it with a long "o", as in "go". According to the *Oxford English Dictionary*, both pronunciations are correct. Of course, you will invariably encounter people who absolutely insist that THE correct way to say it is _____ (insert one of the two options here).

Killdeer are brown above, white below, with two bold black neck-bands, and are robin-sized but with the longer legs of a shorebird. During the breeding season, these migrants can be found across most of North America. They prefer open habitat with vegetation low or completely lacking. Beaches are a favorite place, as are golf courses and nicely manicured parks. Killdeer locomotion is a series of running and stopping. Ostensibly, the purpose of this constantly repeated stop-and-go is to rustle up grub, although not grubs themselves. Flushed insects get flushed down their gullet.

Killdeer, so named for their vociferous *k'dee k'dee k'dee* (some think it is more of a *kill-deer kill-deer kill-deer*), are that bird with the broken-wing act. Get too close to a Killdeer nest—which, I might add, you will likely never see[i] as their plumage offers amazing camouflage—and one of the parents will try to lure you away, running, dragging a wing as though it is severely injured. The idea is that you, as the predator, will say to yourself, "Ooh, yum, an injured bird. This should be easy to catch and eat." Of course, the Killdeer has other ideas: once it has lured you away from the proximity of its nest, its wing miraculously heals and the bird will take flight, describing a huge circle, eventually ending back at its nest.

In terms of age, Killdeer are a relatively long-lived species, with the oldest bird known from banding records being nearly eleven years old when it was recaptured at a Kansas banding site.

Today's bird of the year:

108. Killdeer

Monday, 02 April

S hortly after I moved to Maine in 2002, I became friends with Ron Wanner. Back then, he was manager of a local kayak guide service; now, he manages Cadillac Mountain Sports. Ron is outside every day, walking his dog, hiking, kayaking, bicycling, cross-country skiing. He is also an astute observer of the natural world. He unfailingly lets me know when he sees some of the more charismatic fauna, whether it be Barred Owls *who-cooks-for-you*ing at Compass Harbor, the first Bufflehead of the fall along the Shore Path, or the first Great Blue Heron of the spring.

This last—the heron—Ron has long reported as coming like clockwork the first day of April every year. And you know what? He is right! Now, each year, I try my darnedest to get out on April Fool's Day to look for Great Blues. Unfortunately, this year, the day coincided with Easter Sunday, a family day with its own traditions, so I did not have much time for birding (Craig Kesselheim, of Southwest Harbor, did report a Great Blue Heron in his dooryard that day).

As a result, I began my quest for my FOY (first of the year) Great Blue a day late.

11:24 a.m.   Great Meadow, near Acadia National Park's Wild Gardens of Acadia and Sieur de Monts Spring, is a large, beaver-dammed wetland. Over the years, this locale has been a place where I have found various ducks, Pied-billed Grebe, American Bittern, and, yes,

Great Blue Heron. It is also surrounded by a lovely two-mile walk; perfect for a man and his dog to stretch their legs. Highlights of this walk included my first Mount Desert Island Wood Duck pair of the year, a Barred Owl with a freshly lined nest cavity in the same tree in which it has been nesting in recent years, and a singing Brown Creeper, but sadly, no Great Blue Heron.

12:49 p.m.   On my way to Thompson Island, I made a few stops, including College of the Atlantic's Peggy Rockefeller Farm on Norway Drive. These extensive (for Mount Desert Island) fields will soon be bustling with singing Savannah Sparrows and Bobolinks, but not yet. Still, a Mourning Dove-sized bird perched erect atop a hedgerow tree warranted a quick stop. American Kestrel!

Kestrels are a small falcon that hunt open habitats, such as farmland, in search of large insects, rodents, and small birds. These guys are cavity nesters, so for those of you with suitable habitat, you can build a kestrel box[i] and hang it high in a lone tree or the side of a barn with a southeasterly aspect. Oh, in case it was not obvious, this was a bird for my year-list.

12:51 p.m.   A search of Hamilton Pond did not turn up any herons, but there were seven species of waterfowl: Canada Goose, American Wigeon, Mallard, American Black Duck, Green-winged Teal, Ring-necked Duck, and Bufflehead, all common for this season and always satisfying to find and observe.

1:03 p.m.   Continuing on my heron quest, I added a quick stop at the Route 3 pullout along Northeast Creek. Tide was exactly at slack high. Seven species—Canada Goose, American Black Duck, Bufflehead, Common Merganser, American Crow, Song Sparrow, American Goldfinch—were all what you would expect. But still no heron.

1:09 p.m.   Continuing to the head of Mount Desert Island, clock ticking because I really needed to get back to work, it was finally time to check out Thompson Island, even if just for some quick drive-by birding.

There is an unnamed wetland across the street from Steamboat Landing Gas Station (until recently, long known as Parkadia Exxon), on the east side of Route 3. With no safe pullout to carefully look it over, this is birding-at-fifty-miles-per-hour at its best. Driving north, in a line of cars, I had no option to slow down, but I did manage to tease out a feeding American Black Duck. Nearby was a Ring-billed Gull, easily discernable for its size relative to the duck (Ring-billed Gulls are just a bit smaller than American Black Ducks and their body proportions are less stocky than a Herring Gull). And I saw three American Crows, all foraging on the ground near each other.

Continuing the ½-mile north to the Thompson Island Information Center to make a safe (and legal) U-turn, I waited for the end of the line of traffic so I could drive more slowly south, not rushed by the need to drive the speed limit. As I approached the wetland for this second pass (and my last chance to look for birds for the day), I slowed to forty, thirty, twenty miles per hour. Quick check of the rearview mirror: no cars behind. Now for a quick perusal of the wetlands: There, at the back of the wetlands, against the line of spruce, a lone Great Blue Heron! Success!

Standing nearly five feet tall, Great Blue Herons can be numbered among the charismatic megafauna. These large birds are majestic in both appearance and behavior. They are a shade of gray-blue with nuptial plumes in the spring flowing off the back of their head and feathered down their chest. Their manner of hunting, with slow, deliberate strides, gives a clear sense of purpose in their activity. In flight, deep and broad wings flap strongly, steadily, powerfully.

For years, I monitored a Great Blue Heron colony on Valcour Island (not far from the New York shore of Lake Champlain) that once numbered nearly 1,000 nests. One year, a Great Horned Owl took up residence and the colony was abandoned. Some small number of the Great Blue Herons made their way 12½ miles south to the Four Brothers Islands, a preserve of The Nature Conservancy and one of my research sites. Typically, these herons like to nest high in the treetops, but one nest was low enough that I, as a young field biologist at the bottom of the pecking order, was designated to climb so that we could band and measure the chicks.

I learned a good lesson about the aforementioned pecking order. In a form of ornithological hazing, and as the youngest in my group of biologists by a generation, I was always the one given the difficult tasks (think of Jim Fowler in Mutual of Omaha's Wild Kingdom, when Marlin Perkins would say, "We'll send Jim in to get the lion/crocodile/python;" yeah, that was me). So up I went, on this hot day, sweat pouring off my brow, streaking my glasses, stinging my eyes. Powdered guano dust, dried from baking in the sun, in the air, in my mouth, in my lungs.

Finally, secure in my stance in a crotch of branches, I peered into the nest. A lesser person may have been frightened to the point of giving up their grip and falling to an ignominious end, but I held my ground, staring back at the fierce, prehistoric face challenging me. A young Great Blue Heron chick, pinfeathers well on their way to developing into fledgling plumage, coiled its neck, ready to strike. So, I struck first, shooting my hand out to grab it around the neck (not too tightly, though; I had no intention of hurting the bird). The muscular strength of this pre-fledgling presaged the future of the powerful bird into which it would grow.

As I pulled it out of the nest, its three siblings were all glaring at me as if to say, "Back off pal!" Meanwhile, my bird was writhing, trying to attack me with everything it had, clawed feet grabbing at my hand and wrist, scratching, drawing thin streaks of red through my skin. (Clearly, the memo about the modern invention of work gloves had not reached me.)

Finally, the bird extracted, I handed it down to my mentor, Mike Peterson. With practiced hands, he and New York State Department of Environmental Conservation Forest Ranger Gary Lee quickly affixed a size 7B band, measured the wing chord, did a quick check of the amount of fat, successfully avoided any scratches (I needed to learn that trick), and handed it back to me.

We repeated the process for each of the chicks—each earning me more scratches—as quickly as we could, wanting to minimize our intrusion. The whole time, I was only too glad that there was not a parent on the nest. And within less than a minute after our retreat, a parent, who had been attentively watching and waiting nearby, returned to tend the young.

Great Blue Heron? Check! Mission accomplished, now I could go home and spend the afternoon working on my computer.

Today's birds of the year:

109. American Kestrel   110. Great Blue Heron

Wednesday, 04 April

2:28 p.m. Today, Fogo and I ran from our house, south down Knox Road, west on Gilbert Farm Road, across Route 102, and down Clark Cove Road. The roundtrip is a good 2½-mile run, affording Fogo an opportunity to swim in tidal Clark Cove. (What dog does not want to play in the water?) While running down Gilbert Farm Road, there is a good-sized wetland abutting the road. Although I almost always see Mallards there, I strictly adhere to my mantra: You have to look at every bird.

So, when a lovely male/female pair of ducks flew overhead, a quick glance up revealed these were no ordinary Greenheads. A broad, spatulate bill could only belong to Northern Shoveler. In terms of plumage, it is understandable how, upon a cursory glance, shovelers could be mistaken for Mallards, with both males having iridescent green heads and both females being a similarly mottled brown. But Mallards can range up to 20% larger.

A birder's day is never done. And if you run an ecotour business, your day is most definitely never done. An email comes in, you have to check in case a potential client wants to book a tour. So, when my computer said, "You have mail" (okay, it doesn't actually say the words anymore, but you get the picture), I had to take a quick peek. Better than potential business was an alert from eBird informing me of a local bird just reported that would be a tick for my Hancock

County Little Big Year. I dropped everything, told my family that I had to chase a bird, and would be home in an hour.

5:37 p.m.   It took me nineteen minutes to get to the private Eagle Point Road in Lamoine. Fortunately, a friend who lives on the road invited me to come look at the bird with him, telling me to drive down the road and look for the wreck of an old lobster boat listing in the field. Well, turns out there are TWO wrecks of old lobster boats listing in the field. Fortunately, I kept driving and saw Patrick's truck.

Before I even put my van into park, I could see nine Snow Geese. Yes! Even though it was raining steadily, Patrick and I both got out to watch the geese actively foraging. It almost seemed as if there was military precision in their feeding procession: move forward a few steps, quickly feed on some unidentified vegetation; move forward a few more steps, quickly feed again on some unidentified vegetation; repeat, for the entire time we watched them.

While observing the Snow Geese, I looked each one over carefully, hoping that maybe, just possibly, there was with them their smaller cousin, Ross's Goose. Nope, but it was good to spend time watching this bird uncommon to Hancock County.

So, nineteen minutes of driving to get to Eagle Point Road, nineteen minutes observing the birds, twenty minutes home (I got stuck at a traffic light for a minute). I was gone an hour, just as I had told my family.

As geese go, the Snow Goose is on the small side. While we think of them as being all white with black wingtips, there is a less common color morph where the body is dark brown and the head is white, a "Blue Goose."

The population of Snow Geese has grown tremendously over the past forty years. During my time working and birding in the Champlain Valley of northern New York and Vermont, I would see vast flocks—many thousands, tens of thousands—of these white geese settling in the fields, grazing, making the fields appear covered in snow.

Along with their increasing population has come more human-wildlife conflicts. The bulk of their wintering grounds are centered along the greater Lower Mississippi River valley, from Louisiana and Texas north to Iowa. As bottomland hardwood forests have been converted to rice plantations, vast flocks of Snow Geese have moved their winter range inland, away from coastal marshes, to forage on waste grain. And they stay into early spring, grazing on new shoots. As you can imagine, this does not go over well with farmers. In response, we have seen expanded hunting seasons, including the addition of a spring season, in attempts to bring their numbers down to something wildlife managers consider more reasonable. (Of course, "more reasonable" means a number that eats less crops.)

We humans have a propensity of molding the environment to fit our ends. And when species respond, we feel the need to further manage them rather than change our own behaviors. How I wish we could be better stewards of the natural world.

Here in Maine, we are at the very eastern edge of their migration. In fact, *Birds of North America* has the eastern boundary of their migration corridor almost exactly following the Maine/New Hampshire border. As a result, in Hancock County, Snow Geese are an infrequent sight and years can go by between local sightings. Alas, you have to be at the right place and the right time to see them. Or have a friend like Patrick.

Today's birds of the year:

111. Snow Goose   112. Northern Shoveler

Thursday, 05 April

For this week's Weekly Birding Tour, I decided to offer a more physically active outing than usual: we walked from Sieur de Monts Spring, down the Hemlock Trail to the Park Loop Road, up the road to the Jesup Trail, back to Sieur de Monts Spring, out the Park Loop Road all the way to Precipice, and then all the way back, nearly six miles in all, and all in Acadia National Park. It was unanimous that is was wonderful to get in so much walking!

8:33 a.m.   The intersection where Ledgelawn Avenue dumps onto the Park Loop Road offers an incredible view looking out over Great Meadow where Cromwell Brook drains under the road and out toward Frenchman Bay. Within a small area, there is roadside edge, a freshwater meadow managed by North American Beaver, oak forest, and stands of White Pine, all set in a glacially sculpted rolling topography.

Even though it was cool (the temperature was in the upper 30s Fahrenheit), the heat of the sun warmed the near-ground micro-climate enough to drive some limited insect activity, just enough to attract the first migrant Eastern Phoebe I've seen this year.

Phoebes are a drab flycatcher, gray backed with a hint of olive and white belly. Their constant tail-pumping is a telltale sign in identifying them. They are the first flycatcher that arrives in Maine each spring. In fact, it will be over a month before we see any other flycatcher species.

In the Northeast, many people know phoebes from the placement of a mud and grass nest above the head of a door or window or under the shelter of the eaves. The female will sit on the nest, seemingly nonplussed by our comings and goings (seemingly is the operative word: you can be sure she knows very well what is going on around her), tending first her eggs and then her naked hatchlings.

She is so dedicated to her job that on numerous occasions, I have reached up into a nest, gently grasped the tending female, pulled her off the nest, affixed a uniquely numbered U.S. Fish & Wildlife Service size 0 incoloy band to her leg, then gently placed her back on her nest. The effects seem to be minimal as each time she has gone on to successfully fledge her brood. On more than one occasion, the female I have pulled off was sporting the band I had bestowed upon her in a previous year. (In footnote ix for 01 January, I wrote about a similar such experience John James Audubon had banding an Eastern Phoebe.)

Once the eggs have hatched, both the male and female catch insects to feed the young. In less than three weeks, the young fledge, leave the nest, and are off on their own. Here in Hancock County, it is uncommon for phoebes to have more than one brood.

Beginning in 1880, a group of young men from Harvard University, calling themselves the Champlain Society, would spend summers on Mount Desert Island studying the natural world. Among these young men was nineteen-year-old student of ornithology Henry Spelman. Spelman was known to tramp around the Northeast Harbor area, carrying a smooth-bore collecting gun to shoot birds (for that was the way that bird studies were carried out back then), and prepare them as study skins. Ultimately, these study skins wound up in the Museum of Comparative Zoology at Harvard University.

Jumping forward to the current era, Catherine Schmidt, of the University of Maine Sea Grant Program, and I coauthored an article—'Searching for Spelman's birds'—for the 2018 issue of the Mount Desert Island Historical Society's annual journal, *Chebacco*. During the journal's launch party this evening, I read a few passages from our article, focusing on Spelman. Afterward, I made a quick birding detour on the way home.

5:42 p.m.   This is the time of year that the Mount Desert Island High School's water treatment settling ponds should begin to open up. We are fortunate in living in a place where we are allowed access to the school campus. One end of the Kittredge Brook Trail is here. And there are times of the year when the ponds are one of Mount Desert Island's most significant birding hotspots.

I circled the parking lot to get my best vantage of the first pond. DRAT! Still frozen. I decided to walk around the three ponds anyway. Good thing, too! The second and third ponds were completely open. In the sixteen minutes it took me to walk around them, I only tallied four species. But one of them was a first-of-the-year Wilson's Snipe.

This secretive shorebird likes wet vegetation. A close cousin to the American Woodcock, it has an impossibly long bill used to drill into wet ground for worms and other invertebrates. Its eyes are positioned on the side of its head such that it has a complete, 360-degree field of view; a particularly useful trait when you are a small, delectable bird and your 2½-inch bill is buried in mud, probing for food. This could just be where the expression "eyes in the back of your head" originated.

Today's birds of the year:

113. Eastern Phoebe   114. Wilson's Snipe

Tuesday, 10 April

I n 2009, the Downeast Chapter of Maine Audubon launched a
bluebird trail, installing nest boxes around Hancock County. As
part of that effort, I installed an even dozen bluebird boxes at
the Peggy Rockefeller Farm. Since that time, almost all of them have
been consistently used each nesting season, mostly by Tree Swallows, with only one box used annually by bluebirds.

To date, 253 nest boxes have been installed across Hancock
County and monitored by volunteers, all as part of Downeast Audubon's bluebird trail. This citizen science initiative is making a difference. The numbers of birds fledged in these nest boxes in 2017 speak
for themselves: 181 Eastern Bluebirds, 490 Tree Swallows, 183
Black-capped Chickadees, and 4 Tufted Titmice.

8:00 a.m.   Driving past the Peggy Rockefeller Farm, on my way to
meet Natalie and Fogo for a morning walk, I glanced over at the nest
box that hosts a pair of Eastern Bluebirds each year. Migration is
slowly ramping up and it is high time for bluebirds to return. Right
on cue, there was a pair: one perched atop the box, the other sitting
on a trammel of a nearby wire fence.

Eastern Bluebirds are members of the thrush family. These beautiful blue birds with the burnt orangey-red belly have seen serious
population declines across their range due to loss of habitat, suitable
nesting cavities, and competition with non-native invasive species
such as European Starlings and House Sparrows.

9:53 a.m.   Hamilton Pond. It is on Route 3, so I pass it every time I drive into town. Its shore affords a variety of habitats and it is one of the first freshwater bodies to open up in the spring. And so, I look. Often.

Today, the pond was busy with six species of waterfowl, ninety-three individual ducks in all: Mallard, American Black Duck, Green-winged Teal, Ring-necked Duck, Bufflehead, Hooded Merganser, and one Mallard x American Black Duck hybrid (this particular hybrid had the dark body of an American Black Duck and the green head of a male Mallard).

As I was scanning the pond, I heard a sharp cry that I had not heard since last summer. Osprey! What a joy to see my first Fish Hawk of the season.

Osprey eat fish exclusively. With their keen eyesight, whether from a perch in a tree, on a utility pole, or hovering high overhead, they look for fish. Once their prey is targeted, they make their screaming-eagle dive, sometimes from as high as 100 feet. At the last possible second, they swing their feet forward, talons spread wide, ready to instantly latch into their piscine prey. Meanwhile, simultaneously, they raise their wings straight back. All of this elaborate ritual is designed to streamline their profile as they enter the water, maximizing their efficiency at catching dinner (or breakfast, or lunch) and to minimize harming themselves with the force of impact.

If you have ever watched an Osprey fly after a successful catch, you may have seen them maneuver the fish to carry it headfirst. It is thought that this move is purely for the purpose of aerodynamics.

Osprey are widespread in North America, but ours from the Northeast migrate to Mexico, with some making their way all the way to the Brazilian Pantanal.

Here on Mount Desert Island, among the better places to search for Osprey is Hamilton Pond and the spillway below the Somesville mill pond. In fact, the mill pond may just be one of the best places to watch Osprey ply their craft. There, a fish passage enables the anadromous Alewife to swim upstream to its spawning grounds.

Although many Alewives make it up the passage[i], many more fall prey to Harbor Seals, Bald Eagles, gulls, and, yes, Osprey during their journey. The best time to watch them—both the Osprey and the Alewives—is in May and June. Follow the Osprey's methodical hunt and you will see poetry in motion.

Today's birds of the year:

115. Eastern Bluebird   116. Osprey

Wednesday, 11 April

The Natural History Center's Weekly Birding Tour affords an excuse (not that I ever need one) to seek out new areas to take my regular tour participants. Planning each month's schedule, I ponder what birds might we see, where might we see them, and where could we go that might be interesting while at the same time not excluding anyone due to challenging trail conditions.

This day was about the boggy and wetland habitats of the Schoodic Peninsula. Among the sites we visited were Frenchman Bay Conservancy's Corea Heath Preserve and, across the road, Maine Coastal Islands National Wildlife Refuge's Corea Heath.

This coastal heath is made up of a variety of natural communities. The heath itself is an admixture of sphagnum bog largely surrounded by a shrubby Black Spruce forest, with the heathlands made up of mostly well-drained, acidic soils. Bogs, by definition, are poorly drained, formed in a glacially scoured depression (these depressions can range from less than one acre up to thousands of acres); the only water input being precipitation. Given the long water retention and the floral makeup, the environment is acidic. On a pH scale of 0–14, where the upper end is basic, like lime, and the low end is acidic, the pH of bogs typically ranges from 3.3–5.5.

11:15 a.m.   It is the surrounding Black Spruce forest in which we were particularly interested, especially the wetter, low-lying portions with a sphagnum floor. A dirt road traversing the edge provides much-needed unconsolidated dry soil for birds to dust-bathe. And the *coup de grace* was an eBird report from the previous day. All of this raised our hopes for Spruce Grouse.

Traveling down the dirt lane, Jane Potter called out, "There it is!" Although we weren't going fast, it still took me a moment to react. By the time we piled out of the car, the bird had disappeared into the dense forest. Following a deer path into the woods, I managed a quick look of a hen Spruce Grouse retreating further into the woods. Two thoughts immediately entered my mind.

Hen? The eBird report included a photo of a male, red supercilial (above the eye) combs inflated as part of their sexual display. The hens have an all-brown camouflage. So clearly there is a pair in the area.

My competing thought was not to chase the bird. With a pair in the area and breeding season upon us, we don't want to overly disturb the bird. This is especially important as we are at the very southern end of Spruce Grouse breeding range. Populations at the edge of a range are, by nature, low; so, rather than chase the bird, we walked the road to look for more.

No more Spruce Grouse but we had a nice walk.

Today's bird of the year:

117. Spruce Grouse

Friday, 13 April

For some, Friday the thirteenth bodes ill. For me, this day was fruitful, adding five species to my Little Big Year tally.

Next week is Spring Break for our local schools and Anouk and I will be heading off to the North Country of New York State to visit my mother. As Natalie will be staying home—she is teaching Fisheries, Fishermen, and Fishing Communities at College of the Atlantic—she and I decided to fold in an afternoon walk. Time was limited, so we took advantage of the short hike that starts from the College of the Atlantic campus.

1:00 p.m.   Directly across Route 3 from the college's North Lot is a connector trail that leads into Acadia National Park. As we made our way across campus, walking toward the trailhead, the repetitive screech of a Merlin rose above the monotonous roar of traffic. We both looked up and saw this small, dark falcon zip across the sky.

Merlins are small falcons, namesake of wizards, found throughout the northern forests of North America, Europe, and Asia. They are fierce and known to work cooperatively with their mate to hunt songbirds. Get too close to a Merlin's nest or territory and they will scold you with a loud, raucous, ongoing *ki-ki-ki-ki*. Whereas many raptors developed colloquial names based on their gastronomic preferences (for instance, Ospreys are also known as Fish Hawks and Peregrine Falcons are sometimes called Duck Hawks), Merlins have been called "Pigeon Hawks." This is not any indication of a preference for squab, merely that they are of a similar size and have a similarly rapid wingbeat (I cannot begin to enumerate the number of times I saw a Morning Dove flying away and thought Merlin). Along with so many other raptors and top-level avian predators, Merlin populations experienced a severe decline in the second half of the twentieth-century, a direct result of eggshell thinning induced by the pesticide DDT. Today, Merlin populations are on the rise. For instance, in 2002, Merlins were merely migrants here on Mount Desert Island; last year, I found four nests—a good number for this diminutive predator.

Not far up the trail, I heard the tapping of a woodpecker undertaking an excavation. It did not take long to train my binoculars on the bird. With bold and brilliant red on the forehead and beneath the bill, something of a ladder-back pattern dorsally, prominent white patch on the wing, this could only be a Yellow-bellied Sapsucker.

Sapsuckers are so named for their springtime habit of pecking a latticework of holes in a tree, just deep enough to get the sap going. Once upon a time, people thought they were doing this to drink the sap. The reality is even better: they are laying a trap. The proliferation of holes gets a tree's sap to seep; think tapping a maple tree for syrup, only the sapsuckers want to eat the insects attracted to the sap, which mires them in the sticky ooze. Sapsuckers repeatedly return to feed on the little protein packets that are insects.

Our ½-hour walk over, back at the car, sitting in the driver's seat, some motion in the hedgerow was visible in the corner of my eye. A bird! I trained my binoculars on it: Palm Warbler!

It is always a treat to see Palm Warblers in the spring. They are often the first warbler to return. Bright yellow belly, rufous cap, Palm Warblers quickly go from dribs and drabs to dozens upon dozens in a single outing, then down to virtually none outside their peatland bog nesting sites. The name derives from the first example of this species collected on the Greater Antillean island of Hispaniola and described by German naturalist Johann Friedrich Gmelin in 1789.

As it was associating with palm trees, it was given the name "Palm Warbler," even though their range extends far further north—in fact, all the way to the boreal forests of northern North America—than just the tropical latitudes.

2:19 p.m.   After departing Natalie, I paid a quick visit to trusty ol' Hamilton Pond where I tallied thirteen species, seven were waterfowl, and one of them was a Blue-winged Teal....

Blue-winged Teal hold a special place in my heart: the very first bird I ever banded was a Blue-winged Teal. At ten years old, my brother, Rob, and I started working with Jerry Farrell, banding ducks on the lower Niagara River during spring and fall migration. When we joined Jerry on our first banding excursion, I still recall the thrill of walking up to the duck traps—dog kennel-sized wire-mesh enclosures with a single twelve-inch-square doorway at the bottom—filled with ducks. Jerry, adorned in chest waders, waded out to the trap in nearly four feet of water, lifted the corner of the roof, carefully inserted a landing net (the kind used for fishing), and scooped out duck after duck, placing them in an olive-drab, military surplus canvas duffel bag.

Trap empty, back on shore, Jerry carefully laid the duffel down and set up his field office, which comprised of a clipboard with datasheets for recording band numbers, species, age, and sex; strings of uniquely numbered, stainless steel bands; special pliers for affixing bands; and field guides (I don't recall Jerry ever needing to open them, the information was all in his head).

Then it was time.

Prior to this day's banding foray, Jerry had ascertained that neither of us kids knew much about birds but that we were keen to learn. After instructing us about his methodology, he opened the duffel and reached in. Before pulling out a bird, he said it was a Blue-winged Teal. That did not mean anything to us; after all, a duck was a duck, right?

Jerry pulled out a duck, bold white cheek crescent the obvious field mark. It was the most beautiful thing I had ever seen! I was two feet away from this living, breathing, wild animal.

And then Jerry turned to me and asked me to hold it! He did not ask me if I *wanted* to hold it; he just asked me to hold it! A command couched in the civility of a question.

This one-pound creature, heart beating strong and fast, cold black eye looking at me in defiance, was in my hands. Jerry said, "Male Blue-winged Teal." After affixing a uniquely-numbered band to its leg, he read off the number to us to double-check against the records, then told me to release the duck.

Imagine the power of holding a wild animal, then letting it go, seeing it fly off. And not only that, but the next thing Jerry said was "You are now an ornithologist." That was the best day of my tenth year!

... Both male and female Blue-winged Teal are readily identified in flight by the pale blue upper wing coverts.

Imagine a wing stretched out flat in front of you. Divide the wing into four, first making a line down the middle from the body to the tip, then another perpendicular line bisecting the first. Most of the two outermost fourths would be comprised by the primary flight feathers; the trailing edge closest to the body are the secondary flight feathers; the leading edge closest to the body are the upper wing coverts.

As is typical with most North American ducks, the female Blue-winged Teal is a mottled shade of brown to provide camouflage as

she incubates her eggs. The male has the aforementioned bold white
cheek crescent set against a faintly purple head with a hint of iridescence.

2:45 p.m.   From Hamilton Pond, I proceeded down Norway
Drive. Coming around the bend at Bowden Marine Service, you
leave the spruce-fir forest and come out on the open farm fields of
College of the Atlantic's Peggy Rockefeller Farm. Driving slowly
down the road, a Northern Harrier could be seen silently gliding
along, five feet above the ground, head down, looking for a meal.

Their primary prey, various small field rodents, so frequently urinate and defecate as to leave a veritable trail, both of which waste
products fluoresce in the ultraviolet spectrum. One of the many
wonders of the natural world is that many raptors, including the
Northern Harrier, can see in ultraviolet wavelengths. That means
that harriers can follow a rodent's trail!

When I was young, Northern Harriers were called Marsh Hawks.
This seems a more appropriate name to me as they are often found
hunting in marshlands.

For a wonderful young adult fiction about Northern Harriers, see
if you can find a copy of Dean T. Spaulding's *Where Harriers Dance*,
published in 1998.

Today's birds of the year:

118. Merlin
119. Yellow-bellied Sap-
      sucker
120. Palm Warbler
121. Blue-winged Teal
122. Northern Harrier

Friday, 20 April

The past week was eventful. Saturday through this afternoon, Anouk and I traveled to New York State: Canton, on the edge of the St. Lawrence River Valley and the Adirondack Park, to visit my mother; and Lewiston, the colonial village on the eastern shore of the lower Niagara River, to share my childhood haunts. In Hancock County, migration took a noticeable uptick while we were away with the arrival of the first wave of Broad-winged Hawks, Greater Yellowlegs, Laughing Gulls, Tree Swallows, Winter Wrens, Ruby-crowned Kinglets, Hermit Thrushes, Pine Warblers, Yellow-rumped Warblers, Chipping Sparrows, and Swamp Sparrows. And for amphibians, Big Night[i] heralded their annual emergence.

On Saturday, at the beginning of our New York holiday, as Anouk and I were driving west, passing through Montreal, we were deep into the audio book of *Harry Potter and the Deathly Hallows* when the story was interrupted by a call coming in over the Bluetooth connection. "Rich, can you get down to Hamilton Pond? There is a Violet-green Swallow there right now!" It was Maine Audubon's Doug Hitchcox, one of the top birders in the state. And he knows I live two miles from Hamilton Pond.

Normally, Violet-green Swallows are found from the eastern foothills of the Rocky Mountains west to the Pacific and north well into Alaska. They are not particularly known for vagrancy; that is, for occurring well outside their typical range. As it was the State of

Maine's first-ever record for this species, I was lamenting our week-long sojourn, but with it being seven hours behind us, turning around was not an option.

After a week of western New York fun with Anouk, we returned home. Chomping at the bit to find some of the recent migrants, as soon as we unpacked the car, I was off for a bit of birding.

3:30 p.m.   I made a beeline for the Mount Desert Island High School. The three settling ponds, along with the adjacent habitat, can make for incredible birding. Approaching the ponds, I could hear a small chorus of Green Frogs. Surrounding the ponds, the scattered Red Maples were showing the first signs of spring bud development. Either side of the lane was bustling with Palm Warblers actively feeding. Although they nest on boreal bogs, in migration, they can be found most anywhere. Among the Palm Warblers were my first two Yellow-rumped Warblers of the season.

Back in the day, when I was learning warbler songs, for most of them, I could associate a mnemonic, a memory aid, to remember. Black-throated Green Warblers sing *zee-zee-zee-zoo-zee*. Common Yellowthroats, *witchity, witchity, witchity*. Yellow Warblers say *sweet, sweet, sweet, a little more sweet*. For just about every warbler species, there is a mnemonic. Except Yellow-rumped Warbler. I learned that when I hear that warbler without a viable memory aid, it must be a Yellow-rump.

Feeding alongside the warblers was a mixed foraging flock of Black-capped Chickadees, Red-breasted Nuthatches, and Golden-crowned Kinglets. These three species are here year-round, but they will also feed alongside migrants. And today, that migrant was a pair of Ruby-crowned Kinglets.

Kinglets, both Golden-crowned and Ruby-crowned, are tiny, each measuring up to only 4⅓ inches long. The Ruby-crowns winter in the southern third of North America and breed in the northern third. These little birds can lay as many as twelve eggs in a single nest. For all their frenetic energy, flitting about their forested habitat, energetic studies have shown they only use about ten calories per day (granted, ten calories for a creature weighing less than half an ounce doesn't seem like much, but if my ratio mathematics are any good, it would be nearly thirty-five times more than a 180-pound person consuming 3,500 calories daily).

Continuing the walk, I reached the middle pond where there were Canada Goose, Mallard, Green-winged Teal, and Bufflehead. Then I noticed that one of these ducks was not like the others. Maybe that was because it was not even a duck but a member of the rail family. Gray plumage overall and white bill with a keratinous shield extending up the forehead could only be an American Coot. Having just seen dozens of them at Western New York State's Iroquois National Wildlife Refuge the day before, it was a species fresh in my mind.

Coots are uncommon to Hancock County, but certainly not unexpected. With their range expanding northward, we will likely be seeing more of them. Although duck-like, American Coots do not have webbed feet. Instead, they have extra skin around each toe that serves to increase the surface area, thereby enabling them to reasonably efficiently paddle through the water.

Heading back to the car, the high-pitched, drawn out *say's here* of a Broad-winged Hawk alerted me to its presence. Looking up, triangulating on the periodic call, I found the deep-winged silhouette of a Broad-winged Hawk. The smallest of our local buteos, Broad-winged Hawks are a raptor of the forests. Fortunately, their distinctive call, which they give frequently, at least on their breeding grounds, is a true way of identifying them (unless it is a Blue Jay doing quite a reasonable facsimile, but that is another story).

In October 2006, I had been invited by Jeff Wells and Boreal Songbird Initiative to attend the North American Ornithological Congress in Veracruz, Mexico, to present a paper[ii]. After several days of the conference, my paper presented, Jeff and I, along with three other ornithologists, played hooky to go birding.

My Spanish was better than Jeff's, which isn't saying much, so I negotiated the car rental. With a map in hand, we made our way to Chichicaxtle, out in the countryside, where Jeff knew there was a hawk-watch underway. Somehow, my focus having been on song-birds and preparation of our paper, I had no idea of the magnitude of the raptor migration. I should have clued in when some of the conference printed materials referred to the Veracruz "River of Rap-tors".

Chichicaxtle was small by Mexican standards. A dozen or so homes—what might have been a car repair shop in someone's front yard—and a tiny store selling soda out of someone else's side door. Our directions were to drive through town and turn left on the dirt track that goes through the soccer field. It took us two drive-bys to find the so-called soccer pitch. Well, maybe part of the reason it took us those two drive-bys was that none of us, me (the driver) included, were watching the road. The sky was stippled with movement: hun-dreds and thousands of large birds!

We finally found the parking lot, which was in the shadow of the new raptor research center run by the non-government environmen-tal organization, Pronatura. We spilled out of the car, all in a rush to train our binoculars on the sky. I centered my gaze on a particularly large kettle of Broad-winged Hawks.

In my career as a field biologist, I have learned how to count large numbers of objects: you start by counting every individual. Once you are comfortable with what ten of something looks like, you count by tens (ten, twenty, thirty…). You repeat this process with hundreds (100, 200, 300…), and even thousands if need be. Well, in my field of view, there were nearly 500 Broad-wings! That kettle that initially caught my eye alone had in excess of 2,000 raptors!

A quick look to the north and I was overwhelmed! There was a steady stream of hundreds and thousands of birds winging south. THIS was the legendary Veracruz River of Raptors! Black Vultures. Turkey Vultures. Osprey. Mississippi Kites. Hook-billed Kite. White-tailed Kites. Northern Harriers. Sharp-shinned Hawks. Cooper's Hawks. Gray Hawk. Red-shouldered Hawks. Broad-winged Hawks. Short-tailed Hawk. Swainson's Hawks. Zone-tailed Hawks. Red-tailed Hawks. American Kestrels. Merlin. Peregrine Falcons. And then there were the non-raptorial species, including Anhinga, American White Pelican, Neotropical Cormorant, and Wood Stork. While the aerial field of view was not blanketed in sky-darkening numbers, there was no patch without raptors! Scanning with our binoculars, every single field of view had dozens, if not hundreds, of raptors!

One amazing fact in the story of the River of Raptors is that it was only "discovered" in 1997. Although the fact of its presence is entirely logical, ornithologists only learned of this unique phenomenon relatively recently. Ironically, the locals have long known about this annual event—where upwards of five million raptors migrate past each autumn—which, to them, signals the changing seasons. Most raptors are not keen to fly any considerable distance over open water, so in their fall migration, nearly all of the migratory raptors of North America get funneled to Mexico. The Sierra Madre Mountains further funnel them toward the Gulf of Mexico side of the Mexican isthmus. Counting 700,000 raptors in a day is not unheard of.

Broad-winged Hawks were, by far, the most abundant bird of the day. Black and Turkey Vultures were a distant second. Birds commonly seen in Maine—Osprey, Cooper's Hawk, American Kestrel, and Peregrine Falcon—all showed in respectable numbers. The light/dark contrast of the Swainson's Hawk's underwings can be readily learned when you see 100 or more in an hour. The sharp-winged profiles of the White-tailed Kite and Mississippi Kite boosted my life-list by two. I will never forget the excitement of fifty ornithologists training their binoculars on a lone Short-tailed Hawk, whose smaller size and generally white underparts set it off from all the other thousands of raptors.

In about four hours at Chichicaxtle, I personally saw 100,000, 200,000, perhaps 300,000 raptors! Though accustomed to counting large numbers of birds, I was so enthralled by this phenomenon—seeing more raptors in an hour than I had in my entire life up to that point—that I opted to experience the birds rather than count them. Later, that evening, at the bar at the Hotel Bienvenido in Cardel, an ornithologist from that station told me that was likely the peak flight day of the season, with 432,308 raptors tallied![iii]

For me, a veteran of the Coot Hill Hawk Watch in the Lake Champlain Valley and the Cadillac Mountain Hawk Watch on Mount Desert Island, though both produce respectable numbers, I could only stand and watch in awe. There are a few natural events in life I am convinced that, when people experience them, changes them forever. Watching the birth of your child. Going on a whale-watch and seeing those behemoths of the deep up close. Kayaking amidst a pod of 200 or more Long-finned Pilot Whales schooling past, literally within reach. Holding, and then releasing a wild bird that was just banded. And now, to my list, I will add witnessing the Veracruz River of Raptors.

4:35 p.m.   Hamilton Pond. Again. (And again. And a-gain.) With birds migrating and Hamilton Pond's low water levels, this is a site worth watching. This afternoon, the species I picked up was Swamp Sparrow. Similar to Chipping Sparrow, this bird can usually be identified by its namesake habitat. A ubiquitous little brown bird, a single Swamp Sparrow singing in the cattails was easily heard and then not-so-easily seen.

7:33 p.m.   There were two species I was hoping to pick up and with the day winding down, I was saved while walking Fogo in our woods. First up was Winter Wren. Proportionate to its size, this wren might just have the longest and most complicated song of any North American songbird. And you don't have to take my word for it: look up Winter Wren at Cornell Lab of Ornithology's All About Birds website and listen to the complex warbling of this little bird.

While I was busy being mesmerized by the melodious tune of the Winter Wren, it finally penetrated my consciousness that the other bird I was hoping to find, a Hermit Thrush, was singing in the distance. This is one of the more musical cousins of the American Robin. For me, there are a four species of bird whose songs embody the spirit of northern forests—Common Loon, Black-throated Green Warbler, White-throated Sparrow, and, of course, the Hermit Thrush, whose ethereal tones offer a narrative of the north woods.

This day's birds of the year:

123. Yellow-rumped Warbler
124. Ruby-crowned Kinglet
125. American Coot
126. Broad-winged Hawk
127. Swamp Sparrow
128. Winter Wren
129. Hermit Thrush

Saturday, 21 April

This morning's hotspots were to include visits to College of the Atlantic's Peggy Rockefeller Farm and Hamilton Pond. From my house, I just keep turning left—left out of my driveway, left onto Gilbert Farm Road, left onto Norway Drive, left onto Route 3, and then left onto Knox Road. Eventually, seven miles later, I am back home.

Except, I didn't get that far.

10:39 a.m.   Halfway down Gilbert Farm Road, diving through a scrubby wetland of second- (or third- or fourth- or…) growth alder, a medium-sized red bird flew across the road. The only red bird I expect to see this time of year is a Northern Cardinal and this was too small to be a cardinal. Nor did I see the black wings that would make it an unusually early Scarlet Tanager. That doesn't leave too many options.

A U.S.-first Red Warbler was recently seen in Arizona. This is a Mexican bird that doesn't migrate, nor is it known for grand peregrinations, so that is ruled out....

Or is it? In 2007, a Green Violetear (now officially named Mexican Violetear) showed up locally in Northeast Harbor. I was one of six people fortunate enough to see that amazing rarity. Subsequently, I learned they are prone to extralimital wanderings to Louisiana and Texas, but still, Maine?

... That left Summer Tanager as the reasonable choice. And it is reasonable, too: a few are found every year in Maine, and sometimes here in Hancock County.

So, a quick stop and I was eventually able to relocate the bird. Summer Tanager was the winner!

These guys usually range from Virginia south to Florida and west to southern California.

10:47 a.m.   Continuing on my way, I stopped at the lone barn of the Peggy Rockefeller Farm along the open fields of Norway Drive. In another month, these farm fields will be alive with Tree Swallows and Bobolink, but this day, I was hoping to pick up an early Tree Swallow. No luck.

What I did get, though, was a trilling Pine Warbler atop the tallest of the clump of spruces, which was a bit surprising because this is a species that is typically true to its name, rarely straying from pines. Still, it was a Pine Warbler. In addition to its musical trill, when I finally picked one out in the treetop, it was a small, yellow warbler with wings trending toward a pale gray and two prominent wingbars.

Today's birds of the year:

130. Summer Tanager   131. Pine Warbler

Sunday, 22 April

Rob Packie is one of my local birding friends. Among the many reasons I like birding with him, besides the fact that we share a similar sense of humor, is that he is a local boy, born and bred in Bar Harbor. That local knowledge often comes in handy—like today, when he had the inside scoop on a Blue Grosbeak in the Deer Isle-Stonington area.

6:47 a.m.   Driving down the Route 172, the Ellsworth Road, *en route* to Stonington, an hour and a half from Bar Harbor, and (critically to my Little Big Year) still in Hancock County, three dark birds crossed the road, then flew parallel to us for about five seconds, plenty of time to make an identification—three tannish brown blackbird-sized icterids with pale eyes make them all female Rusty Blackbirds.

This species has seen a significant decline in their population over the past forty years. Alas, no clear cause has been identified.

7:27 a.m.   We arrived at Rob's friends' home, the site of the Blue Grosbeak. Pulling into the driveway, a blue bird in an ornamental shrub quickly darted off. Rob had a key to this house, so we made our way inside to begin our stakeout. This was among the easier avian stakeouts I have undertaken. Within ten minutes, a blue bird (likely the one we saw as we pulled into the driveway) tentatively hopped out from behind the woodshed. Several times it darted back and forth, briefly visible, then retreating. Rob and I changed our position to another window and there it was! A beautiful, blue, male Blue Grosbeak, chestnut wing-bars clearly on display. This time, it stayed put long enough for me to shoot a number of photographs.

Grosbeaks are closely related to cardinals. Their usual range is from the mid-Atlantic coast south to Florida and west to southern California. Their range seems to be extending northward; some ornithologists suggest this may be a result of forest clearing, opening up habitat more suitable to their preferences.

8:30 a.m.   After our success with the Blue Grosbeak, we visited my favorite Deer Isle birding site: Scott's Landing, an Island Heritage Trust preserve. Over the next hour, we slowly walked a mile through a variety of habitats. It was the open field that yielded two year-birds.

Three Tree Swallows swooped into the field, wheeling all about. This is a species I will see through the months of May and June—they breed in nest boxes I monitor at the Peggy Rockefeller Farm—but it is always good to see the first ones return....

Few other birds look to me as though they are flying purely for the joy of it the way Tree Swallows do. Even though their population is large (scientists estimate 20 million Tree Swallows), it is declining, along with all other aerial insectivores, largely due to a loss of their insect food, which are being killed by our intensive use of insecticides, whether on our farms, in our communities, or around our homes.

I remember one particular April day years ago in the High Peaks of the Adirondack Mountains of New York State. I was sitting on the porch of the Marcy Dam Ranger Cabin, four miles in from the Adirondack Loj trailhead, with my interior ranger friend Mike. It was a beautiful day, no wind, the sun was out, the thermometer had pushed well into the 40s Fahrenheit. With a snowpack that was still many feet deep, backcountry skiers were out in force. Mike greeted each party, ensuring their preparedness for the conditions (skies or snowshoes, food, water, extra clothing, emergency plan). At one point, I looked down Marcy Brook and saw two swiftly moving shapes flying up the stream toward us. Tree Swallows! How magical it was to see the very first Tree Swallows of the year as they arrived on their northward migration!

... Continuing our walk through the meadow, a number of Savannah Sparrows and Song Sparrows were active, mostly foraging, a few exercising their lungs with song.

One lesson I strive to constantly practice is to look at every bird. And today it was rewarded. One sparrow was not like the others. It had a streaked breast, much more finely streaked than a Song Sparrow. It lacked the yellow lores (or eyestripe) of the Savannah Sparrow. A white eye-ring was our first clue to its identity. The outer tail-feathers were also white. All of these combined lead to an identification of Vesper Sparrow.

This is a grassland sparrow. Here in Maine, during the breeding season, it is often found on the same blueberry barrens as Upland Sandpipers. Alas, although we have plenty of this habitat in Maine, it is less common in Hancock County, so not only was this a year bird, it was a particularly good one as Vesper Sparrows can be difficult to find.

11:07 a.m.   Our last stop of the day was the home of Ed and Deb Hawkes. Walking around his dooryard, in a patch of pruned *Rosa rugosa*, or Seaside Rose, a faint chip note alerted me to the presence of a bird. Now, on the one hand, I sometimes feel that all chip notes sound alike. But this one sounded different, higher, perhaps more musical, than any I have heard since at least last fall. Could it be a Chipping Sparrow? Yes!

In 1929, ornithologist Edward Howe Forbush wrote of the Chipping Sparrow that it was "the little brown-capped pensioner for the dooryard and lawn, that comes about farmhouse doors to glean crumbs shaken from the tablecloth by thrifty housewives."

Today's birds of the year:

132. Rusty Blackbird
133. Blue Grosbeak
134. Tree Swallow

135. Vesper Sparrow
136. Chipping Sparrow

Tuesday, 24 April

This time of year, with new species of birds arriving nearly every day, I decided to visit a number of different sites. On today's list: Mount Desert Island High School, Stone Barn, and Peggy Rockefeller Farm.

Mount Desert Island High School, which has an open campus policy (meaning that anyone can walk around the campus), may just be the best bird-watching option in Hancock County. And so it is that I visit frequently from April well into November.

8:50 a.m.   Right off the bat, as I walked around the settling ponds, I started hearing Ruby-crowned Kinglets and Yellow-rumped Warblers. Oh, how I love this time of year, if for no other reason than hearing the avian chorus. Despite a light turnout (at least in terms the number of individual birds), I still managed twenty-six species of birds in thirty-nine minutes.

The highlight of this stop turned out to be a bit of an audio puzzle. Walking around the backside of the ponds, coming from the woods was an intermittent *weep*.

In the world of birding, there are no rules, only guidelines. Hearing the *weep*, the guideline that came to bear was that Great Crested Flycatcher, which this callnote most closely resembled, shouldn't be arriving for nearly three weeks. But the tonal quality was a bit off for a Great Crested Flycatcher. Racking my internal avian audio library,

I finally hit upon it: Swainson's Thrush. Of course! That makes much more sense. (In the spring, it sometimes takes me a while to recognize birds that I have not heard in months.)

The bird wasn't too far back in the Tamaracks, so I played two iterations of the *weep* call from iBird Pro on my iPhone[i]. A thrush popped right up. Uniformly olivish back and tail; buffy eye-ring; brown spotted throat and chest; buffy throat and white chest, both with dark spots; belly spots fading to white. Yup, Swainson's Thrush.

On Friday, a Cattle Egret was reported from College of the Atlantic's Peggy Rockefeller Farm. C.J. Walke, the farm manager, sent me an email reporting the bird as hanging out with their herd of Belted Galloway, a heritage beef cattle originating in Scotland. My recent daily sojourns in pursuit of the bird had been fruitless (or birdless; at least in terms of Cattle Egret), so I was excited to try to find it.

10:00 a.m.   I thought to run Fogo at Stone Barn (the farm across the road from the Peggy Rockefeller Farm), whose property is open to the public and welcomes dogs. This would also set me up to look for the Cattle Egret on the Peggy Rockefeller Farm. Lo and behold, the Cattle Egret was in the Stone Barn field! It was foraging near a heritage apple tree for worms, insects, frogs, or just about anything else it can fit down its gullet. This was a lone, small, all-white member of the heron family sporting yellow nuptial accents on its crown and back.

Cattle Egret are native to Africa. It is thought four of them reached South America, perhaps blown across the ocean by a storm, in 1877. From there, adapting well to the New World, their population spread, reaching the United States by 1941. Today, in the Western Hemisphere, I have seen them from the Falkland Islands and southern Argentina all the way north to Maritime Canada.

Continuing our walk through the woods, Fogo and I eventually reached the shores of Northeast Creek. This early in the season, new growth of the various wetland vegetation is only just beginning to hint at emerging and last year's growth is all dead and laid flat by the accumulation of the winter's snow. This certainly makes it easy to peruse the wetland.

And peruse I did. The only waterfowl were two drake Mallards, one sporting a green head, the other blue. (In reality, they are the same iridescent color. It is a property of the constituent components of the hollow feather vane—the barbs, barbules, and hooklets—and how they reflect light. So, in the case of a bird such as a Mallard, their green heads can appear blue, or even black, depending on your angle to the light.) Apart from the Mallards, there was a veritable dearth of bird activity, if not birds themselves, on the Northeast Creek wetland plain, but still....

This is the time for American Bitterns to begin arriving, so I did another careful scan. What I previously took to be a clump of cat-tails, or some other similar vegetation, moved in a very deliberate fashion, and not at the whims of the wind. AHA! Watching closely, a long leg came up and slowly, cautiously, was planted again. Then the body moved to follow. An American Bittern!

American Bitterns have a variety of evocative colloquial names. *Oonk-a-choonk*! Hear the deep bass call of this bird once and you will understand its common moniker of Thunder-pumper. Bitterns are also known as Bog Bull, Stake Driver, and Indian Hen, among others.

The plumage of the American Bittern is about as good a camouflage as you will find in the natural world. Patterned with light and dark brown vertical stripes, as soon as they point their head to the sky, they blend in with the surrounding vegetation.

I recall one morning years ago, driving in the Lake Champlain Valley before sunrise, down the Clark Road past the Webb-Royce

Swamp, an American Bittern walking across the road was caught in my headlights. Sensing danger, it stopped and pointed its head skyward, deciding to blend in with…what? The road? This means of hiding works great in wetland; not so great in the middle of a paved road.

Later, our walk nearly done, Fogo and I once again emerged from the woods and onto the mown field. A lone bird wheeled overhead, its manner of flight more laborious than the Tree Swallows I had been seeing the last few days. Brown upperparts and throat fading to a nearly white brown marked this a Northern Rough-winged Swallow. This species derives its name from the fact that the wing feathers have small hooks, making them appear uneven, or "rough," on their leading edge.

1:13 p.m.   After walking at Stone Barn, I drove to the northern Peggy Rockefeller Farm lot to look for grassland birds. The Peggy Rockefeller Farm is in two slightly disjunct parcels separated by Stone Barn Farm: one at the corner of Norway Drive and Crooked Road, the other a mere quarter mile north on Norway Drive.

Grassland birds are more than Bobolink and Eastern Meadowlark (the former is still two or three weeks out before the first ones arrive; anymore, the latter is a vagrant). I think of grassland birds as anything that either breeds on grasslands or relies on them for a significant portion of their life cycle.

Today's grassland birds included a pair of Canada Geese foraging on grasses; two Killdeer were clearly paired up, running around, calling out *k'dee k'dee k'dee*; a pair of Tree Swallows were scoping out a nest box; and Savannah Sparrows and Song Sparrows seemed to already be staking out territories. It would be a stretch to include a pair of Mourning Doves foraging on seeds in the fields under the *nom de plume* of grassland birds. And, although Turkey Vultures certainly feed on carrion…

STOP! Any time my late mentor, Mike Peterson, and I were out birding, I grew accustomed to his occasional exclamations: "STOP!" I soon clued in that these stops often coincided with roadkill. Mike would then have me pick it up (a square-mouthed grain scoop-style shovel lived in the bed of my 1989 red four-wheel-drive Toyota pick-up truck) to transport back to his house. There, I then locked the hubs and we four-wheeled out to the middle of his meadow. The roadkill was deposited on a four-foot by four-foot wooden platform which could be espied from the comfort of his porch. This was Mike's Turkey Vulture feeder.

… the lone one floating high above was not a grassland bird.

The highlight of this stop was a Field Sparrow! I don't know that Field Sparrows were ever abundant in Hancock County. Carroll Tyson and James Bond, in their 1941 *Birds of Mt. Desert Island, Acadia National Park, Maine*, considered the species a "rare or accidental visitant from the south". In his 1987 edition of *Native Birds of Mount Desert Island and Acadia National Park*, Ralph Long wrote that "this is one of the southern species that has become established as a summer resident on the island since the great fire [of '47]." In more recent years, natural communities have matured to the point that there may not be enough adequate habitat for them.

In spring 2011 and 2012, a male Field Sparrow showed up at Maine Coast Heritage Trust's Babson Creek Preserve and began singing. And singing. And singing. All day long, for weeks upon weeks, this lone Field Sparrow sang its bouncing-ball trill in the vain hopes of attracting a mate. If he had been successful in finding a female, it is quite likely we would been appalled at his behavior: a male Field Sparrow will fly at a female in his territory, striking her, knocking her to the ground. But if we had been Field Sparrows, this would have appeared an entirely normal part of the mating ritual.

Reviewing the day's findings, five birds helps my Little Big Year tally. American Bittern, Northern Rough-winged Swallow, and Swainson's Thrush are three species that I expect to find every year. Cattle Egrets and Field Sparrows are much more vagrant in Hancock County, so those were particularly good additions to the year-list.

Today's birds of the year:

137. Swainson's Thrush
138. Cattle Egret
139. American Bittern

140. Northern Rough-winged Swallow
141. Field Sparrow

Wednesday, 25 April

Today was a disjointed day of birding with a quick morning foray to Stone Barn and then a visit to the head of Mount Desert Island in the afternoon.

7:05 a.m.   Rob Packie told me about a pair of Barred Owls frequenting the trails at the Stone Barn, so I set out to try to find and photograph them. Crossing back through the open field after completing the forested loop, the owls gave me a departing hoot. DRAT! I did not have enough time to backtrack. To make up for it, I heard the rattling chitter of a flight of Tree Swallows. As they wheeled about, I did my best to count (sixteen was my best effort). Among the Tree Swallows, my first pair of Barn Swallows of the year.

Like Tree Swallows, Barn Swallows are amazing aerialists, wheeling and darting. If we were to anthropomorphize, it just looks like too much fun. The reality is that there is a method to the zooming madness: swallows eat on the wing and these guys are chasing food, often flying insects that we cannot see from our land-bound vantage.

Barn Swallows are one of the most widespread species in the world, being found breeding across most of the northern hemisphere and wintering in most of the southern hemisphere (excepting Australia and Antarctica).

1:04 p.m.   I do like to multitask. Parked at pump number three at Steamboat Landing Gas Station at the head of Mount Desert Island, waiting for my van to fill, I had my binoculars glued to my face, looking across Route 3, scanning the adjacent wetland for any sign of avian life. A lone Greater Yellowlegs was my reward.

I am routinely asked what my favorite bird is. That is a difficult question to answer. I am mesmerized by the songs of the Brown Creeper and the Adirondack race of Savannah Sparrow. I dream about flying like a swallow. My favorite type of birding is standing at the rail of a ship, looking for pelagic seabirds. But I have a special place in my heart for Greater Yellowlegs. There is something about shorebirds in general and Greater Yellowlegs in particular that really attracts me. No small part of that is finding several of their nests on the wind-blasted barrens of Newfoundland, a landscape that I simply adore.

For students looking for a graduate project, you should consider Greater Yellowlegs. As Cornell Lab of Ornithology's All About Birds website states, despite their being "common and widespread, their low densities and tendency to breed in inhospitable, mosquito-ridden muskegs make it one of the least-studied shorebirds on the continent." Personally, I like mosquito-ridden muskegs; perhaps I should tackle this project. Anyone want to fund me?

1:06 p.m.   I have written previously about Ed and Deb Hawkes' amazing yard. At last count, they have 150 species of birds on their greater yard-list—greater meaning anything they can see while standing on their property, even if it is a mile offshore. Most every year, they take a birding trip, targeting species to add to their respective life-lists. And while they are away, I am happily recruited to fill their bird feeders, water their plants, and watch their birds.

Before I even opened the door to my van, I could hear a cacophony. Among the songs was what I thought was an American Robin, but if it was, it was a robin that had opera training: the sweet, sing-song melody, a sort of *cherree chirrup, cherree chirrup*. Rose-breasted Grosbeak! Even if I did not see the bird, its sweet melody made me smile; while in my mind's eye, I could visualize the male: black head and upperparts, white underparts, and rosy-red breast.

As I rounded the corner of the house, most of the birds at the feeders flushed, but a small black bird remained at one of the black-oil sunflower feeders. A small black bird? Right, a small member of the blackbird family with a brown head could only be the Brown-headed Cowbird....

Long ago, before the landscape became so fragmented with farms and communities, cowbirds were largely relegated to the prairies where they followed North American Bison, feeding on insects stirred up by the grazing ungulates. Today, cowbirds are found throughout the entirety of the continental United States. They are "brood parasites," meaning the female lays eggs in the nests of other birds who then incubate the eggs and raise the chicks, doing all the work.

The relationship between cowbirds and their host is complicated. A single female cowbird can lay as many as forty eggs in forty nests in a season. In a never-ending battle, the host may evict the intruding egg—Yellow Warblers will actually build up the nest atop a cowbird egg—but the female cowbird, while she has absolutely nothing to do with the care or raising of her progeny, keeps tabs. Cowbirds whose eggs have been evicted from a nest have been known to return to that nest and destroy or kill the eggs or young of the host.

... Immediately behind the feeder with the Brown-headed Cowbird was a crabapple tree, close enough to serve as protective cover for the variety of songbirds but just far enough that squirrels cannot leap to the feeders. Through the dense tangle of branches, I could see the yellows of American Goldfinch, the red of a male Northern Cardinal, the flash of white outer tail feathers of Dark-eyed Junco, and the raspberry reds of male Purple Finch.

Among the raspberry reds was a brown that I initially took to be a female Purple Finch. That is, I thought it was a female Purple Finch until I realized that the bird was 30% longer and fully 50% heavier than the nearby male Purple Finch. Its chest was a buffy brown beneath the darker brown streaking, bold white wing bars, the eyestripe was a bright white, and the clincher: the bill was, well, gross, as in the Middle English definition meaning "thick, massive, bulky." Right, how could I forget? Rose-breasted Grosbeak is one of those species where both the male and female sing.

If I had to choose one particularly noteworthy feature of the Rose-breasted Grosbeak, even more than the rosy-red chest of the male, I would choose its song. On a spectrum of similar songs, there is the familiar, if not ubiquitous, *churree-chirrup* cadence of the American Robin. Moving toward the less musical, there is the similar song of the Scarlet Tanager, but one made all the raspier due to an apparent case of strep throat. And then there is the sweet, musical intonation of the Rose-breasted Grosbeak, once described by twentieth-century naturalist H. Roy Ivor as "so entrancingly beautiful that words cannot describe it."[i] Not being able to top that superlative, I will leave it at that.

Today's birds of the year:

142. Barn Swallow
143. Greater Yellowlegs
144. Rose-breasted Grosbeak

145. Brown-headed Cowbird

Thursday, 26 April

J ohn James Audubon's (1785) birthday.

Today was not a birding day, but it was. Although I did not set out to go birding, I am always birding. Sometimes, that simply means I take a slight detour on my way to and from other activities, just in the simple hope of finding a few birds. And so it was this day....

1:06 p.m.   Driving by the hayfields of College of the Atlantic's Peggy Rockefeller Farm, after the recent heavy rains, a group of gulls were concentrated, probably searching for earthworms. This is where my late birding mentor, Mike Peterson, would say, "The boys are out." Of course, his use of "boys" was simply a generic collective as there is no sexual dimorphism in gulls (in other words, males and females look alike). There were well over one hundred Ring-billed Gulls, about forty Herring Gulls, and Great Black-backed Gulls numbering in the single digits, but one of the last looked small. I stopped the van so I could pull up my binoculars. Yellow legs! That makes one of the black-backed gulls not a Great but a Lesser.

Lesser Black-backed Gull is a bird commonly found in Europe; however, during the past forty years or so, they have been increasingly showing up on the east coast of North America. In fact, they reputedly have a very small breeding population on Isle of Shoals, located six miles off the Maine/New Hampshire border. During winter trips to Mount Desert Rock, twenty-five miles offshore of Bar Harbor, it is not uncommon to see dozens.

While it is not an unexpected bird on our coastal waters, seeing it loafing on a farm field was a surprise, albeit a pleasant one; especially as it meant one less bird I would need to chase offshore; especially one of the less common birds for my year-list.

1:38 p.m.   A relatively quick visit to Hamilton Pond turned up all the usual suspects for a late April day—birds such as Canada Goose, American Black Duck, Ring-necked Duck, Osprey, Belted Kingfisher, Eastern Phoebe, and Yellow-rumped Warbler—sixteen in all. A Barred Owl hooting its *who cooks for you, who cooks for you all* from across the pond was a nice accompaniment to the avian soundtrack, especially being midday.

Scanning the pond through my spotting scope, I was able to more accurately tally the birds. Over the years, I have learned that it is important to carefully scan the shoreline. Good thing this has become second nature! Slowly skirting the shoreline, what I first took for a small duck, possibly a hen Green-winged Teal, turned out to be a small grebe: a Pied-billed Grebe, to be precise.

All grebes have virtually no tail, helping to separate them from ducks. However, unlike their larger cousins, Horned Grebe and Red-necked Grebe, the Pied-billed Grebe has a short, stubby bill, further clinching identification.

The genus for Pied-billed Grebe is *Podilymbus*, which roughly translates from Latin to "feet at the buttocks" (Anouk thinks this is hilarious; heck, I do, too). While on the subject of names, some intriguing colloquial names for the Pied-billed Grebe include Dabchick, Devil-Diver, Hell-Diver, Dipper, and Water Witch.

Today's birds of the year:

146. Lesser Black-backed
     Gull

147. Pied-billed Grebe

Friday, 27 April

8:09 a.m.   Driving north to Bangor, I saw a kettle of nine vultures in the distance. First chance I had, I pulled over to scan the birds. I was immediately struck by the fact that one of them lacked the typical dihedral (that is, its wings were in a straight line and not held at an elevated angle) of the Turkey Vulture, so I just presumed it was Red-tailed Hawk (remember, if it seems big, almost impossibly big, it is likely a Bald Eagle; if it is just big, but not impossibly big, it is likely a Red-tailed Hawk). When I finally got my binoculars on it, I saw a vulture, all dark beneath with contrasting light primaries, those finger-like flight feathers at the end of the wings. Eventually, as I watched, the kettle drifted directly overhead. *Voilà!* I could now see the bird's black head, as opposed to the clearly visible red heads of the Turkey Vultures, further confirming the bird's identity.

While Turkey Vultures are common throughout Maine, Black Vultures are still rare, although no longer so rare as to require a report to the Maine Bird Records Committee.

Black Vultures do not have as developed a sense of smell as Turkey Vultures. In the typical range of the Black Vulture, they are known to follow their bigger cousins, soaring higher, keeping an eye on them. When the Turkey Vulture finds a meal of decomposing meat, Black Vultures will sometimes pack together to mob their bigger cousin away, stealing the meal.

Today's bird of the year:

148. Black Vulture

Saturday, 28 April

7:12 a.m. A morning's birding outing before the gaggle of girls descends upon our house for Anouk's overnight birthday party began with a visit to the home of Ed and Deb Hawkes. Hairy Woodpecker, Eastern Phoebe, Black-capped Chickadee, Ruby-crowned Kinglet, Hermit Thrush, Yellow-rumped Warbler, and Chipping Sparrow were among the common birds readily observed.

Reaching the boardwalk across a corner of their marsh, I paused to look and listen. Spring, with vibrant green shoots of new vegetation only just beginning to emerge and the previous year's growth lain flat by the weight of the winter's snow, is a good time to survey the swamp. My timing was rewarded with easily evident Swamp Sparrows. A male/female pair of Blue-winged Teal, even though they were the only ducks on the open water of the wetland, would have been easy to miss without careful observation.

The bird that made my day, though, was a Green Heron. For all of their stripy camouflage, this secretive, elusive bird really stood out. While the distance was enough so that the intricate detail of the striking greens and burgundies blended into more flattened fields of color, the short (for a heron), stocky, hunch-necked stance was easily discernable.

One fun fact about Green Herons: They are one of the few species of bird that use tools. They do this by taking small bits of food—

perhaps twigs, feathers, insects, etc.—and drop them on the water's surface as a sort of lure to attract their fishy prey.

8:28 a.m.   Each and every time I walk around the Mount Desert Island High School's settling ponds, I am always surprised by how long it takes to do the ¾-mile loop. Of course, the reason for the time is that there are almost always so many birds to see. And while I tallied twenty-seven species on this visit, the highlight was my first-of-the-year Blue-headed Vireo.

Formerly known as Solitary Vireo, the Blue-headed Vireo is the first vireo to routinely arrive in Maine each year. Take a close look at this warbler-sized bird and instantly you'll appreciate the name. In addition to its blue head, it is further identified by "spectacles," prominent white eye-rings connected by a white bridge over the bill.

Blue-headed Vireos are one of those species that give you "birder's neck." Since they inhabit the uppermost canopy of coniferous forests (deciduous forests, too, for that matter), they do not make observing easy. Fortunately, their slow, repetitive *here I am, there you are* song readily identifies them as a vireo. And when they end their series with a *chewy chewy*, then you know you have a Blue-headed Vireo.

Today's birds of the year:

149. Green Heron

150. Blue-headed Vireo

Sunday, 29 April

Having the ability to check email on my iPhone is both blessing and curse. A curse because it is too seductive to ignore for long. However, in my line of work, needing to respond to tour requests and field questions concerning the Maine Bird Atlas, it is an invaluable tool. So, when the hourly "Year Needs Alert for Hancock County"[i] from eBird landed in my in-box alerting me to a Painted Bunting, I had to beg my leave from my family to chase this rare bird.

Normally, Painted Buntings are restricted to a wide swath of the south starting in the southern tip of North Carolina, extending throughout Florida, across to Texas, and sweeping down through Mexico and Central America. The first one I ever saw was at the Audubon Corkscrew Swamp Sanctuary, located south of Sarasota, Florida. I had been given explicit directions for finding one—walk through the nature center, out the back door, to a set of feeders, then watch and wait. Sure enough, there was a pair exactly where I had been told.

With eBird only showing a few dozen records of Painted Bunting in Maine, this is a particularly good bird. Although I had one for my Maine life-list (a Painted Bunting overwintered at a Blue Hill feeder in 2010), I needed to chase this individual for my Little Big Year.

1:39 p.m.   Simultaneous to the Year Needs Alert, Scott Riddell reached out to say the bird had been at his granite platform feeder an hour earlier. On my way, I picked up College of the Atlantic freshman Nathan Dubrow. At Scott's house, we met Ken Shellenberger (he is with the U.S. Coast Guard Station Southwest Harbor; I joke with Ken that his job must be to go birding for the Coast Guard because I have been seeing quite a few recent eBird reports from him). Scott's neighborhood is sort of a residential *cul-de-sac*, meaning little traffic and no issues with us milling about in the road.

After waiting and watching Scott's feeders for about thirty minutes, we fanned out to search for the Painted Bunting. Almost immediately, a whistle from Nathan alerted us to the fact that he found the bunting roosting in a cedar! The foliage was so dense that the bird was nearly invisible. Fortunately, what was visible was good enough to snap a few poor photos, albeit photos showing glimpses of the vibrant reds and blues and greens of the Painted Bunting. Still, they were good enough to make a positive identification, and that was all that mattered.

3:30 p.m.   After three birding stops, I was now at College of the Atlantic's Peggy Rockefeller Farm fields north of Crooked Road. In the distance, I could see that the lone Cattle Egret continued to forage in the Stone Barn fields. Walking along the road, I heard and saw some of the more common birds—American Crow, Barn Swallow, Savannah Sparrow, Song Sparrow, Red-winged Blackbird, and Common Grackle. A high-pitched, sweet, musical song greeted my ears as I was winding down my mile-long walk. Eastern Meadowlark! This has to be in my top three ten favorite songs!

There was a time when meadowlarks were far more common than they are today. Historically, they would have been found in nearly every grassland east of the Mississippi. Alas, dramatic changes to the landscape, primarily agricultural, have severely reduced their population. Females will abandon their nests if people, or their activities, get too close; or, at best, are overly cautious in returning, which prolongs the exposure of eggs or young to the elements and the threat of predation. Conversion of grasslands to non-grassland farmlands, tilling to manage weeds, grazing livestock (which are prone to trample nests), mowing, injudicious use of herbicides and pesticides, and old farm fields returning to forest, all have a negative impact on the viability of Eastern Meadowlarks. Unfortunately, here on Mount Desert Island, that means we likely no longer have breeding meadowlarks (the last one I found nesting locally was in 2004).

Today's birds of the year:

151. Painted Bunting   152. Eastern Meadowlark

Tuesday, 01 May

Between 2005 and 2017, Natalie and I have had the great good fortune of having worked with Garrison Keillor and his former radio show, *A Prairie Home Companion*, on annual chartered cruises to destinations around Northeastern North America, Alaska, the Caribbean, the Mediterranean, the Baltic, England and Scotland, Scandinavia, Spain, and Africa, eleven cruises in all.

For the first cruise, we were just naturalists, lecturing, leading Naturalist on Deck programs, and escorting shore excursions. After that cruise, when Garrison asked us to return for the next one, he said we worked too hard and that he wanted us to hire more naturalists, as well as coordinate the education program. Regretfully, the cruises have come to an end, but not the long-lasting friendships. Among those friendships with many of our fellow travelers was Dan Johnston from Utah.

For the past several cruises, Dan spent countless hours on the bow with Natalie and me, both while we were on duty during our Naturalist on Deck programs and off duty. We spent countless hours scanning the horizon for seabirds. Whether on deck or over a cocktail in a lounge, Dan wanted to geek out over bird identification, pouring through field guides, comparing with photos both he and I took. I thrived on our dialog delving into the minutiae of superciliums and remiges and undertail coverts. The friendship with Dan is one of those easygoing relationships where you feel like you have always known each other. To this day, although we rarely see each other, we regularly exchange texts of our latest bird sightings.

When Dan's East Coast son, Jim, and his wife had a baby in December, it was only a matter of time before Dan came to see his new granddaughter. I also benefitted: with Dan being this close—by Western standards, the five hours from near Boston, Massachusetts, to Bar Harbor, Maine, is just a hop, skip, and drive—it was *fait accompli* that he visit. That made for three days of birding with Dan and Jim.

Of the twenty species of larids (gulls, terns, and skimmer) on the Hancock County checklist, all but two (Herring Gull and Great Black-backed Gull) are migratory. Four of those twenty have black heads as part of their breeding plumage—Bonaparte's Gull, Black-headed Gull, Little Gull, and Laughing Gull. It was just a matter of time before I found my first migrant gull of the season.

3:01 p.m.   Dan, Jim, and I found ourselves at Seawall, a good place to scan the surrounding waters for all form of waterbirds, including gulls. In the United States, Laughing Gulls are an East Coast species. So, when Dan asked, "Is that a Laughing Gull?" I said yes, almost before seeing it. I mean, really, what else looks like a Laughing Gull?

They have long wings lending to flight more gracefully buoyant than most gulls. Couple that manner of flight with upper wings and back a much darker shade of gray than Herring or Ring-billed Gulls but not so dark as Great Black-backed Gulls, prominent white eye-ring split laterally like two halves of a circle not quite coming together, and a blood-red bill and Laughing Gulls are easily identified.

Thanks to the International Migratory Bird Treaty Act[i], Laughing Gull populations, which were nearly decimated by plume and egg hunters during the late nineteenth and early twentieth centuries, have responded more than favorably.

Based on banding data, we know the oldest Laughing Gull was twenty-two years old. The band had been collected when the bird was "caught or found dead due to control operations" in Maine in 2009.

Today's bird of the year:

153. Laughing Gull

Wednesday, 02 May

T he Natural History Center's Weekly Birding Tour is held on Wednesdays. On this day, Dan, Jim, and I were joined by one of the regulars, Jane Reynolds, so I thought we would do something different and head north of Ellsworth for a morning walk.

8:24 a.m.   This was my first time to explore Branch Pond Public Forest. Although one of my birding friends, Chuck Whitney, had told me about it a number of times, I tend to be much more parochial, birding more often than not around Mount Desert Island. As we explored some of the hiking trails of Branch Pond Public Forest, walking 3½ miles over nearly three hours, I had to wonder why I had waited so long to explore this wonderful woodland?

Highlights of our walk included seeing two Yellow-bellied Sapsuckers chasing each other around the towering hulk of a dead and hollowed maple, periodically drumming, raising a reverberating racket that could be heard for quite some distance. Meanwhile, the soundtrack to a portion of our walk was two male Winter Wrens singing their long, melodious song to defend their territories from each other, as well as any other male Winter Wrens in the area. Several pair of Hermit Thrush, clearly paired off, were skulking around the forest floor; one pair playing hide-and-seek with us, constantly keeping a Volkswagen Beetle-sized glacial erratic between them and our troupe. And a male White-throated Sparrow sang one of the defining songs of the North Woods—*Old Sam Peabody, Peabody, Peabody.*

Not far down the Marsh Trail, we immediately heard the song of a Northern Waterthrush, a series of descending couplets, *WEET-WEET, Weet-Weet, weet-weet.* Don't be taken in by the name, though. The Northern Waterthrush is a member of the North American wood-warblers and not a thrush at all. The name "waterthrush" is likely a mash-up of the fact that it has a more thrush-like appearance and that it prefers wet areas, frequently found foraging along calm, wooded waters such as small streams and bog flats. Their favorite foods: a variety of invertebrates, including snails, and even small fish. Where most songbirds only defend their territory on the breeding grounds, both Waterthrush—Louisiana and Northern—also defend their wintering territories.

11:18 a.m.   Our morning walk over, on our way out from Branch Pond Public Forest, driving down the mile-long dirt access road back toward Route 1A, we crossed a single-lane bridge. An Eastern Phoebe darted out from beneath. This was an almost certain indication of breeding, so I made a quick stop in order to properly document it as a record for the Maine Bird Atlas. Indeed, as suspected, a quick look under the bridge revealed a nest.

After confirming that the Phoebe was breeding, we took advantage of the break to identify any other birds in the area. There were only six species, but a Black-and-white Warbler was a wonderful addition to our day's list. And to my Hancock County Little Big Year list.

The Eastern Phoebe was once known as Black-and-white Treecreeper, both as homage to its European look-alike[i] of that name and for its habit of creeping along trunks and branches, very much like the treecreepers of the Old Country. The Black-and-white Warbler has evolved an extra-long hind claw, as well as legs stouter than other wood-warblers; adaptations well suited for their particular habit of locomotion up and down tree trunks. Where most songbirds defend territories by sing-offs, Black-and-white Warblers are more combative, including on their wintering grounds (shades of the Northern Waterthrush, right?).

Look for Black-and-white Warblers among the earlier wood-warblers to arrive in Maine.

Today's birds of the year:

154. Northern Waterthrush

155. Black-and-white War-
bler

Thursday, 03 May

Dan and Jim had to leave today, and I had to get back to work, but not before we snuck in a few hours of birding. There are two significant birding hotspots on Mount Desert Island during spring migration that I wanted to share with them.

A cool morning early in May meant there was no need to be out the door at the crack-of-dawn. Instead, by the time we had a leisurely start to the day, eggs-over-easy for breakfast, and hang-out time with Anouk, we finally left the house just before 8:00.

8:13 a.m.   The birding started slow at Acadia National Park's Sieur de Monts Spring. Named for seventeenth-century merchant, explorer, and colonizer, Pierre Dugua de Monts[i], Sieur de Monts Spring is a hotspot for its range of habitats in a relatively limited geographic footprint. My standard two-mile loop takes us through each of these natural communities.

From the Sieur de Monts Spring parking lot, walk out the Hemlock Trail about one mile to the Park Loop Road. Turn left and walk along the shoulder, facing the oncoming one-way traffic about a quarter mile, then turn left onto the Jesup Trail. Half of the Jesup Trail is a boardwalk. At the end of the boardwalk, take in Wild Gardens of Acadia. All-in-all, it is about a two-mile figure-eight circuit with virtually no elevation change, and yet, you walk through a hemlock forest, a mixed White Pine-Red Oak upland, a Red Maple swamp, a birch hedgerow surrounded on one side by an alder swamp and on the other by a wet meadow, and, across the wet meadow, is the shoulder of the massif comprising Dorr and Kebo Mountains which creates updrafts for raptors and ravens to ride.

This morning, one of the very first birds we heard at Sieur de Monts Spring was a Black-throated Green Warbler. *Zee zee zee zoo zee.* This is a song I will never forget....

Birding the forests along the shores of the Niagara River as a kid, along with my kid brother Rob, two years my junior, we knew Black-throated Green Warblers, at least visually. And its song may well be one of the first we learned.

Between us, our complete ornithological kit consisted of one pair of binoculars, Zeiss, taken off a German officer during World War II by one of our Father's uncles, a 1960s vintage solid state, hand-crank, portable record player[ii], and a 1970 vinyl LP of Donald J. Borror's *Songs of Warblers of Eastern North America*. As the eldest (and, as Rob was fond to point out, having the worst vision), I carried the binoculars. Rob carried the portable record player, ready to cue the track with the desired warbler song.

One day, while we out birding, we heard a song that we did not recognize. We couldn't find it on *Songs of Warblers of Eastern North America*, so between bouts of our mystery bird's crooning, we would try to stealthily sneak closer. Finally, after what must have been thirty minutes or more, we found the bird. A Black-throated Green Warbler. A Black-throated Green Warbler? But they sing *zee zee zee zoo zee*.

Later, we shared our finding with our birding mentor, Jerry Farrell. He told us that many birds have more than one song. Really? How did we not know that? Lesson learned. Turns out the alternate song of the Black-throated Green Warbler is *zoo zee zoo zoo zee*.

... Continuing on, walking through the hemlock forest, one iteration of *ee-o-lay* announced the presence of a Wood Thrush. Wood Thrush are a species that were once much more common. Alas, like so many species of birds (the majority, in fact), the entire Wood Thrush population has declined as a result of deforestation on both their breeding grounds and wintering habitats.

Halfway through our walk, in an alder thicket, we heard the song of the Least Flycatcher. Flycatchers of the genus *Empidonax* are notoriously difficult to identify down to species. Unless you hear them. *Empidonax* flycatchers have distinctive songs; hearing one sing is often all that is needed to confirm the species. (It gets a bit easier when you are banding, have the bird in hand, and can make precise measurements of things such as the length of wing chords and tail feathers.) In this case, the short, harsh *che-BECK* of the Least Flycatcher is diagnostic. With a little effort scanning the woods, we found it singing, perched atop an alder where it could survey its landscape for flying food....

I spent two college summers working as the Nature Director at Camp Bedford, a Boy Scout camp in the north-central Adirondack Mountains. Before starting my job that first summer, I was sent to National Camp School for training to become a nature director.

Lost to the vagaries of time are the names of my fellow prospective councilors and how many of us were there, but it was quite a few. We were learning the skills to run waterfronts, field sports, and arts and crafts. Among the many joys of camp life are the skits, songs, chants, and cheers, often unique to each camp. To help this evolution, we students of National Camp School were required to develop our own, to be performed at an assigned meal. The naturalists, my group, were lucky to draw a dinner later in the week. Every day, our instructor would check in with us, "How are you guys coming?"

"Fine," was our standard answer, even though the reality was that this form of theatrics was the last thing our particular group wanted to do. I mean, look at us: a bunch of crunchy-granola, Birkenstock-wearing, tree-hugging, long-haired nature-nuts. (Well, that was the stereo-type. I, for one, was not very crunchy-granola, did not own Birkenstocks, and have never had long hair. In fact, I have never even owned a tie-dyed t-shirt!) We were not gung-ho field sport drill instructors nor whistle-blowing waterfront types. We were not even into theatrical arts and crafts. We wanted to be one with Nature, listen to the Spring Peeper chorus, follow the peregrinations of our resident beavers, smell the Wake Robin.

The day of our debut was suddenly upon us. We had until dinner to prepare. After the morning's lessons, our instructor was very aware of our lack of effort toward a skit, song, chant, or cheer. To help us focus, he led us indoors, into a room with no windows, and said we had to stay until we were prepared.

For some reason, the small group of us just were not motivated for this particular task. An hour crept by during which we talked about dichotomous keys. Mr. Instructor looked in on us. "Any luck?" No. Another hour had us talking about the breeding distribution of boreal birds, with a particular emphasis on southern range limits. "Any luck?" No. 4:00 p.m. "Any luck? No, but we cleared up any confusion on whether wood-fern is actually a fern. A 5:00 dinner meant our deadline was set.

Finally, I turned to the group and said, "Listen, what are we? We are scientists, right? Field biologists and naturalists. What is the thread uniting our field? Taxonomy. And what is the basic unit of taxonomy? Hierarchy. Kingdom. Phylum. Class. Order. Family. Genus. Species. Let's make that our cheer."

Dinner over, the camp director called for the naturalists. Our small group, all sitting together, stood, and with force, blasted out, "KINGDOM PHYLUM CLASS ORDER FAMILY GENUS SPECIES!" and sat back down. The silence was deafening. No roar of applause and cheers like there had been for all the other performances. I imagined a bunch of jocks scratching their heads, wondering, "What the hell was that?" And the arts and crafts lot shaking their heads, thinking to themselves, "Naturalists."

Ever since, whenever the topic of scientific names comes up, I cannot help myself: "KINGDOM PHYLUM CLASS ORDER FAMILY GENUS SPECIES!"

... Toward the end of our Sieur de Monts Spring tour, walking down the boardwalk, we encountered Glen Mittelhauser, executive director of the Maine Natural History Observatory (and also the coordinator of the Maine Bird Atlas) out doing wetlands fieldwork. In response to our query about good birds, Glen said a Great Crested Flycatcher was just a short piece up the boardwalk. Sure enough, we heard one calling, *whee-eep whee-eep whee-eep*. Even though we did not manage to see it—my memory was that this is quite early for this flycatcher to have arrived—sure enough, there is no confusing the call.

A fun fact about flycatchers: They have a variety of collective nouns. When you encounter a group of them, you can choose among "outfield," "swatting," "zapper," and "zipper" of flycatchers. As in, "There was a _____ (fill in your collective noun of choice) of flycatchers at Sieur de Monts Spring this morning."

9:52 a.m.   Moving on to the Mount Desert Island High School, as soon as we opened the minivan doors, we could hear the rapidly ascending *zeeee-up* song of the Northern Parula. Parula derives from the diminutive of *parus*, which translates as "little titmouse." Mark Catesby, an English naturalist whose legacy is *Natural History of*

Carolina, Florida and the Bahama Islands (published between 1729 and 1747) called the parula a "Finch Creeper," John James Audubon called it "Blue Yellow-backed Warbler." Both names are evocative in their own right. Northern Parulas are a small warbler that make their nests amid hanging clumps of *Usnea* lichen, Old Man's Beard. To see a Northern Parula approach a hanging clump of lichen and then, seemingly, disappear, is not magic. It's a nest site!

Today's birds of the year:

156. Black-throated Green Warbler
157. Wood Thrush
158. Least Flycatcher
159. Great Crested Flycatcher
160. Northern Parula

Friday, 04 May

The pressure was on this day: it felt as though I was running around like the proverbial phasianid with its cranium removed. At 1:00 p.m., I was to meet Dr. Sean Todd and his College of the Atlantic oceanography class to head up to New Brunswick for the weekend—I was co-leading the trip with Sean—to learn about and experience the world's highest tides (they reach over fifty feet between low tide and high tide!). I was worried about missing some really good birds (it was still something of a bitter pill to swallow to have missed a State of Maine first Violet-green Swallow back on 14 April when I was in New York State). As I would be out of state, and out of country, for 2½ days, I was frenetically looking for birds during the morning's errands.

11:30 a.m.   Driving down Indian Point Road, on my way to Somesville to pick up a trailer of kayaks we were borrowing, I passed an old farm. A movement out of the corner of my eye caught my attention. Glance to the rearview mirror: no cars. Sideview mirrors: no cars. Looking ahead: no cars. So, I slowed down to look. Flycatcher behavior; darting out for food and back to its fence-railing perch; dark upperparts, white lowerparts. The clincher was a white terminal band across the end of the tail. Eastern Kingbird! Eastern Kingbirds have one of the wackiest vocalizations of any eastern bird. They make a sound reminiscent of static electricity.

11:34 a.m.   Pulling into the Somesville driveway to pick up the kayak trailer, I was greeted by the rapid *wheet-sa wheet-sa wheet-sa ti-ti-*

ti-ti of the Nashville Warbler. Unfortunately, time did not allow for me to look for it, but a positive identification, based on the characteristic song, was made nonetheless.

Nashville Warblers have two distinct populations: eastern and western. Although they are not so separate as to be considered sub-species, let alone different species, they do exhibit one notable behavioral difference in that the western population wags its tail. A number of bird species do this. While the exact reason is unknown, some ornithologists have posited that tail-wagging may flush insects, making it easier to find food.

12:01 p.m.   Back on the College of the Atlantic campus, I met up with our group of sixteen students. It did not leave much time for anything more than incidental birding, but that was enough to tally eleven species. Among them, a Warbling Vireo was warbling, as they are wont to do. A drab bird with a yellow wash overall and a faint eyestripe all clearly point to this species. Research suggests that Warbling Vireos may, at least in part, learn their song instead of it being innate, as in most songbirds.

Our twelve-passenger vans were loaded with students and all the accoutrements we would need for the next few days. We were still on the college campus driving past the Community Garden when I briefly saw a Blue Jay-sized bird in an apple tree: a rich chestnut-brown above, dark streaks on a cream chest below, intense yellow eye assessing whether I posed any danger. It sported a decurved (downward curving) bill. Brown Thrasher! These guys blend in so well that they are easily overlooked (I only see a few of them each year).

Brown Thrashers always seem to me to be one of the most under-reported, if not under-appreciated, birds. This may be a product of their secretive nature, skulking about in dense cover. It is always surprising to me how I can hear their exuberant song and yet cannot find them. I can be standing in front of the bush where they are clearly singing and still not be able to see it.

If for no other reason, they should get accolades for having an incredible vocal repertoire. According to the *Birds of North America* species account for Brown Thrasher, they have more than 1,100 song types! The species account quoted an E. Murphy as writing: "Much of the reclame [sic] which has fallen to the Mockingbird is really due to the unperceived efforts of the Brown Thrasher. It is the opinion of many ornithologists that the song . . . is richer, fuller, and definitely more melodious than that of *polyglottis*" (*polyglottis* being the scientific species name for the Northern Mockingbird, which is a cousin to the thrasher).

2:32 p.m.   My final bird of the day was seen at forty-five miles per hour. Driving by the wetlands at the head of Mount Desert Island, a large (as in Great Blue Heron large), white wading bird was hunkered down feeding. An entirely unsatisfactory look at a Great Egret, but beggars cannot be choosers, right?

The nearest Great Egret colony to Hancock County is considerably south, south of Portland, even, on coastal islands near Scarborough Marsh. So, what was this guy doing here?

During spring migration, it is not uncommon that some birds fly hundreds of miles further north than their nesting grounds, a phenomenon ornithologists have dubbed "migration overshoot." Whether this is a pioneering foray, looking for potential nesting habitat beyond that already known, or, perhaps, a way of dispersing far enough before the actual nesting season in order to mitigate pressure on food resources, or even the possibility that these are non-breeding birds, stretching their winged wanderlust, is anyone's guess. Whatever the reason, we regularly see Great Egrets this time of year, so this one was not a surprise.

If this Great Egret is a breeder, it will likely be departing soon, looking for more of its own kind. They normally arrive at their colonial nesting sites early, earlier than many of the other species that nest alongside them. It is thought their presence may attract other colonial nesting species such as Great Blue Heron, Snowy Egret, Black-crowned Night-Heron, Glossy Ibis, and Cattle Egret.

Today's birds of the year:

161. Eastern Kingbird
162. Nashville Warbler
163. Warbling Vireo

164. Brown Thrasher
165. Great Egret

Monday, 07 May

Today, I had the privilege of being guest lecturer for Hannah Podurgiel and her two sessions of outdoor science class at Mount Desert Island High School. As you might imagine, given the name of her class, we went outside; specifically, we walked around the high school's settling ponds (one of my favorite birding hotspots) to talk birds and bird ecology while giving the students a lesson on bird identification, both visually and by ear. Nothing beats having real-life examples to observe in a natural setting when giving lessons in ecology.

9:45 a.m.   A Turkey Vulture flew overhead. I shared the manner in which this red-headed scavenger cleans the ick and slime coating their legs after dining on carrion, their primary diet: they squirt guano down their legs. The high ammonium content kills the nasty bacteria and sterilizes (more or less) in the process (I saw and wrote about my first Turkey Vulture of 2018 back on 22 February). While the graphic details of Turkey Vulture dining practices drew comments of "ew, gross" from a few students, "cool" seemed to be the prevailing sentiment. This instantly became a highlight of the morning field trip. I like to think my obvious fascination with all things biological (I am a field biologist, after all) was a lesson for the students in and of itself.

Continuing our walk, the conversation was both free-wheeling and wide-ranging. One of the stated goals of the class was to introduce students to some of the diverse ways people make a living in the natural sciences. I shared that I regularly work as a naturalist on small ships making the Antarctic run. This fact became a focus of our conversation with questions galore about penguins. Of course, these being Mainers, they know about puffins, so I gave a spontaneous lesson in convergent evolution—where two unrelated species in parallel environments (North Atlantic and Southern Ocean) evolve comparable physiological traits (*e.g.*, similar fusiform[i] body shapes and counter-shaded coloration) to fill similar ecological niches (feeding on small cold-water fishes)—comparing and contrasting penguins and puffins.

As we walked and talked, I verbally threw out the occasional *pish, pish, pish,* to attract birds. When a Black-throated Blue Warbler popped up, everyone was excited. Midnight blue above, white below, black facial disk and throat, and a bold white wing patch (which appears almost square on a resting bird), this is a striking warbler, if in an understated sort of way. I shared with the students a mixture of facts and anecdotes, beginning with when Black-throated Blue Warblers were first described by German naturalist Johann Friedrich Gmelin in 1789. He thought they were two species, what with the blue male and drab female having such different plumage.

One anecdote I shared with the students was that I can relate to Black-throated Blue Warblers through our mutual "sweet tooth." While doing research in the Dominican Republic in January of 2001, I had the pleasure of traveling with a group of conservation biologists, including Steven Latta. Among our observations of Neotropical migratory songbirds, we found Black-throated Blue Warblers feeding on "honeydew," a sweet carbohydrate solution that *Homopteran* scale insects excrete as waste after eating the phloem of host plants[ii].

This explained a few things for me as the spring previous to my Dominican trip, I had a Black-throated Blue Warbler regularly come to my hummingbird feeder in the Adirondacks in early May. At the time, I was quite curious about this behavior, never having observed a warbler drink sugar water. More recently, I have again witnessed this behavior in Bar Harbor, only this time I had a better understanding of its significance.

11:43 a.m.   During the second outdoor science class field trip, the birds were much less active. This is as you would expect, considering that we were now into the heat of the day. Looking out over the third pond, I was discussing the late Robert MacArthur's 1950s fieldwork in nearby Bass Harbor and how it resulted in what is widely considered today to be the seminal scientific paper on niche partitioning[iii]—the concept of how birds of similar species (wood-warblers in his case) arrange themselves along an elevational gradient within the forests, feeding at different heights within the canopy— when a medium-sized, plain-looking shorebird suddenly flew in, hovered over some clumped vegetation for several seconds, then took off to parts unknown. Fortunately, in the time it hovered, I was able to get a definitive glimpse, identifying it as a Solitary Sandpiper, while at the same time getting most of the students on the bird, too.

There are eighty-five species of shorebirds in the Family Scolopacidae worldwide. Of these, only two nest in trees: the Solitary Sandpiper of the Western Hemisphere and the Green Sandpiper of the Eurasian continent. In the case of the Solitary Sandpiper, which breeds across much of Canada, from Labrador to British Columbia and on into Alaska, it tends to use former nests of American Robins, Rusty Blackbirds, Eastern Kingbirds, Gray Jays, and Cedar Waxwings in which to lay its eggs.

Over the following months, I have run into some of the students from Hannah's class. They often come up to me to initiate conversations about birds. It is good to know that I may have had a bigger impact on some of them than I realized at the time of our initial meeting.

12:58 p.m.   After leaving the students, I made my way home. Fogo, penned up in the house all morning, was eager to run our trails, so I gladly obliged. It wasn't long before I heard the *teacher, teacher, Teacher, TEACHER* of an Ovenbird.

This thrush-looking warbler, with a dull golden racing stripe cresting its head, gets its name for the construction of its nest. Ovenbirds make their nest on the ground, domed, with its entrance to the side; it is said to resemble a Dutch Oven. Despite the Ovenbird's similarity to a small thrush, I will never (again) confuse it with any other bird.

One day, early in my friendship with the late J.M.C. "Mike" Peterson, we were running the spring banding station at the Crown Point (New York) State Historic Site. Mike had me check the net lanes where I found we had captured a number of birds. When I brought them to Mike, I was excited to present him with an Orange-crowned Warbler! Except that Mike told me to look again. Oh, right. Orange-crowned Warblers are more or less a uniform drab yellow-brown with few distinguishing field marks (this includes an almost indistinguishable hint of an orange smudge atop its head). The bird I had in hand was warm brown above, with heavily streaked under-parts, a prominent white eye-ring, and a bold orangey racing stripe over the top of its head. "Ovenbird?" I tentatively corrected myself. A very dry "Yes" from Mike was laden with undertones of "I thought you knew your birds better than that." This is one identification mistake I never made again.

5:55 p.m.   In the spring, even mundane tasks offer an opportunity to find year birds. For instance, this evening, I was on the College of the Atlantic campus to meet up with the oceanography class to finish unpacking and cleaning gear after our Bay of Fundy weekend. From near the north end of campus, the raspy chortle of House Wren alerted me to its presence. Its voluble vocalization made it easy to find this little bird with the cocked tail.

Although broadly distributed from coast to coast, here in Hancock County, we are at the very northeastern end of the House Wren's breeding range. At the fringes of any given population, you expect far smaller numbers (I have only ever observed a few House Wrens in this part of the world). George B. Dorr (one of the founders of Acadia National Park) is quoted in Ora Knight's 1908 *Birds of Maine*: "Some years ago a pair built in a bird house in my yard." Carroll Tyson and James Bond, in their 1941 *Birds of Mt. Desert Island, Acadia National Park, Maine*, described a pair nesting in Bar Harbor in 1938, and Ralph Long mentioned a pair in a nesting box in 1983.

Closer to the south end of campus, where we were taking care of our gear, a Yellow Warbler was singing its melodious *sweet sweet a little more sweet* song.

Male Yellow Warblers are brilliantly colored, entirely yellow except for bold chestnut streaks accenting its chest. As beautiful as they are, life can be challenging for them. They have been known to get caught in the webs of orb-weaver spiders[iv]. More significantly, though, is the fact that Yellow Warblers are frequently parasitized by Brown-headed Cowbirds.

It is a constant battle between the two: cowbirds lay eggs in the nest of the Yellow Warbler, which, in turn, often builds a new nest atop the parasitized one. And yet, cowbirds are known to keep track of the progress of their eggs. If the host ejects the egg or unfledged chick, the female Cowbird has been further known to destroy the Yellow Warbler's next clutch of eggs. It's a vicious cycle, made worse by the fact that our constant fragmentation of existing habitat continuously creates new inroads for cowbirds to reach territory they historically never knew.

Today's birds of the year:

166. Black-throated Blue
     Warbler
167. Solitary Sandpiper

168. Ovenbird
169. House Wren
170. Yellow Warbler

Wednesday, 09 May

The Natural History Center's Weekly Birding Tour got a slightly early start this morning. Not as early as I would like—heck, sunrise was 5:11 a.m. today—but considering the cool temperatures and dense fog, we still had plenty of time to find birds, which was borne out by the impressive tally of eleven year-birds.

6:52 a.m.   We met at Mount Desert Island High School and immediately began observing birds. A Lincoln's Sparrow, a generalist ground-nester that here on Mount Desert Island has been known to set up nesting territories eight miles to the south around the edges of Big Heath[i], was working the hedgerow near where we parked.

Continuing on our way, two White-crowned Sparrows were in the grass just beyond the third pond. These two will ultimately continue north to nest in the northern half of Canada and throughout most of Alaska, returning to the same breeding grounds year after year. This parochialism leads to regional dialects within their song. I'm curious, if they were to start breeding in Maine, would their vaguely White-throated Sparrowesque song end in "ayuh, chummie"?

As we made our way around the pond, a gurgly, buzzy song, not dissimilar to that of the House Wren, came from the remnants of last year's cattails on the other side of the pond. Seeing it with the spotting scope, we confirmed not a House Wren but a Marsh Wren.

This bird has been documented nesting on Mount Desert Island, but it has probably been several decades since the last nest has been found.

Toward the end of our walk, working our way on the path less traveled through the forest behind the baseball fields, a beautiful, indigo, male Indigo Bunting was cooperatively perched on a branch overhanging the trail.

All four of these—Lincoln's Sparrow, White-crowned Sparrow, House Wren, and Indigo Bunting—are migratory songbirds, although you could make an argument that, at least to our human aesthetic, only the bunting had what we would consider an actual song.

The feathers of the Indigo Bunting contain no blue pigment. Their deep sky-blue color results from light refracting and reflecting from the feathers. Their feathers do contain melanin. You can see this dark pigment, trending toward black, by holding an Indigo Bunting feather up so that light comes from behind.

8:08 a.m.   A few days previous, Craig Kesselheim reported a Snowy Egret at Bass Harbor Marsh. Like the Great Egret I saw Friday, this bird breeds on coastal islands in the vicinity of Scarborough Marsh in southern coastal Maine. And like Great Egrets, this may be a case of migration overshoot. Fortunately, the nature of saltmarsh estuaries (this is one of the two largest on Mount Desert Island) is such that a tall, white egret stands out above the vegetation. In fact, as we drove across Adams Bridge, before we even pulled over to park, the bird was obvious.

Snowy Egrets and Great Egrets could be the poster children for my Little Big Year, coinciding as it does with the 100th anniversary of the passage of the International Migratory Bird Treaty Act. Among the tenets of the Act were proscriptions on hunting birds for their feathers—both Snowy and Great Egrets were heavily persecuted by plume hunters for the millinery trade which was largely driven by women's fashion of the day. Here on Mount Desert Island, Snowy Egrets turn up in small numbers every spring and fall.

8:18 a.m.   Near the outflow end of Bass Harbor Marsh, before the water flows under the bridge, is an unmarked Acadia National Park field offering a variety of shrubby habitat and open meadow bordering the estuarine wetland. Good thing I had reminded everyone to wear Wellies so we could tromp through the area. At the end, we heard the lazy *witchity witchity witchity* of a Common Yellowthroat. Our patience was eventually rewarded as a masked male, replete with brilliant yellow chest, popped up to sing.

As an ornithological history buff, I was intrigued to learn that Common Yellowthroat was the first New World bird species described by science. In 1766, Carolus Linnaeus, the father of the modern binomial system for assigning scientific names, catalogued a specimen from Maryland.

According to banding records, the oldest Common Yellowthroat lived to at least 11½ years.

8:48 a.m.   On the way to Acadia National Park's Ship Harbor, we drove through the hamlet of Bass Harbor. Driving by a house whose yard was a veritable birding Shangri-La, what with feeders surrounded by a variety of shrubs, including forsythia, I noticed a blackbird-sized yellow bird in one bush. A quick stop for a better look revealed an avian treat: black throat bib, dark pointed bill, gray wings with white wingbars. An Orchard Oriole! Their normal breeding range takes them north to Massachusetts, east to the Mississippi, and south through Florida.

I cannot see an Orchard Oriole without thinking of my friend, Deb Hawkes. For years, she worked at a Bar Harbor law office. And for several years, about this time of year, she would call to say there was an Orchard Oriole in the apple tree in the law office's dooryard.

Given the fact that Orchard Orioles turn up in our area almost every year, it makes me wonder whether climate change may be influencing their range to the point where they someday might breed in Maine.

8:50 a.m.   We finally made it to Ship Harbor. Species trickled in. Ultimately, our list for this site would stand at twenty-seven, seven of which were wood-warblers—Black-and-white Warbler, Common Yellowthroat, Northern Parula, Blackburnian Warbler, Black-throated Blue Warbler, Yellow-rumped Warbler, and Black-throated Green Warbler. It was the Blackburnian, my first of the year, that really was memorable.

Old "Fire-throat" is one of my visually favorite birds (I even have an original watercolor of a Blackburnian Warbler by local artist June Hallowell (1929—2015) sitting on my desk, just to the right of my computer). It is a bird with a bright yellow-orange throat blending into a yellow belly streaked with black on the sides. Alas, the Blackburnian's habit of haunting the upper reaches of the coniferous forest canopy makes it less visible than some of its cousins who frequent the bottom half of the forest.

10:22 a.m.   Just west of Acadia National Park's Seawall Picnic Area is a field extending from Seawall Road down to the ocean. While this grassy area was created as a leach field for the Seawall Campground, the fact that it is not regularly mown, coupled with a bordering scrub of alder and spruce and larch, makes it a diverse habitat that attracts a correspondingly diverse array of birdlife.

There were a variety of warblers and sparrows and finches, all singing away. Down at the shore, a cobble seawall rings the cove. With warblers actively feeding in the shoreside alders and the sun at our backs, we settled on the cobble beach to just sit and watch for a bit. Keeping us company was a Gray Catbird working the beach hedgerow, constantly squawking its pseudo-mimicked couplets, occasionally intoning a cat-like mewl.

A slightly larger bird worked its way through the depths of the alders, barely discernable, only showing the briefest glimpse of a portion of its brown back or a portion of its white belly, not revealing any significantly identifiable body parts.

And then, as if the gods were parting the clouds, a full view of the underside of a long, spotted tail! [Cue the angels singing.] A cuckoo! And not just any cuckoo, but a Yellow-billed Cuckoo! We spent another chunk of time, perhaps ten or fifteen minutes in all, sitting, watching, straining our eyes for a better look. Finally, we did manage to see the yellow bill (well, mostly it is the lower bill that is yellow).

I love cuckoos! This cuckoo was a smaller version of the Hispaniolan Lizard-Cuckoo which I have seen and banded in the Dominican Republic. Not many birds eat hairy caterpillars, but Yellow-billed Cuckoos do. When we experience outbreaks of nuisance insect pests such as gypsy moths and tent caterpillars, this cuckoo is ready to feast. In times of abundant food supply, they will not just lay eggs in their own nests, but also those of robins, catbirds, and Wood Thrushes. Each cuckoo can eat as many as 100 caterpillars in a sitting.

1:27 p.m.   With the Weekly Birding Tour over, I made my way home. Poor Fogo. He is accustomed to lots of exercise, so I took him for a 2½-mile out-and-back run to Clark Cove. Of course, our runs are as much about birding as they are him getting exercise, which means I always have my binoculars.

At Clark Cove, I let Fogo off leash so he could frolic at the ocean's edge. Running hell bent for leather to the water, he flushed nine yellowlegs that I had not previously noticed (otherwise, I would have kept him leashed). Fortunately, they landed a short distance away, seemingly unperturbed by the big, goofy, curly-haired dog.

As soon as the yellowlegs landed, I noticed two things: 1) They all had yellow legs. 2) Two of them were smaller with smaller bills.

Yellowlegs are among my favorite birds and to see Lesser Yellowlegs side-by-side with Greater Yellowlegs really makes my day. I only wish that we had seen these two species together during my Weekly Birding Tour: it is so much easier to show the differences in similar birds when you can see both in one field of view of your binoculars.

Lesser Yellowlegs range between nine and ten inches long, head to tail; Greater Yellowlegs range from 11½—13 inches long. Size is not always that easy to ascertain if the birds are not side-by-each. In that case, the bill serves as an equally good, if not better, reference. The Lesser Yellowlegs' bill, while still long, is significantly shorter than that of the Greater Yellowlegs. More importantly, though, is the fact that the bill of the former is straight while the latter had a slight but noticeable upward curve (also referred to as recurved).

On the return trip home, we passed a house with a productive feeder set-up. These folks, who I have not yet met, get some great birds visiting their yard. The first thing I noticed was the addition of orange halves to the top of the feeder poles. Orange halves can only mean one thing: orioles. It did not take long before a brilliantly-plumaged male Baltimore Oriole showed.

Although this bird was not singing, if we had heard the vaguely robinesque song, it would have been more of a whistling, wonderfully rich singsong. Baltimore Orioles have an interesting way of feeding: they insert their slender, pointed bill into the fruit of their choice (like inserting a straw into a kid's juice box)—typically ones that are dark and succulent—and then open their bills to drink with their tongue, a method known as "gaping." If you see a bird you think is an oriole, but it doesn't seem quite right, it may, indeed, be one. It is not until their second autumn that they attain the brilliant plumage we associate with the Baltimore Oriole.

Today's birds of the year:

171. Lincoln's Sparrow
172. White-crowned Sparrow
173. Marsh Wren
174. Indigo Bunting
175. Snowy Egret
176. Common Yellowthroat
177. Orchard Oriole
178. Blackburnian Warbler
179. Yellow-billed Cuckoo
180. Lesser Yellowlegs
181. Baltimore Oriole

Thursday, 10 May

Mid-afternoon and I finally had a chance to go birding. More importantly, Fogo needed to run, and Stone Barn Farm is a good place to go. I took a tennis ball and a racket with which to bat it for him to chase and get tuckered out (as if that is possible).

2:17 p.m.   Between bats of the ball, while Fogo tore downfield like a shot, I would scan for birds. Standing in the middle of a hayfield does not present much in the way of birds other than Tree Swallows, so I scanned them closely. Training your binoculars on a swallow is the final exam of optics handling, what with the manner in which they dart around, then instantaneously change direction mid-flight.

I was listening and watching, watching and listening. A different chittering song caught my ear. And then I found the culprit. Brown above, white below, with a brown "necklace" across the upper chest: a lone Bank Swallow. These are a colonial species—that is, they sometimes nest in large numbers—excavating tunnels in sandy banks, often in gravel pits or in stream banks (and hence, the name: Bank Swallow).

Eventually, I drove down the road to the barn in the middle of College of the Atlantic's Peggy Rockefeller Farm fields. A lone black bird perched atop a ten-foot-tall alder strongly suggested a Bobolink. Walking closer to better check out the bird, I saw that indeed it was.

My first Bobolink of the year, a single male. Far more would be coming within days.

Bobolink are a member of the Icteridae, the blackbird family, which also includes orioles, grackles, and, of course, Red-winged Blackbirds. The male Bobolink has a rich, creamy hood that strongly contrasts with his mostly dark body. It tends to perch atop stems of uncut grasses and sedges, a shrubby tree, a fencepost, anywhere to get a vantage of his meadowed realm, and then he sings one of the most unusual, bubbly songs of any northeastern bird.

Bobolinks are champion migrants. They fly each autumn to extreme southern South America, then return the next spring. They orient along Earth's magnetic field, thanks to the presence of iron oxide in their head. Depending on the season, this helps them align to the proper north-south direction.

In terms of mating, the males are polygynous, meaning they choose multiple females, and the females are polyandrous (mating with multiple males), so the genetics of each clutch of eggs shows multiple male parentage.

In the same clump of alders on which the Bobolink was singing, I heard (*pleased-pleased-pleaded-to-MEETCHA*) and then saw a Chestnut-sided Warbler. These birds frequent scrubby, edge habitats and second-growth woodlands.

2:55 p.m.   Hamilton Pond was my second and last birding stop of the day. At the landing on the western end, two photographers were set up with their long lenses trained on a fishing Osprey. "You know you need a permit to shoot photos here, don't you?" I jokingly said to the photographers, my friends John Rivers and Paul Renault.

Scanning the far shore, Paul asked what those shorebirds were. Thank goodness for spotting scopes. I could see two were Greater Yellowlegs, with their yellow legs standing out and bills with a hint of being slightly recurved. The third was substantially smaller and puzzled me for a moment.

This small "peep" sandpiper finally turned, revealing its telltale white rump. White-rumped Sandpipers are another champion migrant, traveling between their breeding grounds in the high Arctic and wintering in southern South America, with a significant chunk of their migratory route taking them over the open waters of the Atlantic Ocean.

Today's birds of the year:

182. Bank Swallow
183. Bobolink
184. Chestnut-sided Warbler

185. White-rumped Sandpiper

Saturday, 12 May

Saturday morning. We are quickly coming upon that time when the dawn chorus is significant and the best birding is the hour or so after sunrise. I awoke at 4:30 a.m. in anticipation of getting an early start birding. Alas, I had not counted on an overnight frost.

5:21 a.m.   Due to the cold, birding at the Mount Desert Island High School started off slower than I had hoped, but sightings still trickled in. The grass was coated in a rime of frost. Steam wafting from the three relatively warm settling ponds made for foggy viewing. The first bird I saw was a duck in the first pond. Small, all brown, with a windswept white teardrop pattern around its eyes made for easy identification of a female Wood Duck. I have seen many already this year, but I never tire of watching this cavity-nester.

In a stand of spruce near the beginning of the trail, a number of Yellow-rumped Warblers were warming up, beginning to feed. A high, thin, up-and-down song sounding a bit like a Black-and-white Warbler turned out to be a different warbler: my first American Redstart of the year.

Although sexually dimorphic (males and females look different), American Redstarts have bright patches at the base of their primary flight feathers, contrasting against their otherwise dark upperparts. This is true for both males and females. They flash these feathers during their frenetic movements to startle insects. In an apparent nod to convergent evolution—where unrelated species evolve similar features to fit similar ecological niches—other unrelated birds around the world, some also called redstarts, do similar tricks.

Working my way around the ponds, a large, stand-alone Red Maple was budding. By the time I got to it, the sun had risen enough to frame it in light. This light warmed up the buds and branches enough to get the poikilothermic (or cold blooded) insect-life going, which, in turn, gave good reason for the birds to begin hopping around, foraging like mad in efforts to replenish the fat stores they burned overnight to keep warm. Among the Nashville Warblers and Northern Parulas and Yellow-rumped Warblers and Black-throated Green Warblers, one bird showed flashes of ruddy across its sides and throat. Bay-breasted Warbler!

This is one of those uncommon boreal birds that birders always hope to see. Bay-breasted Warblers migrate north to the forests of northern Canada. They are subject to the episodic whims of their prey—spruce budworm—more than most species. In this era of pesticide treatments (where our efforts to play god by managing landscapes with chemicals, which comes at the expense of species such as Bay-breasted Warbler), it has been a long time since the last major spruce budworm outbreak (my memory puts it at 1984). As such, it has been a long time since we have had a surfeit of this large boreal specialty. Still, I usually manage to see a few each year.

Standing there, watching the Bay-breasted Warbler, my back to the ponds, I heard the *weet weet weet* call of a Spotted Sandpiper. Sure enough, there it was, on the same minute island as the nesting Canada Goose, white breast a background for the eponymous spots. This, the most widespread of North American sandpipers, has many colloquial names, including jerk, perk bird, teeter-bob, and tip-tail, all for its manner of constantly dipping its tail the way that they do. Unlike most of our other resident birds, in Spotted Sandpipers, it is the females that arrive first in the spring. They then establish and defend territories as they await the return of their mates.

Winding down my walk, crossing the short boardwalk near the baseball fields, I heard the *weet-weet-weet-e-o* of a Magnolia Warbler. Although the French name *Paruline à tête cendrée* (the warbler with an ash-colored head) is lovely, it does not do justice to the magnificent yellow underside highlighted with black streaking.

Scottish-American poet, ornithologist, naturalist, and illustrator, Alexander Wilson, considered by some as the "Father of American Ornithology," was the first to identify a Magnolia Warbler for science. He named it "Black-and-yellow Warbler," collecting it in a Magnolia in Tennessee. (It seems a lot of our North American birds were first identified by science in the southeastern U.S., or what would become the southeastern U.S.) Wilson used "Magnolia" in the scientific name, *Setophaga magnolia*, which eventually became the common name, too[i].

7:47 a.m.   On my way home, I paid a brief visit to Sweet Pea Farm where I found two Wilson's Warblers flitting about the vegetation around a roadside (well, more of a drivewayside, but that doesn't roll off the tongue near as well) pond. This small, all-yellow warbler with the black topknot is a ground-nesting species.

At the head of the drive into the farm is a house with a hummingbird feeder. There I saw my first Ruby-throated Hummingbird of the year. Attracting hummingbirds is easy. In a suitable hummingbird feeder, simply put out a solution one part sugar and three parts water. No dye is necessary; in fact, it is best to avoid any dyes. Boiling the mixture will kill most bacteria and extend its shelf-life but be sure to let it cool to room temperature before filling your feeders. Believe it or not, banding records show the oldest Ruby-throated Hummingbird lived to over nine years!

7:59 a.m.   My last stop of the morning was at the Northeast Creek pull-off on the shoulder of Route 3. A raft of Common Mergansers, heavy on the mostly white males, is always a delight to see, as was the female Belted Kingfisher with her chestnut belly band. However, it was the repetitive calling of a Red-eyed Vireo that caught my attention.

The mnemonic I use to remember the song is "*Here I am, there you are*" repeated over and over and over. It does this all day long. If I was to name this species, I would have called it the Bleary-eyed Vireo: I'd be bleary-eyed, too, if I sang all. day. long.

Today's birds of the year:

186. American Redstart
187. Bay-breasted Warbler
188. Spotted Sandpiper
189. Magnolia Warbler
190. Wilson's Warbler
191. Ruby-throated Hummingbird
192. Red-eyed Vireo

Sunday, 13 May

Hamilton Pond is a birding hotspot. In early spring, when the ice starts to go out, migratory waterfowl use this manmade waterbody as a stopover. And again in late fall, up until the pond freezes, waterfowl use it as a staging ground along their southward journey. Over the years, some of the noteworthy birds I have observed on Hamilton Pond include Canvasback, Redhead, Pied-billed Grebe, and Black-crowned Night-Heron. I have seen Red-shouldered Hawks overhead, especially during spring migration. And songbirds of all sorts—various flycatchers, Ruby-crowned Kinglets, and Palm Warblers, to name but a few—frequent the varied shoreline habitats.

The old dam in the southwest corner of Hamilton Pond gave way during a February storm a few months back, dropping the water level some three to four feet, exposing relict tree trunks. The good news was that no personal property was impacted as a result of the breached dam. The bad news was that Hamilton Pond was an essential water source for the Bar Harbor Fire Department[i]. The REALLY good news (at least for birders) was that the drained pond exposed the rich muddy pond bottom, offering a veritable buffet for migrating shorebirds. Practically overnight, the pond went from a place where shorebirds were only seen in dribs and drabs along the edges August through October as they migrate south to a shorebirding hotspot.

Natalie was off for a weeklong National Working Waterfront conference in Michigan, leaving Anouk and me at home for some quality daddy-daughter time. And then I made a mistake: I checked email and saw that Kenneth Shellenberger found a Stilt Sandpiper at Hamilton Pond. "Anouk, I am going to Hamilton Pond for half an hour to look for a rare bird. Do you want to come?" "Birds, schmirds."

2:13 p.m.   From my house to the west end of Hamilton Pond is a four-minute drive. A quick scan of the western end revealed no shorebirds. At the eastern end, a ½-mile away, I heard the *tew-tew-tew* of a Greater Yellowlegs as soon as I stepped out of the car, giving me a direction to train the spotting scope. Greater Yellowlegs are one of my favorite species and here there were three together. As much as I wanted to watch them, I was on a mission.

Panning my scope to the right, not even half a field of view, a smaller Lesser Yellowlegs hove into view. Greater on the left, Lesser on the right, afforded a good opportunity to compare and contrast the two similar species.

A number of "peep" sandpipers wandered into the field of view. The Least Sandpiper sports yellowish legs and a black bill with just a hint of decurve (curving slightly downward). As the name suggests, they are the smallest sandpiper in the world. I tallied six of these "peeps." Their manner of traveling in small flocks is something for which they are known. Oh, Least Sandpiper was species 193 for the year-list.

With my spotting scope taking in these three sandpiper species, a fourth entered the view. Stilt Sandpiper! This was a breeding adult with a swath of ruddy below and behind the eyes and atop the head, making it easily identifiable.

Stilt Sandpipers are rare in Hancock County. When they do turn up, it seems that more often than not, it is in spring. Canadian ornithologists, studying this species, made an interesting observation:

female Stilt Sandpipers that have the longest bill mate with males that have the shortest bill; this is especially true for first-time breeders. (No word if the reverse was true.)

For me, not only was this the 194th species for my year-list, turns out it was a life-bird, too! Not bad for fifteen minutes of birding!

Today's birds of the year:

193. Least Sandpiper   194. Stilt Sandpiper

Monday, 14 May

I should know better than to take binoculars when I take Fogo running: it becomes more of a birding outing and less about exercise. The Witch Hole Pond Carriage Road loop is 3⅓ miles. I'm a slow runner and so normally do it in about forty minutes. Thirty-three species and nearly an hour later, I finally made it around the pond.

8:14 a.m.   As I sat on one of "Rockefeller's teeth," the affectionate name bestowed by workers upon the Newfoundland Retriever-sized granite blocks lining portions of the Carriage Road to honor John D. Rockefeller, Jr.'s, penchant for being present and following the progress of the road construction, an American Bittern called out, *oonk-a-choonk*, a sound that resonates great distances.

Beginning my run-stop-walk-stop-repeat routine, I slowly tallied passerines....

Passerines are the perching birds. Although, technically, they are members of the order Passeriformes—birds with three toes forward, one back, all joining at the same level on the foot pad—and are made up of some 140 families of birds, there are finer points to the definition. For the sake of this discussion, in Hancock County, we will include the following families among the passerines: tyrant flycatchers, shrikes, vireos, corvids, chickadees, larks, swallows, kinglets, nuthatches, treecreepers, gnatcatchers, wrens, starlings, mimics, thrushes, waxwings, Old World sparrows, pipits, New World sparrows, blackbirds, wood-warblers, cardinals, grosbeaks, and tanagers, collectively, our local perching birds.

... There are many things that can make a day of birding a good day: Ovenbirds being the most abundant species of the day is one of them! As I progressed, it quickly became apparent that this would be the case—by the end of the loop, I counted twenty-four Ovenbirds (Black-capped Chickadees and Yellow-rumped Warblers tied for second place with ten birds apiece).

I almost always run this loop anti-clockwise. In fact, when Natalie and I walk it together (which is often), she doesn't even ask which way I want to go; knowing what a creature of habit I am, she automatically turns right across Duck Brook Bridge to go in my preferred direction. For some inexplicable reason, today, I went left after crossing the bridge.

The trail has intersections spaced nearly at the mile marks, making it easy to track your progress. Whether by design or a result of the needs of the landscape, this is how it panned out.

One-third of the way through the loop, just after the first intersection, is nestled little Half Moon Pond. Although its perimeter is lined with plants tolerant of an acidic environment, surface water flows in and flows out, making it a fen rather than a bog. Where the pond drains, its course follows the Carriage Road for a short while, ducks beneath, then continues through the spruce forest to an old beaver pond that is more a graveyard for drowned spruce.

It was in this water course that a beautiful Little Blue Heron stood, showing off its bluish-gray body, burgundy head, and two-tone bill. As they do not have the showy nuptial plumes, also known as "aigrettes," of their Great Blue Heron cousins, the Little Blue

Heron was not among the heavily targeted species during the plume trade of the late 1800s and early 1900s. While little data is available on historic population levels, the *Birds of North America* Little Blue Heron species account suggests their population may be slowly expanding.

Today's bird of the year:

195. Little Blue Heron

Tuesday, 15 May

As a regional coordinator for the Maine Bird Atlas, coupled with my professional background as field biologist and birder, I was asked to assist with the training of the six field technicians hired to work for the Atlas this year.

We were ten in total: Glen Mittelhauser, executive director of the Maine Natural History Observatory (and one of the finest naturalists in Maine, I might add); Adrienne Leppold, of Maine Department of Inland Fisheries and Wildlife and director of the Maine Bird Atlas; Evan Adams from the Biodiversity Research Institute; and I were the instructors; Sean Ashe, Matt Dickinson, Connor Marland, Logan Parker, Nathaniel Sharp, and Chris West were our students. What a great student-to-instructor ratio!

I have long considered myself as having excellent hearing, especially when I am with people my age and older. But spending the day with a bunch of young men—for, just through the luck of the draw, they were all men—ranging in age from twenty to twenty-nine, I quickly realized that sure, my hearing is still pretty darned good…but not quite as acute as I had thought. Some of the warblers they seemed to easily pick up were a struggle for me. But I did hear them once pointed out. And I managed to hear a Least Flycatcher that none of them picked out. (Or was I just hearing things?)

During the course of the morning, I quickly realized this group of field technicians were all top-notch birders in their own right. Our training was really about teaching the protocols specific to atlasing in general and the Maine Bird Atlas, in particular. As we swapped stories, I also discovered their introduction to birds had many parallels to mine. For instance, they all grew up birding and were all a little bird nerdy. This group of young men were, as they say in Maine, "wicked smaht." To qualify for a position on the Atlas team, they had to take the Birder Certification Online[i] and score at least 90%.

Most of their field work will consist of point counts—where they stop and count every bird they can identify over a ten-minute period. Since most of the point counts will be conducted by ear, we met at the Maine Natural History Observatory offices in Gouldsboro for its woodland setting and a noticeable dearth of automobile traffic noise pollution.

Every time I get off-island, even if still in Hancock County for my Little Big Year, it is a reminder of how much truly interesting habitat there is around the State of Maine. Forests of oak, beech, maple, spruce, fir, hemlock, tamarack, pine. Mountains. Grasslands. Beaches. Wetlands ranging from bogs to open lakes and ocean. The panoply of natural communities means an opportunity to find an equally diverse array of bird species. And so, we set off.

8:28 a.m.   Although our day started at 5:00 a.m. and we had already conducted four practice point counts, this was the first one that added a new bird to my year-list. The raspy, singsong vocalization sounding like an American Robin with a sore throat could only be a Scarlet Tanager. It is amazing to me that this brilliant red bird (almost the same red of a Northern Cardinal but with a hint of day-glo mixed in) with starkly contrasting black wings can virtually disappear in the treetops. You'd think it would stand out. I'm sure there must be research somewhere on the way brightly colored birds blend into the greenery. Or maybe I just need to take an art class to learn more about color.

Scarlet Tanagers are between a warbler and a cardinal in size. On the breeding grounds, which span from the Mighty Mississippi to the east coast and from the latitude of the Carolinas to just north of the Canadian border, they tend to frequent either pure deciduous forests or those with some conifers mixed in. Scarlet Tanagers are particularly susceptible to nest parasitism by Brown-headed Cowbirds, especially as we increasingly fragment the forested landscape.

According to the U.S. Bird Banding Lab, the record age for a Scarlet Tanager is nearly twelve years old. This record goes to a bird banded in 1990 in Pennsylvania and found eleven years and eleven months later in Texas.

In my years, I have had any number of surreal experiences. Being on stage with Garrison Keillor for the recording of an episode of *A Prairie Home Companion*, may rank right at the top.

In 2005, Natalie and I were hired by Garrison to work as naturalists on a Holland America Line cruise-ship he was chartering for a weeklong roundtrip journey from Boston to Prince Edward Island and then back to Boston (this was a fundraising cruise for Minnesota Public Radio). Though I never considered myself a cruise-ship kind of guy (wilderness adventure is more my pace), I was in heaven! Imagine, a week at sea, working as naturalists for this amazing radio persona who was such an integral part of my childhood experience. Heck, he has been a part of much of my adult years, too.

I must confess that I come from a long line of wise-asses. Invariably, part of my humor sneaks into my work and I regularly color my discussions on avian ecology with a repertoire of birding humor, using fictitious bird names that are tantalizingly similar to the real thing. Rosy-breasted Pushover replaces the real-life Rose-breasted Grosbeak; in lieu of the brilliantly colored Scarlet Tanager, I use Scarlet Teenager—my favorite.

During that first week at sea with Garrison, his amazing staff, all the regular performers we knew from the radio show, and 1,200 of his fans, he invited us on stage. Standing in the wings, waiting for our cue to walk into the limelight, Natalie turned to me. She must have intuited that I was working up something goofy to say as she cautioned me to be my professional best. Really? Has she ever even listened to the show?

Before I knew it, we were on stage!

Garrison:	[Addressing me] So, you are an ornithologist. Are you also a birder?
Me:	Yes.
Garrison:	[Turning to the audience] Are there any birders here tonight? [Mild applause.] Birders are a weird lot. [Uproarious laughter!] They keep life-lists and state lists and year lists...
Natalie:	And yard lists. [More laughter.]
Garrison:	... and they are always looking for some rare bird. Rich, is there any bird you haven't seen that you hope to see on this cruise?
Me:	Well, in fact, there is. When we are in Prince Edward Island, walking on the vast sand beaches, this incredible natural community where the ocean meets the island; when the sun is out, the air temperature in the eighties; and the waters of the Northumberland Strait is hovering around seventy-four degrees, we will have the perfect conditions for seeing two species that I would be eager to see: the Rosy-breasted Pushover and the Scarlet Teenager.

The audience loved that! Garrison chuckled, too (it was one of two times in our thirteen-year relationship that I managed to get him to crack his otherwise staid demeanor).

Garrison: In case you haven't noticed, birders have their own sense of humor.

One year later…

In a skit during the weekly Saturday evening broadcast of *A Prairie Home Companion*, imagine my surprise (and pleasure) when I heard Garrison describing birds with his Radio Actors (sound effects man Fred Newman, Sue Scott, and Tim Russell) sounding them out:

Garrison: There was a seagull…

Fred: RAWK!

Garrison: … and there was a cardinal…

Fred: [Muttering a Latinized incantation.]

Garrison: … and there was a Scarlet Teenager…

Radio actors: [Doing their best falsetto impression of a bunch of teenagers gabbling away.]

Within minutes, my telephone was ringing off the hook and emails were flying in from across the hemisphere: "Rich, Garrison stole your joke! I hope you get royalties!"

The fact that Garrison thought enough of one bit of my humor was royalty enough!

10:46 a.m. This was the penultimate practice point count for the day. Continuing along the logging road we had been birding all morning, a variable song, described by some as *suey de swee-ditchety*, was my only other new bird species of the day: Canada Warbler.

This striking bird with the bright yellow chest and black necklace looks quite similar to a Magnolia Warbler but lacks the white highlights, instead having solid blue-gray upperparts. Their habit of frequenting cool, wet forests (often alder-lined steams with dense undergrowth) during the breeding season, habitats that are generally not convenient to our access, means there is a lot we do not know about this species. Any graduate students out there, this is a chance to make your mark.

During the course of the morning, we identified a total of fifty-two species, fifteen of which were warblers. The highlight for me was not observing the two species of birds new for my Little Big Year; rather, it was the privilege of spending the morning with a group of such amazing birders. Thank you, Glen, Adrienne, Evan, Sean, Matt, Connor, Logan, Nathaniel, and Chris.

Today's birds of the year:

196. Scarlet Tanager   197. Canada Warbler

Thursday, 17 May

My morning started with a run to Clark Cove. I was determined to run the whole way, not letting myself get distracted by birds. To that end, I intentionally left my binoculars at home.

8:13 a.m.   Well, I was partially successful: I made it to Clark Cove without stopping. A number of shorebirds foraging along the water's edge "forced" me to pause. Three small sandpipers were clearly "peeps," but determining their species was too much without binoculars. Dang it! Why did I leave them behind?

The yellow legs of a pair of Greater Yellowlegs was visible even without optical aids. And when they took flight, their characteristic and diagnostic *tew tew tew* flight call confirmed what I already knew.

A large, chunky shorebird with a black front and black-and-white mottling on the back was the first species of the day to be added to my year-list. This Black-bellied Plover was on its way to the furthest north margins of the continent to nest. Black-bellied Plovers are warier than most shorebirds, often serving as an interspecies sentinel; that is, they keep an eye out for potential predators and the other species of shorebirds keep an eye on them.

Considering all of the birds I heard on the run to Clark Cove, I decided to start an eBird checklist. When you factor in the many stops on my return trip, my average pace ended up being that of a fast walk. (So much for not getting distracted by birds.)

Not far up Clark Cove Road, in the scrubby second- (and third- and fourth-) growth habitat lining the roadside, a thin, slightly rising song, Black-and-white Warblerish, drew my attention. I knew it to be a Cape May Warbler, but I really, REALLY wanted to see it! A little patience was rewarded with a brief look confirming what I knew: an overall yellowish cast that goes from the yellow underside to the strikingly yellow face with chestnut highlights on the cheeks to a more olive-yellow back and wings.

The Cape May Warbler is not from New Jersey. Rather, that is where it was first described: in the early 1800s, a specimen that had been collected by naturalist George Ord in Cape May was identified by Alexander Wilson as a species new to science (interestingly, it would be another 100 years before another Cape May Warbler was again reported in Cape May). This is one of our true boreal specialties, breeding in a broad swath of northern forests from Nova Scotia through Alberta, so we only tend to see them here in Hancock County during spring and fall migration[i]. On the breeding grounds, Cape Mays are insectivorous, being particularly well known as a spruce budworm specialist. On their Greater Antilles and Yucatán wintering grounds, their curled and semi-tubular tongue is used to feed on nectar.

Ornithologist James Bond wonderfully describes following a pair of Cape May Warblers nesting near Acadia National Park's Seawall. Over a period from 28 May through 15 June 1936, Bond made careful observations, from pair bonding through nest building to egg laying, ultimately with six eggs. He reports that the "nest, apparently the first to have been found in the United States, was situated thirty-eight feet above the ground against the trunk of a black spruce approximately four feet from the extreme top of the tree."[ii]

Crossing Route 102 and Red Rock Corner, heading east on Gilbert Farm Road, a large—and as far as I can determine, unnamed—

wetland on the south side of the road is seasonal home to Common Grackle and Red-winged Blackbird. In the past, it has not turned up near as many species as I would expect for such a seemingly high quality wetland. So, I was more than a little surprised to hear the Guinea Pig-like grunting of a Virginia Rail. I didn't find the bird, but that's okay; there is nothing with which to confuse the vocalization of this laterally compressed bird. (The expression "thin as a rail" comes from the head-on narrow profile of this species, which enables it to move quickly through otherwise virtually impenetrable habitat.)

While looking for the Virginia Rail, I heard a somewhat soft and sort of slow *CHE-bec* (many field guides describe the call more as a *fee-BEER*, but my ear disagrees). My first Alder Flycatcher of the year! Visually, Alder and Willow Flycatchers are virtually indistinguishable from one another, but if you hear them, there is no question which is which. When they don't vocalize, short of having them in your hand so you can measure features such as wing chords, they are designated "Traill's" Flycatcher.

The name "Traill's" Flycatcher is an homage John James Audubon bestowed, writing, "I have named this species after my learned friend Dr. Thomas Stewart Traill of Edinburgh, in evidence of the gratitude which I cherish towards that gentleman for all his kind attentions to me." Eventually, the species was split into Alder Flycatcher (*Empidonax alnorum*) and Willow Flycatcher (*Empidonax traillii*).

12:10 p.m.   Back to my favorite spring birding hotspot, the Mount Desert Island High School settling ponds. There was a good showing of birds, with thirty-five species making their way into my field notebook in forty-four minutes.

Shortly into my walk, a swallow darted out from the pump house. My first impression, based purely on the facts that it was a swallow and that it was at the high school ponds, was Barn Swallow. But then I realized the bird did not have a deeply forked tail; instead, it was closer in size and shape to that of a Tree Swallow but with a white forehead. Ahh, Cliff Swallow! These birds tend to nest in colonies, but not always, making nests of mud dabbed on a cliff or wall, sometimes on, or even in, a building. Over the years, I have found a few nesting sites in Hancock County but the nearest I knew of to the high school was 2½ miles away on the south edge of Bar Harbor village.

Around the backside of the pond, along the "wall" of tamarack and alder, a good variety of wood-warblers were actively feeding, putting on quite a show. Among the Black-and-white Warblers, Nashville Warblers, Common Yellowthroats, American Redstarts, Northern Parulas, Magnolia Warblers, Blackburnian Warblers, Yellow Warblers, Pine Warblers, Yellow-rumped Warblers, and Black-throated Green Warblers were two Blackpoll Warblers.

Named Blackpoll for the black cap, or "poll," on their head, they sing a song that can reach 10,000 hertz, far higher than all our other local birds. More impressive is their fall migration. Before departing on their three-day, 1,800-mile nonstop epic journey to South America, much of it over the open Atlantic, Blackpoll Warblers gorge themselves, doubling their weight to provide the energy they need to survive. If they encounter any significant weather or headwinds, their chances of surviving decrease as they burn through vital fat (*i.e.*, stored energy) reserves. (I wish I could just burn through my fat reserves....)

Today's birds of the year:

198. Black-bellied Plover
199. Cape May Warbler
200. Virginia Rail

201. Alder Flycatcher
202. Cliff Swallow
203. Blackpoll Warbler

Saturday, 19 May

After leading a morning Birding by Ear workshop for the Maine Master Naturalist program at Acadia National Park's Sieur de Monts Spring, I took my group to College of the Atlantic for the indoor portion of the program. At the edge of the parking lot was a glorious Red Flowering Quince. The short walk from our cars to McCormick Lecture Hall took over half an hour, and it was all the fault of a tiny little bird. Well, more like seventeen of them. The quince was abuzz with Ruby-throated Hummingbirds!

While focusing on the hummingbirds, enjoying their amazing abilities of flight, zipping up, down, back and forth, hovering, inserting their long bill and still longer tongue into the flowers to feast, the sound of a vireo slowly percolated its way into the show.

Two vireos are common this time of year: Blue-headed, with its lazy *here-I-am, there-you-are*, slowly repeated, long pauses between iterations, sometimes ending in *chewy-chewy* and Red-eyed, which tend to be high in the canopy. You can use the same mnemonic for their song as for the Blue-headed, but in the case of the Red-eye, they cannot help themselves, they have to sing rapidly and incessantly. All day. All night. All the time.

This vireo, the one that caught my attention, was singing faster than the Blue-headed but slower than the Red-eyed. Its song was actually sung as opposing couplets, the first ending on a higher note, as though asking a question; the second ends on a lower note, answering its own question. It would be easy to confuse this with the Red-eyed Vireo's song, the latter being more abundant and more voluble.

Normally, Philadelphia Vireos are found breeding in deciduous regrowth, younger woods, perhaps the result of some landscape-scale disturbance, whether logging or fire or a microburst (an intense downdraft of air with the potential to cause considerable damage) or some other natural phenomena. This one was singing from the middle of the quince!

Once again, patience has its own rewards. In this instance, Philadelphia Vireo! The vireo finally moved to a position allowing a relatively unobstructed view. Yellow underparts, drab upper, eyestripe much more subdued than in Red-eyed. It's almost as if the Red-eyed Vireo is the big brother athletic star and the Philadelphia is the younger brother, stuck in the shadow of its bigger-than-life sibling. Be that as it may, Philadelphia Vireos are a wonderful, if too-often overlooked, species.

Today's bird of the year:

204. Philadelphia Vireo

Monday, 21 May

As of today, my Hancock County Little Big Year list is at a very respectable 208 species. While the year is far from over, I am approaching a point of diminishing returns where the number of species I might still reasonably expect to find during the next six months shrinks with every species I add. By my quick tally, I have a realistic chance at twenty-eight additional species, birds such as a shearwater or two, both storm-petrels, a number of shorebirds, a jaeger or two (four or five would be ideal), Bonaparte's Gull, Common and Arctic Tern (any other tern would be a bonus), Black-billed Cuckoo, a nightjar or two, a few flycatchers, American Pipit, a few more warblers, and Nelson's Sparrow would all round out the list. Anything beyond those is a bonus, pushing the year-list into territory I only dreamed of.

And so, when a bird rare to Hancock County is reported, I need to chase it down. That was the case with this morning's early start. Least Bittern is uncommon throughout Maine and particularly rare (or maybe it is just incredibly secretive, which it is) in Hancock County. Laurie Yntema reported one she heard at Corea Heath at dawn yesterday. This morning, I was out the of the house by 4:00 a.m.

4:51 a.m.   As soon as I arrived at the parking lot for Frenchman Bay Conservancy's Corea Heath Preserve, I jumped out of the car and immediately started hearing birds. The avian cacophony was so great that initially I had trouble separating them out. I wanted to hear them all! Instead, I tackled the calls systematically. The ethereal, flute-like song of the Hermit Thrush. The singsong melody of the American Robin. OH! There's the downward spiral song of the Veery: *VEER Veer veer*. My first year-bird of the morning.

Veeries tend to nest in damp and forested woodlands with a dense understory. On Mount Desert Island, they have become increasingly hard to find, but beaver swamps can be a good place to look for them, and that is part of the make-up of Corea Heath.

A Sora shouted out its descending whinny call, clearly announcing its presence to the world. And not one, but two other Soras answered. During the course of my visit, they were garrulous, alternating descending whinnies and their *ker-wee* calls. A small, secretive rail found in aquatic marshes, Soras can be surprisingly common; a fact belied by the difficulty in actually seeing them.

Knowing that a Least Bittern had been heard the previous dawn, to refresh my memory, I listened to audio tracks of its various vocalizations on the hour drive. At Corea Heath, while listening to the Sora trio, the Least Bittern gave out a loud, harsh, almost cackling call. During the rest of my visit, it intermittently called and sang its low, chuckling tune. Walking along the road to triangulate the sounds, a slight bushwhack led me to a vantage, perhaps twenty feet above the wetland. Looking through my spotting scope, every time the bittern called, I would scan the general area from whence it came. This went on for a good twenty minutes when finally, a small wader, smaller than a crow, with a tan-brown body, contrasting black upperparts, and white edging to the wing, stepped fully into view. As quickly as it stepped into view, it promptly stepped out, occasionally calling and singing but did not show itself again.

Most range maps show a sliver of Least Bittern population extending along coastal Maine into New Brunswick. This may well be, but with their secretive nature, it is no wonder they are seldom seen hereabouts. A perusal of eBird does not show any occurrence records for Mount Desert Island and just a few for Hancock County.

In his 1987 edition of *Native Birds of Mount Desert Island and Acadia National Park*, Ralph Long writes, "In 1968 a pair of least Bitterns inhabited Beaverdam Pond south of Bar Harbor where they nested in a clump of cattails .... These are apparently the first nest records of the Least Bittern from Maine."

Like the American Bittern, when facing danger, Least Bitterns freeze, standing erect, head pointed to the sky, counting on their brown striped plumage to camouflage them in their wetland surroundings. And it does this incredibly well; it's as though they disapparate.

All the while that I was tracking the Least Bittern, I continued adding to my morning's list. And to my year-list. Well, one more to the year-list. I heard a sound like no other bird, a sound often dubbed into movies, incongruously in scary scenes, regardless of habitat, or in settings of coastal heath in Scotland and Ireland and Wales, usually with waves crashing against rocky cliffs in the background and winds battering anything not rooted to the ground. Upland Sandpiper! If you don't know what this sounds like, this is one "song" you have to look up—an alien-sounding rising trill that drops off in a sort of downward audial spiral at the end.

Whereas most members of Order Charadriiformes, Family Scolopacidae are associated with water edge, Upland Sandpipers are found in prairies and prairie-like habitat. Here in Maine, you hear it early in the morning on blueberry barrens. Read bird accounts from the by-gone era of seventeenth- and eighteenth-century gentlemen naturalists and you may come across mention of Bartram's or Bartramian Sandpiper, named in honor of American naturalist William Bartram (1739—1823), and this would be the bird.

I have never seen more than one or two Upland Sandpipers at a time, but if there were a group, appropriate collective nouns include "bind," "contradiction," "fling," "hill,", or "time-step." (Actually, any of these can be applied to any sandpiper.)

Today's birds of the year:

205. Veery

206. Sora

207. Least Bittern

208. Upland Sandpiper

Tuesday, 22 May

Birdathon! For fifteen years, I have been coordinating a team as part of the Downeast Audubon Birdathon. All proceeds send local Hancock County youths to summer nature camp. This year, we are sending kids to three camps: National Audubon's Hog Island Audubon Camp, located on an island in Muscongus Bay, between Portland, Maine, and Mount Desert Island; Acadia Institute of Oceanography in Seal Harbor, here on Mount Desert Island; and Huntsman Marine Science Center in St. Andrews, New Brunswick. Our team—the Acadian Flycatchers—focuses on Mount Desert Island and, weather permitting, surrounding offshore waters via local tour boat.

As this is a fundraiser and we want to identify as many species as possible (we raise money by soliciting sponsorships from local businesses), we start our day at 3:00 a.m. to afford time to chase a few owls previously staked out (alas, no owls cooperated this year). Throughout the day, our team grows and contracts, amoeba-like, as people's schedules allow. For the morning, our core team of Don Lima, Roberta Sharp, and I we were joined by Seth Benz and Rob Packie.

4:27 a.m.   After our unsuccessful owling effort, we headed into Acadia National Park. At the T-intersection where Ledgelawn Avenue meets the Park Loop Road is Great Meadow, a large grassy wetland[i]. Before the sun rose, we added eleven species to our tally. The *oonk-a-choonk* of an American Bittern was expected. The *kidick-kidick* of a Virginia Rail was a pleasant surprise, especially as we had never found a rail during previous birdathons (although we do occasionally find them at other times during the spring and summer).

The six of us, standing there, inventorying the surround-sound bird audio track all around us, were surprised by a Common Nighthawk that flew silently, low overhead; long, narrow wings marked with white "windows" at the base of the primary feathers beat powerfully as it sped through, gleaning aerial plankton.

As a result of the Common Nighthawk's bat-like manner of flight, they are sometimes called "bullbats." Common Nighthawks are a medium-sized bird, part of a family referred to as goatsuckers for their alleged fictional ability to fly into a barn and suck milk from the teat of a goat or cow. Contrary to their name, nighthawks are neither exclusively nocturnal (actually, they are more crepuscular) nor hawks.

9:54 a.m.   While at Northeast Creek, where we picked up our only Common Mergansers of the day, a pickup truck zoomed into the parking area and skidded to a halt. Out came Ed Douglas, an excellent local amateur photographer, who came specifically to invite us to his incredibly birdy property nearby. And thus, there we went.

As we were observing birds close-up, Rob asked, "What bird is that?" referring to a warbler-sized bird perched atop a thin dead snag. Seth instantly answered, "Olive-sided Flycatcher. Look at its 'britches'." Indeed, Olive-sided Flycatchers exhibit a pattern of plumage that looks as though they have a pair of pants hitched up around their waist. We didn't hear it sing, but surely its song must be a favorite of home-brewers everywhere: an emphatic *quick-three-beers!* This is a bird of boreal forests, showing a particular affinity for recently burned areas as they offer an abundance of dead snags from which to perch and then fly out to catch insects....

Years ago, sometime in the early 2000s, I was walking down the Jesup Path, through the medium-sized wet meadow that is part of Acadia National Park's larger Great Meadow complex. To the west, from high up on the ridge of Dorr Mountain, a faint *quick-three-beers!* drifted down to my ears. This Olive-sided Flycatcher continued to regularly sing out the entire time of my observation.

As most of the birding at Sieur de Monts Spring's two-mile Jesup Trail and Hemlock Trail figure-eight loop is within the forest, binoculars are the tool of choice, which means I rarely carry my spotting scope here. Fortunately, this was not one of those times. As a result, I was able to train my scope on the bird sitting atop the tallest spire of a dead White Pine emerging above the surrounding canopy some ¼-mile away.

Later that spring, Rob Packie and I were walking down the same section of the Jesup Trail and I recounted to him that experience. According to Rob, nearly every time since, whenever he and I walk down the Jesup Path, I tell him the story. Over. And over. And over. For some inexplicable reason, it took a long time for the fact that I had told him this story on numerous occasions to penetrate my thick skull. It has become a joke that Rob teases me about any time we are birding along the Jesup Trail, preempting any repetition of the story.

... Earlier today, I thought I had heard one faint iteration of an Olive-sided Flycatcher song but kept it to myself. Now that we were looking at an actual one, I mentioned that I thought I had heard one earlier in the day when we were at Sieur de Monts Spring. Of course, Rob had to tell my oft-repeated Olive-sided Flycatcher story. As you might imagine, that became the morning's running joke. The fact that Rob was the one to observe today's Olive-sided Flycatcher was somewhere between ironic and poetic justice.

Walking down Ed's driveway, bordered on both sides by blooming pin cherry and scrubby alder, we saw an abundance of birds.

Warblers kept adding up: Ovenbird, Black-and-white Warbler, Common Yellowthroat, American Redstart, Northern Parula, Magnolia Warbler, Yellow Warbler, Chestnut-sided Warbler, Blackpoll Warbler, Pine Warbler, and Black-throated Green Warbler. In one pin cherry, a tree that was particularly ebullient with blossoms, a Tennessee Warbler was an especially good find.

Tennessee Warblers breed in the Canadian boreal with fingers of their population dipping south into the U.S. in places such as the forests of northern Maine and the Adirondack Mountains of northern New York. Historically, James Bond has documented occasional breeding of Tennessee Warbler on Mount Desert Island, but it has been many decades since the last confirmed local nesting.

10:59 a.m.   Our last stop before our afternoon boat tour with Acadian Nature Cruises was Ed and Deb Hawkes' property. From their home, a ½-mile loop leads through a grassy saltmarsh situated along the western edge of Mount Desert Narrows. We inadvertently flushed two furtive sparrows while walking along shoreline. These birds had orange-brown facial discs, streaked upperparts, streaked and buffy breast, and white belly. Nelson's Sparrows!

Once known as Nelson's Sharp-tailed Sparrow, it had its name shortened by the ornithological powers that be to simply Nelson's Sparrow (the bird was named in honor of Edward William Nelson, a nineteenth- and twentieth-century American naturalist and ethnologist). This was not only a bird for our birdathon, it was also one for my year-list. We paused to observe the two sparrows as they furtively crept in and out of the sedge-covered shoreline, much in the manner of a Meadow Vole.

12:50 p.m.   At noon, we left Seth, Rob, and Ed (who had joined us at 6:00 a.m. at Sieur de Monts Spring) and met Tammy Packie and Jeff DiBella for the boat portion of our birdathon aboard the m/v *Acadian*.

Gary Fagan, operator of Acadian Nature Cruises, gave us free passage on his boat in exchange for a favor in return: that the birdathon team do some natural history interpretation once we reach Petit Manan Island (Petit Manan Island is part of the Maine Coastal Islands National Wildlife Refuge, which spans 250 miles of the Maine coast and is comprised of sixty-some islands and four mainland parcels). Deal!

While waiting for the boat to depart, Don, Roberta, Tammy, Jeff, and I evaluated the birds we might get on the boat tour and came up with the magical number of fourteen species:

> Common Murre
> Razorbill
> Atlantic Puffin
> Common Tern
> Arctic Tern
> Roseate Tern
> Wilson's Storm-Petrel
> Leach's Storm-Petrel
> Northern Fulmar
> Cory's Shearwater
> Great Shearwater
> Manx Shearwater
> Northern Gannet
> Great Cormorant

From Bar Harbor, we steamed across Frenchman Bay, around Schoodic Point, to Petit Manan Island and back. Rounding Schoodic Point, a pair of Common Terns flew past, squawking their harsh call.

Terns are easily distinguished from gulls at most any distance from the way they row through the air, long wings beating, lifting their bodies on the down-stroke and letting their bodies fall on the up; whereas gulls have enough mass that for most of them, their bodies scribe a straight course through the air.

Both Common and Arctic Terns nest on Petit Manan Island, which is to the east of Hancock County, situated in coastal Washington County. This meant that unless the birds were observed in transit, any observed only at Petit Manan Island could not be counted for my Little Big Year, although they would still be valid birdathon birds. Alas, the only Arctic Terns we saw that day were flying around the south side of Petit Manan Island. And those guys seemed to be heading toward the island, likely returning from a foraging run.

As an interesting aside, Common Terns sometimes nest close to the high tide line. When they do, they will add material in attempts to raise them above high water.

Well, we missed most of our target birds—we were a week earlier than our usual annual birdathon date, so it was likely just too early for most of the pelagic species—but Red-throated Loon and Lesser Black-backed Gull were good additions to the day. As the saying goes, a bad day of birding is better than a good day in the office. And being on a boat, this was not only a good day of birding, no matter how many species we observed, it was a GREAT day of birding!

For what it is worth, here's our complete list from the boat trip: Common Eider, White-winged Scoter, Black Scoter, Red-throated Loon, Common Loon, Double-crested Cormorant, Bald Eagle, Spotted Sandpiper, Razorbill, Black Guillemot, Atlantic Puffin, Laughing Gull, Ring-billed Gull, Herring Gull, Lesser Black-backed Gull, Great Black-backed Gull, Common Tern, and Arctic Tern.

8:33 p.m.   Our last stop of the day was the Hancock County-Bar Harbor Airport. Ed Douglas had given us intelligence of a Killdeer nesting there in a gravel parking area. This was probably not the best choice for the Killdeer. Whether it was the late hour or the possibility that the bird had succumbed to an oblivious driver, we did not find the bird. However, we did see a Veery. While it was not a bird for my year-list, it was a Veery good finish to an excellent day of birding that netted us 102 birdathon species.

Today's birds of the year:

209. Common Nighthawk
210. Olive-sided Flycatcher
211. Tennessee Warbler

212. Nelson's Sparrow
213. Common Tern

Wednesday, 23 May

I needed a break. The birdathon, as much fun as it was, was a lot of work (solicitation letters need to be drafted and sent to area businesses; there is wrangling the herd of cats that is my team, each with different schedules; scouting beforehand to help increase our tally; leading the day itself, which goes from 3:00 a.m. to about 9:00 p.m.; and then collecting pledges; sending thank you letters; and writing the follow-up article for the Downeast Audubon Newsletter). I find one of the best ways to decompress is to go hiking. With that in mind, Natalie and I hiked up Huegenot Head. Of course, even when on a break, I couldn't entirely stop birding.

10:01 a.m.   Near the beginning of our hike, a Least Flycatcher was easily spied. And while I always appreciate seeing them—I saw my Little Big Year Least Flycatcher 03 May—I only wish we had observed it yesterday for the birdathon.

Near the summit of Huegenot Head, the forest transitions to one of Jack Pine, certainly more boreal than the lower elevation birch-beech-maple forest. At the top, Natalie and I each took a few minutes to do our separate things. Natalie found a flat spot to practice some yoga; I took in the solitude of being above the noise of traffic and listening to the wind in the trees and the birds.

A small flycatcher, a dull yellowish overall, including its belly, with bold wingbars, landed just a few feet from me. Yellow-bellied Flycatcher! Unlike other *Empidonax* flycatchers, Yellow-bellies are easily identified. While I knew I would see one somewhere in Hancock County, I do not always get them so close to home here on Mount Desert Island. It felt like a lucky find! This is another bird of the boreal forest, especially one made up of conifers and peatlands.

Yellow-bellied Flycatchers largely migrate from Central America to the boreal forests of North America. Arthur Cleveland Bent, author of the twenty-one-volume *Life Histories of North American Birds* (published 1919—1968), referred to this species as a "woodland waif", writing: "In its summer home its voice betrays it, but there, also, the searcher must invade the moist, gloomy morass of northern forest bog, beneath the shade of spruces and firs, and endure the attacks of hordes of black flies and mosquitoes, to even get a glimpse." That description says it all.

Today's bird of the year:

214. Yellow-bellied Flycatcher

Thursday, 24 May

For today's Weekly Birding Tour with The Natural History Center, we explored the trails of Acadia National Park's Compass Harbor after rambling about the nearby Hemlock and Jesup Trails at Sieur de Monts Spring.

9:31 a.m.   Among the tour participants today was Leslie. She was a tourist visiting from Cape May, New Jersey, new to our group, and making her first visit to Maine. Her *joi de vivre* was contagious! Every bird was special to her. We could have watched one chickadee for an hour and I think Leslie would have been ecstatic. Even so, she expressly stated wanting to see warblers.

Walking the trails of Compass Harbor, there were a lot of birds in the canopy, giving us all a case of birder's neck as we craned back to scan the treetops. Warbler sightings trickled in: Ovenbird, Nashville Warbler, Common Yellowthroat, American Redstart, Northern Parula, Magnolia Warbler, Yellow Warbler, Chestnut-sided Warbler, Black-throated Blue Warbler, Pine Warbler, Yellow-rumped Warbler, and Black-throated Green Warbler. Twelve species in all. An excellent tally of warblers for a single location!

Coming upon the Compass Harbor waterfront, we startled a Whimbrel who took flight, squawking its epithets at us as it flew away. Fortunately, everyone was able to get a clear, if short, look at the large shorebird with the very long, decurved (downward curving) bill.

Whimbrels evolved this particular bill such that the curve matches the curve of the burrow of Fiddler Crabs, one of their primary foods. This adaptation comes in quite handy on their wintering grounds.

Whether Whimbrels are flying north to the high Arctic during their spring migration, like this one, or south on their autumnal peregrination, Maine is only a brief feeding stopover during their hemispheric journey.

Today's bird of the year:

215. Whimbrel

Monday, 04 June

So many writers weave expressions of angst into their missives, writing of depression, regret, tension. In *The Happy Isles of Oceania: Paddling the Pacific*—a piece of travel-writing that was quite impactful on me as a young adult—travel writer Paul Theroux frequently dwells on the demise of his marriage and the grim reality of a future alone. For me, generally, I am not a person who experiences great angst. A graph of the sine wave of my emotional being would show crests and troughs that barely deviate from the median.

That said, the past two weeks were a bit difficult, which is by no means meant to equate my mindset to someone who is truly struggling. In fact, considering the amplitude of my normal emotional highs and lows, my current trough was probably within the realm of normal variation for many people. Still, I was struggling with trying to balance the fiscal need to be away for work with my intellectual and emotional investment in my Little Big Year.

I had been off to the Great Lakes for a two-week naturalist gig on a small ship full of Road Scholars[i]. This is normally an adventure I would relish. Having grown up in Lewiston, New York, between Lake Erie and Lake Ontario on the banks of the lower Niagara River, this was the world of my childhood. It is also an area steeped in history with a fascinating natural history. However, my absence from Maine was during a time when shorebird numbers were increasing as the entire population heads north to their high Arctic breeding grounds. Untold thousands of shorebirds pass through Hancock

County. Of course, I would have a chance to see most of these on their autumnal migration southward. Alas, it has been more than 100 years since the days of the large flocks of shorebirds that darkened the skies. All of this said, missing two weeks during their peak migration increased the potential of missing species for the year.

While I was away, a number of the usual migrants returned or passed through, including Eastern Wood-Pewee and Willet. More importantly, pelagic birds had begun to return—think shearwaters and phalaropes. On the Acadia Birding Festival's 02 June pelagic tour, a Brown Booby was observed off Schoodic Island. DRAT! I have seen them in the Caribbean, but having one in Maine, in Hancock County, during a Little Big Year, would have been a megararity for the year-list (it was the first Hancock County record and the third for the State of Maine).

Being away made me realize how much I came to identify with this one-year project. It had morphed from something of a lark with a purpose to being an integral part of my identity. The constant focus on birds resulted in an increased physical and spiritual connection to the natural world, a state of being to which I have always assigned a high value but something that is all-too-easy to take for granted…until you are removed from it.

Late last night, I returned from the Great Lakes. This morning, after seeing Anouk to her school bus, I was chomping at the bit to go birding.

8:31 a.m.   Hello Mount Desert Island High School, old friend. When I need to see birds, you never disappoint.

It was a gray day, threatening to drizzle. This week's schedule was filled with preparations for next week's trip to Newfoundland. Every couple of years, Natalie and our friend, colleague, and marine biology professor, Sean Todd, teach a class at College of the Atlantic entitled "This Marvelous, Terrible Place: The Human Ecology of Newfoundland." While I do the odd lecture for the class, my role comes to bear during the actual trip to Newfoundland when I become a co-leader. (Anouk comes, too, and Sean has designated her the morale officer.) I absolutely LOVE Newfoundland! It is a geography that, from the first moment I set foot on The Rock, I felt at home. I always look forward to the class, but this year, it meant eighteen more days traveling outside of Hancock County during the tail end of spring migration. Which also meant I had zero birding seconds to lose this one week home.

Despite a few warning rain droplets fired across the figurative bow, I felt a quick tour of the high school could be productive.

And it was! As I approached the settling ponds, a veritable cloud of swallows was feeding over the ponds, wheeling about, scooping up aerial insects. In fact, there were far more swallows than I could readily account for by the presence of only two bird nesting boxes. Tree Swallows are cavity nesters. Considering the proximal stand of dead Tamarack and Black Spruce, there may well be a profusion of nesting cavities. Or not. I don't typically see so many swallows wheeling about except in very early migration when they are merely looking for food and have not established territories.

A few swallows seemed notably small. There were some brown Bank Swallows flying among the counter-shaded[ii] (white below and gun-metal blue above) profusion of Tree Swallows. A smaller number of chestnut-chested swallows zigged and zagged, deeply forked tails flaring as they stalled, marking them as Barn Swallows.

One swallow stood out: a bit larger than the Barn Swallows, perhaps 30—40% larger than the Tree Swallows. In the poor ambient lighting, everything appeared flat, low contrast, making it challenging to clearly discern color. Still, this intriguing bird appeared more a flat color, somewhere on the blue-to-black spectrum. What was particularly noteworthy was that it was a uniform color above and below, no counter-shading. Purple Martin!

As with the other swallows, Purple Martins are also cavity nest-ers. The eastern population of Purple Martin nests almost exclusively in nest box colonies anymore (look for those big white nest bird houses, or better yet, a cluster of gourd-like bird houses, both with loads of holes for birds to go in and out and both on a tall pole near water). Given the slightly later date for this sighting than I would have expected, it is quite possible it is a young bird, as older ones arrive earlier on their breeding grounds to stake out territories.

Purple Martins were once far more abundant than they are today. In 1831, John James Audubon wrote, "Almost every country tavern has a martin box on the upper part of its signboard; and I have ob-served that the handsomer the box, the better does the inn generally prove to be." Given the voracious appetite Purple Martins have for consuming flying insects, this was both good marketing and partic-ularly good pest control, which was always good for the comfort of a tavern's guests.

The hanging of a bird house is not a new practice. Before Euro-peans arrived, Native Americans hung empty gourds to serve as mar-tin houses. The fact that we needed to put up houses for Purple Martins, even back in colonial times, speaks, albeit indirectly, to the fact that we had so altered the landscape that this aerial insectivore could not find enough suitable natural nesting sites.

As I have written in the past, the back corner of the settling ponds, the northwest corner, is often a spot where I find interesting birds. This day, I could hear a particular *bee-buzz* of a song coming intermittently from not too far into the woods. *Bee-buzz*. This is not a bird I hear regularly. In fact, it has been years, perhaps a dozen or more, since I last heard it. Working my way through my mental audio catalog of bird song, I finally realized I was hearing Blue-winged Warbler. Blue-winged Warbler! Although they are rarely seen in Hancock County, somehow, when a Blue-winged Warbler does turn up, I always manage to miss them, so this bird was a particularly meaningful find.

The Cornell Lab of Ornithology's All About Birds website has this to say about the song: "Blue-winged Warblers sing a raspy *bee-buzz* that sounds like an inhale (*bee*) and an exhale (*buzz*)."[iii] That is exactly it! So, I waited. And listened. And waited some more. And listened some more. The bird was not singing regularly. For a while, it started to sound as though the bird was moving off. And then it got closer. And closer. Finally, a small yellow bird with the merest hint of black mask and wings that were on the blue end of the gray spectrum popped out on the end of a branch!

The typical breeding range for Blue-winged Warblers is the very southern corner of Maine, west to the Mississippi River, and south to a latitude equivalent to the southern borders of Kentucky and Arkansas, with a disjunct population breeding in the north of Alabama. We are gradually finding Blue-winged Warblers in Hancock County, which is outside of its known breeding range. With human development and management of the landscape, we are seeing more shrubbier habitat, well-suited for Blue-winged Warblers. Whether these increased observations are the result of an expanding population, migration overshoot, post-nesting dispersal, or some other factor, is still a mystery.

As an aside, the DNA of Blue-winged Warblers and Golden-winged Warblers are 99.97% similar. Even though Blue-wings and Golden-wings have different songs, habitats, and wintering grounds, they readily hybridize. If you have ever heard of "Brewster's" Warbler or "Lawrence's" Warbler, these are hybrids showing features of both their progenitors.

9:09 a.m.   One of the many fascinating features of eBird is the ability to set up "alerts," informing of bird reports that you might need for your county-, state-, or life-list. This year, the year of my Little Big Year, I set eBird to inform me of birds reported in Hancock County which I need for my year-list. While I was in the Great Lakes, I began to get numerous reports for Eastern Wood-Pewee. This week was my last chance for a while to find one until I return from Newfoundland.

The Eastern Wood-Pewee is a late-returning flycatcher of deeper woodlands, readily identifiable by its musical intonations of *pee-o-wee*. In typical flycatcher fashion, it is not shy about singing. I have seen many, many Eastern Wood-Pewees in my life. I've even banded a fair few. Time being tight—a mid-morning tour in less than an hour was awaiting—I made a quick foray to Acadia National Park's Sieur de Monts Spring to search for my first-of-the-year pewee.

I walked a few hundred yards down the Hemlock Trail, accompanied by the incessant, repetitive song of Red-eyed Vireo (*here-I-am, there-you-are*), repeated over and over, *ad infinitum*; the burst of song of an Ovenbird (*teacher Teacher TEACHER*), the flight calls of American Goldfinch overhead (*perchickory, perchickory*), a lone Barred Owl calling out (*who cooks for you, who cooks for you all*). By the time I reached the Barred Owl nesting tree, I heard a high, musical *pee-o-wee* filtering through the morning chorus.

My avian target found, my birding day was complete. This was a good start to my one-week-between-trips-away to find some spring migrants. The sine wave of my emotional being was back up, perhaps even a little more than usual.

Today's birds of the year:

216. Purple Martin
217. Blue-winged Warbler

218. Eastern Wood-Pewee

Tuesday, 05 June

L iving next to a National Park is wonderful! It is a ready playground: you can walk, hike, run, bicycle, snowshoe, or cross-country ski, whatever conditions allow. Sometimes, you can even do several of these in one day. This afternoon, Natalie and I walked the Carriage Road to Aunt Betty Pond and back (followed by a bicycle ride, but I had no birds to report there).

What's more, you can get out into the Park any time of day. During the work week, Natalie prefers afternoon walks for the way it bisects her day. I like to start my day with a morning walk for the increased opportunity to see and hear my feathered friends. Sometimes we get out together in the morning for an hour, sometimes it is the afternoon. Today, afternoon won out.

1:37 p.m.   As we walked along the Aunt Betty Pond Carriage Road, a portion wends its way behind Acadia National Park Headquarters and is generally within earshot of Route 233 traffic. A mile or so in, the Carriage Road veers off to the southwest, affording the solitude of woodland therapy.

This day, time did not allow us to take in the entire six-mile loop; instead, we walked out a 1½ miles and then back. What we did manage, though, was to see the vegetative regrowth of an area that had undergone a controlled burn at some point in the recent past—this is part of Acadia National Park's ongoing effort to manage the landscape for the elements of the natural world, as well as for the human landscape. In the case of the latter, controlled burns are often used to maintain scenic vistas. Associated with scenic vistas are specific habitat types, better characterized as natural communities.

This particular pocket natural community is one of grasses and Lowbush Blueberry (the authors of *The Plants of Acadia National Park* write of Lowbush Blueberry: "Fruit a sweet and delicious blue berry, flavor of Maine specimens unparalleled elsewhere in the *UNI-VERSE*"—the emphasis is mine but I like to think that they intended it) nestled amongst a mixed forest. The intervals of fire management have fostered a forest of relatively young trees with a dense understory.

Chirry, chirry, chirry, chorry, chorry.

Mourning Warbler!

This bird is not routinely found on Mount Desert Island. Yet, this was the perfect habitat, if a little small in acreage, in which to find it.

Mourning Warblers are stunning. Both male and female have yellow underbellies, olive backs, and slate-gray heads, although the male's colors really pop out and has the addition of a black gorget, or throat patch.

In most birds, the parents carry the eggshells off, away from the nest when the young hatch. It would not do to have telltale clues (*e.g.*, eggshell bits) pointing their figurative finger for predators to find a nest directly above. Female Mourning Warblers do it differently: they eat the eggshells. Perhaps this replenishes the calcium lost in making the eggs in the first place.

One other fun fact about Mourning Warblers: when predators lurk too close, both male and female adults will feign a broken wing in attempts to lure their antagonist away.

Today's bird of the year:

219. Mourning Warbler

Wednesday, 06 June

1 0:04 a.m. Nothing like birding at thirty-five miles per hour. Driving, along the Norway Drive sheep pasture of College of Atlantic's Peggy Rockefeller Farm, windows down, enjoying the flow of fresh air, I did not immediately acknowledge the insect-like buzzy call briefly carried on the westerly breeze, rising and falling, Bernoulli fashion, as I drove past.

WAIT! Was that a Grasshopper Sparrow? That was a Grasshopper Sparrow!

I practically stood on the brakes and quickly turned around, parked along the narrow shoulder of the road, and waited for the call to repeat. A minute passed, maybe more. There! There was the buzzy song I knew from my days banding birds at the Crown Point (New York) State Historic Park banding station: Grasshopper Sparrow. It was definitely insect-like but not an insect, emanating from some distance out in the field. I was amazed I even heard it. If I had been a few seconds sooner or a few seconds later, I would certainly have missed it.

Back in the 1980s and 1990s, working at the spring banding station at Crown Point State Historical Site on the New York shores of the southern end of Lake Champlain, I have banded a number of Grasshopper Sparrows. Alas, it has easily been twenty years since I have observed one, so I was eager to see this bird.

Grabbing my binoculars (they are nearly always within arm's reach), I climbed the A-frame ladder over the fence and waded through the knee-deep grass a dozen steps in the direction of the call, then waited. After a pause, the bird sang again. A few more steps forward and wait. Song. Repeat. Closer and closer I edged. Finally, a nondescript bird materialized atop a stalk of grass, periodically throwing its head back to belt out its short, insect-like song.

In the world of LBJs—little brown jobs—Grasshopper Sparrows are particularly drab. That said, they do exhibit a few key field marks. Certainly, their song is definitive. As sparrows go, this is a small bird, seemingly not much larger than its eponymous food. (Okay, maybe not that small.) Its beak seems disproportionately robust for its size, perhaps the avian equivalent of Cyrano de Bergerac. It sports a thin, white eye-ring. And a portion of the supercilium, or eyestripe, in front of the eye trends toward an orangey-yellow (or a yellowy-orange in some).

I closed to about 150 feet, plenty close for viewing this bird not commonly found in Hancock County. In fact, to find it reliably in Maine usually means a visit to the Kennebunk Plains in the southern part of the state.

As delightful as it was to hear and see this species, I worry for their future as we continue to convert grasslands into parking lots, housing developments, suburbs, and mono-culture farmland. According to the Breeding Bird Survey, Grasshopper Sparrows have seen a 72% decline in their population since 1966. Throughout its range, most state wildlife agencies list Grasshopper Sparrows as being endangered, threatened, or a species of special concern.

Today's bird of the year:

220. Grasshopper Sparrow

Friday, 08 June

I have written this previously, but when undertaking a big year, whether globally, continentally, or locally, there comes a point of diminishing returns when you have found the majority of likely birds and you begin targeting those few that are left. In this day's case, it was Bonaparte's Gulls. I had been casually looking for them for a month, making frequent visits to Acadia National Park's Thompson Island, a place where I find them every single year. Although these gulls can be seen throughout May, their numbers notably build during June. With my imminent departure in a few days for a fifteen-day trip to Newfoundland, I was hoping to find one of these black-headed beauties soon; otherwise, I may have to wait until they pass through in the autumn to find them.

12:13 p.m. Pulling into my favorite Thompson Island parking spot, I noticed two things: it was nearly low tide and there were dozens of gulls foraging in the shallow pools of the extensive mudflats. Walking to the shore's edge, two shorebirds flushed, calling out *chu-wee, chu-wee.* Landing a short distance away, I could see they were on the smaller side and had the short, thick bills characteristic of a plover. Add to the mix the black neckband and the birds were readily identifiable as Semipalmated Plovers....

Spend enough time discussing plovers and, invariably, someone will express a strong opinion for the correct way to say the word. Think about it. How do you say it? Do you say plover to rhyme with clover? Or do you say plover as it rhymes with lover?

My short answer is that I am happy when people identify a plover, regardless of how they pronounce it. That said, I have long held that when a question of pronunciation or etymology arises, I defer to *The Oxford English Dictionary*. In that venerable reference, they conclusively state the pronunciation is "plɐ•vəɹ", that would be plover that rhymes with lover. Although the dispute may be settled, I will never correct someone for saying plover with a long o.

… As I continued my quick scan, my gaze almost immediately landed on six "peep" sandpipers. And indeed, they were small with a wash of streaking across the breast, longish dark bill with a hint of a droop at the end, dark legs—all of these details marked them as Semipalmated Sandpipers.

The descriptive "semipalmated" forename for both the plover and the sandpiper is a reference to the partial webbing between the intersection of where the digits of the toes join the tarsometatarsus (think foot bone).

Two species quickly added to the year-list, my spotting scope set up, I began scanning the gulls. There were a few large Herring Gulls about and a load of nearly identical-but-smaller Ring-billed Gulls. I looked first to the flying gulls, hoping to find the flittier, almost butterfly-like motion of a Bonaparte's Gull in flight. *Nada.* So, I shifted my focus to the gulls foraging the intertidal. More Ring-bills, lots and lots of Ring-bills.

Wait, one had a black spot behind the eye, a head with a gray wash, and a black bill. And another. And another. I must have become complacent in my scanning, because suddenly, they were everywhere!

Bonaparte's Gulls may just be my favorite larid (member of the Family Laridae). This is a preference based on experience with countless thousands of gulls. At the Four Brothers Island Preserve on Lake Champlain, I have herded unfledged Ring-billed Gull chicks as part of an annual banding program, stalked adult Ring-billed Gulls around five-foot-tall clumps of Garlic Mustard, cuddled Herring Gull chicks, and been "bit" and pecked and generally intimidated by Great Black-backed Gulls. I have counted millions of Black-legged Kittiwakes in Alaska and photographed them in Newfoundland. And I have watched the life-and-death struggles of a two different pair of Kelp Gulls on the Antarctic Peninsula (the tag-teaming Brown Skuas won the first battle I observed; in the second, the Kelp Gulls managed to avoid catastrophe by ducking at just the right moment). But still, I love Bonaparte's Gull best....

My first Bonaparte's Gulls were at the end of Digby Neck, Nova Scotia, on Brier Island. It was the fall of 1986. A few months out of university and starting a new job at the Atmospheric Sciences Research Center atop Whiteface Mountain in New York's Adirondack State Park, I was sent off to an Environmental Protection Agency Mountain Cloud Chemistry Project workshop in Bar Harbor. At the conclusion of the conference, and being all the way in Maine, I hopped aboard the Blue Nose ferry to Yarmouth, Nova Scotia, then made my way to Brier Island, the terminus of the Digby Peninsula. Something about the remoteness of this place beckoned. Once there, the car parked, I unpacked my trusty 1986 Cannondale SM500 mountain bike and began exploring.

Pedaling out Gull Rock Road, I was met with a strange sight: a good number of twig nests in the spruce lining the road. Low in the trees, high in the trees, in the middle of the trees, always toward the ends of branches. It was autumn, nesting season was long since over, so no birds were in attendance to help me easily identify their makers. That said, there were clues in the form of loads of feathers scattered about. Short white feathers clinging to the needles of the spruce. Longer, black-tipped white primary feathers. Clearly some kind of gull was the culprit, but I had never heard of gulls nesting in trees.

Continuing all the way out to Hog Yard Cove, the southernmost point of Brier Island, I was greeted by hundreds, perhaps even thousands of gulls sitting on the water roiling with the turbulent tidal currents of the mouth of the Bay of Fundy. Nearly all of these gulls were small, smaller than the Ring-billed Gulls of my Niagara River gorge youth. The basic plumage included black dots behind their eyes. Bonaparte's Gulls!

As for those mystery nests, returning to the Adirondacks, I shared my observation with my mentor and friend, Mike Peterson. He told me they were likely the nests of Bonaparte's Gulls, a tree-nesting species of gull that nest in colonies.

… Now, watching the Bonaparte's Gulls flying and foraging off Thompson Island, my day was complete.

Today's birds of the year:

221. Semipalmated Plover
222. Semipalmated Sandpi-
     per

223. Bonaparte's Gull

Sunday, 10 June

T his may just wind up being the best birding trip of the year! Not for the variety. And not for the fact of the privilege of experiencing a bird rare in Maine. No, it was for the sheer adventure of it!

It was invigorating to arrive at the South Gate trailhead to the Great Pond Mountain Wildlands[i] at sunset and bicycle in 3½ miles on the Valley Road, the sky a backdrop brilliant with the purples, reds, and oranges of the recently set sun. Quickly left behind were all sounds of civilization, leaving me immersed in the "quiet" of nature.

All too often, writers refer to the absence of man-made sound as some sort of preternatural quiet. These sorts of statements always irk me as they demonstrate our bias in favor of the human-dominated land- and soundscape. We have become so accustomed to the incessant drone of automotive traffic, the unhealthy hum of power transmission lines, the background din of all manner of apparatus heating and cooling our homes and businesses, and every other sound accompanying the built landscape, that its absence has come to be equated with silence. Not so! In actuality, there is always sound. Just listen.

Notice the wind passing through the trees. It is not just some generic sound from a movie soundtrack. As the speed of the breeze changes, so too does its tenor. For any given velocity, it produces a different sound as it passes through different trees—spruce, pine, aspen, oak—and over different landscapes—ponded waters, meadows, forests, mountaintops. So it was that the crunch of my bicycle tires rolling over a gravel road was accompanied by the so-called "sound of silence."

8:46 p.m.   A half hour earlier, I parked my car, unloaded my steadfast Cannondale mountain bike (the same one I was riding when I found all the Digby Island Bonaparte's Gull nests thirty-two years ago), and began the 3½-mile ride in to the locale where Cheri Domina had reported a Chuck-will's-widow a few nights previous.

To ensure a more complete coverage of all species of breeding birds during the five years of the Maine Bird Atlas, the Department of Inland Fisheries & Wildlife coordinates a number of special projects, including nighttime surveys for nightjars. On the evening of 06 June, imagine Cheri's surprise, as she was doing a nightjar survey at Great Pond Mountain Wildlands, when she heard a Chuck-will's-widow, a bird more typically found south of the Mason-Dixon Line, singing its little heart out. Last night (09 June), she led a walk for Downeast Audubon and the bird was still there! Given the fact that early tomorrow morning (11 June) I was off to Newfoundland with a group of College of the Atlantic students, this was my sole window to search for the bird.

Bicycling in, the first bird to greet me was a singing Veery. Its downward spiraling song—*VEER Veer veer*—is one I heard every spring during my Adirondack days but one I seldom hear near my home or anywhere on Mount Desert Island. With the sun recently set, the dusk chorus was a tonic to my need to commune with wilderness. Mourning Dove. Hermit Thrush. American Robin. These made up the soundtrack of my evening's ride.

Sometimes, when your senses pick up some unexpected phenomena, it takes a moment or three for your brain to acknowledge the message the synapses of your central nervous system are trying to convey. So, when I heard a loud and repetitive noise from the forest, a quarter mile from the meadow where it was first reported, I kept on pedaling, not fully realizing what I was hearing: *chuck-will's-widow chuck-will's-widow chuck-will's-widow*, over and over, incessantly.

HOLY COW! The Chuck-will's-widow!

\-------------------------

The only other Chuck-will's-widow on my life-list was recorded in 1999. My friend Brian McAllister, along with two of his friends—Drew and Frank—and I participated in the World Series of Birding[ii], New Jersey Audubon's annual competition pitting teams against one another to see which can find the most species of birds in twenty-four hours (oh, and to raise money for New Jersey Audubon's conservation programs, too).

The evening before the big event, we all went to bed early, Frank and Drew in their trailer, Brian in his tent, me in mine. At midnight, the alarm on my Casio dive watch went off—*bee-bee-bee-beep, bee-bee-bee-beep, bee-bee-bee-beep*. In my sleep-deprived stupor—for we had been scouting for several long days, learning and relearning birds seldom seen in the Adirondacks, as well as developing our plan of attack for the Big Day—I hit the button to turn off my alarm. But it kept going, morphing in my brain: *bee-bee-bee-beep, bee-bee-bee-widow, chuck-will's-widow, chuck-will's-widow*. And with every iteration of *chuck-will's-widow*, the ceiling of my tent was pumping up and down, as if keeping tempo.

Suddenly, the fog was gone from my brain, I was wide awake. "Brian," I whispered in that undertone where you want your voice to carry but don't want to disturb anyone. Or anything. "Do you hear it?"

"Yes," his reply barely audible, "I think it's close."

"It is! It's sitting on top of my tent!"

Chuck-will's-widows are the largest of North America's nightjars[iii], the family of birds that includes nighthawks. In addition to insects, Chuck-will's-widow are known to occasionally take small songbirds, and sometimes even bats!

At Great Pond Mountain Wildlands, this was certainly the night of the goatsuckers, those wide-mouthed crepuscular birds that swoop about catching loads of insects. Of course, they were doing more than feeding. While the Chuck-will's-widow kept up its audio vigil, I heard a distant sound that the field guides label "booming." This time of year, when the male Common Nighthawk is trying to impress a female, he flexes his wings in acrobatic diving displays, fanning his primary flight feathers. As the wind rushes through the feathers of this adjusted position, it makes a preternatural sound. While "booming" might not be the word I would choose, I can offer up no better choice, so "booming" it is.

I looked to the heavens, hoping to see the flash of white at the base of the primaries to get a visual confirmation of what I already knew by the booming sound was a Common Nighthawk. While searching, a passel of cigars-with-wings (for that is an apt description for the shape of flying Chimney Swifts: long, sweeping wings attached to a cigar-shaped body) wheeled about, also actively catching and feeding on insects.

On so many levels, Chimney Swifts are a fascinating species. They are incredible aerialists, only landing to nest or sleep. Due to their incredibly short leg structure, which prevents them from perching on any horizontal surface, they must be on a vertical surface, like the inside of an old chimney. Likewise, their nests are glued, using a combination of natural materials and their sticky saliva, to the inside, vertical surface of a chimney (pre-settlement, they would have nested inside hollowed trees and on cliff faces). And that is how they derive their name: for their habit of nesting in chimneys.

There seems to be something onomatopoeic about nightjars (by the way, Chimney Swifts are not nightjars, but a closely related family all of their own). Chuck-will's-widow sings *chuck-will's-widow*. There is another nightjar that sings its name: the Eastern Whip-poor-will. Sure enough, as I stood there, rooted to the mysterious sounds coming out of the dark—Chuck-will's-widow singing and booming nighthawks—I caught a distant and faint intonation: *whip-poor-will, whip-poor-will, whip-poor-will*.

Eastern Whip-poor-wills were once relatively common throughout Hancock County. I recall one June 2001 evening, sitting on the deck with friends at their Otter Creek home. The sun had set, the alpenglow on the west face of Gorham Mountain long subsumed into a black silhouette against the night sky, a chorus of *whip-poor-will, whip-poor-will* rose from the field below. For years, that was the last Eastern Whip-poor-will I found in Maine (and remains the last one I have found on Mount Desert Island). Today, they can still be found in Hancock County, especially at Great Pond Mountain Wildlands, but their global population has dwindled precipitously.

My night's quest complete—having found my two target nightjars, with the bonus of Chimney Swifts—I began the uphill bicycle trek back to my car. It was not long before I passed another field and four more Eastern Whip-poor-wills were speeding me on my way. *Whip-poor-will, whip-poor-will, whip-poor-will*.

Today's birds of the year:

224. Chuck-will's-widow   226. Eastern Whip-poor-will
225. Chimney Swift

Monday, 11 June

Newfoundland! The Rock! Among my favorite places on the planet!

This morning, Natalie and I are co-leading a group of fourteen College of the Atlantic students on an eighteen-day journey to New-foundland. Early up and at 'em, vans loaded, sleepy students nested into their seats, we drove in two twelve-passenger vans. Content from the previous night's soul-reviving run of nightjars and swifts, I had absolutely no expectation of adding any year-birds to my list during the brief time we would be driving north and east through Hancock County on our way to North Sydney, Nova Scotia, and the ferry to Port aux Basque, Newfoundland.

8:10 a.m.   Not far down Route 9, known throughout the Pine Tree State as "The Airline," a medium-sized hawk flew across the road wrestling a snake that clearly had no desire to become a meal. Whether the bird was carrying the snake to a nest to feed young or just to a perch to feed itself, I could not ascertain in my brief fifty-five miles per hour glimpse.

What I did gather, though, was that this bird was a bit larger than a Broad-winged Hawk with very reddish underparts, especially the chest and forewings—the so-called "arm" of the wing—with a white "window" at the base of the primaries and an obvious white terminal band on the tail. The general impression of size and shape of the bird was a Red-shouldered Hawk. Not quite the long look I would have preferred, but not a bad way to say *sayonara* to Maine until the end of the month.

Today's bird of the year:

227. Red-shouldered Hawk

Sunday, 01 July

I t was good to be home! I do love Newfoundland and Labrador—the landscape, the people, the climate, everything about it, really—but being away, again, this time for nearly three weeks, was challenging, especially considering that this was a crucial time to pick up birds. I was chomping at the bit to do some Little Big Year birding.

I did have some wonderful birding experiences during my Newfoundland and Labrador travels. In Maine, we see Greater Scaup only during spring and fall migration. Seeing a mated pair of them, on territory at Pinware Provincial Park in Labrador was delightful. Common Goldeneye is a purely winter visitant along coastal Maine. We had a pair of these on territory on Western Brook Pond in Gros Morne National Park in Newfoundland.

Despite mass marketing of Atlantic Puffins to attract tourists to Maine, I never tire of seeing them. In Maine, you have to take a boat ride to their offshore nesting islands to reliably see puffins. In Newfoundland, there are many places where you can walk right up, sit down, take photos, and have them at arm's length—no boats required!

We had truly amazing numbers of birds. At Witless Bay Ecological Reserve in Bay Bulls, there were hundreds of thousands of Atlantic Puffins and Common Murres whirring about in veritable clouds. And Cape St. Mary's Ecological Reserve is one of North

America's most remarkable gannetries with thousands of Northern Gannets nesting along the upper tiers of 400-foot cliffs that plunge steeply to the sea while lower down are stratified layers of Black-legged Kittiwake, Common Murre, and Razorbill.

Finally, while I was manning the grill at the Bonavista Neck camp of our dear friends, Minnie and Lindsay Russell, I glanced up and saw a Snowy Owl! Instantly, I abandoned my post, grabbed my spotting scope from the van, and set it up to show all our students, Minnie and Lindsay, and Natalie and Anouk. After a good ten minutes, the bird took wing, flying a quarter mile to light atop another utility pole. When I turned back to the original pole, a second Snowy Owl had come in! Later, with the two owls still in sight, we loaded up the vans to drive the quarter mile down the road for ice-cream at Little Dairy King. With the sun set and dark infusing the landscape, we saw our third Snowy Owl of the day. These three owls were a great addition to our Newfoundland and Labrador adventure!

July and August are typically the time for family vacations. Now that we had returned from our travels, it was time to dive headlong into the full-on summer season, leading families on outings to learn about the natural world of Acadia National Park, Mount Desert Island, and Downeast Maine. While that might not allow as much dedicated birding as I desired (when guiding, my focus is on my guests, even when it is a birding tour), it did mean plenty of time outdoors where birds can be seen and heard.

First up was a private tour for a family of four that began at Acadia National Park's Sieur de Monts Spring, one of my favorite birding hotspots. I come back to Sieur de Monts Spring again and again when I lead tours, or even when I just want to go birding, because it has such a variety of natural communities, from valley bottom Red Maple swamps to riparian corridors, sedge meadows, mixed forests, long abandoned pasture lands, upland hemlock forests, and more. For the astute observer, there are signs of the Great Fire of '47. Emergent "flag trees" on the side of Dorr Mountain show the prevailing direction of the winter winds. Wild Gardens of Acadia offers snapshot glimpses of some of the local plant associations. And there is a bubbling spring, the source of the name Sieur de Monts Spring. All of this and more makes for a wonderful nature walk.

9:37 a.m.   For an outing that was not exclusively bird focused, we still tallied nineteen species, all typical of Sieur de Monts Spring this time of year. One species of bird is heard often enough that I am not surprised when its usually distant and constantly repeated song, *cuh-cuh-coo cuh-cuh-coo cuh-cuh-coo*, slowly creeps into my consciousness: Black-billed Cuckoo. As you might imagine, the name "cuckoo" derives onomatopoeically from its song. In French, they call this species *coucou*, which is also an informal greeting between friends, "*Coucou, mon ami*" (hello, my friend).

The cuckoos of North America are sometimes referred to as "rain crows" out of the belief that they call just before it starts to rain. In Europe, cuckoos are known nest parasites, meaning a gravid female will lay her eggs in the nest of other birds. While the Black-billed Cuckoo of North America will do this on occasion, they are more apt to build their own nests.

There are many fun facts about Black-billed Cuckoos: the way they periodically shed their stomach lining, hacking it up like one big hairball; the rapidity in which they fledge (an average of seventeen days from the time the egg is laid); the bittern-like manner in which young birds point their bill skyward and remain still when threatened. Additionally, they are relatively short-lived. According to data from the Bird Banding Lab, the oldest one was banded in 1965 in Ontario and was recaptured in 1969 in Connecticut.

If you are in, or even near, their territory at the right time of year, this secretive and elusive bird can readily be heard if you listen carefully enough.

Today's bird of the year:

228. Black-billed Cuckoo

Tuesday, 03 July

Today, I had the privilege of leading a family of four on a tide-pool tour along Acadia National Park's Ship Harbor Trail. As Ship Harbor drains, a shallow tide race, about a foot-and-a-half deep, forms, bending Rockweed and Sugar Kelp in the current, evoking images of prairie grass undulating in the wind. After we had identified much of the marine flora and fauna of this shallow area, we continued on our way to the southern terminus of the trail to look at more traditional rocky tide-pools. While birding was not the focus of the trip, by now you should realize that I am ALWAYS birding.

11:00 a.m.   Standing in the rocky tide-pool at the southern tip of the Ship Harbor Trail, water barely an inch from the hem of my Patagonia Stand-Up shorts, head down, looking for the ever-elusive Jonah Crab, I heard the grating call of an Arctic Tern (in comparison to the call of the Common Tern, it really is harsher sounding). I looked up to see a single tern flying surprisingly close, perhaps twenty feet above and less than one hundred feet away. I quickly raised my binoculars to spy a tern with an all-red bill and pale wing-tips, confirming my audial identification.

I was surprised by this sighting. Yes, Arctic Terns breed on the coast of Maine; some not very far away—as the tern flies—on Petit Manan Island, a breeding island in the Maine Coastal Islands National Wildlife Refuge. I think of them as generally flying out to sea to feed and not flying inshore as this one was. Of course, birds fly, and so there is nothing to stop them from coming close. One of the many reasons I like field biology is that there are no rules, just guidelines, and the birds do not always like to follow them.

It has long been known that Arctic Terns are long distance migrants, racking up 25,000 migratory miles each year. Or so we thought. Ornithologists have learned that figure was actually a farcry from reality. Thanks to the ever-decreasing size of technology, eleven Arctic Terns were fitted with miniature geolocators. The result, as detailed in a 2010 study published in the *Proceedings of the National Academy of Sciences*[i], put the figure at closer to 50,000 miles! Now, take that figure, multiplied over a lifespan that can be more than thirty years, and you have a bird that flies a distance comparable to three roundtrips to the moon!

Today's bird of the year:

229. Arctic Tern

Monday, 09 July

The past week I had been getting out for early morning birding before starting my daily tours. This particular morning, I made my way to Orland for a quick walk at Great Pond Mountain Wildlands hoping a change of scenery might add to my Little Big Year.

7:22 a.m.   Hiking in the Valley Road, the feeling of *déjà vu* was understandable. It was a day shy of a month ago when I was last here, bicycling in at dusk in my successful pursuit of Chuck-will's-widow. This time, however, I hiked a circuit that took in the Esker and Drumlin Trails.

Early in the walk, a hen Ruffed Grouse and three precocial chicks nearly startled the bejeesus out of me as they flushed from the edge of the trail. In *A Sand County Almanac*, Aldo Leopold wrote[i] "the autumn landscape in the north woods is the land, plus a Red Maple, plus a Ruffed Grouse. In terms of conventional physics, the grouse represents only a millionth of either the mass or the energy of an acre. Yet subtract the grouse and the whole thing is dead."

Several Veery were singing their downward spiraling *VEER Veer veer*, a song I rarely hear on Mount Desert Island. Now that was worth the trip! Vireos, warblers, sparrows, finches, twenty-four species in all.

The highlight of my day, though, was first hearing and then seeing a flock of four Evening Grosbeak. These large, yellow finches, not dissimilar to oversized American Goldfinch, were once far more common than they are today.

While their estimated global population of 4.1 million seems healthy, from 1966—2015, the North American Breeding Bird Survey has shown that Evening Grosbeaks have declined by 97% in the eastern United States. Cornell Lab of Ornithology's All About Birds website[ii] offers no clear reasons for this decline. What they did posit was the following:

Recent declines may be due to logging and other development in the boreal forests of northern North America; to disease outbreaks such as salmonella, West Nile virus, and House Finch eye disease; or to reduced numbers of spruce budworm and other forest insects, in part due to aerial spraying by the U.S. and Canada. As climate change alters the landscape over the next century, Balsam Fir is expected to recede from New England, and Evening Grosbeaks may disappear from this region.

Today's bird of the year:

230. Evening Grosbeak

Tuesday, 10 July

Whenever Martha and her husband visit Bar Harbor, they book nature tours with me. This year, her son, Robert, a fledgling birder, and his wife came along, so the focus of our tour was birds. Robert had two particular requests: he wanted to target seabirds typical of the Maine coast and find Peregrine Falcons.

During the course of the morning, we scoured the eastern side of Mount Desert Island looking for Robert's target birds, visiting birding hotspots such as Great Meadow, Sieur de Monts Spring, Ocean Drive, and Fish House Road, all in Acadia National Park. We also visited College of the Atlantic's Peggy Rockefeller Farm, Northeast Creek, and Hadley Point.

I like birding tours such as this. Although we were all calling it a birding tour, it was really a general natural history tour, weaving in botany, geology, and human history. Starting at 5:00 a.m., not long after sunrise, meant we practically had Acadia National Park to ourselves. The birds are at their best, singing, defending territories, foraging, announcing the presence of predators.

7:22 a.m.   We began our drive down Acadia National Park's Ocean Drive where we paid a quick visit to Sand Beach to see if there might be any shorebirds working the tide line.

It is always fun to go birding with new birders: the chance for them to find new life-birds is so much higher than with those more seasoned. Within minutes, we saw Common Eider, Black Guillemot, and Great Black-backed Gull, all seabirds and all life-birds for Robert!

We also saw three hoary shorebirds chasing the waves as they rolled in and out, sewing their long and stocky bills in and out of the sand just vacated by the receding water.

Sanderlings!

While most field guides collectively name the five smallest *Calidris* sandpipers—Baird's, Least, White-rumped, Semipalmated, and Western—"peep" sandpipers for their diminutive size, Cornell Lab of Ornithology's All About Birds website also includes Sanderling in that list. They are, indeed, small, but they are up to a ½-inch longer bill-to-tail than Western Sandpipers, the next largest, making them (Sanderlings) the largest of the "peeps."

When watching Sanderlings chase the receding waves, probing for marine invertebrates, it would be easy to overlook the fact that they also ingest a significant amount of sand. That, along with the calcium-based mollusk shells and keratin-based crustacean exoskeletons, offers no nutritional value. Sanderlings rid their bodies of this detritus by regurgitating miniature pellets *à la* owls.

Film animation company Pixar really and truly grasped the essence of Sanderlings in their 2016 short film entitled *Piper*. Watch this nearly five-minute long film and you will experience what it is to be a Sanderling.

By 9:00 a.m., we had tallied forty species, seven of which were seabirds, and five of those were life-birds for Robert. Not bad for a mid-July morning.

Today's bird of the year:

231. Sanderling

Friday, 13 July

After my morning tour, I parked on one of Bar Harbor's side streets so I could walk around town to run some errands. As always, I had my binoculars but was not anticipating a year-bird in downtown Bar Harbor during the middle of summer.

3:44 p.m.   Walking down Roberts Avenue, a one-way residential side street connecting two of Bar Harbor's main business drags, Cottage Street and Mount Desert Street, an incessant, nasal, two-note *cah-ah, cah-ah* caught my attention. Fish Crow? Fish Crow!

Within North American, American Crows are the most commonly seen crow species. This is true everywhere, but especially away from the water. Depending on where in North America you live, American Crows can range in size from fifteen to twenty-one inches in length, beak to tail, with the larger birds being found the further north you go.

This fact of size increasing with latitude is known as Bergmann's Rule. Bergmann's Rule states that in a species with a broadly distributed range, the colder the climate (which generally equates with being further north), the larger the individuals. When you think about it, this makes sense: larger individuals have greater thermal mass and thus will keep warmer. Conversely, those smaller species living further south less mass and are able to more readily shed heat. I cannot begin to count the times that tourists from southern states have commented on seeing a lot or ravens. Ravens are generally solitary, in pairs, or in small immediate family groups, so I tell them they are seeing crows. Of course, this causes disbelief. Then I explain Bergmann's Rule. I sometimes wonder how many people leave Bar Harbor at the end of their holidays and spread the gospel of Bergmann. (By the way, Bergmann's Rule applies to all species, not just birds.)

Fish Crows, on the other hand, run a bit smaller than American Crows, ranging in size from fourteen to sixteen inches in length. Gauging size can be deceptive, short of having the bird in hand along with some sort of ruler or caliper. Where American Crows are ubiquitous most everywhere, Fish Crows tend to congregate around water along a wide swath of an arc extending down the lower half of the Mississippi River, along the Gulf coast states, throughout most of Florida, and up the Atlantic coast toward Massachusetts (with southern Maine at the northern extremis). Be careful in your identification, though; where you find Fish Crow, you will also find American Crow.

The easiest way to differentiate the two—Fish Crow and American Crow—is by their calls. We all know the stereotypically harsh *cah, cah* of the American Crow. On the other hand, Fish Crows have a nasal, two-note *cah-ah, cah-ah*. Be careful when listening. Female American Crows will give a nasal begging call to courting males. Juvenile American Crows, fresh off the nest, also have a nasal call. The difference being that in both cases, the *cah, cah* is distinctly made up of single notes.

To the best of my knowledge, no Fish Crow had ever been reported in Hancock County prior to 2018. They are reported annually to our north and west in Penobscot and Knox Counties, albeit in very small numbers. With the warming climate and their range expanding north and inland, it was only going to be a matter of time before one showed up in Hancock County.

In 2014, on the eighth of our eleven cruises working as naturalist on ships chartered by Garrison Keillor and his radio show, *A Prairie Home Companion*, we cruised the North and Baltic Seas. For me, one of the highlights of this adventure was that it was the second (and last) time I managed to get a chuckle out of the big man on stage (and that was out of my twenty-some appearances in front of an audience with him!). Unlike my earlier times on stage with GK, this time, I didn't write down the experience afterward, but my memory of the event is vivid:

Garrison: So, Rich, what birds are you excited about on this cruise?

Me: I'm glad you asked, Garrison. Here in Europe, the corvid family is really fascinating! Specifically, I'm interested in the crows. There are two species of crows that are really quite common, and they look nearly identical: the Carrion Crow and the Hooded Crow. To tell them apart, you have to count the pinion feathers. The Hooded Crow has nine pinion feathers and the Carrion Crow has ten, so the difference is just a matter of a pinion.[i]

Garrison always appreciates a good play on words, and this must have been a particularly good one as a hearty chuckle escaped his lips before he quickly regained composure. A short while later, backstage, sound effects man and Radio Actor Fred Newman came up to me and shook my hand, telling me "that was a good one!" Fred went on to say that he is always messing with Garrison, purposely going off script trying to illicit a good guffaw.

There have been a few occasions walking through some major airport between flights (usually on our way to join Garrison) when Natalie and I have been approached by people asking, "Aren't you the naturalists?" Of course, there is a whole unspoken second part of the sentence: "for Garrison Keillor?" Invariably, they follow up with some comment on it just being "a matter of a pinion."

Today's bird of the year:

232. Fish Crow

Thursday, 19 July

I have been keenly interested in birds since the ripe, young age of about ten, beginning with the first time I joined Jerry Farrell and began banding ducks on the banks of the lower Niagara River. Banding ducks morphed into a lifelong passion for birds. As kids, there were countless days when my brother Rob, two years my junior, and I sallied forth into the woods around our Lewiston, New York, home in pursuit of feathered gems.

These sojourns were not necessarily quests for the rare. I remember the two of us spending countless hours watching American Goldfinch (we called them Wild Canaries), the yellow males brilliantly yellow in their breeding plumage, foraging in the poplars on the hillside adjoining our house. Belted Kingfishers fishing along the shores of the lower Niagara were a riveting study in form and function. During the winter, the incessant, if not voluble, *ararat, mount ararat*, of hundreds, maybe even thousands, of Oldsquaw (for that was their official name back when we were kids; today, they are Long-tailed Ducks) gabbling among the ice-flows drifting north on the inexorable currents of the mighty Niagara River was a never-ending source of fascination.

Later, while attending college, I launched on a decades-long quest to see and band all the boreal birds of New York's Adirondack Park. Every social and professional group has their own jargon, and in the world of bird-banding, "fondle" was an accepted term for banding birds (as in "I fondled twenty birds today" or "I banded twenty birds today"). By the time I left the Adirondacks in 2002, my life fondle-list had included Spruce Grouse, Gray Jay, Boreal Chickadee, Olive-sided Flycatcher, Yellow-bellied Flycatcher, Tennessee Warbler, Cape May Warbler, and Bay-breasted Warbler, just to enumerate a few of the 178 species I have banded.

Now that I live in Bar Harbor, I have developed a dual obsession with shorebirds—the sandpipers and plovers—and seabirds—those pelagic species for which you have to search far offshore. Today, I managed to see some of both!

College of the Atlantic's Dr. Sean Todd, Steven K. Katona Chair in Marine Sciences and director of Allied Whale, had requested my pair of eyes on their team of observers conducting whale surveys. To sweeten the deal, he dangled the carrot of encouraging me to multi-task by conducting seabird surveys at the same time. (Distribution at sea of seabirds is among the most poorly understood of any order of birds, so any time I am on a boat, I undertake surveys, counting the birds in a methodical manner. And the best way to aggregate and share this data is through the citizen science eBird portal.)

Go on a boat ride? Offshore? All day? YOU BETCHA!

Well, today was that day!

At 8:17 a.m., the lines were cast and we set off on College of the Atlantic's forty-six-foot research and support vessel, m/v *Osprey*. First stop, Mount Desert Rock, twenty-five nautical miles[i] south of the college's campus, out in the open Gulf of Maine. The college acquired the three-acre island and all the facilities—a seventy-foot lighthouse, a lightkeepers' house, and a boathouse—from the U.S. Coast Guard in 1996. This is now the base for College of the Atlantic's offshore marine operations.

8:59 a.m.   *En route* to the Rock, as Mount Desert Rock is affectionately known by those associated, I undertook fifteen-minute transect surveys (this is one standard methodology for seabird surveys). With time fixed and distance easily calculated thanks to the modern convenience of GPS, we have the precise statistical ability to estimate birds per unit area.

Mostly we were seeing Herring Gulls, along with some Great Black-backed Gulls. During the fifteen-minute survey midway on our trip to the Rock, an immature Northern Gannet breezed by. While not a new species for my Little Big Year, they are among my favorite birds (remember, there is one in the logo of my business, The Natural History Center).

Gannets and gulls are large birds with wingspans in excess of four feet. I had to remind myself to recalibrate my observations to take in smaller birds (think swallow size). When I did, I saw a small, black bird, its erratic flight must surely be the avian equivalent of dancing.

Wilson's Storm-Petrels are one of the tubenoses. This is not a true family of birds; rather, it is an assemblage of birds among a number of families all sharing a particular physiological adaptation to their marine environment: a large, nostril-like conduit atop their bills that is less an olfactory organ and more part of their salt-regulation system.

The metabolisms of all organisms need freshwater. At sea, this can be a significant hurdle to overcome. But overcome it they have. Tubenoses, including storm-petrels (which have a particularly prominent—for their bill size—tube), can drink briny oceanic water directly. Their kidneys take a first stab at filtering out the salt from the water. A nasal salt gland, located at the back of their head, finishes the job. The end result is straight H_2O for the birds and a viscous sodium solution dripping steadily out of their tube and down the tip of their bill.

In the northwest Atlantic, there are two species of storm-petrels and I was on the lookout for both. Wilson's Storm-Petrel is, by far, the more common. In fact, it is so common that College of the Atlantic's Dr. John Anderson once proclaimed it the most abundant bird species on Earth. In hindsight, he may have been referring collectively to all twenty-eight species of storm-petrel.

This South Atlantic breeder comes north for the austral winter. When you see a storm-petrel in the northwest Atlantic, the vast majority of the time it is a Wilson's Storm-Petrel. Our locally breeding storm-petrel, Leach's, is much less frequently seen, but more on that shortly.

While watching the storm-petrels, two larger—much larger—petrels (or shearwaters, for petrels and shearwaters are essentially the same thing) flew past. The first was a Great Shearwater. It glided by, black-capped, the wingtips of its forty-four-inch span grazing the water's surface, effortlessly banking in its pursuit of a meal. Close on its tail was a slightly smaller Sooty Shearwater, perhaps drafting the larger bird (the way bicycle racers do, or even Canada Geese when flying in their trademark "V" formation).

With something like eighty-three species of petrels and shearwaters—and this does not include the storm-petrels, diving-petrels, giant-petrels, or even the albatross—our task is made easier by the fact that we only have four shearwater species that frequent our waters.

Like storm-petrels, shearwaters and petrels are tubenoses. Unlike storm-petrels, shearwaters and petrels are in a different family, the Procellariidae (fulmar are in this family, too).

As wonderful as it was to see a Great Shearwater, you might not want to get too close. As a means of self-defense, they can eject a foul-smelling oil from their tube. I wonder if my father, Joel Mac-Donald, experienced that.

Back in 2002, my father was on his way to meet Natalie and me during our Gulf of Maine Expedition, a five-month educational sea kayak adventure we undertook to raise awareness about issues facing the coastal communities of this vast, international watershed. The day before he met us, he went on a Zodiac whale-watch tour out of

Nova Scotia's Digby Peninsula. The Zodiac paused to watch several critically endangered North Atlantic Right Whales. A Great Shearwater was flying its back and forth pattern as it searched for food, getting closer and closer to the Zodiac. At one point, flying close—too close, it turns out—to the boat, it flew smack dab into my father's chest, then flopped over in the bottom of the boat. Great Shearwaters need a long runway to take off, so this bird was stranded. Fortunately, the guide picked up the wayward bird and set it in the water, but no mention was ever made of a foul-smelling oil being ejected.

Sooty Shearwaters are easily identified, being all dark brown, trending almost to black, with white linings in the underwing (much in the manner of the American Black Duck). Whereas the Great Shearwater is relatively common in the Gulf of Maine during the southern winter, the Sooty is far less common in these parts. So, when an all-dark shearwater hove into view, I was excited to tick this bird.

Sooty Shearwaters had their fifteen minutes of fame (okay, maybe it was like fifteen seconds) in the 2011 movie, *The Big Year*, starring comedic actors Jack Black, Owen Wilson, and Steve Martin. In the opening sequence, showing an improbability (for that is the collective term for a group of shearwaters) of Sooty Shearwaters, Brad Harris (played by Jack Black) says, "Take the little Sooty Shearwater of Tasmania, for example. Before setting out on its first migration to Hawaii, he has to shed half of his body weight[ii]." That is just a tiny piece of this fantastic flier's life story.

9:28 a.m.   As we continued on our way to the Rock, during this fifteen-minute observation period we had a mess of ten Wilson's Storm-Petrels. Flitty in their flight, almost butterfly like, with a squared tail and obvious white rump, they are readily identifiable. Still, I look at every one, hoping for something slightly different.

Soon enough, I saw the stiffer-winged flight of a Leach's Storm-Petrel. They are seemingly paler than Wilson's Storm-Petrels and have a unique light-colored patterning in the wings, a tail that is obviously forked, and significantly less white on its rump, all field marks useful in identifying this species.

Leach's Storm-Petrels nest on coastal islands in both the North Atlantic and North Pacific. Being small, they are readily preyed upon by the larger seabirds, especially gulls and skuas. To get around this, both male and female Leach's Storm-Petrels evolved the habit of foraging far offshore by day, sometimes up to well over 100 miles from their nesting islands, returning only at night to incubate their eggs or feed their young, secure deep in nesting burrows.

I think a life at sea is ideal. Surely it must agree with these seven-inch-long birds with an eighteen-inch wingspan, too, as they can live up to an average of twenty years (the record is thirty-six).

9:44 a.m.   Moored at Mount Desert Rock, Captain Toby Stephenson orchestrated operations, sending supplies to shore while picking up a few of the island's staff to help in the whale survey. With all hands on deck, this meant scanning for telltale blows, or spouts, as we described miles-long straight-line transects. Each transect was parallel to the other, separated by one nautical mile. This distance is such that any spouts spied by an astute observer overlaps between transects. Simultaneously, I kept on with my bird surveys.

I was pleasantly surprised to see a Merlin perched on the western corner of the light-keepers house—it seemed a long way offshore for this small falcon. Then, a lone Razorbill quickly flew by, too-small wings whirring fast just to keep the bird airborne. A careful scan of the roosting and nesting gulls turned up a Lesser Black-backed Gull. The birds I was most interested in, though, were a small group of six skittish Red-necked Phalarope.

These guys are pelagic (among birders and ornithologists, "pelagic" means offshore, far offshore) shorebirds. Although it sounds like something of an oxymoron, phalaropes are, indeed, in the sandpiper family. And they do spend most of their lives offshore. Like any other seabird, they readily sit on the water, capable of moving about with their semipalmated, or partially webbed, feet (they will also perch on flotsam or jetsam). And like any seabird, they generally only come to land to nest.

By the time I normally see Red-necked Phalaropes in the Gulf of Maine, their plumage is eclipsing, molting into their drabber winter feathers, so I rarely see them with their eponymous red throat. These little birds with a nearly needle-thin bill breed in the high Arctic. Contrary to the overwhelming majority of North American birds, the female Red-necked Phalarope is the one with the showy plumage. Females are the aggressors, fighting for the privilege to mate; and once their eggs are laid, they take off to entice another male, leaving the initial male to incubate and raise her young, traits exactly the opposite of warblers.

10:07 a.m. Not long after departing the Rock, a Cory's Shearwater hove into view. These are always uncommon in the Gulf of Maine, preferring warmer waters, but not so much that we are surprised to find them. With global warming raising temperatures of the waters of the Gulf of Maine, we are finding them increasingly often.

I have long contended that Cory's Shearwater should have been named Great Shearwater as they are the largest of the North American shearwaters (of course, we would have to come up with an alternate name for the bird bearing this moniker). Among the many fascinating facts relating to this family, shearwaters have an organ called a proventriculus, a sort of reservoir just above their stomach, to store fish oil. This oil is dense in protein, a vital source of energy for a bird that flies nearly all the time. Granted, all of the shearwaters, petrels, and albatross have the ability to lock their wings in place, fully extended, requiring virtually no energy to subtly maneuver their flight feathers to make course corrections. Still, having a ready supply of reserve energy is never a bad thing.

11:22 a.m. As the *Osprey* continued working our way west and I continued with my bird surveys, we came upon an improbability of

Great Shearwaters. Twenty-eight, to be exact. Flying among them was a much smaller bird, all dark above and all white below. A Manx Shearwater!

This is a species that historically bred almost exclusively in burrows on islands in European waters, especially those around the United Kingdom and Ireland. Over time, it has expanded its range. Since 1973, there have been small breeding colonies ranging from Newfoundland to Massachusetts, including the first confirmed breeding and fledging of a Manx Shearwater in Maine in 2009 on Matinicus Island!

11:37 a.m.   During this observation period, three good-sized birds approached the *Osprey* from behind. My first clue to their identification was that they were all dark above and mottled dark below. The real telltale sign, though, was the prominent patch of white at the base of their primary flight feathers. Right off the bat, I knew these were jaegers (they were too small to be skuas, although both jaegers and skuas share the Genus *Stercorarius*). So, I looked to their definitive field marks: their tails.

One was clearly larger overall than the others. Its tail was showing the two central tail feathers beginning to emerge beyond the others, but very rounded. The other two birds showed a similar tail feather development except that they were clearly pointed.

Very exciting! The larger bird, the one with the rounded tail feathers beginning to protrude, was a Pomarine Jaeger; the other two were Parasitic Jaegers.

Jaeger comes from the German for hunter and the Pomarine Jaeger is that, a hunter. At sea, these deep-chested birds with powerful flight musculature can overtake most any seabird. They harass, even attack, smaller seabirds. The smaller seabirds then give up their catch or risk becoming the jaeger's next meal.

Parasitic Jaegers are kleptoparasites. Unlike another kleptoparasite, the Brown-headed Cowbird, who plants its eggs in the nests of other birds, the Parasitic Jaeger steals food from other birds.

4:00 p.m.   The day's trip proved to be of mixed results. For me, it was a success! I was ecstatic, having added nine pelagic species to my Little Big Year tally. Unfortunately, for the whale survey crew, it was a bust. We saw loads of Harbor Seals and Gray Seals and Atlantic White-sided Dolphins, but no large whales. Throwing in the towel, we worked our way back toward the Rock.

During this observation period, a lone Northern Fulmar made an appearance. Fulmars can be confusing as they come in a variety of color morphs, ranging from almost gull-white to a sooty-dark. Fortunately, they all have a unique deep-chested, stiff-winged appearance differentiating them from gulls. To top it off, though, the ends of their primary flight feathers often show white, a sort of "window," almost jaeger-like.

There are two fulmars species globally: the Northern Fulmar in the north latitudes and the Southern Fulmar of the Southern Ocean (I have been fortunate enough to see both!). Northern Fulmars were long known by whalers for following ships and eating offal. As a breeding bird, they do not become sexually mature until they are eight to ten years old, sometimes even much older. Banding records from Scotland show fulmars living to be up to fifty years old! Today, the nearest breeding Northern Fulmar is in the Witless Bay Ecological Reserve in Bay Bulls, Newfoundland, south of St. John's.

4:49 p.m.   The last bird to be added to my Little Big Year list for the day was found on Mount Desert Rock.

Back at the Rock once again, I was able to go ashore where I connected with Nathan Dubrow, a College of the Atlantic student going into his second year. He has spent the summer on the Rock. And man-o-man, did he ever rack up an impressive list of birds for a tiny island twenty-five nautical miles from the mainland! (In a subsequent conversation with Nathan, I learned that over two seasons on the Rock, he tallied 168 species of birds!)

In his typically laconic fashion, the first thing he uttered to me was two words: "Lark Sparrow." We quickly made our way to the lone patch of *Rosa rugosa*, or Seaside Rose. Nathan started a lip-smacking pishing that immediately attracted a Song Sparrow. With just a little patience, the chestnut-cheeked Lark Sparrow popped up, perching very cooperatively on a rocky outcrop, in perfect sunlight, posing, turning, affording excellent photographic opportunities.

Through recent studies, we are learning how important offshore islands are to both migratory birds and vagrants, such as this Lark Sparrow. What this little brown bird, normally found from the Mississippi Valley west to the Pacific, was doing all the way east on Mount Desert Rock is anyone's guess, but they do show up, with annual regularity, in Maine. And often on offshore islands. I'm just glad this one showed up when and where it did. Thank you, little buddy.

7:27 p.m.   Our long day over, we were docked once again at the College of the Atlantic pier. For me, any day on the water is a good day, and this had been an incredible day! We were out at the time of year when the most procellariids are visiting the Gulf of Maine. This was not the first time I hit a home run with shearwaters and storm-petrels, but that is by no means the norm. I was particularly excited to have picked up all seven I hoped to find for the entire year! One Jaeger would have been a treat; the second was a real bonus. The one or two Lark Sparrow reports we get annually in Maine are usually far from Hancock County. And when we do get them, they are usually from an offshore island such as Mount Desert Rock. Lastly, I was pleased to have contributed so many seabird surveys to the eBird database.

Yes, this was about as good as a day of birding gets in my book.

Today's birds of the year:

233. Wilson's Storm-Petrel
234. Great Shearwater
235. Sooty Shearwater
236. Leach's Storm-Petrel
237. Red-necked Phalarope
238. Cory's Shearwater

239. Manx Shearwater
240. Pomarine Jaeger
241. Parasitic Jaeger
242. Northern Fulmar
243. Lark Sparrow

Monday, 23 July

As part of their Summer Programs, College of the Atlantic has a wonderful offering: Family Nature Camp. For more than a decade now, I have had the great pleasure of being one of the leaders at Family Nature Camp, sharing my passion for everything in the natural world with multiple generations of campers.

Think of the camps many of us went to as children. If you went to camp along the Maine coast, it may well have included activities such as sunrise birding to hear the dawn chorus, maybe even seeing a Barred Owl or three; hiking up a mountain to learn about alpine ecology; tide-pooling along the rocky coastline; and canoeing and kayaking. Now, imagine this camp except that it is for the entire family: kids, moms, dads, even grandparents are welcome.

1:30 p.m.   Today, we launched our sea kayaks from the college's beach. In our five tandems and three solos, we paddled to the west end of Bar Island, around its north shore, crossed to Sheep Porcupine Island, getting just beyond it as far as green bell number seven between Sheep Porcupine Island and Burnt Porcupine Island. With a freshening breeze coming out of the southwest, we retraced our route back to the college.

During our paddle, we tallied thirteen species of birds, including typical waterbirds such as Herring Gull, Great Black-backed Gull, and Double-crested Cormorant. Although the Bald Eagles we saw were likely the pair nesting on Sheep Porcupine Island, and therefore it was no surprise to see them in this area, they were a highlight of the paddle. Turkey Vultures, once rare in Maine, are now commonplace. While watching several circling over Bar Harbor, I imagined a Gary Larson-esque cartoon with Turkey Vultures swirling, anticipating a tourist keeling over and hence a fresh meal. American Crows were foraging in the intertidal zone. Two Common Ravens glided high overhead, their wedge-shaped tail visually separating them from their smaller, square-tailed cousins. Black-capped Chickadees and Black-throated Green Warblers were voluble enough to be heard, even above the din of our group of enthusiastic paddlers.

Some form of migration is underway nearly year-round. And for shorebirds—sandpipers and plovers—who have to contend with a very short Arctic summer in which to court, mate, tend eggs, and fledge young, getting out before the snow flies is a very real concern. Of course, we were a bit early for that. So, in this case, the shorebirds we saw were likely those unsuccessful in their attempts at attracting a mate.

This would likely be true of the five Semipalmated Sandpipers we observed. Meanwhile, the three Spotted Sandpipers working the shoreline, tails perpetually bobbing, were almost certainly local birds as they are one of the few shorebirds that nest in Maine.

A lone Red Knot was mixed in with the Semipalms. Red Knots are famous for their big migrations and their habit of amassing on the banks of Chesapeake Bay, especially in and around Delaware, where they gorge themselves on Horseshoe Crab eggs, fattening up for migration. They are, perhaps, equally infamous for their significant population crash, a direct result of our over-harvesting Horseshoe Crabs—fewer Horseshoe Crabs means fewer Horseshoe Crab eggs and thus, less essential food to fuel Red Knot migration—and habitat conversion on their Tierra del Fuegan wintering grounds in southernmost South America.

On the return trip, I steered us to quickly circumnavigate the rocky ledge between Bar Island and Sheep Porcupine Island, a place where I regularly see shorebirds. Good thing! We saw a lone, large, stout shorebird with an unusually long bill. A Short-billed Dowitcher!

Its name, dowitcher, may come as a reference to its sewing-machine like manner of feeding, rapidly sticking its bill in marine sediment and pulling it out with equal rapidity. Perhaps this manner of feeding reminded some early naturalists of a dowager (an elderly widow) sewing in her parlor.

The name Short-billed Dowitcher, especially in comparison to Long-billed Dowitcher, is a bit misleading: the former's bill is short, and that by a very little bit, only in comparison to the latter. It is amazing to think that the nest of the Short-billed Dowitcher was not officially discovered by naturalists until the 1950s. That gives me hope that there are still interesting things to find in the natural world.

Today's birds of the year:

244. Red Knot   245. Short-billed Dowitcher

Friday, 27 July

My last Family Nature Camp tide-pool tour of the season was a bit sad. I derive great satisfaction sharing my love for, and knowledge of, the natural world with people eager to learn. Without exception, participants in College of the Atlantic's Family Nature Camp are just that: eager to learn. Alas, it will be another year before I see many of these families again.

3:16 p.m.   Low tide at the Bar Harbor gravel bar was forecast for 5:13 p.m. With the tide going out, we followed, working our way lower and lower into the intertidal zone as more and more of the bar was exposed (for about two hours either side of low tide, you can walk the third of a mile across to Bar Island). Many of the kids seemed to feel a gravitational attraction to the stone wall of the Harborside Hotel shoreline. In so doing, they inadvertently flushed one of my favorite birds: a Ruddy Turnstone!

A long, chattering alarm call, suggestive of turnstone, was enough for me to drop my dip net and raise my binoculars to the fleeing suspect. You could almost call it "piebald" (typically meaning patches of contrasting colors, usually black and white), except it has three primary colors instead of two: black and white forward parts and white belly bracket chestnut wings (oh, and let us not forget the nearly Day-Glo red legs). I enjoy this bird so much that I have carved from wood and painted more of these birds than any other species.

Of the 350 or so species of shorebirds worldwide, there are only two turnstones: the more cosmopolitan Ruddy Turnstone and the Black Turnstone of Alaska. Ruddy Turnstones can be found on six of the seven continents (who knows, with global warming, they may even turn up in Antarctica one day). In the Americas, they breed in the high Arctic and winter on both North American coasts from the continental United States to northern South America.

Ruddy Turnstones are born precocial and ready to take their first flight at about nineteen days of age. When they migrate, it is all by instinct. The adults leave before the fledglings, so the juvenile birds have to figure it out on their own. With Ruddy Turnstones living to be about sixteen years old, they have plenty of time to figure it out.

Today's bird of the year:

246. Ruddy Turnstone

Monday, 30 July

This week, I was leading a special College of the Atlantic program—Downeast Expedition—and today was the first of a weeklong series of adventures. Over the years, I have had the privilege of working with the college in a variety of capacities, including associate professor, mentor, friend, and instructor in their Summer Field Studies and Family Nature Camp. Downeast Expedition, being a new program, only had six people: two families, one with children. The upside was that they received loads more personalized attention; the downside was that with so few people, the college might not offer the program again next year.

Today, we drove the hour to Winter Harbor, on the eastern side of Frenchman Bay. In Maine, the locals say, "Yuh cahn't get they-uh from hee-uh." This is particularly true when you can stand in Bar Harbor, look the six or so miles across the bay at Winter Harbor, but have to drive forty-one miles around, an hour's drive time, to board the forty-foot *Tricia Clark*, the oldest puffin tour boat in Maine....

For over forty years, the *Tricia Clark* was the boat used by Barna Norton to take groups of birders to Machias Seal Island to see Atlantic Puffins. The island is in an area known as the "Gray Zone" as it is claimed by both the United States and Canada. For decades, Norton would land his tours on the island, proclaiming it American territory. There are stories that circulate of how Norton would plant the American flag to further lend credence to his claim of American sovereignty over the island. However, since at least the early 1830s, the island has been home to a variety of lighthouses, all staffed by Canadian lightkeepers. To this very day, Canadian lightkeepers rotate year-round for two-week stints on Machias Seal Island. With fishermen from both countries fishing the Gray Zone, resolving its political status has not been in anyone's interest as there will only be one winner and one very definite loser—the losing country instantly loses access to some very productive lobster fishing grounds. The result: neither country has pushed the issue. The Gray Zone and Machias Seal Island remain one of North America's only disputed border zones and may not ever get resolved.

… While the *Tricia Clark* is the oldest puffin tour boat in Maine, maybe even on the Atlantic seaboard, nowadays it is operated by a brand new company: Winter Harbor Puffin Cruise. We left the protected confines of Winter Harbor, making our way south through Frenchman Bay, along the west side of the Schoodic Peninsula. Rounding the peninsula, we passed Schoodic Island with its colony of ground-nesting Double-crested Cormorants. (This is the same island where Kyle Lima and I observed my first Snowy Owl of the year back on 20 January.) From there, we continued east toward Petit Manan Island, which is part of the Maine Coastal Islands National Wildlife Refuge.

The refuge was created for the birds (and pupping seals, too, but it is the birds in which we were most interested today). Petit Manan Island has a 123-foot-tall lighthouse, the second tallest in Maine[i]. The island is an important nesting site for Common Murre, Razorbill, Black Guillemot, Atlantic Puffin, Laughing Gull, Herring Gull, Great Black-backed Gull, Common Tern, Arctic Tern, and the Federally-listed endangered Roseate Tern.

10:03 a.m.   Heading east of Schoodic Island, approximately one nautical mile, a smallish gull was floating on the water. A blackish smudge behind the eye clearly identified it as one of the so-called "black-headed" gulls, albeit an immature bird (hence, the head has not yet attained its black hood). My initial impression was Laughing Gull, but hearkening the words of my longtime late mentor, Mike Peterson ("You have to look at every bird"), I looked again, this time even more carefully.

Yes, there was a distinct smudge behind the eye. An additional dark mark above the eye on an otherwise all-white head was noteworthy. Legs, feet, and bill were on the reddish end of the spectrum. Back and wings were the paler gray of the Herring Gull floating nearby, but this bird was visibly smaller. As we approached, the bird took flight, affording me a clearer view of the wings. The bottom side of the primary flight feathers, or primaries, those long feathers at the end of the wings, was black. Finally, I observed a black band on the tail. Put all of these field marks together and the bird was identifiable as not just one of the "black-headed" gulls, but as THE Black-headed Gull.

Actually, the name is a bit of a misnomer. If you look closely, it is apparent that the hood of the adult Black-headed Gull is actually more of a dark chocolate brown. It is a small gull, though, smaller than Laughing Gull, closer in size to Bonaparte's Gull. Long a European Gull, a nest was found in Newfoundland in 1977. Since then, their North American population has been slowly increasing.

So, the lesson when looking at black-headed gulls, know your field marks and look at every, single, one.

Today's bird of the year:

247. Black-headed Gull

Monday, 20 August

Early in our relationship, Natalie shared her dream of a major kayak expedition. On 04 May 2002, we embarked on the Gulf of Maine Expedition, paddling sea kayaks around the perimeter of the Gulf of Maine on a five-month educational adventure. What an amazing experience! This was the realization of a childhood dream. Few things make me happier than being on an epic journey, exploring wild landscapes, camping every night, with my best friend, travel buddy, and the love of my life.

It was during the course of the Gulf of Maine Expedition, traveling slowly, all senses alive with the sights, sounds, smells, tactile sensations, and tastes, intimately connecting us to our environs, that we began hatching the vision that would grow into The Natural History Center. Now, years later, I run The Natural History Center whose mission is making the natural world accessible through experiential opportunities in the field.

As much as I enjoy—no, love—what I do, it is not all asters and daisies. One pitfall of running such a business, where our tour season coincides with Anouk's summer vacation, is that it is always challenging to take time off during the summer. In this the ninth year of our business, we committed to a few days' vacation. With Anouk in her tweens, we set aside a three-day weekend for a kayaking trip among the islands of the Deer Isle archipelago. As an added bonus, my cousin Hannah and her partner Tyler joined us.

20 August

We launched our kayaks at Old Quarry Ocean Adventures, a truly wonderful campground nestled within the spruce forest on the east side of Webb Cove in the town of Stonington. Stonington is set in a landscape surrounded by hundreds of glacially carved islands steeped in a history of excavating granite. We then paddled out to Maine Coast Heritage Trust's Saddleback Island to set up base camp for the next three days and two nights.

Today, the third day of our trip, we took one final circuitous paddle among the islands on our way back to Webb Cove and Old Quarry Ocean Adventures. During the course of a leisurely four hours and six miles of paddling, we tallied forty-five species of birds, ten of which were shorebirds. From the end of July through August and September, shorebirds are regular, if not abundant, visitors to this region, as well as the broader coast of northeastern North America, as they wing their way south.

It is easy to state that the avian highlight of this tour was the shorebirds. At first, we heard the sweet call notes of Semipalmated Sandpipers flitting by us in twos and threes, wings beating in the rapid flight so typical of the small, "peep" sandpipers. There were large Black-bellied Plovers, a few still retaining their namesake black bellies, visible as the stockiest, if not the largest, of the day's shorebirds. Semipalmated Plovers worked the rocky shorelines. Least Sandpipers lived down to their name as the smallest of the "peeps." Spotted Sandpipers sometimes cried their two-note calls of alarm; other times, they teeter-tottered along the shoreline in their unique manner. The rapid, three-note *tew tew tew* of Greater Yellowlegs were occasionally joined by the two-note *tew tew* of Lesser Yellowlegs. Distant groups in the tens and twenties of small shorebirds were too far removed to identify as anything but "peep *sp.*" in my eBird checklist. All of these contributed to the day's total of well over 300 individual shorebirds; maybe not a huge number but far more than I typically see in a year in Bar Harbor, Mount Desert Island, and Acadia National Park combined.

8:45 a.m.   Hell's Half Acre is a small island nestled within a few hundred feet of the northern arc of Devil Island. (There has to be some interesting history to those names, don't you think?) Tide was draining with dead low tide forecast for 11:19 a.m. Significant amounts of intertidal beach were exposed, largely made up of shell ground by wave action over years innumerable.

A group of twenty Black-bellied Plover were working the intertidal zone, foraging for their varied diet of marine invertebrates of the wormy sort. I derive no end of pleasure from watching the antics of shorebirds and so raised my waterproof Opticron Savanna 8x32 binoculars from their secure home nestled in the top of my Kōkatat Guide life-jacket to watch. With their scurrying, feeding, and occasional nervous fluttering, I eventually observed that one of these was not like the others.

Not dissimilar in size, this bird had a warmer cast to it, less well-defined breast markings, and a prominent pale eyestripe. It took me a few moments to sort through my mental key to come up with American Golden-Plover. American Golden-Plover! This is a bird I see infrequently, sometimes going years between sightings. It makes sense since most of my birding is in New England and Atlantic Canada and the migration route of the American Golden-Plover has it traveling north and south each year through the middle third of North America. In the world of shorebirds, American Golden-Plovers have one of the longest migrations of any shorebird. They breed in the high Arctic and winter on the grasslands of southern South America.

Several hours later, returning to Webb Cove at the close of our paddling day, I could see a good number of shorebirds working the mudflats near a derrick abandoned these many decades. Black-bellied Plover were easy to pick out, as were Greater Yellowlegs. Once again, I scanned the foraging birds for the pure joy of watching them. One bird stood out as being bigger, stockier, and having a slightly recurved, or upward curving, bill. A godwit! But which one?

Looking through my binoculars, the bill clearly had a darker tip and a more orangey-yellow base. The uniformly colored underparts marked it a juvenile bird. When it flew, startled—perhaps by its shadow, maybe by the clanging machinery of the nearby lobster processing facility, or, who knows, it could have seen an alien spaceship—it flew briefly, only to quickly settle down once again. Whatever the reason for its brief flight, that was all I needed: in flight, it exhibited dark underwing linings and a white rump: the markings of a Hudsonian Godwit!

In migration from its breeding grounds in the northernmost reaches of North American to the southernmost extent of South America, the Hudsonian Godwit is known to sometimes make nonstop flights of thousands of miles.

Once quite numerous, godwit numbers are now greatly diminished, never having recovered from the pressures of nineteenth-century market hunting coupled with the more recent loss of habitat both along its migration corridor and on its wintering grounds. Seeing any godwit is a real thrill. When we do see a godwit in Maine, it tends to be a Hudsonian.

Today's birds of the year:

248. American Golden-
    Plover

249. Hudsonian Godwit

Saturday, 25 August

Natalie, Anouk, and I are not ones to turn down any opportunity to get out on the water, so when George and Kelly Dickson proffered an invitation for an evening of sailing, food, and games aboard their thirty-five-foot 1978 Ericson 35-2, we jumped at the opportunity. We sailed up Frenchman Bay to anchor off Hancock Point for dinner and board games; then, with the sun setting, sailed south, back toward Bar Harbor.

7:39 a.m.   Halfway through our return run, the setting sun illuminating the western sky with every shade of yellow, the shadow of the Earth darkening the eastern horizon, Natalie stated, in the form of a question to which she already knew the answer, "Is that a Black-crowned Night-Heron?"

Pale underparts, red eye, head capped in black and tucked in, yellow legs barely extending beyond the tail, a squat, stout bird flew toward us, overhead, and then away, off into the distance. This is one of the two typical aspects in which we find the Black-crowned Night-Heron (the other is the compact bird, a statue along a crepuscular shore, waiting to strike at unsuspecting piscine prey).

Perhaps no other writer so clearly evoked an image of the Black-crowned Night-Heron as Arthur Cleveland Bent in his wonderful series *Life Histories of North American Birds*: "How often, in the gathering dusk of evening, have we heard its loud, choking squawk and, looking up, have seen its stocky form, dimly outlined against the gray sky and propelled by steady wing beats, as it wings its way high in the air toward its evening feeding place in some distant pond or marsh!" That was exactly our experience.

Today's bird of the year:

250. Black-crowned Night-Heron

Monday, 27 August

When people think of exploring the saltwater nooks and crannies of the coast of Maine by boat, whether skiff or sailboat or canoe or kayak, they often conjure images of dramatic rocky shorelines, stippled with over 3,000 islands[i], often bought to life through the works of artists such as Hudson River School painters Thomas Cole and Frederick Church.

As a guide of nature and adventure tours, my guests regularly profess their desire to paddle around the nooks and crannies of the Porcupine Islands, the islands sheltering Bar Harbor; however, this area is often at the mercy of afternoon sea breezes, ocean swells, and reflecting and refracting waves, often the result of ocean swells, boat wakes, or a combination thereof. At times, this coastal paddling can be rewarded by encounters with Bald Eagles, Harbor Seals, and Harbor Porpoise. On one occasion, I spied a Humpback Whale! And on at least two others, Minke Whales were only a few paddle-lengths away! As popular as the Porcupine Islands are as a paddling destination, conditions can quickly run afoul of the skills of beginning and intermediate paddlers.

The marine forecast called for a stiff afternoon breeze, so I opted to take my group sea kayaking around the protected waters of Mount Desert Narrows [ii], looking for birds—waders, shorebirds, and gulls—Harbor Porpoise, Harbor Seals, and the wide variety of intertidal life. As we made our way around Thomas Island, a Great Egret worked the shoreline, not far from a Great Blue Heron, exemplifying the size disparity between the two: even though Great Egrets are tall, they are still visibly smaller than the Great Blue Heron. An immature Bald Eagle was shadowing an adult, just south of The Twinnies, begging for food, perhaps not quite ready to truly be off on its own.

To see these three large birds in short succession was to appreciate the fact that these are large birds. Great Blue Herons get to be fifty-four inches tall, have a seventy-nine-inch wingspan (that's just over 6½ feet), and can weigh up to 5½ pounds. That seems surprisingly light for such a big bird. In comparison, the smaller Great Egret stands noticeably shorter at forty-one inches, has a fifty-seven-inch wingspan, and weighs up to two pounds. For a bird (Great Egret) that is ¾ the height of the Great Blue Heron, its mass is less than half. Now, to give a little perspective, Bald Eagles stand up to thirty-eight inches tall, but have an eighty-inch wingspan and can weight up to fourteen pounds. Next time you see a Bald Eagle fly, look at its massive wings and think back on these relative numbers.

11:14 a.m.   On the western side of The Twinnies, Bar Harbor Oyster Company, a small aquaculture farm, provided a great chance to see mariculture up close. Today, the mostly submerged oyster rafts served double-duty as roosting platforms for a host of gulls and cormorants.

A scan of the gulls on the rafts instantly revealed large numbers of Ring-billed and Herring Gulls. Ring-billed Gulls are noticeably smaller than Herring Gulls, a quick identification clue when you see them side by side. Smaller even than the Ring-billed Gulls are Bonaparte's Gulls. The petite Bonaparte's Gulls, with the smudge of black behind their eye denoting the fact that many of them have already molted into winter plumage, were as abundant as their larger cousins. That was not surprising considering that by late July, Bonaparte's Gulls begin queuing up for their southward migration.

As we paddled toward the oyster rafts, only a few Bonaparte's Gulls remained as most took flight. Still, I scanned each and every gull (Mike Peterson, you would be proud). Binoculars up, our momentum slowly carried us forward to within about ten feet of a small gull. At first, I thought it was another Bonaparte's, but then I realized it was smaller yet! But what?

This bird had the black spot behind the eye typical of one of the black-headed gulls in basic, or winter, plumage. However, it retained a dark smudge of a cap on the back half of its head. Bright orangish-red legs were a standout feature. And finally, with wings folded over the back, there was virtually no dark showing on the wingtips. I was leaning toward it being a Little Gull, the smallest gull in the world, but was still not completely confident in the identification. Fortunately, it eventually took wing, revealing dark underwing linings. Little Gull, indeed!

This is another one of those members of the Laridae family that is common to much of Europe and Asia, along with Black-headed Gull and Lesser Black-backed Gull, that has made its way to North America. Although we may have no way of ever knowing if it is truly a native of North America, it was first documented in the Western Hemisphere in 1819 and not discovered nesting until 1962. According to Cornell Lab of Ornithology's All About Birds website[iii], Little Gulls are usually found in ones and twos and threes, often in the company of Bonaparte's Gulls.

Paddling back to our launching site, we discussed the beauty of the day and how we wished we had a modern-day Thomas Cole or Frederick Church with us to capture the light reflecting off the water and onto the islands, perhaps spotlighting one of the day's memorable birds.

Today's bird of the year:

251. Little Gull

Wednesday, 29 August

S ummer is my busiest season. Every day is filled with nature tours, some occasionally several days long. I try my best to work every day from mid-May through mid-October as winter is much leaner in terms of work. Inevitably, once or twice a summer, tours are cancelled last minute. That was the case this morning.

I awoke, fully expecting to be out the door to meet my guests at their hotel at 8:00. Upon arrival, they asked if it would be permissible to cancel as they really wanted a down day. ("Of course, we'll still pay you for the day.")

Yes! Suddenly, I had an unexpected day off. So, I called my friend Ed Hawkes to see if I could coax him—it never takes much—into a social jaunt to look for shorebirds. He is a combination friend, bird-carving mentor, father figure, and just someone I really and truly enjoy spending time with. I was quite pleased to be spending the day with him. With a rising tide predicted to be high at 1:20 p.m., conditions were good for the chance to see shorebirds.

We loaded our spotting scopes and headed to Acadia National Park's Thompson Island. Thompson Island is located at the northern end of Mount Desert Island, just over one mile west of The Twinnies, the area my guests and I paddled yesterday. Other than a few Greater Yellowlegs and some very distant "peep" sandpipers (as well as a bunch of Bonaparte's Gulls), there was little in the way of shorebirds.

Next up, Raccoon Cove and Marlboro Beach. They are in the northwest corner of Frenchman Bay, about five miles from Thompson Island as the Willet flies.

8:48 a.m.   Scanning the length of Raccoon Cove through our spotting scopes, we could see a number of Greater Yellowlegs toward the far side, their brilliant yellow legs making them readily identifiable.

Yellowlegs have long been one of my favorite species. They are not particularly flashy, other than their legs, but they have a musical *tew tew tew* that carries a great distance on the wind. Besides, they are northern breeders . . . and I am drawn to northern climes.

Two birds were standing on a distant rock that was quickly being swallowed by the rising tide. Though one was clearly a Greater Yellowlegs, the other seemed drabber but beefier. Its legs were most certainly not yellow, leaning toward a more grayish color. Its bill was noticeably more robust. The clincher was when tide finally forced it to take flight: a striking white pattern spanning the length of the wings, accompanied by a distinctively raucous call, revealed the bird to be a Willet!

There are many intriguing facts about Willets. It is one of the few shorebirds—along with Killdeer, Piping Plover, Spotted Sandpiper, and Upland Sandpiper—to breed in the State of Maine. When feeling threatened by a potential predator, they will drag a seemingly broken wing, Killdeer style, in effort to lure the antagonist away from their nest. With a bill that is particularly sensitive to finding invertebrate food items buried unseen in the substrate, they can forage day or night.

And, perhaps most relevant to the inducement for writing this book—the 100-year anniversary of the Migratory Bird Treaty Act— Willets have shown a tremendous comeback from decades of market hunting which greatly suppressed their population to alarmingly low numbers. Thank goodness for the foresight of some of our fore-bears.

Today's bird of the year:

252. Willet

Saturday, 01 September

I awoke during the wee hours and decided to step outside to listen (this is something I regularly do). Songbirds, which migrate at night when there are fewer predators to evade, regularly intone various one-note flight calls. Tonight, conditions were good for a night flight: relatively calm, barometer up, a light northerly breeze offering no impediment to the birds' southerly progress. On a clear and calm night such as this, a trained ear can differentiate some of the individuals from the migrating hoards. And with the aid of a bit of technology, even more can be identified.

2:00 a.m.   Outside, laid out on our picnic table, staring heavenward, listening, I was hearing three or four birds calling every minute. That meant that three or four were flying low enough overhead as to be within earshot of where I lay in our dooryard. A few calls were particularly clear, perhaps because they were flying lower than the others. A Swainson's Thrush. A Yellow-rumped Warbler. Most, thirteen, to be exact, were difficult to identify to species....

Since the advent of radar[i], a whole field of study dedicated to night flight has evolved. Radar uses radio waves to determine the position, range, and speed of objects. In its infancy, radar operators sometimes noticed unusual patterns blanketing their displays after dusk. On those occasions, it seemed the nighttime sky was filled with clouds on even the most cloudless of nights. These were discounted as noise but, over time, it was learned that these seemingly anomalous returns were the signature of untold millions of birds taking to the sky to continue their nightly migration.

Although the first published effort to quantify the night flight sounds of songbirds was in 1896, it was not until the latter half of the 1950s that the first truly serious efforts to monitor and understand songbird night flight through their vocalizations[ii] were undertaken. In 1998, the not-for-profit organization Old Bird was created by William R. Evans. Dedicated to this esoteric branch of ornithology, Old Bird has, almost single-handedly, made nocturnal flight call study a twenty-first-century scientific pursuit through the use of computers, homemade microphones, and free software to analyze the nearly indistinguishable chips and chirps of migrating birds. Today, anyone with patience and motivation can identify those species migrating across the sky in the depths of night[iii].

... Lying and listening in the dark from the vantage of our picnic table, the bird that got me excited, though, was the Dickcissel. With something of a synthetic call, almost two notes, it is unmistakable once you learn it. And I just heard one! Although I hear a few every year in migration, Maine is outside its typical range, so I see them far less frequently. It seems there could be a graduate research project somewhere in here as we do identify a good number of them in Maine through their autumnal nocturnal flight calls.

Dickcissels, with plumage reminiscent of a meadowlark, are a large, sparrow-like bird with the core of their breeding range centered in the heartland of the prairie states. According to Breeding Bird Survey data, Dickcissel numbers declined precipitously between 1966 and 1978. Since then, it seems their numbers may have stabilized at this lower number. It is quite possible this is a reflection of dramatic changes in their grassland landscapes that eventually levelled off.

Here in Maine, if you are going to actually get lucky and see one, the best time and place to look is during the fall and winter among large flocks of House Sparrows, especially those congregating on farms.

Today's bird of the year:

253. Dickcissel

Wednesday, 05 September

There are distinct tourist seasons here in coastal Maine. With the summer tourist season—the season when Bar Harbor and Acadia National Park are filled with families on vacation slowing—I resumed offering my Weekly Birding Tours. It may have been a bit early in the fall season as none of my regulars were able to tag along; however, I did have the pleasure of being joined by Richard and Lucie from Québec City. Richard was bilingual and Lucie was a francophone. This was an excellent opportunity for me to practice my French. (Natalie is a native French speaker, what with her Belgian Walloon roots and all; but all-too-often, when I try to speak the romantic language at home, my darling daughter says, "Daddy, please don't speak French, it hurts my ears." *Mes oreilles.* My ears.)

Today we hit a number of my usual seasonal birding hotspots, starting with Acadia National Park's Sieur de Monts Spring. Bird activity was bustling at the parking lot but unexpectedly poor on the Jesup and Hemlock Trails.

8:28 a.m.   The Ocean Drive section of Acadia National Park's Loop Road was also slow., though we did see our first Red-necked Grebe of the season. Several Common Loon offered focus for a good discussion of plumage and life history. Double-crested Cormorants were perched on Old Soaker, wings spread, like John Milton's Satan on a cross. In addition, there were also Black Guillemots, Herring Gulls, and Great Black-backed Gulls to be viewed.

From the vantage of Otter Cliff, a large, deep-winged tern, almost gull-like in flight, flew by at eye level as we were watching the various seabirds. Dark undersurface to the primaries. A shallowly forked tail. The real clincher was the deep red bill. In fact, that field mark alone is enough to easily identify this bird as Caspian Tern, the largest tern in the world!

Their breeding grounds are widely scattered coast to coast. Here in Maine, we see small numbers of Caspian Terns during migration, especially in the fall as they wing their way south from their Newfoundland breeding grounds to their wintering grounds in Florida and the Antilles, both Greater and Lesser.

10:03 a.m.   Our last stop of the morning was at Acadia National Park's Fabbri Picnic Area. This is one of those birding spots that I hesitate to call a hotspot, but when it *is* good, it can be REALLY good. And today was really, REALLY good!

We were struck by the number of birds actively foraging in the upper canopy. That said, the density of the canopy, combined with the birds' rapid movements, made it challenging to identify every last one. And then there was the challenge of getting us all cued on the same bird at the same time.

From the Fabbri parking lot, we walked back into the picnic area. Richard and I were craning out necks, trying to get on one at a time. Meanwhile, Lucie's search of the shrubbier vegetation down low was quickly rewarded with a larger-than-life warbler-type bird: bright yellow chest, uniformly olive-brown back, white belly and vent, distinct eye-ring almost making the bird seem as though it was wearing glasses. Yellow-breasted Chat!

The breeding range of the Yellow-breasted Chat is much to our south, extending north as far as Long Island, New York. This is one of those species that often exhibits post-nesting dispersal—meaning young birds (and sometimes adults, too) strike out in all directions of the compass before beginning their proper autumnal southward sojourn (they also undergo migration overshoot, reaching latitudes well north of their breeding range during spring migration before returning south to environs where they are better expected). We know more than just a few birds do this as Yellow-breasted Chat are found annually here on Mount Desert Island.

Despite being larger than warblers, with a more robust bill, more diverse vocalizations, and some very un-warbler-like behaviors, Yellow-breasted Chats were long lumped within the family of New World Wood-Warblers. Taxonomists have generally been uncomfortable with this positioning in the avian family tree. In 2017, ornithologists finally decided that chats are, in fact, not warblers. To reflect this new thinking about chats, they created a new family—Icteriidae—a family all its own. Do not be confused by the similarity this family name shares with the blackbird family—Icteridae—the two names differ by a single "i". In both cases— Icteriidae and Icteridae—the names derive from ancient Greek meaning "jaundiced one." This is a specific reference to the prominent yellow of both the chat and many of the orioles (which are in the blackbird family).

Further back in the understory, a Blue-gray Gnatcatcher was actively foraging. This tiny songbird is about the size of a kinglet, but with a dull gray cast to it and no obvious markings other than a white eye-ring and a long tail whose outer feathers flash white. As we watched this diminutive bird foraging for insectivorous food, we could see why it is sometimes referred to as the "Little Mockingbird". Though it is substantially smaller than the Northern Mockingbird, it shares a proportionately long tail, elongated body shape, and overall drab gray coloration.

Blue-gray Gnatcatchers are not long-lived (about four years). This little bird is near the bottom of the pecking order and has many obstacles to overcome during its short life. That may explain why they have been documented producing up to seven nests in a season.

Toward the end of our visit to Fabbri, a short and high, sharp call note, almost a *tchak*, had my radar up for an Orange-crowned Warbler. Eventually, we found a relatively nondescript bird in the brushy habitat at the entrance to Fabbri intermittently giving the call that confirmed it as an Orange-crowned Warbler. Despite breeding from Alaska to Labrador, wintering around the southern fringe of the continent from North Carolina south through Florida, down into most of Mexico, and north to northern California, their secretive ways make this one of the most overlooked of North American species.

Songbirds migrate at night and land before sunrise to feed during the day, building energy for the next night's flight. When a weather system drives them to ground is known as a fallout. The last time I saw so many birds at Fabbri, it was clearly a major fallout with hundreds of warblers in the understory shrubbery. Although today wasn't quite that scale, it still merits listing the results from our forty-five minutes of birding in which we tallied thirty-one species, mostly passerines, including fourteen types of warbler:

> Ring-billed Gull
> Herring Gull
> Accipiter *sp.* (our glimpse of this bird was so rapid that we could not narrow it between Cooper's Hawk and Sharp-shinned Hawk)
> Belted Kingfisher
> Downy Woodpecker
> Red-eyed Vireo
> Blue Jay
> American Crow
> Black-capped Chickadee
> Red-breasted Nuthatch
> Blue-gray Gnatcatcher
> Golden-crowned Kinglet
> Gray Catbird
> Cedar Waxwing
> American Goldfinch
> Dark-eyed Junco

Song Sparrow
Yellow-breasted Chat
Black-and-white Warbler
Tennessee Warbler
Orange-crowned Warbler
Common Yellowthroat
American Redstart
Cape May Warbler
Northern Parula
Magnolia Warbler
Black-throated Blue Warbler
Pine Warbler
Yellow-rumped Warbler
Black-throated Green Warbler
Canada Warbler

Not bad for a morning of birding after a night flight that was considered by some experts to be only medium-good, at best.

Today's birds of the year:

254. Caspian Tern
255. Yellow-breasted Chat
256. Blue-gray Gnatcatcher
257. Orange-crowned Warbler

Friday, 14 September

I n the Gulf of Maine, the great whales—Humpback, Fin, and North Atlantic Right—are migratory. They travel between their calving grounds in the warm waters of the lower latitudes to the biologically productive cold waters of the north to feed during the warmer months. Thanks to these gentle giants, an entire whale-watching industry has developed from Cape Cod to Nova Scotia.

The pelagic birding season coincides with the presence of the whales: late May through late October. Few things make me happier than standing on the bow of a ship, land a sliver on the horizon (if it is even visible at all), scanning from starboard to port looking for phalaropes, skuas, jaegers, murres, razorbills, puffins, kittiwakes, terns, storm-petrels, fulmars, and shearwaters. In coastal Maine, a good day of pelagic birding can easily yield fifteen species.

Nine months into my Little Big Year, I have managed to whittle down my pelagic wish-list: Razorbill, Black-legged Kittiwake, and Atlantic Puffin, all in January; Dovekie and Thick-billed Murre in February; and Common Murre in March; all from shore. A pelagic trip with College of the Atlantic in July more than doubled my list of pelagic species, adding Red-necked Phalarope, Pomarine Jaeger, Parasitic Jaeger, Wilson's Storm-Petrel, Leach's Storm-Petrel, North-ern Fulmar, Great Shearwater, Sooty Shearwater, Cory's Shearwater, and Manx Shearwater.

That did not leave many pelagic species to find, but I was still seeking Red Phalarope, Great Skua, and South Polar Skua. With fall rapidly approaching, every opportunity for me to get out on a boat or ship meant finding me glued to the rail, binoculars poised, looking for those elusive remaining target birds.

On Tuesday, 11 September, I boarded the m/s *Victory II*, a 200-passenger cruise-ship, in Bar Harbor. For the next eight days aboard, I would be working as a naturalist and lecturer. We cruised to Halifax, Nova Scotia, then returned to Bar Harbor for the day today before continuing to southern New England. What a pleasure to not only work on a small ship, but for part of that voyage to steam through Hancock County waters, a corner of the world I know so well.

5:45 a.m.   The sun was just beginning to lighten the eastern sky. Having crossed the Gulf of Maine overnight, from Nova Scotia to Maine, we approached Frenchman Bay and Bar Harbor. Although sunrise was not until 6:10 a.m., nautical twilight[i] at 5:06 a.m. began making the horizon discernable and civil twilight at 5:41 a.m. allows for enough light to make objects visible and identifiable.

The first birds we saw were a number of Northern Gannets, flying at all altitudes, mostly well above the sea surface, wings stiff and minimal flapping. Conversely, an even greater number of Great Shearwaters glided low, hugging the surface. A few Great Black-backed Gulls and a lone Double-crested Cormorant almost completed the morning's list.

By 7:00 a.m., about fifteen miles from Bar Harbor, a lone seabird crossed our bow. Dark wings with significant white patches displaying at the base of the primaries marked the bird as a member of the genus *Stercorarius*. A large, stocky bird with deep, powerful flight. Tail short, somewhat wedge-shaped. Head and underparts a uniform pale brown-gray. South Polar Skua! All these field marks helped differentiate this South Polar Skua, with its strongly contrasting body and wings, from the more uniform brown of the Great Skua.

South Polar Skua have a migration the reverse of the typical North American birds we are more familiar with. After courting, mating, and nesting in the Antarctic, they wander widely, with unknown numbers[ii] frequenting the North Atlantic during the austral winter. South Polar Skuas are typical of the skua and jaeger family, using their powerful chest musculature to rapidly chase down other seabirds to steal food. If you ever make it to the nesting grounds of the South Polar Skua, be sure to protect your noggin or you may end up with a rap to the head you will not quickly forget as they do their best to chase you away. (I share this warning from direct experience!)

That evening. . . .

6:33 p.m.   I have to say, it always feels a bit incongruous to arrive in Bar Harbor via ship, spend the day, and then leave. This is my home, after all! This time, though, leaving on a ship afforded me yet another opportunity to look for pelagic seabirds. With sunset a mere fifteen minutes away, I spent half an hour affixed to the bow, beginning as soon as we left the mouth of Frenchman Bay and headed out into the open Gulf of Maine.

Great Black-backed Gulls were the commonest species as we steamed away from Bar Harbor. Two sparrow-sized Wilson's Storm-Petrels worked a windrow looking for food. Great Shearwaters skimmed the water, banking low, subtly dragging wingtips, shearing water. A lone, immature Northern Gannet soared on unflapping wings like a giant white cross in the sky.

For me, though, the avian highlight had to be the four Red Phalaropes feeding along a deep-current upwelling (they eclipsed my usually-favorite Northern Gannet as the highlight because they added a species to my Little Big Year). These small sandpipers—one of our two truly pelagic sandpipers—were swimming in small circles, stirring up marine invertebrates from just a few inches deep; a delectable meal if you are a phalarope. Even though Red Phalaropes are small (they get to nearly nine inches in length), they are the largest of the phalaropes. These birds had already molted their breeding plumage, leaving a monochrome palette of whites and grays with accents of blacks.

In most avian species, the breeding plumage of males tend to be the more brilliant. Not so in Red Phalaropes, here it is the females. During the breeding season, females are the aggressors, fighting for the males. And once they have claimed their mate, paired, and laid eggs, they bid *adieu* and, quite literally, fly off in pursuit of another male to start the process all over. (If this sounds familiar, it is because this set of facts are the same with Red-necked Phalaropes.)

Today's birds of the year:

258. South Polar Skua   259. Red Phalarope

Thursday, 11 October

I finally returned home after nearly a month working as a naturalist aboard the two Victory Cruise Lines ships: m/s *Victory I* along the New England and Canadian Maritime coasts and then m/s *Victory II* plying the Great Lakes. I was ecstatic to see my family and return to my Little Big Year in earnest. The low overcast and drizzle imparted the sky with the dusky hue of sunset, still an hour-and-a-half hence.

3:23 p.m.   An hour previous, my flight from Chicago had landed at Bangor International Airport. Now, driving south from Ellsworth on Route 3, upon reaching the midpoint of the causeway between the mainland and my home turf of Mount Desert Island[i], I took my ritual deep, cleansing breath, as though passing through a holistic door into clearer skies and cleaner air. I was home!

Caught in the slow-moving leaf-peeper traffic heading onto the island, the draining tide not quite to the midpoint, I chanced a quick glance to the still-mostly-filled saltwater pool between Acadia National Park's Thompson Island and Mount Desert Island proper. Three ducks floated in an undefined formation. Small ducks. Long tails erect. Continuing south, it took a moment for these ducks to fully register. Small! Long tails erect! Where the road forks at the Steamboat Landing Sunoco station, I made a U-turn to retrace my path and check out those ducks.

Ruddy Ducks!

Well past breeding plumage, these now-drab birds still had a defining bold, white cheek patch. Ruddy Ducks are well distributed across North America, largely below the forty-fifth parallel (although the breeding range does stretch up into pockets of Alaska). In any plumage, but especially breeding, these are truly magnificent ducks. That they are so different looking than most any other North America duck is reflected in the fact of their being our continent's only member of the genus *Oxyura*.

In fact, worldwide, there are only six widely distributed *Oxyura* species. There is the Andean Duck of South America, where it is found at high elevations, while the Lake Duck occurs at lower elevations in Argentina and Chile. The White-headed Duck can be found around the Mediterranean basin on into central Asia. The Maccoa Duck is found in the highlands of eastern and southern Africa. And the Blue-billed Duck is a resident of Australia and Tasmania.

And then there is our Ruddy Duck. My experience with them is limited to occasional sightings, usually during the winter around Sears Island near Belfast, Maine, in Waldo County. Growing up in western New York, I would see them in larger numbers when I made spring birding forays to Iroquois National Wildlife Refuge. John Charles Phillips (1876—1938), a naturalist and author of hundreds of books and magazine articles, offered an intriguing perspective: "Its intimate habits, its stupidity, its curious nesting customs and ludicrous courtship performance place it in a niche by itself. Even its eggs are unique in appearance[ii] and are deposited in a slipshod, irregular manner that is most extraordinary. Everything about this bird is interesting to the naturalist, but almost nothing about it is interesting to the sportsman."[iii]

Yes, Ruddy Ducks are intriguing to naturalists, both for their striking appearance and their general lack of concern with people; perhaps that is part of what marks the "stupidity" of this species. On the other hand, sportsman have long considered that Ruddy Ducks "taste like low tide on a hot day"[iv]; at least, that is how they were described in a 06 December 2010 article in *The Atlantic*.

Whichever your perspective, Ruddies are a wonderful little duck to watch.

Today's bird of the year:

260. Ruddy Duck

Friday, 12 October

I love my job! I get to lead birding tours. Up mountains. On crisp fall days with valleys filled with the autumnal colors of maples and birch and beech and every other deciduous tree of Downeast Maine. Today, in celebration of their tenth wedding anniversary, I had the pleasure of leading Arkansans Renee and Brent on a hike up Acadia National Park's Gorham Mountain.

10:33 a.m. For nearly ten minutes, we had the Gorham Mountain summit to ourselves. Dark-eyed Juncos, flitting about the Pitch Pines so common on Acadia's alpine granitic ledges, were intoning their sweet *tew-tew-tew* call. Black-capped Chickadees were plentiful, some hanging upside down from the ends of branches in order to glean insects in a cold-induced torpor. Golden-crowned Kinglets won the award for most abundant species of the day, twenty-four of them in all.

All of these birds were exciting to see and hear. The highlight of our hike has to be the first bird we saw running across the bedrock as we reached the summit cairn: American Pipit!

The tail-bobbing walk would have been enough to identify this bird; all the other field marks—size significantly larger than a warbler, gray-brown above, streaked under-parts, white eye-ring, small (for its size) bill—further confirmed what we already knew.

In Hancock County, look for American Pipits during migration, especially in the fall, as they head south from their Arctic nesting grounds. They may be drab little things, but they can certainly brighten any birder's fall landscape.

Today's bird of the year:

261. American Pipit

Tuesday, 16 October

L ow tide this morning was 10:00 a.m. That meant the Hog Bay mudflats would still be exposed by the time I got there. Hopefully there would be some shorebirds. If I was going to drive the thirty minutes to Hog Bay, it was worth including a circuit of the Schoodic section of Acadia National Park, too, which only adds another twenty miles. This made particular sense, what with the strong westerlies blowing near gale force (I would prefer the winds out of the south to increase the possibility of seabirds being pushed closer to shore, but beggars cannot be choosers).

10:52 a.m.   The best vantage of Hog Bay is from South Bay Road in Franklin. I set up the spotting scope and slowly began scanning the entirety of the mudflats of the drained bay. It did not take long to start tallying shorebirds.

Semipalmated Plover were scattered about in four groups; twenty-six was my tally. One Black-bellied Plover, by itself, feeding out in the middle of the bay, was easily identified by its size and distinctly stocky, short-billed plover shape. Two more Black-bellied Plovers towered over the group of Semipalmated Sandpipers they were feeding alongside. Two Sanderlings, appearing nearly all white at this distance, were feeding alongside three Semipalmated Sandpipers. A flock of twelve unidentified "peep" sandpipers flew by, driven rapidly by a stiff tailwind.

I am forever invigorated by watching shorebirds! That said, the particular one that made my morning was a Pectoral Sandpiper feeding amongst one of the groups of Semipalmated Plovers. Pectoral Sandpipers are a medium-sized shorebird exhibiting a clear demarcation between a heavily streaked chest and a strongly contrasting white belly. My first clue that this was something different was the fact that this bird looked to be nearly twice the size of the nearby plovers. Pectoral Sandpipers are an uncommon species in Hancock County, although that may be as much a function of their paucity and limited habitat options as the fact of few birders in our area.

After nearly forty minutes watching shorebirds, I moved on to the Schoodic Section of Acadia National Park, where I visited all my favorite birding spots, including West Pond marsh, Arey Cove, and Schoodic Point.

1:23 p.m.   My last stop, both at the Schoodic Section of Acadia National Park and of the day, was where I found my thrill, at Blueberry Hill . . . parking area, that is. With the stiff northwesterly breeze, Blueberry Hill was in a bit of the lee of Schoodic Peninsula. Between my vantage and Schoodic Island, a half mile to the southeast, the winds were clearly making waves. Beyond Schoodic Island the winds were much stronger, perfect conditions for the Northern Gannets effortlessly wheeling about, plunge-diving, each appearing as a flying cross, pearlescent against the stormy sky.

While carefully scanning the gannets and gulls swooping low and flying high, I slowly ticked off species for my day list. A skein of eleven Black Scoter, one Surf Scoter in their formation, whipped past, moving so fast that you would have thought they had a tailwind rather than a headwind. Common Eider, like the scoter, were winging it southwest along the coast. A lone Black Guillemot, bold white wing patch clearly visible against its black plumage. There were three species of gulls: Ring-billed, Herring, and Great Black-backed. A Common Loon in flight presented a distinct form. I only saw two Double-crested Cormorants; most of their brethren having already departed for points south. Two Common Raven, wedge-tailed, were playing on the wind with nary a flap. All told, fourteen species.

While scanning beyond Schoodic Island, three small, dark-hued geese whipped past. Brant! These are uncommon in this part of the world. We do get small numbers of Brant, but not the throngs of thousands seen further to the south. I always find this surprising as they nest in the high Arctic and the Atlantic seaboard is a major fly-way.

My first experience with a Brant was back in my Adirondack days while I was working at The Nature Conservancy. One late fall lunch, I walked across the street to meander through the property of the Keene Valley Country Club. With the buildings and grounds were closed up for the season, the place was deserted. The pool, with just a few inches of rainwater puddled in the deep end, was otherwise empty. Or, almost empty. A Brant was floating in the foot of water! And it was unable to get out. As the gate to the pool was locked, I hopped the fence, removed my hiking boots, rolled up my pant legs, lowered myself into the pool, and corralled the Brant into a corner of the deep end. It appeared this bird was in trouble; a view only reinforced by the ease with which I caught it.

Turns out my suspicions were correct. I took the bird to my wild-life veterinarian friend, Nina Schoch. She later told me the bird was emaciated but that she was able to nurse it back to health and arrange to have it released closer to its wintering grounds. Although we didn't band it, chances were good that it could live into its twenties.

Two more birds for my Little Big Year list, neither of which were species I had included on my list of anticipated year-birds, had me pondering the point of diminishing returns. Just how many species might I see in Hancock County this year?

Today's birds of the year:

262. Pectoral Sandpiper   263. Brant

Wednesday, 17 October

There is a particular joy in really getting to know a piece of land intimately. Over time, you begin to see not just seasonal changes, but the daily patterns of a living, breathing landscape writ small.

Over the long term, you can watch trees grow from saplings to maturity, closing in the canopy, blocking light from reaching the forest floor. One day, the forest is intact with nary a blemish to any trunks; the next, a litter of wood splinters at the base of several trees causes you to look up to find vertical excavations, the work of an industrious pair of Pileated Woodpeckers.

As time elapses, a tree loses branches. Fewer branches mean fewer limbs to hold leaves. Photosynthetic activity diminishes, the tree senesces and eventually comes down, thereby creating a hole in the canopy which allows sunlight to reach a patch of forest floor, enabling seeds to sprout and saplings to reach for the sky.

Meanwhile, there is a whole understory of floral activity. Skunk Cabbage generates heat, melting the snow around it, getting a head start accessing both sunlight and available nutrients. Trillium, both the genus and the common name (a species I have long known as Wake Robin), flowers April through June, carpeting the forest floor in some locales. The creeping rhizomes of the delicate Star Flower shoot up whorls of leaves from which one or two pure white flowers erupt.

Moving a rotting log can reveal a hidden world of invertebrate life: Red-backed Salamanders and the very occasional Spotted Salamanders, Pill Bugs (sometimes known a Potato Bugs, Roly Polies, and Doodle Bugs), centipedes, millipedes, and every other sort of invertebrate that feeds on decaying leaf litter. Meanwhile, overhead, Gray Treefrogs intone their raccoon-like trilling call.

Snow, rain, dry, cold. Each month brings seasonal changes.

For me, one of the most significant changes during the course of a year is the birds. In my yard, "Newfoundland" Robins can make an appearance as early as February. Palm Warblers and Yellow-rumped Warblers can arrive by the end of March or early April. The ethereal tones of the Hermit Thrush announce the official arrival of the Neotropical migrants. Winter's quiet gives way to the cacophonic dawn chorus of late spring. Juvenile Barred Owls plead with their parents, begging for food through much of the summer. With August comes the end of bird song while migration ramps up. Hawks are overhead through September. Yellow-rumped Warblers, primarily young of the year (what are known in the world of bird-banding as "hatch year" birds), are abundant as they fatten up for their southward migration. October is the month of the sparrows, the epitome of LBJs (Little Brown Jobs). And by 01 November, a good day of birding can end with a list that includes ten or more species of sparrows. November is often rarities month. And December is Christmas Bird Count Season.

Today, taking Fogo for one of his many daily walks around our back four acres, I heard a soft call note of a thrush different from our common thrush, the Hermit Thrush. This call note was more of a short, harsh *wheer*, compared to the fuller and much more familiar *tchup* or *chuck* or *quoit* or *eeee* of the Hermit. My gut said Gray-cheeked Thrush, but I felt compelled to use the process of elimination.

Using the iBird Pro app on my iPhone, I started working my way through the list with the most common thrushes and played first the call and then the song of a Hermit Thrush. No response. Continuing with my suspicion that the mystery bird was a Gray-cheeked Thrush, I next played the call of its close cousin, Bicknell's Thrush. Again, no response. Despite the potential of other thrushes—particularly, Wood Thrush, Veery, or Swainson's Thrush—I decided to follow my instinct and played the call of the Gray-cheeked Thrush. The bird flew right in, to within ten feet, and responded by calling back at me. Viewing it through my binoculars, I could see this bird was a drab gray-brown. The cheeks appeared a flatter gray, less warm than I think of with Bicknell's Thrush. And there was no distinct eye-ring. I felt comfortable calling it a Gray-cheeked Thrush.

And that is what I reported to eBird.

Within twenty-four hours, Louis Bevier, a Colby College research scientist, among the finest ornithologists I know, and one of the eBird reviewers for the State of Maine, sent me an email, the core of which follows:

The calls of Bicknell's and Gray-cheeked are not diagnostic based on present knowledge. There is the lone paper by Bill Evans[i] on flight calls, suggesting a potential difference, but the claim has not been confirmed. Moreover, recent work suggest overlap. Most cannot be i.d.'d by sight either (need wing length), and only a few large and cold gray birds that can be confirmed with photos as *aliciae* type Gray-cheeks are assignable to Gray-cheeked. It's tough news that in New England, Gray-cheeked is a tough bird to confirm without specimen or in hand evidence.

Kent McFarland and others who have spent considerable time studying Bicknell's and Gray-cheeked (Quebec and Maritime populations) Thrushes agree that these should be left as GC/BI (in lit.). There was a discussion about the topic of calls initiated by Dan Lane on Xeno-canto[ii] and then later discussed by Nathan Pieplow. This demonstrated much overlap and variation.

I think calls among Gray-cheeked and Bicknell's populations need a lot of study before we can declare they are identifiable. There is just way too much variation within an individual, let alone making the leap to the air with flight calls. These might be changed at a later date, but we risk building a false or at best undocumented narrative about the status of each by accepting these as identified to one or the other based on unconfirmed evidence.

We have not treated this consistently in eBird, and I am trying to address it now. (There are a ton I have accepted as GCTH that ought to be slashes.)

Can you change these to the slash? These remain a real bugaboo in eBird for New England.

I knew that Louis was right. I also knew that the bird I saw was new for my Little Big Year list, whether a Gray-cheeked Thrush or Bicknell's Thrush. Short of the actual song, this would have to stay listed as Gray-cheeked/Bicknell's Thrush; it's certainly one of the two but we cannot further narrow it down.

Until 1998, these two species were treated as Gray-cheeked Thrush; however, through the analysis of recombinant DNA, scientists determined that Bicknell's Thrush was not a subspecies but a full-blown species of its own, despite the near impossibility of confidently identifying the two by sight and sound alone. Gray-cheeked Thrush breed across the top of North America, in the taiga forests from Alaska to Newfoundland, and overwinters in northern South America (although its precise winter range is poorly understood).

Contrast that with Bicknell's Thrush, which has two distinct breeding ranges: 1) alpine habitat above 3,000 feet in the Adirondack Mountains of northern New York, the Green Mountains of Vermont, and the White Mountains of New Hampshire and Maine (historically, populations were also found in the Berkshire Mountains of Massachusetts and the Catskill Mountains of Downstate New York, which is where Eugene Bicknell first identified the species in 1881), all in the northeastern U.S., and 2) lower elevations, down almost to sea level, along the Gaspé Peninsula of Québec. Its winter range is relegated almost entirely to the island of Hispaniola, the island home to the Dominican Republic and Haiti.

I have far more experience with Bicknell's Thrush than its cousin, having censused their distribution through much of the Adirondack Mountains and banded them in the Dominican Republic. My experience with Gray-cheeked Thrush is limited to a handful of individuals banded at the spring banding station at Crown Point (New York) State Historic Site on the shores of southern Lake Champlain.

Even though I have had experience with Bicknell's Thrush, I've learned my backyard still holds many natural history mysteries. And I love that this is the case.

Today's bird of the year:

264. Gray-cheeked/Bicknell's Thrush

Wednesday, 24 October

O nce again, I found myself at Acadia National Park's Sieur de Monts Spring, leading an hour-long nature walk for Road Scholar[i]. On these walks, we talk extemporaneously about topics that can be illustrated by the landscape around us. This day, I was struck by the topics of forest composition, sparrows, and the Great Fire of '47.

Late on Friday, 17 October 1947, the Bar Harbor Fire Department received a call about smoke coming from the cranberry bog in the Northeast Creek wetlands, in the northernmost portion of Mount Desert Island. Ultimately, this turned into a conflagration that burned in a southeasterly direction, consuming 17,188 acres. This fire took ten days to control and nearly a month to completely extinguish.

While wildfires are always terrifying—perhaps even more so on an island where egress is limited—there can be a positive side, at least in terms of the natural world. Vegetative cover regenerates, offering new habitat that can bring in new species. The standing dead trees that remain after a fire can harbor insects, sometimes giving rise to population spikes in bird species such Black-backed Woodpecker. Damaged canopies may see an increase in various "worms," caterpillars that provide protein blasts to warblers such as Cape May and Bay-breasted. Areas opened up by fire may turn into grasslands, affording new foraging opportunities for species such as Field

Sparrow and Eastern Meadowlark. In the case of the Great Fire of '47[ii], all of these scenarios eventually played out.

There is no such thing as "balance" in the natural world—it is ever changing. Sometimes, though, when viewed through the lens of our short and impatient human lives, the changes are not so evident. Over time, as habitat matures, species composition continues to adjust with some departing and some arriving. For instance, different species of trees tell different stories of the changes seen by the landscape. These were all subjects we discussed on our walk.

8:53 a.m.   Making our way down the Hemlock Trail, a lovely, wide lane of finely crushed gravel, our pace was slowed by frequent talking stops. The surrounding forest of Eastern Hemlock, Balsam Fir, and White Pine offered opportunities to explore evolutionary adaptations to survive northern winters.

Two Hermit Thrush very cooperatively foraged along the edge of the trail, showing off the contrast between their rufous tails and their more-brown backs.

Sparrows were everywhere! While White-throated Sparrows were most abundant (forty of them were tallied in an hour), twenty Dark-eyed Juncos came in a distant second with eighteen Song Sparrows nipping at their heels (in one case, quite literally, as a particular Song Sparrow seemed to be chasing juncos away from its foraging area). We also observed four Fox Sparrows, two Lincoln's Sparrows, and a lone Swamp Sparrow.

As we returned to our starting point, a chorus of sweet flight calls announced the presence of a trio of Pine Grosbeaks. They whirred about overhead, with me saying out loud, "Please land, please land." And they DID! Right in the tip-top of a Red Maple. Three plump, reddish birds with the outsized beaks made it clear why they wear the name "grosbeak" ("grosbeak" derives from the French *gros bec*, or "big beak").

Pine Grosbeaks are in the finch family. When you see them alongside their Purple Finch cousins, you can see that the close similarities extend beyond physical appearance, taking in habitat, latitudinal range, and, to a large extent, diet. Although Pine Grosbeaks look physiologically similar to the Rose-breasted Grosbeaks that regularly visit our spring and summer feeders, they are actually in different families (the Rose-breasted Grosbeak is a member of the cardinal family).

With a predilection for the buds, cones, seeds, and fruits of the trees of the boreal forest (which means we also find Pine Grosbeaks both in North America and across northern Eurasia), these birds are less migratory and more irruptive, heading south when northern food supplies crash. Unfortunately, this means we don't see them every year. With luck, these three may just be announcing a southerly irruption for the coming winter.

Being a northern species, Pine Grosbeaks don't see many, if any, people. As such, they are quite tame, seemingly slow-moving. In Newfoundland, a place near and dear to my heart, Pine Grosbeaks are known as "mopes" for this very behavior.

My birding day could have ended there. I had a good morning, but I did not add any new birds to my Little Big Year list. Or did I?

My recollection was that I had already seen Pine Grosbeak early in the year. As I was reviewing my eBird records, today's Pine Grosbeak was listed as a year-bird for Hancock County. What? I went back to check my files and, indeed, this was a new species for my Little Big Year. HURRAY! It would have been easy to miss this one.

Today's bird of the year:

265. Pine Grosbeak

Monday, 12 November

Three days ago, a dead whale was found offshore south of Bar Harbor and Mount Desert Rock, somewhere in the vicinity of Bank Comfort. All that was known was that a large whale carcass, entangled in rope, buoy still attached, had been found floating.

The very real concern was that this whale might be a North Atlantic Right Whale. If so, this would be the eighteenth known to perish this year! Given that the entire population of critically endangered North Atlantic Right Whales is thought to number around 425[i] and that the population has been declining in recent years, this is quite worrisome. In fact, this is especially disturbing as some marine biologists have suggested that North Atlantic Right Whales could become extinct by 2040.

That there are any extant North Atlantic Right Whales is truly amazing.

Before Christopher Columbus "discovered" America, Basque whalers had eliminated the European population of these whales and began whaling (and fishing) in the waters of Newfoundland and Labrador[ii].

There are many facets to North Atlantic Right Whales that made them the "right" whale to hunt. They are noted for being slow movers, especially so when skimming along the surface filter feeding.

North Atlantic Right Whales are one of the few great whales lacking a dorsal; making identification much easier. These two features made these whales easy to spot and hunt. And, most importantly to the whalers, when North Atlantic Right Whales are killed, they float (most of the large whales do not). This last point was a boon in retrieving hunted whales. Finally, when you add in their slow (even by whale standards) reproductivity, this was a recipe for their current plight.

With North Atlantic Right Whale numbers so low, when a dead whale is reported, Herculean efforts are made to identify the species and the cause of its demise. (Of course, a badly decomposed whale can complicate identification.) Much additional effort has been put toward mitigating future deaths resulting from human activity (anthropogenic causes of mortality in North Atlantic Right Whales include ship strikes, disease caused by pollution, lack of prey due to warming sea waters and overfishing, and entanglement in offshore fishing gear).

By the time the report of this particular animal made its way to Allied Whale, the marine mammal research arm of College of the Atlantic, and the troops were mobilized, the whale could have floated most anywhere.

Allied Whale is the local organization in charge of rescuing or recovering stranded or dead marine mammals, but this was far from a solo effort. There were, in fact, many players involved. To increase the chances of finding the whale, the U.S. Coast Guard ran a drift analysis to focus our search area. Both U.S. Coast Guard and National Oceanic and Atmospheric Administration sent observation planes aloft in an effort to locate the whale. Maine Marine Patrol sent out their vessel, p/v *Dirigo*. Given the area to be covered, Bar Harbor Whale Watch proffered their high-speed tour boat, m/v *Friendship V*, to Allied Whale. To round out the effort, skilled observers such as myself were invited along so as to have more eyes scanning the sea surface.

What, you may ask, does all this have to do with birds? Two words: Great Skua.

Actually, the answer is just a little bit more involved in that few things make me happier than standing at the rail of a ship and looking to the sea. So, when Allied Whale asked if I wanted to be an observer, an extra set of eyes to search for the floating carcass, there was no question regarding my answer.

My methodology for tracking seabirds, while also assiduously looking for the whale, was to conduct thirty-minute surveys. Fortunately, Cornell Lab of Ornithology's eBird app makes this easy, linking in GPS, tracking time and effort, and suggesting expected species. During the very first bird survey, begun as we departed the pier in Bar Harbor, I began seeing pelagic birds; specifically, Black-legged Kittiwake and Northern Gannet. But no whale.

10:48 a.m.   Barely into my second survey, Toby Stephenson, captain of College of the Atlantic's research vessel and skipper for the day of *Friendship V*, called out, "Skua!" Seasoned naturalist Megan McOsker confirmed the skua, adding, "I think it is a Great Skua." Although we were here to search for the whale, every one of us is passionate about all aspects of the sea, including pelagic birds, and in the northwest Atlantic, the skua is arguably the apex avian predator. Skuas are an offshore bird and I love seeing them, so I was particularly intrigued.

Of the seven species of skuas and jaegers worldwide, all members of the genus *Stercorarius*, it is possible to see up to five of them in the Gulf of Maine: Pomarine, Parasitic, and Long-tailed Jaeger (although this last is always a longshot) and South Polar and Great Skua.

As this particular skua flew across the bow, it exhibited the prominent white patch at the base of the primary feathers typical of all Stercorariids, instantly narrowing identification from the 10,721 known extant bird species to one of the five aforementioned. This bird then landed just off the port bow, surprisingly close to the ship, affording the three of us on the *Friendship V*'s bridge a good look.

Its large size and powerful flight, akin to a gull on steroids, further narrowed identification down to either Great Skua or South Polar Skua. This bird was uniformly dark brown, showing no contrast in the shades of brown between its head, nape, and back. That, coupled with the time of year—by now, South Polar Skuas should all be in, or on their way to, the Antarctic where they breed during the austral summer—and the three of us were unanimous in naming it: Great Skua.

Great Skua, a vital tick for my Little Big Year. Alas, still no whale.

Great Skuas breed across the North Atlantic from Iceland to Norway. Having no need to go anywhere near land, non-breeding birds, as well as post-breeding adults, wander widely across the North Atlantic, from mainland Europe to North America. Skuas are particularly well-suited for the pelagic life. They have a nasal salt gland, their internal desalinization plant, which meets all of their freshwater needs. Being powerful aerialists, they can cover tremendous distances in pursuit of food. This often means finding other birds with food, giving chase, and forcing them to disgorge or risk being eaten themselves. Great Skuas are an apex predator. Although their global population is estimated at about 30,000, if you want a chance to add one to your North American life-list, that requires going well offshore to search.

I could end this day's entry right here. It was an incredible day! I was on a boat, offshore, with a bunch of people passionate about the biology and ecology of the oceans. We saw whales and seals and, of course, birds. The three-acre offshore island of Mount Desert Rock was regularly within view. The seas tested our sea-legs and the brisk winds burned our cheeks. (Alas, despite our best efforts and the observational skills of over two dozen observers, we never found our target whale carcass.)

So, what were some other highlights of the day?

Not long after getting good looks at the Great Skua, Zack Klyver, Bar Harbor Whale Watch's naturalist extraordinaire, called out, "Whale! 12:00!" (12:00 is a directional reference—think of looking down on the ship as though it is a flat clock: the bow is 12:00; the stern is 6:00; ninety degrees off the starboard, or right, side is 3:00; ninety degrees off the port, or left, side is 9:00; every other "time" is relative to those coordinates.) Continuing closer, I was finally able to discern the blows from the spume. And when I say blows, it is because there were not one, but two, whales!

Thar she blows!

Whenever I am aboard a whale-watch boat and we see the distant, telltale breath of a whale, I so want to call out, "Thar she blows!" As much as I want, I rarely do. (Sometimes, I think these things simply to amuse myself.) A pair of tall, columnar blows meant Fin Whales. Fin Whales are the "greyhounds of the seas." They are fast, able to sustain speeds of twenty-five miles per hour!

Toward the end of my second survey period, five White-winged Scoters flew downwind. In the middle of this line of scoters was a duck with obvious white. I didn't have long to train my binoculars, but it was enough to see this was an eider. And not just any eider, but a beautiful, male King Eider!

All day long, sightings of Black-legged Kittiwakes, the true "sea" gull, and Northern Gannets trickled in. Other than a few distant, and very much alive, Fin Whales, we found no sign of our mystery carcass.

At one point, a longish, duck-sized, counter-shaded (that is, white lowerparts and dark uppers) bird winged past, wings beating too rapidly to be a duck. It was low to the deck, hugging the wave troughs, making it challenging, at best, to get a good look. Finally, I saw enough field marks to call out Common Murre.

Earlier in the day, back when we were still at the pier, Toby raised the question of whether we might see any dovekies, the tiny cousin to the puffin. I offered my opinion that it was early in the season to see many, if any. At about 12:30, while I was once again on the bridge, Toby shouted, "Dovekie!" Look as I might, I could not get on the bird. No worries, though, as five minutes later, when I was back on deck, a Dovekie flew alongside the *Friendship V*, perhaps fifty feet off the starboard, keeping apace of us for a good five seconds.

The *Friendship V* was repositioned about ten miles south of Mount Desert Rock for the next survey period. A flock of fifty-two Canada Geese sped past, low to the deck in the well-formed "V" formation so typical of this species. One goose was noticeably smaller than the others, but try as I might, I could not convince myself it was a Cackling Goose.

South and east of Mount Desert Rock, over Bank Comfort, we had more Dovekies. As a matter of fact, Dovekie sightings trickled in all afternoon. Two Atlantic Puffins had already shed the nuptial plating of their clown bills, now showing much more gray. Two Common Loons sped past high overhead. Five more loons, lighter in color, loosely in formation, revealed themselves to be Red-throated Loons. And we saw the first of (what would ultimately become) ninety-seven Northern Fulmar. Lots of seabirds, but no dead whale.

The last notable bird of the day was a lone Great Shearwater, observed as the sun was getting low on the western horizon. This bird may have been a little confused as it should already be in Tristan da Cunha in the South Atlantic, courting a mate and establishing a nesting territory.

By the time we returned to Bar Harbor, we had been aboard the m/v *Friendship V* approximately 7½ hours and covered nearly 140 miles. The morning seas that ranged five to seven feet settled down in the late afternoon to something more like three. Same with the winds, which were initially blowing a stiff northerly, eventually reduced to half that intensity.

Few people have the opportunity to spend much time offshore birding. To give an idea of what the day was like, the following is the day's list of birds from the time we left Bar Harbor until dark (numbers in parentheses are the total number of those species observed through the day):

Canada Goose (52)
American Black Duck (6)
King Eider (1)
Common Eider (31)
Surf Scoter (10)
White-winged Scoter (5)
Black Scoter (4)
Bufflehead (4)
Great Skua (1)
Dovekie (13)
Common Murre (2)
Black Guillemot (2)
Atlantic Puffin (2)
Black-legged Kittiwake (6)
Herring Gull (113)
Great Black-backed Gull (7)
Red-throated Loon (5)
Common Loon (7)
Northern Fulmar (96)
Great Shearwater (1)
Northern Gannet (30)
American Crow (8)

Today was a phenomenal day! It was one of those personal highlights that will always be among my significant memories. For the good folks from Allied Whale, I can only imagine the frustration at not finding the whale. We had so many resources out looking for this whale and, sadly, no success on that front. I desperately fear for the future of the North Atlantic Right Whale.

Still, I have nothing but the greatest gratitude to everyone involved in this Herculean effort to search for our mystery whale. It was so deeply satisfying to spend the day with this group of dedicated and passionate people so attuned to maritime ecology. For me, it was a truly wonderful day of pelagic birding!

Today's bird of the year:

266. Great Skua

Sunday, 02 December

T oday was gray with snow that turned to sleet that turned to rain that turned to a soaking, daylong drizzle. Despite my best efforts to stay indoors, intent on reading and trying to finish a bird-carving at my basement workbench, when eleven-year-old Anouk needed a photograph for our family Christmas card it meant firing up the ol' laptop. Anouk has an amazing eye for design and composition and took the lead for designing our family holiday card. It is a marvel to see our children grow, taking on responsibilities, developing skills.

Of course, when you get too close to a computing device, there is an insidious flow of electrons sucking you in. *NPR NPR NPR,* whispers the computer. And so, you make a quick scan of the day's headlines. *Facebook Facebook Facebook.* Ah yes, the social media black hole that has devolved from a forum to keep up with family and friends into an anonymous and faceless, if not nameless, bulletin board for meaningless memes and polarizing politics. *Email email email.* Sure, why not? I'm already frying brain cells.

Apparently, I need a $1,000 Canada Goose jacket to be in style. I now know the world's best golf destinations, places where it never snows (apparently, they did not get the memo that I am a skier, not a golfer). Some company is offering me "three months for the price of two," but they didn't state what it is that you actually get. The bank of Nigeria continues to recognize my fiscal acumen and wants to give me $6 million (I think I first received this exact same email in the 1990s, back in the Dark Ages of the internet). And I can have my choice of Russian brides (sorry to disappoint ladies, but I am happily married). PHEW! This is exhausting. Thank Darwin for the delete button.

The one email that did catch my eye, though, was from eBird, with the subject reading "Year Needs Alert for Hancock County." Okay, now this is promising, especially this late in the year. This email reported that a Red-headed Woodpecker was seen on the "Quiet Side" of Mount Desert Island, near Southwest Harbor, in the hamlet of Manset.

Bird reports sometimes take time to gain momentum. Several days ago, a retired couple in Manset started observing the Red-headed Woodpecker, a bird they knew from their time living in Massachusetts. Word got out. My friend, Billy Helprin, saw it yesterday but did not report it to eBird until today. That got another friend, Craig Kesselheim, to check it out. Craig is a dedicated eBird practitioner, so it was not long after his report hit the ether that a report was spit out to my in-box, waiting for me when I checked my email.

Sorry kiddo, a rare bird calls. Here's the photo you wanted and now I'm off to see if I can rack up another notch for my Little Big Year.

The directions to the bird were vague; intentionally so, I realized. My intent was to walk around Manset and look for suet feeders on the hunch that, given the time of year and the paucity of food, this bird would be keeping to a tight patch of habitat. The big question was where to look. Normally, I would not mind walking around for an hour or two, searching, but in the steady drizzle, I was a bit less excited by the prospect.

So, I did what any contemporary birder would do, I texted Craig. A few quick exchanges and he offered to meet at the Manset town dock and lead me to bird of the year number 267.

1:13 p.m.   We pulled into the driveway of the exact house with the suet feeder the woodpecker has been frequenting. We were met by one of the owners as she was walking out of her studio. "The bird was just here but may have flown to the neighbor's yard," said she. The words were barely out of her mouth when Craig shouted, "There it is!"

Flying away from us, undulating through the air in a flight pattern so typical of woodpeckers, there was no mistaking this unique bird. Red-headed Woodpecker! Half the wings are white: from the last primary feather to the body, all the flight feathers are boldly white, contrasting markedly with the black of the "meat" of the wing (what would be equivalent of our arm to the wrist). The white continues through the uppertail coverts, that part of the body immediately above where the tail inserts.

The bird flew to the neighbor's suet feeder dangling from an apple tree. Hanging from the feeder, wings folded over its back, it continues to show a vast expanse of white. This particular bird was a juvenile, lacking the red head and solid black back of an adult. Instead, the back was finely barred in a ladder-like pattern and the head was dark gray, transitioning seamlessly into the other dark parts.

What a surprise to find this bird in Hancock County! In fact, it is a rare bird throughout Maine, even though it breeds not far away in Massachusetts. Since moving to Bar Harbor in 2002, this Red-headed Woodpecker was only the second one I have seen in Maine (the first one was in Bar Harbor in 2013).

There are numerous fun facts about the charismatic Red-headed Woodpecker. It was the "spark bird" for Alexander Wilson (arguably the father of American ornithology), meaning it was the bird that "sparked" his passion for our feathered friends. It makes an appearance in Longfellow's epic poem, *The Song of Hiawatha*. It is known to cache food for later consumption. For me, however, with my love of language, one of the most intriguing facets of this species is its collection of colorful appellations, such as White-shirt, Half-a-shirt,

Shirt-tail Bird, Jellycoat, Flag Bird, Flying Checkerboard, and Tricolored Woodpecker.

Alas, there has been a marked decline in the population of Red-headed Woodpeckers in the past sixty years, a decline can be directly attributed to habitat loss.

Today's bird of the year:

267. Red-headed Woodpecker

Sunday, 30 December

A ll year long, my nemesis bird has been Boreal Chickadee. I have made numerous forays into suitable habitat to look for this brown-capped denizen of northern forests. There was a time when it was much more common throughout Hancock County. For instance, I recall Boreal Chickadees in my campsite at Blackwoods Campground during my first visit to Acadia National Park back in 1986. Alas, global warming has sent this little parid packing.

With less than forty-eight hours left in my Little Big Year, it was time to make one more foray in search of Boreal Chickadee.

Throughout the year, there have been scattered reports of the bird but none I felt reliably could produce one. I thought back to one of the purposes of my Little Big Year: to boldly bird where few birders have birded before. In plain language, that would mean exploring the northernmost reaches of the county.

Stud Mill Road—just Stud Mill in local parlance; as in, "Yes deah, ah'm goin' up-ta-da Stud Mill." It is the east-west super-highway of private logging roads, reaching from Penobscot County, through northernmost Hancock County, and well into Washington County, some ninety miles (give or take) in all. One of the many good things about this road is that it is open to the public, so long as you yield to the logging trucks. And yield you will because the logging trucks are speeding down the road like they own it. Which they do.

This is beautiful country with forests of spruce and fir, oak and maple. Streams darkened by the tannins of decaying vegetation hint at the promise of heritage strain Brook Trout and lakes just out of sight, beyond the tree-line. Sunkhaze Meadows National Wildlife Refuge marks the western end of Stud Mill and Moosehorn National Wildlife Refuge the east. This is a region under-explored by birders that, in season, can yield such boreal specialties as Black-backed Woodpecker, Olive-sided Flycatcher, Yellow-bellied Flycatcher, Philadelphia Vireo, Canada Jay, Red Crossbill, White-winged Crossbill, Lincoln's Sparrow, Rusty Blackbird, Tennessee Warbler, Cape May Warbler, Bay-breasted Warbler, Blackpoll Warbler, Canada Warbler, and Boreal Chickadee.

Boreal Chickadees are more particular in their habitat requirements than their black-capped cousin. In the past, the area off Stud Mill Road around Alligator Lake has been particularly good at producing a Boreal Chickadee or two. The best way to find a Boreal Chickadee, once you are in the right habitat, is to listen. To hear their call—a distinctive, harsh *zeer-zeer*—means being on foot, walking, stopping, and listening.

9:02 a.m.   Before making the hour drive to the Stud Mill, I had no idea walking would be so treacherous. Our usual winter deep freeze was interrupted by warming and rain, then plunged back into more seasonal temperatures in the single digits Fahrenheit. Coupled with the weekday traffic of logging trucks piled high with the raw materials of their trade, this made for extremely icy roads.

Now, if you are going to travel on icy roads, it is probably best they be dirt, like those of the Stud Mill and surrounding network. Gravel roads are not smooth with grit and stones rising through the ice, providing texture that affords grip for both vehicular tires and hiking boots. Even so, while walking along the roads was doable, I would not have dared to bring along some of my less ambulatory birding friends.

I began with Alligator Lake Road, one of Stud Mill's many off-shoots. During the first ½-mile: nothing. Not a single bird. The only sound coming from my feet crunching on the frozen substrate and the wind filtering through the coniferous canopy. Every cleared tract and overgrown logging road were fair game to explore. It was a good hour before I heard my first sound of life and that was a lone Red Squirrel scolding me.

Walking, walking, walking, interspersed with a bit of slipping. The crusted snow-covered side trails a much appreciated respite.

It was clear that I was not the only one to walk these trails. Quite literally, I was following in the tracks of several Moose. Meanwhile, the large pads of a Snowshoe Hare dwarfed the far more abundant tracks of Red Squirrels. A few rodent tunnels had collapsed (could they have been Meadow Voles or Field Mice? Or even Common Redpolls?).

I saw evidence of bird life, too. Three toes forward, one toe back, too small for Wild Turkey, could only be grouse. As much as I hoped for Spruce Grouse, the habitat was not thick enough with its preferred Black Spruce, so it was most likely a Ruffed Grouse.

A bit later, continuing down this narrow lane, I nearly had a heart attack as a burst of sound came practically from my feet. A Ruffed Grouse took to the air, probably equally startled by me.

Once my heart rate returned to near normal, I continued down the track. There was the faint murmurings of a Black-capped Chickadee. In my experience, Black-capped Chickadees and Boreal Chickadees do not often tend to forage together, so I was tempering my hope. Still, this was my first chickadee, so I started pishing, pursing my lips and uttering a gentle, repetitive *pish pish pish*, a sound that often attracts the curiosity of Black-capped Chickadees. And as often as not, where there are chickadees, there are nuthatches and kinglets foraging right alongside. But today, all that responded were three Black-caps.

The distant *cronk*ings of a Common Raven may not be melodious, but it is always music to my ears. A lone Red-breasted Nuthatch was working its way down a tree trunk, gleaning little protein blasts from insectivorous foods secreted in the relative protection of bark crevices while in their winter torpor. The *jip-jip* of a White-winged Crossbill suddenly materialized into a flock of eighteen flying overhead, passing as swiftly as they appeared.

After nearly two hours, I returned to the car (knowing the Stud Mill would not be near as smooth as a paved road, I opted for the all-wheel reliability of Natalie's Subaru Outback over my front-wheel-drive minivan). Nary a Boreal Chickadee. DRAT! So, I opted to walk the other direction.

The road was lined with dense spruce forest, a mix of Red Spruce and Black Spruce, with a few White Birches thrown in. If the ground had not been snow-covered, I would have likely seen a forest floor of sphagnum moss, typical of well-shaded northern forests. I had just stopped, thinking that I had pushed my time more than I planned.

Zeer-zeer. Zeer-zeer.

Boreal Chickadee!

I quietly pished. No response (not that I expected any from this shy denizen of northern forests). I waited, triangulating on the sound. The birds, for there were at least two of them, were back in the woods a good piece. I took a few steps in that direction, the snow crunching under my feet a cacophony. Pause. The birds were still there. A few more deafening steps and pause. *Zeer-zeer.* I slowly and, despite all my best efforts, noisily, crept forward.

Finally, in a spot with just a bit of a wooded view, I stopped and waited. One minute. Two. Three. Four full minutes of the Boreal Chickadees foraging within earshot but largely out of sight. My ears, coupled with occasional glimpses of furtive silhouettes through the density of spruce, told me I was there. Binoculars up, I was tracking the shadows when, finally, one landed momentarily in my field of view.

The kin of this brown-capped wonder have led to me having many a wonderful birding experience over the years, hiking mountains, skiing in the backcountry, paddling remote boreal brooks, all in pursuit of Boreal Chickadees.

And now my Little Big Year was complete! I bracketed the year with chickadees: Black-capped Chickadee on my first day and Boreal Chickadee on this, which would prove to be the last day of my Hancock County Little Big Year.

How wonderful to bracket my Little Big Year with the state bird of Maine: the chickadee. When the state legislature selected the chickadee as the state bird, they did not differentiate between Black-capped and Boreal (perhaps that has something to do with the latter also sporting Hudsonian Chickadee and Acadian Chickadee as common names back in the nineteenth and early twentieth century).

Walking back to the car along this road surrounded by boreal forest, I felt elated at having observed 268 species of birds in Hancock County in one year. I never dreamed I would see and hear so many species in such a limited geographic area in a single year. Especially not in Maine. I knew that this evening, as I sat at my computer, this would be the last daily write-up of my Little Big Year. The hyper-focus and daily commitment to birding and writing for the past year was both thrilling and exhausting. If I had to choose one word to describe my birding during the 2018 calendar year, I would like to think it was "meaningful."

Meaningful to me, as I strove to raise awareness about birds. Meaningful in that it elevated my commitment, if that were even possible, to be an advocate for the birds. Meaningful, I hope, to at least a few of the people with whom I crossed paths this year. And, perhaps, meaningful to some of my readers of this book.

Today's bird of the year:

268. Boreal Chickadee

Tuesday, 01 January

New Year's Day.

268!

"That, my friend, is a very big year."

Those were the words of Steve Martin honoring Jack Black's 741st North American species in the movie *The Big Year* as they stood looking across a montane snowscape at a Pink-footed Goose. And those words describe how I felt looking back at my Little Big Year: it was a very big year.

Exactly one year ago, I set out to identify as many species of birds as possible within the geographical confines of Hancock County, Maine—the county in which I live—during the course of 2018. How many birds might I find? Setting a goal seemed a good way to start, so I initially set the bar conservatively, aiming for 225 species. By 10 June, with just under six months remaining in my Little Big Year, I handily reached that threshold when I heard several Eastern Whippoor-will singing at Great Pond Mountain Wildlands. It was only logical to reset the bar for the remainder of the year. With most of the expected species identified, how high could I go? Two hundred fifty seemed a reasonable new target. When I hit that benchmark when a Black-crowned Night-Heron flew overhead at sunset on 25 August, then what? 260? 270?

Of course, this was not about shattering records or having the biggest life-list. It was not a competition except, perhaps, with myself. My Little Big Year was about learning, setting personal goals, and following them through to completion. It was about honoring the anniversary of the Migratory Bird Treaty Act and heralding the Maine Bird Atlas. It was about celebrating the Year of the Bird. Most importantly, it was about immersing myself in an ecology that drives my natural history passion and brings great joy to my life.

In many ways, this first day of 2019 was a virtual repeat of its counterpart 365 days previous. Like that day, I joined Don Lima and his adult son, Kyle, on the Schoodic Christmas Bird Count. There were two notable differences between that day and this: it was about 30° Fahrenheit warmer and we were joined by an additional birder, Fyn Kynd, of Belfast, Maine. Fyn is an eighteen-year-old birding wunderkind (actually, both Fyn and Kyle are something of birding prodigies).

Several decades ago, when I was their age, I shared Kyle's and Fyn's passion for birds but lacked their vision for where I wanted this avocation to take me. If Kyle and Fyn are any indication of their generation, I take heart for the future of birding and conservation of the natural world.

Spending the day birding with these three friends, I reflected upon the past year. For some, the ultimate measure of an effort such as this is the bottom line. And my bottom line was 268: I observed 268 species of birds in Hancock County during the course of 2018. To get to 268 species meant birding. A LOT of birding! To better appreciate that number begs some analysis.

During the course of the year, I got out birding on 190 separate days, sometimes for the time it took to walk Fogo around our back woods; sometimes for a day that stretched from dawn to dusk. Calculating all my time invested—time getting to a birding locale, time birding, time returning from birding—the sum is 22 days, 19 hours, and 27 minutes! Of that total, 8 days, 23 hours, and 33 minutes were spent in cars; 1 day, 18 hours, and 48 minutes were spent on the water in boats of every sort (canoes, kayaks, ferries, research vessels, and pelagic tour boats); and 12 days, 4 hours, and 20 minutes was spent afoot, walking, hiking, cross-country skiing, bicycling, or even just standing or sitting.

Among the various forms of transportation, I managed to cover 7,012.4 miles! That breaks down to 378.9 miles walking, hiking, cross-country skiing, or bicycling, 306.3 miles in boats, and 6,369.0 miles in a car.

As a tour leader, I firmly believe getting out and enjoying nature is an important step in making a connection with the natural world. More importantly, time out in the natural world helps develop a conservation ethic. It is not lost on me the carbon footprint of this pursuit and I find that difficult to reconcile. The environmental impact of birding is something rarely discussed. As a result of my Little Big Year and the associated transportation numbers, I find myself keen to explore means for addressing this challenge going forward.

All of the bird observations that went into my Little Big Year were reported to eBird: 696 checklists in all. Obviously, that means that many days had far more than one checklist submitted. One of the features of eBird is that you can submit place-based checklists. For instance, if my day had me birding at Acadia National Park's Sieur de Monts Spring, Great Head, and Otter Cliffs, that would be three separate checklists. Generating that many checklists seems a large number, and it is, but this is what gives power to the database that is eBird: the more checklists submitted from specific locales, the better resolution scientists get when looking at population trends and distributions. Having submitted so many checklists, I derive great satisfaction in knowing that I made a valuable contribution to the world's largest citizen science project.

While putting such effort into a project, in addition to statistics, it is inevitable that there are going to be emotional ups and downs, as well. Fortunately, in my case, there were mostly ups. As I mentally recap my year, it is the highlights that first come to mind.

Topping my list for what made the year so wonderful and memorable was simply meeting and birding with scores of friends, family, local birders, birders that are not so local, people on my birding and nature tours, students from College of the Atlantic, Road Scholars, and members of the local community, all engaging in conversation and camaraderie. I regularly made a point of sharing my yearlong effort and its threefold purpose of celebrating the Migratory Bird Treaty Act centennial and the Year of the Bird, along with heralding in the launch of the five-year Maine Bird Atlas, all in hopes that more people might be inspired to care about birds through these conversations.

One of my many friendly engagements occurred in April in the hamlet of Bernard. Don Lima and I were driving to a regular birding spot when we caught sight of a flock of black birds up in a tree set back from the road. Somehow, we managed to completely overlook the fact that there was a house between us and the tree. Literally. We pulled over, hopped out of the car, and began scanning the birds. A man came out of the house across the road to our stern, accosting us gruffly, "What are you doing?"

I think it dawned upon Don and me simultaneously how this looked: two middle-aged guys, standing on the side of the road, binoculars screwed to our eyes, looking, for all intents and purposes, toward a house. Quite innocently we answered about the birds in the tree—Common Grackles—how we were just bird-watching, and the fact that such a flock of these birds at this time of year was unusual.

The man relaxed, telling us he just wanted to make sure we weren't spying on his daughter, who lived in the house below our Common Grackles. Then he began talking about the birds, that he had been seeing them for over a week and was glad to learn their identity.

Thinking on this experience reinforced the wonderful, rural island community where I live. How many places in the United States
could this seen unfold and go from confrontation to mutual interest?

Equally as gratifying as the social side of my Little Big Year was
spending so much time out-of-doors (of course, I never need an excuse to get out in the natural world). There were weather-blasted
days on mountains, wind and cold burning my cheeks, invigorating
me, making me feel so very alive. There were misty sunrises at Sieur
de Monts Spring, walking the Hemlock Trail to the dawn chorus and
a trio of begging, screeching, whining juvenile Barred Owls who
were really saying, "Mommy, daddy, feed us!" There were the times
on Day Mountain, among my favorite quick hikes, Fogo prancing in
the mud while I navigated the single-plank boardwalk, Golden-
crowned Kinglets softly chittering away in the surrounding Black
Spruce, Hermit Thrush singing their ethereal song in the distance.
Cross-country skiing the Carriage Road around Witch Hole Pond.
Bicycling in the dark at Great Pond Mountain Wildlands. Thrice-
daily walks in our back woods with Fogo. And the list goes on.

As I have written with every instance: few things make me happier than being on the water. There were numerous opportunities,
such as the trip I guided when we launched kayaks at Hadley Point
and paddled around The Twinnies on a rising tide. Greater Yellowlegs worked the drowning mudflats while a pair of Great Egrets
fished in the *Spartina* grass shallows not far from a Great Blue Heron.
Meanwhile, large numbers of Bonaparte's Gulls were winging about,
flapping in their unique, buoyant flight. Even without finding the
Little Gull sitting on the superstructure of Bar Harbor Oyster Company's aquaculture rafts, this would still have been one of my top
water days of the year, simply for all the bird activity.

I was fortunate to be on the 19 July trip on College of the Atlantic's research and support vessel, m/v *Osprey*. This was the first of
several trips on the college's boat during the year to search for seabirds and dolphins and whales. This particular trip included a visit to
the Mount Desert Rock research station twenty-five miles offshore.

I spent the entire day at the rail of the boat, alternating between binoculars to look at the charismatic megafauna and camera to photograph the same. So entranced was I that I didn't even break for lunch or snacks or water.

The only thing better than being on the water (as if such a thing could even exist) was hiking above tree-line, what with the unique alpine ecology, wind in my face, and expansive views. This is especially true on those winter days, the scratchy sound of wind whooshing over the glacially carved frozen landscape, keening through spruce and fir and pine, all with an absence of combustion-engine noise pollution. Even the drone of aircraft 38,000 feet above disappears on days such as this. That lack of manmade noise is a significant part of my personal heaven. And to top it off, on these winter sojourns, it is not uncommon to have the entire mountain to myself. It doesn't get much better than hiking a loop that takes in both Penobscot and Sargent Mountains (two of Acadia National Park's highest peaks), especially in winter when Snowy Owls sometimes grace their summits.

This was exemplified by a 04 December solo hike up these two mountains. From the moment I parked my car to the time I returned, some six hours later, I did not see a single soul. Once I cleared tree-line on the south ridge of Penobscot Mountain, I saw my first Snowy Owl of the day! Continuing up the mile-long ridge, the wind was blowing brutally, making the already chilly single-digit temperatures feel far colder. Every square inch of flesh was covered, whether by Gore-Tex-clad winter clothing, Buff face shield, and Smith ski goggles. In the lee of my favorite glacial erratic, I set up my spotting scope to scan across Jordan Pond to the summit ridge of Pemetic Mountain. Another Snowy Owl!

Later, after summiting Penobscot, I dropped down into a col on the way to Sargent Mountain, then began hiking up my second peak of the day. Walking by the frozen Sargent Mountain Pond had me thinking about a July trip with College of the Atlantic's Family Nature Camp to go swimming there. No swimming this day. Shortly after I cleared tree-line, I saw my third Snowy Owl. While watching it, another flew in, landing a mere dozen feet away. Halfway to the summit, I glanced to Gilmore Peak and saw a fifth Snowy Owl. And near the summit of Sargent, I practically tripped over a sixth Snowy Owl. The wind blowing the entire time, I never bared more than an oval of my face above my nose. I was in heaven!

Even though I did not write up this Penobscot and Sargent Mountain hike as I did not see any birds new for the year, the day was no less special and was still part of my Little Big Year. This particular outing had special meaning as it has been my habit for the past eighteen years to hike these two mountains on this day as a birthday present to myself.

If those were some of my particularly memorable moments, nearly dipping (birder parlance for missing) on Boreal Chickadee was a persistent low point for me. Until the penultimate day of the year. There were two 2018 reports of Boreal Chickadee from Mount Desert Island: one 26 May, the other 19 June. I write intriguing because I am out and about in the wild environs of Acadia National Park nearly every day and I have not seen or heard this brown-capped bird on the island in nearly fifteen years, leading me to believe this species is now absent from the island. Fortunately, a daylong 30 December effort not only netted me the species for Hancock County, but it wound up being the last species on my year-list. In the end, my year was bracketed by chickadees: Black-capped Chickadee was my first bird of the year and Boreal was the last.

My actual low points this year came in two forms. First, there was the ever-declining environment. Second was the species I missed.

To the untrained eye, signs of the declining natural world may not always be readily apparent. We know from national, hemispheric, and global studies that populations of most species of birds are in a state of decline (insects and amphibians are in even more dire straits). Certainly, as I am out birding, I see fewer birds today than I did forty years ago. Thirty year ago. Twenty years ago. Even ten years ago.

The root cause of this is a direct result of how we treat natural landscapes. Habitat loss, both near and far (especially wintering grounds) and everywhere in between has a ripple-effect: less habitat, less food, less wildlife. Today's accounts of birds are in stark contrast to eighteenth- and nineteenth-century reports. Past stories tell of flights of birds darkening the sky in migration, and not just Passenger Pigeon. For instance, there were vast numbers of curlews and god-wits, millions strong. Today, we only see single numbers of them in Maine.

Climate change, like habitat loss, impacts bird populations. Those Boreal Chickadees for which I had to venture into the northern reaches of Hancock County were once a regular occurrence in ap-propriate habitat on coastal Mount Desert Island. Up until the 1970s, American Three-toed Woodpecker and Blackback Woodpecker were birds you could find on Mount Desert Island with some regu-larity. Due to a warming climate, the former has shifted its southern range forty or more miles north and we are losing the latter locally.

We are now seeing an increasing number of birds in Maine that are more traditionally associated with the U.S. mid-Atlantic region. Species such as Tufted Titmouse and Northern Cardinal are now in Bar Harbor. During the winters, Red-bellied Woodpecker and Car-olina Wren appear ever more regularly. In fact, for the first time ever, in 2018, a pair of Red-bellied Woodpeckers, a species whose range is normally to the south of New England, nested in Penobscot, a town on the western edge of Hancock County.

The ways in which we drive climate change is not tied exclusively to the combustion of fossil fuels. We routinely convert landscapes, whether it be from forest or grasslands to farms or farms to subdi-visions and shopping malls or damming free-flowing rivers or any of the host of other ways we subdue the natural world. By destroying natural landscapes, among the unintended consequences are that we remove the vital ecosystem services they perform, such as sequestering carbon, filtering runoff, mitigating flooding, and providing a source of food and habitat for so many species.

Furthermore, all of these alterations we make to natural landscapes need roads. Sometimes roads seem a living thing: roads beget roads; roads get paved; eventually they get widened.

A direct result of more miles of roads, and bigger and faster vehicles, is more roadkill. As we speed down our asphalt corridors, we take for granted the fact that roadkill means an unnatural loss of an individual animal, many of which species are facing additional pressures in a world where we humans are driving the change.

Roads also present another impasse some bird populations face. Many birds become roadkill themselves as they feed on roadkill. Or they fly across the road in pursuit of prey.

I once saw a Peregrine Falcon chasing a Northern Flicker in a high-speed game of life and death. The flicker flew from the forest on one side of Route 73 in the Adirondack Mountains, across the road, to the forest on the other side with the Peregrine hot on its tail. Alas, birds generally are not in the habit of looking both ways when they cross the road. As a car came speeding by, the flicker barely made it. The falcon was not so lucky. A puff of feathers told of the impact. And then it was tumbling through the air. I ran up to the injured Peregrine who looked at me with a malevolent stare, all the while dragging a wing with a compound fracture, humerus bone poking through the lesser covert feathers. I threw a jacket over the bird to blind it (which also calmed the bird) and took it to a wildlife rehabilitator. Unfortunately, the wing was too badly damaged for the bird to be healed and released to the wild.

A different impact roads have on the landscape is that they open up more feeding opportunities, especially in the form of that same roadkill I previously described. Turkey Vultures, especially, have appreciated the expanded buffet. By the second half of the twentieth century, Turkey Vultures started becoming a regular part of the Maine landscape.

With the increasing number and expanding width of roads, so too has the natural world seen more and more fragmentation of habitat. Many species need intact landscapes, habitats not bisected nor punctured by roads. Increased fragmentation enables a significant rise in nest parasites such as Brown-headed Cowbirds.

These are just a few forms of environmental degradation. Habitat conversion also has direct impacts on pollution. Among the benefits of intact ecosystems is their ability to filter runoff. Or mitigate flooding. Or bind heavy metals raining from our skies (a byproduct of the combustion of fossil fuels).

Intact landscapes also provide shade, cooling the surroundings, including waterways. Remove vegetative cover and we see warming waters which affects insect and fish species composition.

I could go on and on, listing the myriad ways in which a degraded natural world is less able to independently function, to support robust populations of species. Nowhere is this more acutely evident than with the loss of birds.

When I hear about environmental successes, the pessimist in me has to counter them with the reality that any gains are being exponentially outpaced by losses. Don't get me wrong, it is vitally important to do all that we can to preserve as much of the natural world as possible, but we need a global mind shift toward the health of the planet. This will also result in a dramatic improvement in the human condition.

My second low is nowhere near as distressing as our collective destruction of the natural world. It was actually a series of lows which came in the form of misses; that is, birds that would have contributed to my Little Big Year had I observed them. There were fourteen of those for which I can account:

Although Carolina Wren breed further to the south of us, this is a bird we see sporadically during virtually every winter; unfortunately, not by me this year. One at a Winter Harbor feeder 01 January was the first of at least three Hancock County reports through the year. This was a particular disappointment as we probably went right by this house and feeder that day while doing the Schoodic Christmas Bird Count.

On 23 March, a Greater White-fronted Goose was found feeding and resting on Graham Lake, near the Green Lake National Fish Hatchery. This is a very rare bird in Hancock County, being a species with a range more typically encompassing the western half of North America, Greenland, and Europe. When I received the call about this bird, Natalie and I were skiing up Acadia National Park's Cadillac Mountain. The next morning, Ed Hawkes and I were on the search! Alas, the goose seems to have been a one-day wonder.

On 14 April, while Anouk and I were driving west through Montreal, on our way to visit my mother in the St. Lawrence River valley of northern New York, my cell-phone rang. It was Maine Audubon's Doug Hitchcox, one of the top birders in the state, calling to report Maine's first-ever Violet-green Swallow! And it was at Hamilton Pond, just three miles from my Bar Harbor home (a fact that Doug knew well). Although we couldn't turn around (believe me, it was tempting), we activated the local birding phone tree and lots of birders were able to see it. Just not me. Grrrr....

Between May and early October, there were at least five reports of Prairie Warbler from around the county. Alas, this bird eluded me. Every time I learned of one, I was either away, too late in getting there, or simply could not locate the bird. The typical breeding range of the Prairie Warbler, which is beautifully patterned in shades of yellow with black accents, spans from the southeastern U.S. to the southwestern corner of Maine.

On 02 June, while I was working on a small ship plying the Great Lakes, everyone on the Acadia Birding Festival pelagic cruise was treated to a Brown Booby just off Schoodic Island, a first for Hancock County. I have seen plenty of them in their usual Caribbean haunts, but this bird was clearly far off course. To the best of my knowledge, this was only the third report of Brown Booby in Maine, with one from 2011 in Portland and another in 2013 on Eastern Egg Rock, neither of which were in Hancock County.

On 08 June, a report of a Black Tern was submitted to eBird with the location being "Bar Harbor whale/pelagic trip--Schoodic Point Area, Hancock County, Maine, US". While there was no other information, I have, on rare occasion, seen Black Terns in that vicinity myself, but not this year. Normally, at this time of year, Black Terns are on their northern freshwater nesting grounds.

A Federally-endangered Roseate Tern, observed in the mouth of Frenchman Bay 13 June near Egg Rock was one of only two reported from Hancock County waters in 2018. For years, they have nested on Petit Manan Island—one of sixty-some islands in the Maine Coastal Islands National Wildlife Refuge—just across the county line in Washington County. Alas, their numbers have been dwindling to the point that, for perhaps the first time, it appears no Roseate Terns successfully nested in Maine in 2018.

Nathan Dubrow spent the summer working on Mount Desert Rock. Twenty-five miles offshore of Bar Harbor, this three-acre rocky ledge gets some impressive birds, including a 22 August Prothonotary Warbler. This is a bird with front parts a brilliant yellow. Generally found well south of Maine, a Prothonotary Warbler or two seem to find their way to Hancock County every few years.

On 28 August, Nathan photographed the first of a small handful of scattered reports of Baird's Sandpiper. This medium-sized shorebird normally ranges to our west, beginning from the longitude of the Great Lakes and extending all the way to the Pacific. The only Baird's Sandpiper I have ever seen was in 1994 at the Dead Creek Wildlife Area in Vermont with my late friend and mentor, Mike Peterson.

Later that day, Nathan again exhibited his skill as a birder, seeing and photographing a Long-tailed Jaeger off Mount Desert Rock. More common in the Pacific Ocean than the Atlantic, they do occur here, but in my years of living in Maine, I have only been fortunate enough to see one of these slender, raptorial-like pelagic seabirds off our coast.

A single Yellow-throated Vireo was reported for Hancock County at Compass Harbor 09 September. If not for the thick vireo bill, this bird could be mistaken for a warbler. Once again, I was off working on a small ship, this time traveling from Nova Scotia to Cape Cod and southern New England.

On 15 October, while I was leading a nature tour near Bar Harbor, the Schoodic Institute was conducting their Schoodic Point Sea Watch. The sea-watchers, counting birds flying by on their autumnal migration, were treated to the fly-by of a Short-eared Owl. This was the only Hancock County report for the year of which I am aware.

Late 10 November, not long before our 4:11 p.m. sunset, I received a text about a probable Mew Gull at the Mount Desert Island High School (Mew Gulls are both western and Eurasian). Of course, I went to look. It was raining sideways and blowing hard. There were forty-some Ring-billed Gulls actively feeding on the football field but I could not turn one into a Mew Gull. The text stated that a Bald Eagle flew over and flushed the birds—that happened to me, too. Alas, no Mew Gull.

On 18 November, the University of Maine at Orono's Marsh Island Birding Club visited Schoodic Point. This group of student birders included my young friend, Kyle Lima. In his eBird report, Kyle wrote: "First impressions lead to an immediate ruling out of [Common Loon]. Bill was small, head was brownish-black with nape becoming gray washed. Thin black line running through white throat at chin area. Border of dark and white of neck was sharp and straight. Back was dark brownish and white speckled." Photos helped confirm the bird as Pacific Loon. Pacific Loons do, indeed, show up along the Maine coast most every winter, though this year, I missed them.

Those were the missed birds I could confirm from official reports. There were likely other misses, too, such as a rumored Great Gray Owl on the Quiet Side of Mount Desert Island. No additional details were forthcoming so I could not ascertain the veracity of that report.

One final category of missed birds were the species for which I kept constant vigilance but that went unreported in Hancock County in 2018. Specifically, these were Canvasback, Redhead, Sandhill Crane, American Oystercatcher, Long-billed Dowitcher, Yellow-crowned Night-Heron, Glossy Ibis, American Three-toed Woodpecker, Willow Flycatcher, and Hoary Redpoll. All are birds that are occasionally observed in Hancock County.

As much as I greatly desired to see every possible species of bird that passed through Hancock County, I have no regrets about the ones I missed. In total, of the fourteen species I missed, the one hypothetical, and the ten that were never reported in 2018, all were species I have seen before. Five of the fourteen would have been new for my Hancock County life-list. And that would have been nice. All the same, I never tire of seeing the same birds over and over. I'm that guy that is just as happy sitting at the Town Pier watching the Herring Gulls or spending hours mesmerized by the comings and goings of Black-capped Chickadees and American Goldfinch at a set of feeders.

Now that my Little Big Year is over, I am feeling equal parts of a sense of relief and loss. The relief is in no longer needing to be so hyper-focused as I was for the past twelve months. Part of my routine was in writing each account before the day was out, while details were fresh in my memory. Keeping up in this fashion meant that come the New Year, all I had left to write was the concluding chapter. This chapter.

Usually, I enjoy juggling many projects. For my Little Big Year, I had put most of those projects on hold. This single-mindedness of purpose was actually out of my comfort zone. It is good to sometimes step out of character and push your personal boundaries. With my Little Big Year, I did that. Now, not only could I expand focus back into my more usual comfort zone, pursuing multiple interests, but I actually had the time to do so once again.

With the conclusion of my year-long effort, Natalie asked me whether I appreciated my Little Big Year habit. Conversely, she wanted to know if it was ever drudgery.

There was a sort of comfort in the routine of my Little Big Year. Before bed, review the weather forecast for the coming days. Was the weather going to be good for birding? That depended on the time of year. A frigid winter day with a bluebird sky meant small birds foraging in mixed flocks. A southerly blow could mean seabirds blown close to shore or, in the spring, a pulse of migrants arriving overnight. A spring frost that gives over to warmth as the morning progresses could be a banner day of birding at the Mount Desert Island High School. An autumnal northwesterly blow might spell r.a.p.t.o.r.s. As in, loads of them migrating past the Cadillac Mountain Hawk Watch.

Rise in the morning. A quick check of email for the latest eBird alerts helped finalize my day's plan. Where might I go birding to find a year-bird? Am I leading a tour? Can I tweak our itinerary to take us somewhere birdy and still meet the stated interests of my guests? In the afternoon, checking in with members of my local birding community. Ed and Deb: Any good birds on their daily walks? Or at their feeders? Rob: What has he seen that day? Craig: What's the news from the Quiet Side? Sue and Harold: Anything new in Penobscot? Seth: What are you seeing at Schoodic? Don, whose job took him not just all over the state, but all over Hancock County: Have you seen anything, anywhere, that I should chase?

Birding. I was always birding. Even when not out chasing birds. Laying abed, picking out the individual songs in the dawn chorus. Sitting at a meal at our dining room table, one ear (and sometimes both) peeled for the birds. Even in the winter—the gentle, bell-like trill of the Dark-eyed Junco can still be heard. Through the closed window. Above the hubbub of the breakfast conversation. And, it goes without saying that during absolutely any and all time spent outdoors, I was looking for and listening to the birds. It was exhilarating!

And it was exhausting.

The reality is that most of my life, I have ALWAYS been looking for and listening to the birds. This year, the difference was an order of magnitude of intensity. I can generally turn off the birding when needs be. Doing a project with my daughter Anouk, I focus on her. Planning an adventure with Natalie, I am entirely present. Sitting with a small group of friends, over beers and margaritas, talking about life, the universe, and everything, I'm all in.

During my Little Big Year, I didn't turn it off. It got to the point where I couldn't. I did not recognize how both all-consuming and exhausting that can be until New Year's Day 2019 when doing the Christmas Bird Count with Don Lima and company. I was now birding for the pure joy of it. It was a social event with friends. There were numerous times when Don would interrupt our conversation, "Did you hear that?" No.

No, I didn't hear that kinglet. That chickadee. That nuthatch. I had found my birding off-switch! It only took a year of intensive birding to find it.

That brought me back to the second part of Natalie's question: Was it ever drudgery? I can honestly say it wasn't. Exhausting, yes. Drudgery, no. How can an activity that connects you with the natural world ever be drudgery? For me, it can't.

On the contrary, there were many benefits to the hyper-focus I had during my Little Big Year. I know I am a good birder: a combination of my lifelong interest in birds and my career studying them, leading tours, and teaching ornithology meant that they were a broad topic in which I was always learning. My year of intensive birding helped me become an even better birder. It is like any exercise: the more you do it, the stronger you get. I was strengthening those birding "muscles"!

After a year of intensive birding, I am glad to have pursued this project.

Would I do it again? Yes and no.

To avoid the carbon footprint of my Little Big Year, next time, perhaps in a few years, I'd like to try one entirely self-propelled. A zero-carbon big year. That would mean only counting birds observed entirely under my own power, walking or bicycling, from my house. Or making a trailer to attach to my bike and towing my kayak to the sea. Or cycling to a trailhead to ski or snowshoe. It would mean much more time birding my back woods and my neighborhood. There would be bike-camping trips to help deal with the distances involved. Although the number of birds from such a challenge would easily be seventy less species than this year, the result would be all-the-more rewarding for having not burned fossil fuels to find and see my feathered friends.

Spending so much time birding reminded me of my brother, Rob. He loves to hunt and fish. How many times have I heard him say that despite coming home empty-handed, he had a great day? What made it great was simply being outside, listening to the wind in the trees, hearing the birds, seeing signs of wildlife, perhaps watching a babbling mountain brook or seeing unique landscape features. There are so many ways to appreciate the natural world and they all begin with stepping out your door. That is true with birding.

In the end, it is not about seeing the most birds; instead, it is about appreciating what I do see and hear. After a day of guiding or working in my home office, I may be tense. Then I head outside to go birding and that tension melts away. In our culture, where there is so much pressure to rush and work and buy and win, it is always invigorating to go slow, appreciate the natural world, and breath.

Checklist of Little Big Year Birds Observed in Hancock County

T his is a list of all the birds observed during my big year, their common name and scientific name. They are presented in taxonomic order; that is, in evolutionary order based on taxonomy current as of January 2019. (Please note: That means that the numbers preceding the names in this list do not correspond to the numbers in the text at the end of each chapter.) For instance, in the text, Canada Jay was my 87th bird of my Little Big Year but in the following list, it is the 161st species. Furthermore, to serve as an index, the dates after each species name is when I first observed it in 2018. If you wish to read about a particular species, turn to the entry for that date.

Ducks, Geese & Waterfowl—Family Anatidae:
    Snow Goose, *Anser caerulescens* .... (first observed 04 April)
    Brant, *Branta bernicla* .... (16 October)
    Canada Goose, *Branta canadensis* .... (28 February)
    Wood Duck, *Aix sponsa* .... (11 March)
    Blue-winged Teal, *Spatula discors* .... (13 April)
    Northern Shoveler, *Spatula clypeata* .... (04 April)
    Gadwall, *Mareca strepera* .... (25 February)
    American Wigeon, *Mareca americana* .... (07 March)
    Mallard, *Anas platyrhynchos* .... (01 January)
    American Black Duck, *Anas rubripes* .... (01 January)

Northern Pintail, *Anas acuta* .... (08 January)
Green-winged Teal, *Anas crecca* .... (23 February)
Ring-necked Duck, *Aythya collaris* .... (11 March)
Greater Scaup, *Aythya marila* .... (15 January)
Lesser Scaup, *Aythya affinis* .... (01 January)
King Eider, *Somateria spectabilis* .... (03 January)
Common Eider, *Somateria mollissima* .... (01 January)
Harlequin Duck, *Histrionicus histrionicus* .... (01 January)
Surf Scoter, *Melanitta perspicillata* .... (01 January)
White-winged Scoter, *Melanitta deglandi* .... (01 January)
Black Scoter, *Melanitta americana* .... (01 January)
Long-tailed Duck, *Clangula hyemalis* .... (01 January)
Bufflehead, *Bucephala albeola* .... (01 January)
Common Goldeneye, *Bucephala clangula* .... (01 January)
Barrow's Goldeneye, *Bucephala islandica* .... (07 February)
Hooded Merganser, *Lophodytes cucullatus* .... (04 January)
Common Merganser, *Mergus merganser* .... (20 January)
Red-breasted Merganser, *Mergus serrator* .... (01 January)
Ruddy Duck, *Oxyura jamaicensis* .... (11 October)

Pheasants, Grouse & Allies—Phasianidae:
Ruffed Grouse, *Bonasa umbellus* .... (27 January)
Spruce Grouse, *Falcipennis canadensis* .... (11 April)
Wild Turkey, *Meleagris gallopavo* .... (01 January)

Grebes—Family Podicipedidae:
Pied-billed Grebe, *Podilymbus podiceps* .... (26 April)
Horned Grebe, *Podiceps auritus* .... (01 January)
Red-necked Grebe, *Podiceps grisegena* .... (01 January)

Pigeons & Doves—Family Columbidae:
Rock Pigeon, *Columba livia* .... (01 January)
Mourning Dove, *Zenaida macroura* .... (01 January)

Cuckoos—Family Cuculidae:
Yellow-billed Cuckoo, *Coccyzus americanus* .... (09 May)
Black-billed Cuckoo, *Coccyzus erythropthalmus* .... (01 July)

Nightjars & Allies—Family Caprimulgidae:
Common Nighthawk, *Chordeiles minor* .... (22 May)
Chuck-will's-widow, *Antrostomus carolinensis* .... (10 June)
Eastern Whip-poor-will, *Antrostomus vociferus* .... (10 June)
Swifts—Family Apodidae:
Chimney Swift, *Chaetura pelagica* .... (10 June)

Hummingbirds—Family Trochilidae:
Ruby-throated Hummingbird, *Archilochus colubris* .... (12 May)

Rails, Gallinules & Coots—Family Rallidae:
Virginia Rail, *Rallus limicola* .... (17 May)
Sora, *Porzana carolina* .... (21 May)
American Coot, *Fulica americana* .... (20 April)

Plovers & Lapwings—Family Charadriidae:
Black-bellied Plover, *Pluvialis squatarola* .... (17 May)
American Golden-Plover, *Pluvialis dominica* .... (20 August)
Semipalmated Plover, *Charadrius semipalmatus* .... (08 June)
Killdeer, *Charadrius vociferus* .... (30 March)

Sandpipers & Allies—Family Scolopacidae:
Upland Sandpiper, *Bartramia longicauda* .... (21 May)
Whimbrel, *Numenius phaeopus* .... (24 May)
Hudsonian Godwit, *Limosa haemastica* .... (20 August)
Ruddy Turnstone, *Arenaria interpres* .... (27 July)
Red Knot, *Calidris canutus* .... (23 July)
Stilt Sandpiper, *Calidris himantopus* .... (13 May)
Sanderling, *Calidris alba* .... (10 July)
Dunlin, *Calidris alpina* .... (02 January)
Purple Sandpiper, *Calidris maritima* .... (04 January)
Least Sandpiper, *Calidris minutilla* .... (13 May)
White-rumped Sandpiper, *Calidris fuscicollis* .... (10 May)
Pectoral Sandpiper, *Calidris melanotos* .... (16 October)
Semipalmated Sandpiper, *Calidris pusilla* (.................... 08 June)
Short-billed Dowitcher, *Limnodromus griseus* .... (23 July)
American Woodcock, *Scolopax minor* .... (02 March)
Wilson's Snipe, *Gallinago delicata* .... (05 April)
Red-necked Phalarope, *Phalaropus lobatus* .... (19 July)
Red Phalarope, *Phalaropus fulicarius* .... (14 September)
Spotted Sandpiper, *Actitis macularius* .... (12 May)
Solitary Sandpiper, *Tringa solitaria* .... (07 May)
Greater Yellowlegs, *Tringa melanoleuca* .... (25 April)
Willet, *Tringa semipalmata* .... (29 August)
Lesser Yellowlegs, *Tringa flavipes* .... (09 May)

Skuas & Jaegers—Family Stercorariidae:
Great Skua, *Stercorarius skua* .... (12 November)
South Polar Skua, *Stercorarius maccormicki* .... (14 September)
Pomarine Jaeger, *Stercorarius pomarinus* .... (19 July)

Parasitic Jaeger, *Stercorarius parasiticus* .... (19 July)

Auks, Murres & Puffins—Family Alcidae:
Dovekie, *Alle alle* .... (03 February)
Common Murre, *Uria aalge* .... (09 March)
Thick-billed Murre, *Uria lomvia* .... (11 February)
Razorbill, *Alca torda* .... (01 January)
Black Guillemot, *Cepphus grylle* .... (01 January)
Atlantic Puffin, *Fratercula arctica* .... (03 January)

Gulls, Terns & Skimmers—Family Laridae:
Black-legged Kittiwake, *Rissa tridactyla* .... (01 January)
Bonaparte's Gull, *Chroicocephalus philadelphia* .... (08 June)
Black-headed Gull, *Chroicocephalus ridibundus* .... (30 July)
Little Gull, *Hydrocoloeus minutus* .... (27 August)
Laughing Gull, *Leucophaeus atricilla* .... (01 May)
Ring-billed Gull, *Larus delawarensis* .... (01 January)
Herring Gull, *Larus argentatus* .... (01 January)
Iceland Gull, *Larus glaucoides* .... (20 January)
Lesser Black-backed Gull, *Larus fuscus* .... (25 April)
Glaucous Gull, *Larus hyperboreus* .... (01 January)
Great Black-backed Gull, *Larus marinus* .... (01 January)
Caspian Tern, *Hydroprogne caspia* .... (05 September)
Common Tern, *Sterna hirundo* .... (22 May)
Arctic Tern, *Sterna paradisaea* .... (03 July)

Loons—Family Gaviidae:
Red-throated Loon, *Gavia stellata* .... (04 January)
Common Loon, *Gavia immer* .... (01 January)

Southern Storm-Petrels—Family Oceanitidae:
Wilson's Storm-Petrel, *Oceanites oceanicus* .... (19 July)

Northern Storm-Petrels—Family Hydrobatidae:
Leach's Storm-Petrel, *Oceanodroma leucorhoa* .... (19 July)

Shearwaters & Petrels—Family Procellariidae:
Northern Fulmar, *Fulmarus glacialis* .... (19 July)
Cory's Shearwater, *Calonectris diomedea* .... (19 July)
Great Shearwater, *Ardenna gravis* .... (19 July)
Sooty Shearwater, *Ardenna grisea* .... (19 July)
Manx Shearwater, *Puffinus puffinus* .... (19 July)

Boobies & Gannets—Family Sulidae:
Northern Gannet, *Morus bassanus* .... (29 January)

Cormorants & Shags—Family Phalacrocoracidae
Great Cormorant, *Phalacrocorax carbo* .... (01 January)
Double-crested Cormorant, *Phalacrocorax auritus* .. (06 March)

Herons, Egrets & Bitterns—Family Ardeidae:
American Bittern, *Botaurus lentiginosus* .... (24 April)
Least Bittern, *Ixobrychus exilis* .... (21 May)
Great Blue Heron, *Ardea herodias* .... (02 April)
Great Egret, *Ardea alba* .... (04 May)
Snowy Egret, *Egretta thula* .... (09 May)
Little Blue Heron, *Egretta caerulea* .... (14 May)
Cattle Egret, *Bubulcus ibis* .... (24 April)
Green Heron, *Butorides virescens* .... (28 April)
Black-crowned Night-Heron, *Nycticorax nycticorax* (25 August)

New World Vultures—Family Cathartidae
Black Vulture, *Coragyps atratus* .... (27 April)
Turkey Vulture, *Cathartes aura* .... (22 February)

Osprey—Family Pandionidae
Osprey, *Pandion haliaetus* .... (10 April)

Hawks, Eagles & Kites—Family Accipitridae
Northern Harrier, *Circus hudsonius* .... (13 April)
Sharp-shinned Hawk, *Accipiter striatus* .... (01 January)
Cooper's Hawk, *Accipiter cooperii* .... (08 January)
Northern Goshawk, *Accipiter gentilis* .... (10 January)
Bald Eagle, *Haliaeetus leucocephalus* .... (01 January)
Red-shouldered Hawk, *Buteo lineatus* .... (11 June)
Broad-winged Hawk, *Buteo platypterus* .... (20 April)
Red-tailed Hawk, *Buteo jamaicensis* .... (24 January)
Rough-legged Hawk, *Buteo lagopus* .... (01 January)

Owls—Family Strigidae:
Great Horned Owl, *Bubo virginianus* .... (16 February)
Snowy Owl, *Bubo scandiacus* .... (20 January)
Barred Owl, *Strix varia* .... (23 March)
Northern Saw-whet Owl, *Aegolius acadicus* .... (20 January)

Kingfishers—Family Alcedinidae:
Belted Kingfisher, *Megaceryle alcyon* .... (15 February)

Woodpeckers—Family Picidae:
Yellow-bellied Sapsucker, *Sphyrapicus varius* .... (13 April)

Red-headed Woodpecker, *Melanerpes erythrocephalus* (02 December)
Red-bellied Woodpecker, *Melanerpes carolinus* ...... (08 January)
Black-backed Woodpecker, *Picoides arcticus* .... (27 January)
Downy Woodpecker, *Dryobates pubescens* .... (01 January)
Hairy Woodpecker, *Dryobates villosus* .... (02 January)
Pileated Woodpecker, *Dryocopus pileatus* .... (03 January)
Northern Flicker, *Colaptes auratus* .... (23 February)

Falcons & Caracaras—Family Falconidae:
American Kestrel, *Falco sparverius* .... (02 April)
Merlin, *Falco columbarius* .... (13 April)
Peregrine Falcon, *Falco peregrinus* .... (29 January)

Tyrant Flycatchers—Family Tyrannidae:
Olive-sided Flycatcher, *Contopus cooperi* .... (22 May)
Eastern Wood-Pewee, *Contopus virens* .... (04 June)
Yellow-bellied Flycatcher, *Empidonax flaviventris* .... (23 May)
Alder Flycatcher, *Empidonax alnorum* .... (17 May)
Least Flycatcher, *Empidonax minimus* .... (03 May)
Eastern Phoebe, *Sayornis phoebe* .... (05 April)
Great Crested Flycatcher, *Myiarchus crinitus* .... (03 May)
Eastern Kingbird, *Tyrannus tyrannus* .... (04 May)

Shrikes—Family Laniidae:
Northern Shrike, *Lanius borealis* .... (11 March)

Vireos—Family Vireonidae:
Blue-headed Vireo, *Vireo solitarius* .... (28 April)
Philadelphia Vireo, *Vireo philadelphicus* .... (19 May)
Warbling Vireo, *Vireo gilvus* .... (04 May)
Red-eyed Vireo, *Vireo olivaceus* .... (12 May)

Jays, Magpies, Crows & Ravens—Family Corvidae:
Canada (Gray) Jay[i], *Perisoreus canadensis* .... (18 February)
Blue Jay, *Cyanocitta cristata* .... (01 January)
American Crow, *Corvus brachyrhynchos* .... (01 January)
Fish Crow, *Corvus ossifragus* .... (13 July)
Common Raven, *Corvus corax* .... (01 January)

Larks—Family Alaudidae:
Horned Lark, *Eremophila alpestris* .... (02 January)

Martins & Swallows—Family Hirundinidae:
Northern Rough-winged Swallow, *Stelgidopteryx serripennis* (24 April)
Purple Martin, *Progne subis* .... (04 June)

Tree Swallow, *Tachycineta bicolor* .... (22 April)
Bank Swallow, *Riparia riparia* .... (10 May)
Barn Swallow, *Hirundo rustica* .... (25 April)
Cliff Swallow, *Petrochelidon pyrrhonota* .... (17 May)

Tits, Chickadees & Titmice—Family Paridae:
Black-capped Chickadee, *Poecile atricapillus* .... (01 January)
Boreal Chickadee, *Poecile hudsonicus* .... (30 December)
Tufted Titmouse, *Baeolophus bicolor* .... (08 January)

Nuthatches—Family Sittidae:
Red-breasted Nuthatch, *Sitta canadensis* .... (02 January)
White-breasted Nuthatch, *Sitta carolinensis* .... (01 January)

Treecreepers—Family Certhiidae:
Brown Creeper, *Certhia americana* .... (01 January)

Wrens—Family Troglodytidae:
House Wren, *Troglodytes aedon* .... (07 May)
Winter Wren, *Troglodytes hiemalis* .... (20 April)
Marsh Wren, *Cistothorus palustris* .... (09 May)

Gnatcatchers—Family Polioptilidae:
Blue-gray Gnatcatcher, *Polioptila caerulea* .... (05 September)

Kinglets—Family Regulidae:
Golden-crowned Kinglet, *Regulus satrapa* .... (01 January)
Ruby-crowned Kinglet, *Regulus calendula* .... (20 April)

Thrushes—Family Turdidae:
Eastern Bluebird, *Sialia sialis* .... (10 April)
Veery, *Catharus fuscescens* .... (21 May)
Gray-cheeked/Bicknell's Thrush, *C. minimus/bicknelli* (17 October)
Swainson's Thrush, *Catharus ustulatus* .... (24 April)
Hermit Thrush, *Catharus guttatus* .... (20 April)
Wood Thrush, *Hylocichla mustelina* .... (03 May)
American Robin, *Turdus migratorius* .... (08 January)

Catbirds, Mockingbirds & Thrashers—Family Mimidae:
Gray Catbird, *Dumetella carolinensis* .... (22 February)
Brown Thrasher, *Toxostoma rufum* .... (04 May)
Northern Mockingbird, *Mimus polyglottos* .... (09 February)

Starlings & Mynas—Family Sturnidae:
European Starling, *Sturnus vulgaris* .... (01 January)

Wagtails & Pipits—Family Motacillidae:
American Pipit, *Anthus rubescens* .... (12 October)

Waxwings—Family Bombycillidae:
Bohemian Waxwing, *Bombycilla garrulus* .... (26 March)
Cedar Waxwing, *Bombycilla cedrorum* .... (15 February)

Finches, Euphonias & Allies—Family Fringillidae:
Evening Grosbeak, *Coccothraustes vespertinus* .... (09 July)
Pine Grosbeak, *Pinicola enucleator* .... (24 October)
House Finch, *Haemorhous mexicanus* .... (04 January)
Purple Finch, *Haemorhous purpureus* .... (23 February)
Common Redpoll, *Acanthis flammea* .... (09 February)
Red Crossbill, *Loxia curvirostra* .... (06 January)
White-winged Crossbill, *Loxia leucoptera* .... (13 January)
Pine Siskin, *Spinus pinus* .... (05 February)
American Goldfinch, *Spinus tristis* .... (01 January)

Longspurs & Snow Buntings—Family Calcariidae:
Lapland Longspur, *Calcarius lapponicus* .... (23 February)
Snow Bunting, *Plectrophenax nivalis* .... (13 January)

New World Sparrows—Family Passerellidae:
Grasshopper Sparrow, *Ammodramus savannarum* ...... (06 June)
Chipping Sparrow, *Spizella passerina* .... (22 April)
Field Sparrow, *Spizella pusilla* .... (24 April)
Lark Sparrow, *Chondestes grammacus* .... (19 July)
American Tree Sparrow, *Spizelloides arborea* .... (08 January)
Fox Sparrow, *Passerella iliaca* .... (02 January)
Dark-eyed Junco, *Junco hyemalis* .... (01 January)
White-crowned Sparrow, *Zonotrichia leucophrys* .... (09 May)
White-throated Sparrow, *Zonotrichia albicollis* .... (02 January)
Vesper Sparrow, *Pooecetes gramineus* .... (22 April)
Nelson's Sparrow, *Ammospiza nelsoni* .... (22 May)
Savannah Sparrow, *Passerculus sandwichensis* .... (29 March)
Song Sparrow, *Melospiza melodia* .... (04 January)
Lincoln's Sparrow, *Melospiza lincolnii* .... (09 May)
Swamp Sparrow, *Melospiza georgiana* .... (20 April)
Eastern Towhee, *Pipilo erythrophthalmus* .... (29 March)

Yellow-breasted Chat—Family Icteriidae:
Yellow-breasted Chat, *Icteria virens* .... (05 September)

Blackbirds—Family Icteridae:

Bobolink, *Dolichonyx oryzivorus* .... (10 May)
Eastern Meadowlark, *Sturnella magna* .... (29 April)
Orchard Oriole, *Icterus spurius* .... (09 May)
Baltimore Oriole, *Icterus galbula* .... (09 May)
Red-winged Blackbird, *Agelaius phoeniceus* .... (25 February)
Brown-headed Cowbird, *Molothrus ater* .... (25 April)
Rusty Blackbird, *Euphagus carolinus* .... (22 April)
Common Grackle, *Quiscalus quiscula* .... (01 January)

New World Warblers—Family Parulidae:

Ovenbird, *Seiurus aurocapilla* .... (07 May)
Northern Waterthrush, *Parkesia noveboracensis* .... (02 May)
Blue-winged Warbler, *Vermivora cyanoptera* .... (04 June)
Black-and-white Warbler, *Mniotilta varia* .... (02 May)
Tennessee Warbler, *Oreothlypis peregrina* .... (22 May)
Orange-crowned Warbler, *Oreothlypis celata* .... (05 September)
Nashville Warbler, *Oreothlypis ruficapilla* .... (04 May)
Mourning Warbler, *Geothlypis philadelphia* .... (05 June)
Common Yellowthroat, *Geothlypis trichas* .... (09 May)
American Redstart, *Setophaga ruticilla* .... (12 May)
Cape May Warbler, *Setophaga tigrina* .... (17 May)
Northern Parula, *Setophaga americana* .... (03 May)
Magnolia Warbler, *Setophaga magnolia* .... (12 May)
Bay-breasted Warbler, *Setophaga castanea* .... (12 May)
Blackburnian Warbler, *Setophaga fusca* .... (09 May)
Yellow Warbler, *Setophaga petechia* .... (07 May)
Chestnut-sided Warbler, *Setophaga pensylvanica* .... (10 May)
Blackpoll Warbler, *Setophaga striata* .... (17 May)
Black-throated Blue Warbler, *Setophaga caerulescens* ... (07 May)
Palm Warbler, *Setophaga palmarum* .... (13 April)
Pine Warbler, *Setophaga pinus* .... (21 April)
Yellow-rumped Warbler, *Setophaga coronata* .... (20 April)
Black-throated Green Warbler, *Setophaga virens* .... (03 May)
Canada Warbler, *Cardellina canadensis* .... (15 May)
Wilson's Warbler, *Cardellina pusilla* .... (12 May)

Cardinals, Grosbeaks & Allies—Family Cardinalidae:

Summer Tanager, *Piranga rubra* .... (21 April)
Scarlet Tanager, *Piranga olivacea* .... (15 May)
Northern Cardinal, *Cardinalis cardinalis* .... (02 January)

Checklist

Rose-breasted Grosbeak, *Pheucticus ludovicianus* (25 April)
Blue Grosbeak, *Passerina caerulea* .... (22 April)
Indigo Bunting, *Passerina cyanea* .... (09 May)
Painted Bunting, *Passerina ciris* .... (29 April)
Dickcissel, *Spiza americana* .... (01 September)

Old World Sparrows—Family Passeridae:
House Sparrow, *Passer domesticus* .... (04 January)

Acknowledgements

My Little Big Year was far from a solo effort. During the course of the year, I birded with many, many individuals, and had bird sighting intelligence from many more. Although not everyone was mentioned in the text, I appreciated each and every one of you! To the best of my recollection, the people who had some hand in making this book possible include (in alphabetical order):

Evan Adams, Dr. Tom Adams, Anatolia Andriole, Anika Am Stutz, Steve Am Stutz, Dr. John Anderson, Sean Ashe, Lucian Avila-Gatz, Connie & Bill Banford, Tim Barnett, Carol Beam, Anne & Greg Benz, Seth Benz, Louis Bevier, Cecelia Blackett, Gary Blazon, Nan Boardman, Velma Bolyard, Wayne Bolyard, Renee & Brent Borovsky, Bill Carpenter, Alison Dibble, Jeff DiBella, Matt Dickinson, George & Kelly Dickson, Cheri Domina, Ed Douglas, Sherry Downing, Nathan Dubrow, Nina Duggan, Merrie Eley, Gary Fagan, Jean Forbes, Lyn Gatz, Lucie Gauvin, Fred Guard, Susan Guilford, Emily Gumpert, Peggy & Mike Gumpert, Bill Hancock, Lynn Hävsall, Ed & Deb Hawkes, Billy Helprin, Doug Hitchcox, Lynn Horowitz, Will Hunt, Lauren Hunt, Ken Hutchins, Charlie Jacobi, Karen Johnson, Dan Johnston, Jim Johnston, James Kaiser, Scott Kaiser, Patrick Kark, Garrison Keillor, Craig Kesselheim, Joanne Kilton, Zack Klyver, Paula Kulas, Fyn Kynd, Marie Larossee, Steven Latta, Gary Lee, Ellen Lehto, Adrienne Leppold, Kelly & Doyle & Max & Becket Lim, Don Lima, Kyle Lima, Aggie Linforth, Alan & Marsha Lobel, Mary Lyman, Anouk MacDonald, Bronson MacDonald, Claudia MacDonald, Fogo MacDonald, Joel MacDonald, Ramsey MacDonald, Rob MacDonald, Harlan Mahoney, Jennifer Barillo &

Acknowledgements

Brett & James & Carly Maiorano, Connor Marland, Brian McAllister, Mackette McCormack, Pamela McCullough, Tara & Liam McKernan, Megan McOsker, Ronan McWilliams, Richard Mélançon, Martha & Charlie Mitchell, Martha Mitchell, Robert Mitchell, Robbie & Hilary Mitchell, Glen Mittelhauser, Pepin Mittelhauser, Kate Morse, Clark "Chip" Moseley, Truth Muller, Carol & Wally Muth, Elizabeth & Ken Norris, Rob & Tammy Packie, Logan Parker, Anne Patterson, Tim Perrier, John M.C. "Mike" Peterson, Anne Piazza, Tyler Piebes, Karen & Jonathan & Ava & Ori Pinn, Hannah Poduergiel, Jane Potter, Paul Renault, Jane Reynolds, Grayson Richmond, Scott Riddell, Ann Rivers, John Rivers, Stacy Roland, Lindsay & Minnie Russell, Jenna Schlener, Catherine Schmidt, Nina Schoch, Nathaniel Sharp, Roberta Sharp, Sue & Harold Shaw, Ken Shellenberger, Mike Sheridan, Linda Shingleton, Kurt & Robyn Silberstein, Donne Sinderson, Dean Spaulding, Myriam Springuel, Natalie Springuel, Toby Stephenson, Hannah Stevens, Mary Thill, Leslie Tiller, Dr. Sean Todd, Lauren Tucker, Ron Wanner, Dr. Jeff Wells, Chris West, Brendan White, Chuck Whitney, Laurie Yntema, Fred Yost, Karen Zimmerman, and Tristan Zimmerman.

I would also like to thank the many participants from my Road Scholar trips; all of the wonderful families from College of the Atlantic's Family Nature Camp and the many trips I led for them; the residents of Crabtree Neck who joined me on a walking tour sponsored by Crabtree Neck Land Trust; Mount Desert Island High School science teacher Hannah Podurgiel and the students of her Outside Science class; Glen Mittelhauser, coordinator for the Maine Bird Atlas, and his seasonal technicians (Sean Ashe, Matt Dickinson, Connor Marland, Logan Parker, Nathaniel Sharp, and Chris West) during two days of training; the Maine Master Naturalists participating in my Birding By Ear workshop; and all the people on The Natural History Center's many nature and adventure tours. My sincere apologies to anyone I inadvertently forgot to include on this list.

My mother, Claudia MacDonald, did a thorough read and copy-edit of this book. Thanks, Mom! And my birding friend and fellow author, Jane Potter, did a read of the manuscript (Jane is a wonderful author, look up her books on Maine Authors Publishing and start with *Margaret's Mentor*). Thank you, Mom and Jane, for helping me make this book as good as it is! Any errors you find were likely things they noted as needing fixing and I overlooked.

This book would not have been possible without the support of my family. Special thanks are due to my wife, Natalie Springuel, for being a sounding board, my editor, and for all her support during my Little Big Year. This book is a far better read as a direct result of Natalie's tireless big-picture editing, reading, and re-editing. Thank you, Natalie!

Endnotes

My Little Big Year

[i] Since its inception, the World Series of Birding (WSB) has been hosted by New Jersey Audubon (NJA). Although it is the big names that garner the attention, it is open to anyone, regardless of skill. To make the WSB appealing to a broader audience, NJA lets each team decide whether they want to blanket the entire state in twenty-four hours or limit their efforts more regionally. For instance, in 1999, three friends and I participated in the WSB, and birded just Cape May County in southern New Jersey. In the end, the WSB is about having fun and raising money for charity.

[ii] *The Big Year*, directed by David Frankel, was released in 2011. At the beginning of the movie, when they flash through the usual verbiage declaiming its basis, the following text scrolls: "This is a true story. Only the facts have been changed."

[iii] Sandy Komito, *the* Sandy Komito immortalized in Mark Obmascik's book, *The Big Year* (2004), tallied a whopping 745 species in 1998! Eventually, that number was bumped up to 748 after several contested species were accepted by state avian records committees. In those days, North American big years did not include Hawaii. As of 2016, North American big years officially (with the governing body being the American Birding Association) include Hawaii. In that same year, a new North American Big Year record was set with a whopping 835 species! And equally impressive, 783 of those were observed in North America, exclusive of Hawaii!

[iv] Richards, J. (1970). *Atlas of Breeding Birds of the West Midlands*. London: published for the West Midland Bird Club by Collins. 276 pp.

[v] Laughlin, Sarah B., and Douglas P. Kibbe (eds.). (1985). *The Atlas of Breeding Birds of Vermont*. Woodstock, Vermont: Vermont Institute of Natural Science. 456 pp.

vi Adamus, Paul, Bonnie Bochan, and Peter Cannell (coordinators). (1984). *Atlas of Breeding Birds in Maine: 1978—1983*. Augusta: Maine Department of Inland Fisheries & Wildlife. 366 pp.

vii Migrant traps are those places forcing birds to congregate at some point in their migration. Peninsulas regularly make for some of the best-known migrant traps. For example, Point Pelee, on the Ontario shores of Lake Erie, is renowned as a fall birding hotspot as birds queue up, waiting for the perfect weather window to fly across the broad lake.

eBird

i For anyone not around in 1999, or too young to remember, there was great concern that our digital infrastructure was not designed to transition from calendars with years starting 19 versus 20. Great money and effort went into addressing this perceived problem. In the end, the year 2000 came with much fanfare and few e-problems.

ii See ebird.org/news/ebird-2017-in-review, accessed 29 November 2018.

iii See ebird.org/content/ebird/about, accessed 24 January 2018.

01 January

i Frank M. Chapman. (1901). 'The Christmas Bird Census.' *Bird-Lore*. 3(1): 28-33. Available online at: www.audubon.org/sites/default/files/first_bird-lore_1901_nas.pdf, accessed 28 February 2020.

ii Quote taken from the invasive species page of the U.S. Forest Service's Pacific Northwest Research Station (www.fs.fed.us/outernet/pnw/invasives/index.shtml, accessed 04 January 2018).

iii A.W. Schorger. (1952). 'Introduction of the Domestic Pigeon.' *Auk*. 69(4): 462-463. Available for download from the Searchable Ornithological Research Archive at sora.unm.edu/node/20104, accessed 06 May 2020.

iv Ted Gup. (1990). 'Opinion: 100 years of the starling.' *The New York Times*. Available online at www.nytimes.com/1990/09/01/opinion/100-years-of-the-starling.html. Related perspectives can also be found at people.wku.edu/charles.smith/biogeog/COOK1928.htm and www.scientificamerican.com/article/call-of-the-reviled, all accessed 05 January 2018.

v From the Charter and By-laws of the American Acclimatization Society, published in New York in 1871 by G.W. Averell (16 pp.).

Endnotes

[vi] Michael P. Moulton, Wendell P. Cropper, Jr., Michael L. Avery, and Linda E. Moulton. (2010). 'The earliest House Sparrow introductions to North America.' *Biological Invasions.* 12(9): 2955-2958. Available for download from the University of Nebraska – Lincoln's DigitalCommons at digitalcommons.unl.edu/cgi/viewcontent.cgi?article=1945&context=icwdm_usdanwrc. Another interesting historical compilation can be found online at www.sialis.org/hosphistory.htm, accessed 05 January 2018.

[vii] "I found my thrill, on Blueberry Hill" was popularized by Fats Domino in 1956.

[viii] A "super moon" occurs when the Moon is at its closest in its orbit around the Earth. Given the relationship of the gravitational pull between the Moon and the Earth, these events cause particularly low low tides and extra high high tides.

[ix] The Niagara River is unique in being one of the few major rivers in the Northern Hemisphere that flows north. In this case, it flows from Lake Erie, north to the geographic feature that is the falls. The falls are actually three: Niagara Falls, Bridal Veil Falls, and Horseshoe Falls. Niagara Falls (most people lump the narrow Bridal Veil Falls with this) has immense sedimentary, water-blasted boulders at its base; Horseshoe Falls is the longer and higher, cascading nearly 190 feet. Somewhere in the neighborhood of 10,000 years ago, the cataract was seven miles north, pouring over the edge of the Niagara Escarpment in Lewiston, New York, but has eroded back to its current position. Everything below the falls, north to Lake Ontario, is the lower Niagara River. Lewiston, of course, is where I grew up and cut my egg teeth birding.

[x] Banding has a long history, whether used to transmit messages or identify individual birds in pursuit of scientific knowledge. The earliest documented use of banding occurred when Quintas Fabius Pictor (born ca. 254 B.C.E.), referring to the Second Punic War (218—201 B.C.E.), wrote, "When a Roman garrison was besieged by the Ligurians, a swallow taken from her nestlings was brought to him for him to indicate, by knots made on a thread tied to its foot, how many days later help would arrive and a sortie must be made."

In 1595, a metal ring on the leg of one of King Henry IV's Peregrine Falcons confirmed the bird's identity when it was lost in France and was found a day later in Malta.

John James Audubon, curious as to whether Eastern Phoebes return year after year, reached into a nest to grab the nestlings and tied silver threads around the each of their legs. A year later, the return of two of them to the neighborhood was confirmed.

It was not until 1902 that a systematic program to band birds was begun in North America. Today, bands are generally a metal alloy stamped with a unique number. Licensed banders capture birds, affix a band to a bird's leg, make a variety of measurements, and release the bird unharmed. Whenever a bird is found with a metal band, whether by other researchers or private individuals, the band's unique number offers important identifying information. Over the past 100 years, much of our knowledge of migration has come directly as a result of banding. If a bird with a band is found, you can report it to the Bird Banding Laboratory online at www.pwrc.usgs.gov/BBL/bblretrv.

For a short and fascinating read on the history of bird banding, turn to an article by Harold B. Wood (1945), entitled 'The history of bird banding,' published in *The Auk*, 62(2): 256-265, available on-line at https://sora.unm.edu/sites/default/files/journals/auk/v062n02/p0256-p0265.pdf accessed 06 May 2020.

xi The taxonomic order I typically follow is that of the American Ornithological Society's (formerly the American Ornithologists' Union) 'Checklist of North and Middle American Birds' (available on-line at http://checklist.aou.org). Ornithologists have long used the best available knowledge to determine this evolutionary order, with birds that evolved earliest at the beginning of the list and those more recently evolved toward the end.

02 January

i The Cornell Lab of Ornithology maintains a marvelous free website providing information about the birds of North America, including identification, life history, sound recordings, and range maps. For Horned Lark, browse www.allaboutbirds.org/guide/Horned_Lark (accessed 02 January 2018).

ii For two miles, Ocean Drive wends its way along the rocky shoreline of Mount Desert Island's southeast coast. Ocean Drive is part of the twenty-seven-mile Park Loop Road, one of the most scenic drives in Maine. During the winter, most of the road is closed to automobile traffic, but a mile-long stretch is left open for the public to drive. It is one-way, so during the off-season, you can only access it from the end of Schooner Head Road in Bar Harbor.

iii Some birds, especially finches, like to ingest small bits of gravel to aid the gizzard (a portion of the stomach) in grinding food so that the stomach's enzymes can more readily digest and extract nutrients. When driving down the road, especially smaller roads with good tree cover very close, look for birds feeding on the road's shoulders.

03 January

i To learn more about King Eiders, as well as to see some photos, browse the All About Birds website at www.allaboutbirds.org/guide/King_Eider (accessed 03 January 2018).

ii There is an excellent book coauthored by Steven Kress that tells the story of Maine's puffins: Dr. Stephen W. Kress and Derrick Z. Jackson. (2015). *Project*

Puffin: The Improbable Quest to Bring a Beloved Seabird Back to Egg Rock. Yale University Press. 376 pp.

[iii] Atlantic Puffin colonies are maintained and monitored on Eastern Egg Rock, Matinicus Rock, Seal Island, and Petit Manan Island. There is also a vibrant puffin colony on Machias Seal Island, which is officially claimed by both the U.S. and Canada. And as of summer 2018, at least one pair successfully nested on Great Duck Island.

[iv] Two online articles offer good reading on the subject of North American puffin dispersal: 'Puffin mystery solved with first tracking evidence' (www.audubon.org/news/puffin-mystery-solved-first-tracking-evidence) and 'Where do Maine's Atlantic Puffins go for the Winter? (www.audubon.org/news/where-do-maines-atlantic-puffins-go-winter). A similar story from Europe—'Puffins' winter odyssey revealed'—is also available online (news.bbc.co.uk/2/hi/science/nature/8452423.stm), all accessed 04 January 2018.

[v] A fun aside: during the fall of 2017, I had the pleasure of leading a Road Scholar night-sky tour to Norway. Among the program participants was a surname that instantly rang a bell: Schmidt-Nielsen. During the 1960s and 70s, Knut Schmidt-Nielsen was pioneering research on seabirds and the way they metabolize saltwater. It turned out that one of the women in my program was his daughter!

04 January

[i] Bar Harbor's Shore Path closely follows the shoreline, stretching nearly ¾ of a mile from the Town Pier to Wayman Lane (where the hospital is located). This gentle walk takes you back in time as you follow in the footsteps of the Astors and Fords and Rockefellers who all likely took in the scenic vistas as they strolled from "cottage" to "cottage" ("cottage" being the name of these palatial summer homes, bigger than any house in which I have ever lived), many of which still abut the Shore Path today. Created in 1880 by some forward thinkers, with its views of historic "cottages" and inns to the shoreward and the Porcupine Islands to the seaward, this easy path is worth taking in, whether birding or not.

[ii] There is a saying in Maine that "nothing good comes out of the east." In short, whenever there is an easterly component to the wind, it usually is during inclement weather or presages it.

[iii] "Pleased" is a strong word for a House Sparrow. For a reminder on what I mean, see my discussion on Rock Pigeon, European Starling, and House Sparrow written for 01 January.

[iv] One recent study offers a particularly lucid and sobering look at the impact of domestic cats on birds: Scott R. Loss, Tom Will, and Peter P. Marra. (2013). 'The

impact of free-ranging domestic cats on wildlife in the United States.' *Nature Communications*. 4: 1-7. For those interested in exploring further, the following offers a thorough literature review: Nico Dauphine and Robert J. Cooper. (2009). 'Impacts of free-ranging domestic cats (*Felix catus*) on birds in the United States: a review of recent research with conservation and management recommendations.' *Proceedings of the Fourth International Partners in Flight Conference: Tundra to Tropics*. 205-219.

ᵛ Tides are largely driven by the gravitational tug of the Moon. Although geography and bathymetry can influence tidal magnitude, in Maine, the time between a low tide and a high tide (or a high tide and a low tide) is six hours thirteen minutes—two cycles each of low tide and high tides take twenty-four hours and fifty-two minutes.

When estimating the amount of water moving in and out of an area, you can apply the "Rule of Twelfths." In short (and for simple mathematics, we will estimate the tide cycle at six hours), it states that in the first hour of the tide cycle, one-twelfth of the total volume of water to be exchanged will move. In the second hour, two-twelfths will move. In the third hour, three-twelfths will move. In the fourth hour, three twelfths will move again. In the fifth hour, two-twelfths will move. In the sixth hour, one-twelfth will move. If you were to plot this, it makes a sine curve with the most water moving in the middle (or third and fourth) hours, resulting in the strongest currents occurring in the middle two hours of the six-hour tide cycle.

08 January

ⁱ When I first met John M.C. "Mike" Peterson, his life was focused on birds: he banded them nearly full time; at least, whenever he wasn't birding or writing about them. He didn't drive, and I loved to drive, so several times each week I would pick him up at his Elizabethtown, New York, home and we would go birding around northern New York, especially the Champlain Valley.

In 1989, he hired me to be a warden for the Four Brothers Islands Nature Preserve, the only preserve of the Adirondack Chapter of The Nature Conservancy dedicated solely to birdlife. Mike once told me (in jest, I always believed) that the only reason he hired me is because I had a pick-up truck with a trailer hitch and had my own carpentry tools.

On the first day I met Mike, we hooked up the trailer to my truck and the lights did not work. I was able to quickly troubleshoot, replace a length of wire, and get them working. While I worked, Mike regaled me with stories. We finally made it to the Willsboro boat launch. I backed the trailer to the top of the launch and set the parking brake. As I readied the boat for launching, a big ol' fisherman made his way to me and said in a thick, eastern Adirondack accent, "I hope you're goin' out there to kill those gawd-damned birds." Although I had no idea what he was talking about, I was duly intimidated.

And thus, Mike introduced me to the cormorant and the controversy surrounding this native species (in short, people, primarily fishermen, think cormorants eat too many fish, a notion generally not borne out by the science), along with a lifelong passion for truth, accuracy, and clarity in science and in reporting.

Over the years, we banded thousands and thousands of birds together (more than 140 species), participated in dozens of Christmas Bird Counts, occasionally collaborated on the *High Peaks Audubon Newsletter*, and every spring spent days and days between Mother's Day and Memorial Day banding birds at Crown Point State Historic Site.

Mike imparted two particular lessons I will always remember him for: 1) When dealing with the press or kids, speak in soundbites. 2) Keep your fingernails well-groomed because you never know when your hands are going to show up in a photo (I believe he was implying because of a bird you are holding).

Alas, on 02 May 2017, Mike passed away. Good-bye, my friend. I hope we can bird together one day again.

10 January

[i] One of the things I do with my Weekly Birding Tours, or, for that matter, any of The Natural History Center's programming, is track the birds people see. When they reach 100 species of birds identified in our programs, they earn an embroidered patch for their accomplishment. For more details, browse www.thenaturalhistorycenter.com/mdi-bird-club.

[ii] In 1604, French explorer/navigator/cartographer Samuel de Champlain was mapping the coast of much of what would eventually become Maine, New Brunswick, and Nova Scotia. During those explorations, he ran aground on a ledge. I can just imagine how it might have happened: a sailor at the rail, throwing a lead line with its seven-pound weight over the side, counting out knots on the line as it passed through his hand, "Nineteen fathoms" (with one fathom being six feet, that means the water would be 114 feet deep). He would haul the lead line up and repeat the process: "Nineteen fathoms." Repeat: "One fathom." *GRIND!!!* The ship came to a wood-splintering halt on a submerged ledge.

With tide going out, Champlain was stuck on a ledge, grounded for nearly a whole tide cycle. The time between a high tide and a low tide is six hours and thirteen minutes. The time between a low tide and high tide is six hours and thirteen minutes. That meant Champlain had to wait for the tide to go completely out and then come most of the way back in before floating his vessel once again.

In the meantime, he directed two launches to be set and row along the shoreline in opposite directions. Eventually, they met and realized they were stuck off a large island. Standing on the deck, looking to the shore, mountains with rocky summits rising up, Champlain named it *les Île de Mont Désert*, which roughly translates to the island of barren mountains.

The name has long been Anglicized to Mount Desert Island. Today, the big local controversy is the correct pronunciation of our island. Do you say Mount Desert Island, with "Desert" pronounced like the hot, sandy place, or do you pronounce it "dessert," like the tasty, after dinner delicacy? My informal survey suggests residents are split, with people in the latter camp arguing that it is closer to how Champlain would have said the name. Whichever side you support, everyone is in agreement that Mount Desert Island can be simply referred to as MDI, with each of the three letters pronounced individually: M. D. I.

iii The Great Fire of 1947 may well have been the singular most traumatic event to happen to Mount Desert Island since the glaciers. A fire started in Fresh Meadow, the peat bog near Dolliver's dump, in the afternoon of 17 October 1947. The autumn winds kicked up, fanning the flames, creating a conflagration that raged down the east side of MDI, eventually cutting off all access and egress to Bar Harbor. The fire was contained by 27 October with over 17,000 acres burned. The cultural and natural landscape of Mount Desert Island was forever changed.

iv While a kid, birding with my younger brother, Rob, I once rhetorically stated that between a Red-breasted Nuthatch and a Brown Creeper, I could never remember which one tends to forage up a tree trunk and which one tends to go down. Rob, ever the straight guy to my goofball, replied, "That's easy. The creeper goes up, kind of like your underwear creeps up."

v See www.allaboutbirds.org/guide/Northern_Goshawk, accessed 10 January 2018.

15 January

i You can listen to this pivotal speech, or read the transcript, online at http://openvault.wgbh.org/catalog/A_76C3B93B557D4976A032C27C72ACED18#at_90.041_s, accessed 15 January 2018.

ii General impression of size and shape is variously simplified as giss (which would be the most accurate acronym), gizz, or jizz. Although the last two are the most commonly used, they are all pronounced jizz.

20 January

i UMO, with each of the letters pronounced individually, stands for University of Maine, Orono. The Orono campus is the flagship of the University of Maine system, which was established in 1865 as a land grant college.

ii Plans to make your own nest-box can be found on-line at the site for Cornell Lab of Ornithology's NestWatch: nestwatch.org/learn/all-about-bird-houses/birds/northern-saw-whet-owl, accessed 20 January 2018.

Endnotes

[iii] Acadia Wildlife Center is a not-for-profit wildlife rehabilitation clinic accepting all wild animals, whether injured or just unable to fend for itself (such as baby animals). Before picking up any critter you suspect of being in distress, check in with the licensed professionals at Acadia Wildlife Center (or your local wildlife rehabilitator if you do not live in Hancock County). For more information, browse www.acadiawildlife.org.

[iv] Birdsacre combines Cordelia Stanwood's (1865—1958) home (now operating as the Homestead Museum) with a nature center, all on the 200-acre Stanwood Wildlife Sanctuary. Located on Route 3 just south edge of Ellsworth, this non-profit organization is dedicated to Stanwood's life and achievements. A network of trails is open to the public year-round with an educational lineup that includes their popular owl program, starring live owls. For more information, browse their website at www.birdsacre.com.

[v] One winter evening, after dark (remember, sunset is before 4:00 on the Winter Solstice), I was driving west from Bar Harbor on Eagle Lake Road with my daughter Anouk, who was about four years old at the time, and her friend Aggie. Something small flashed in my headlights as it bounced over the car in front of us. Alas, I knew from the experience of seeing this very same thing happen several times before that it was a bird. We quickly pulled over and found an injured Northern Saw-whet Owl standing—wobbling may be a more accurate description—wing dangling by its side. The girls hovering behind me, I carefully picked up the bird and placed it in the pocket of my down jacket, a warm, cozy, dark place to offer it a semblance of calm and security. We took the owl to Acadia Wildlife Foundation where Ann Rivers took it in.

This particular story had a happy ending: several weeks later, Ann called and said the bird was ready to be released. Her preferred policy is to have animals released near where they were found. So, Anouk, Aggie, and I picked up the owl and took it back to the same roadside turnout where we had first recovered it. Opening the transport box, the bird looked around for a moment, then flew off into the forest. Several minutes later, Anouk, Aggie, and I heard a series of bill-claps and a squeaky, mouse-like call. We liked to think it was the owl thanking us for saving its life.

27 January

[i] For more information about Kittredge Brook Preserve, including a map, browse www.mcht.org/preserves/kittredge-brook-forest.

[ii] Since 02 July 2017, the Bird Banding Lab only accepts reports of bird bands online or by mail. Their website—www.reportband.gov—makes it easy, with the added benefit of instantaneously learning about "your" bird, its species, and when and where it was banded.

Many bands still have imprinted either "WRITE BIRD BAND LAUREL MD 20708 USA" or "AVISE BIRD BAND WASH DC". Sending the band, or, better yet, a note with the band number and a very short description of how you came to find the band will immensely add to our understanding of birds. Be sure to include your mailing address and they will send you a postcard with information about the banded bird.

iii Audubon seems to have supplanted the name of Eastern Phoebe with Eastern Wood-Pewee. He sometimes used bird names that are different today. And sometimes he got the names wrong. This is not to detract from his monumental work, which is massively impressive even by today's standards; instead, it is an acknowledgement that even the best of us make mistakes.

29 January

i Rachel Carson. (1962). *Silent Spring.* Boston: Houghton Mifflin Company. 368 pp.

ii Situated as it is adjacent to Acadia National Park's Sand Beach, Great Head is a popular hiking area. The trail ranges from easy for most of it to moderate to a few short sections of difficult. How many people have hiked the trail and come upon the "pile of rubble, clearly manmade as many of the stones retain remnants of mortar" and not known its history?

In 1915, Louisa Morgan Satterlee, daughter of J.P. Morgan, had a stone tea house built on the southern tip of Great Head. I can envision a scene:

Mrs. Satterlee and Mrs. Anthony and others of their friends, sitting, sipping tea, dressed in the long dresses and low-profile hats full of lace, fashion appropriate for outdoor activity of the day. Someone notices a bird in the mist-net, or maybe a wire cage bal-chatri trap. The women file down the path, following Mrs. Anthony, who removed the bird, brought it back to the tea house, affixed an appropriate band, and proceeded to make measurements. The women were so intrigued by these feathered jewels that they wanted to preserve them for all time, and so eschewed the fashion of the day which included all manner of feather adornment in their hats. They would have been among the pioneers of the early Audubon Societies, diligently working to enact legislation to reverse declining bird populations by banning market hunting.

Regardless of the accuracy of my imagined scenario, the pile of rubble we see today is what is left of that once striking structure, part of a larger 110-acre estate called "Great Head." This property had been a wedding present from Mrs. Satterlee's father. In its heyday, the landscape included gardens designed by renowned garden designer Beatrix Farrand and would have been tended by up to five gardeners.

Alas, the Great Fire of '47 destroyed the estate, severely damaging the tea house. In 1949, the property was donated to Acadia National Park, which, in turn, removed the remaining structures out of concern for safety.

To learn more about the story of Great Head, browse www.swhpli-brary.net/digitalarchive/items/show/9112 and www.ellsworthameri-can.com/maine-news/great-heads-long-lost-eden, both accessed 06 May 2020.

[iii] *Birds of Acadia National Park and Mount Desert Island, Maine: Including Offshore Waters, Surrounding Islands, and Mount Desert Rock*, a book I hope to complete during 2020.

[iv] May Thacher Cooke. (1937). 'Some longevity records of wild birds.' *Bird-Banding*. 8(2): 52-65. In this article, Cooke listed two Black-capped Chickadees (one re-trapped six years after being banded, another seven years) and a Chipping Sparrow (retrapped six years after being banded), both initially banded and caught again years later at Great Head, Bar Harbor, Maine.

03 February

[i] In Hancock County, we are fortunate in having a number of conservation organizations protecting our landscape, including Blue Hill Heritage Trust, Frenchman Bay Conservancy, Great Pond Mountain Conservation Trust, Island Heritage Trust, and Maine Coast Heritage Trust.

[ii] In my opinion, the international conservation organization offering the biggest bang for the buck is The Nature Conservancy. For decades, they have been proactively tying their conservation activities in the U.S. to the Caribbean, South America, and beyond by working with in-country partner organizations. (Full disclosure: from 1995—2002, I worked on the science staff of The Nature Conservancy.)

[iii] For more information about the MDI Bird Club, browse www.thenaturalhisto-rycenter.com/mdi-bird-club.

[iv] To learn more about Frenchman Bay Conservancy, its preserves and other efforts to protect the landscape of Downeast Maine, browse www.french-manbay.org.

05 February

[i] The Four Brothers, originally named *Îles de Quatre Vents* (Isles of the Four Winds) in 1609 by French explorer Samuel de Champlain, have long been bird-nesting islands. In 1988, I began working part-time for High Peaks Audubon Society as warden of this preserve owned by The Nature Conservancy. Every year, we conducted a nesting bird census and banded a sample of the chicks. With around 15,000 Ring-billed Gull nests, somewhere in the neighborhood of 1,500 Herring Gull nests, perhaps 1—2 dozen Great Black-backed Gull nests, a peak of over 2,000 Double-crested Cormorant nests, a few hundred Great Blue Heron nests,

and a smattering of Caspian Tern, Great Egret, Snowy Egret, Cattle Egret, Black-crowned Night-Heron, and Glossy Ibis nests, this added up to quite a few birds banded over the years.

ii These seven mountains are among the forty-six peaks in the Adirondacks taller than 4,000 feet. Well, that was the claim when they were originally surveyed. Subsequent efforts to more precisely determine their elevations found four to be shy of the 4,000-foot threshold. Still, in a nod to tradition, they retained their collective name: the Adirondack High Peaks. Anyone who ascends all of them are called 46ers.

09 February

i Sullivan, Maurice. (1940). 'Ivory Gull from Mount Desert Island, Maine.' *The Auk.* 57(3): 403. Available online at https://sora.unm.edu/node/18011, accessed 06 May 2020.

ii Anonymous. (1946). 'Bird notes.' *Maine Audubon Society Bulletin.* 2(2): 48-53.

iii Perhaps no single person embodied the spirit of everything bird more, at least in regard to Mount Desert Island, than James Bond (04 January 1900 — 14 February 1989). He had the corner on the triangular trade of ornithology. Although Bond made his life's work the study of Caribbean avifauna (his opus *Birds of the West Indies* is a definitive resource to this day), he summered on Mount Desert Island. Between times, he could be found in Philadelphia where he held various appointments on the scientific staff of the Academy of Natural Sciences. In a memoriam in *The Auk* (106(4): 718-720), it was written that Bond was "among the last of a traditional breed, the independently wealthy, non-salaried curator, who lacked university degrees." Lack of advanced university degrees certainly did not hinder Mr. Bond.

Beginning in the mid-1920s, he made near-annual visits to Mount Desert Island until his death. During the early summer of 1936, while undertaking field observations near Acadia National Park's Seawall, he documented the first Cape May Warbler nesting not just in Maine, but anywhere in the continental United States. This paper (*Auk* 54(3): 306-308) made an important distinction in the behavior of warblers: that singing male Cape May Warblers "had no particular 'singing tree' as many warblers have, but each bird confined itself to a very restricted locality".

Bond's other mark was through no design of his own—it certainly meant absolutely nothing to him—but is known across the world. Everyone knows his name! Bond. James Bond. Stories abound of how Ian Fleming, progenitor of fictional British secret agent 007, "borrowed" Bond's name. One unsubstantiated story had Fleming and Bond meeting at a party in Jamaica (it was Northeast Harbor, Maine, in another telling) and that Bond introduced himself as "Bond, James Bond." As good as that story is, the real story is its equal. (For a short-but-fun accounting of how Ian Fleming appropriated James Bond's name for his protagonist, read Mary Wickham Bond's 1966 book, *How 007 Got His Name*.)

Ian Fleming had a home in Oracabessa, Jamaica, and was a keen bird-watcher. In a letter to James Bond's wife, long after the success of his first novel, *Casino Royale*, Fleming discusses writing a thriller "to take my mind off the dreadful prospect of marriage ...":

> "I was determined that my secret agent should be as anonymous a personality as possible. Even his name should be the very reverse of the kind of "Peregrine Carruthers" whom one meets in this type of fiction.

> "At that time one of my bibles was, and still is, *Birds of the West Indies* by James Bond, and it struck me that this name, brief, unromantic and yet very masculine, was just what I needed and so James Bond II was born ..."

[iv] Bond, James. (1967). *Native Birds of Mount Desert Island*. Philadelphia: The Academy of Natural Sciences. 26 pp.

[v] Long, Ralph H. (1982). *Native Birds of Mount Desert Island and Acadia National Park, third revised edition*. Southwest Harbor, Maine: Beech Hill Publishing Company. 41 pp.

18 February

[i] The idea for what has become Maine Huts & Trails was first envisioned in the 1970s. Today, the not-for-profit that is Maine Huts & Trails weaves a quilt of public, private, and tribal lands, some in conservation easements, some owned outright. Depending on the season, you can ski, hike, snowshoe, or mountain bike hut-to-hut. Currently, there are four lodges, but the grand vision includes adding more, ultimately making it possible to travel from the Mahoosuc Mountain Range near the New Hampshire border to Moosehead Lake in north-central Maine, all while staying at huts inspired by those of the European Alps. For more information, or to become a member and support this organization, browse their website at www.mainehuts.org.

[ii] During the evening of 18 February 2018, hours after seeing the bird, sitting at a trestle table in the Stratton Brook Hut, while writing this account, I used the then accepted common name of Gray Jay. However, a few months later, the American Ornithological Society accepted a proposal to change the name to Canada Jay. This see-sawing of names—it was Canada Jay from early the 1800s through 1957, Gray Jay from 1957—2018, and now it is Canada Jay once again—can certainly make for confusion. Although I have chosen to leave the day's accounting as I wrote it, please note that the name is now officially Canada Jay.

iii Natalie and I have long been year-round outdoor adventurers. During the winter, we look for more than a ski center experience, we want to be off the beaten track, camping or staying in cabins. Gaspésie National Park offers a variety of weeklong ski circuits. On our particular loop, all of the huts were named in French after local birds: *La Mésange*, the Chickadee; *La Paruline*, the Warbler; *Le Pluvier*, the Plover; *L'Hirondelle*, the Swallow; and *Le Huard*, the Loon.

23 February

i Despite what the bird feeding industry might have you believe, hummingbirds do not need colored water—there is some science that suggests the dyes used in coloring water for hummingbirds might not be beneficial at all. Instead, save yourself some money and make a simple sugar water solution. Mix one part sugar in three parts water in a pot and boil for five minutes. This kills off most of the bacteria and will extend the life of your solution a few days. Let it cool to room temperature and then either fill your feeder or store in your refrigerator. I make it in two-quart batches so that there is always some ready in my refrigerator.

Beginning late April, I keep my hummingbird feeders filled. It is always a joy to see them return. Consider keeping a journal, noting seasonal milestones, such as when the first hummingbird comes to your feeder. Over the years, you can see if you observe any change in their arrival dates.

25 February

i Ed Hawkes is, by far, the finest bird-carver I know. He can draw up plans for a bird, take a block of basswood or tupelo or jelutong, draw up plans, lay them out, cut out a blank, and carve the bird, bringing out the finest feather details, down to the level of individual barbs, and paint all manner of complex shades and iridescent hues. When he is finished, stand back ten feet to consider the bird: you would swear it was about to take flight. To learn more about nationally award-winning master bird-carver Ed Hawkes, or to order a customized carving, browse his website: www.hawkescarvings.com.

ii The Conservation Reserve Program falls under the auspices of the U.S. Department of Agriculture. Through this program, which has its roots with the Agriculture Act of 1956, farmers are paid to take farmland out of production in order to create habitat that reduces soil erosion and improves water quality. Among the intended results are the benefits for all manner of wildlife, from pollinators to migratory birds. For more information on the Conservation Reserve Program, browse www.fsa.usda.gov/programs-and-services/conservation-programs/conservation-reserve-program or www.nrcs.usda.gov/wps/portal/nrcs/detail/national/programs/?cid=stelprdb1041269 (both accessed 06 May 2020).

ⁱⁱⁱ The North American Waterfowl Management Plan was established in 1986 between the U.S. and Canada (Mexico became a signatory nation in 1994) aiming to conserve waterfowl and their habitats through the combined efforts of stakeholder federal, state, and provincial agencies and non-profit organizations. For more information on the North American Waterfowl Management Plan, browse www.fws.gov/birds/management/bird-management-plans/north-american-waterfowl-management-plan.php or www.nawmp.org (both accessed 06 May 2020).

02 March

ⁱ I don't mean to downplay the role of human-driven global warming. This is, most assuredly, the biggest catastrophe to hit Earth since a meteorite crashed into the Yucatán Peninsula sixty-five million years ago. Any inference to climate change should not be construed as a political statement; rather, it is a scientific fact (the science is in near unanimity on this point). For a good starting point to learn more about our current global climate catastrophe, browse the website for the Intergovernmental Panel on Climate Change (www.ipcc.ch) and search for the "assessment report." The links section is also quite good.

06 March

ⁱ According to their website, Maine Coastal Islands National Wildlife Refuge "contains more than sixty-one offshore islands and four coastal parcels, totaling more than 8,200 acres. The complex spans more than 250 miles of Maine coastline" (for more information about Maine Coastal Islands National Wildlife Refuge, browse www.fws.gov/refuge/maine_coastal_islands). These islands are closed to the public during the nesting season, 01 April through 31 August, but can be viewed from the water—there are a number of tour operators up and down the coast offering nature tours to these islands. In Hancock County, tour operators include Acadian Nature Cruises (www.acadianboattours.com), Acadia Puffin Cruise (www.acadiapuffincruise.com), and Bar Harbor Whale Watch (www.barharborwhales.com).

ⁱⁱ Old Soaker is little more than a slip of rocky island offering a modicum of protection to Newport Cove and Sand Beach. With a name like Old Soaker, it should come as no surprise that it gets recycled. For instance, NASA geologist Dr. Katie Stack Morgan, drawing on memories from childhood visits to Acadia National Park and vicinity, has been attributing Maine place names to Martian features, including appelling 'Old Soaker' to a four-foot rocky slab showing apparent water wear (other Acadian names transposed to Mars include 'Fresh Meadow,' 'Gilley Field,' and 'North Bubble'). Closer to home, 'Old Soaker' is the name given to Atlantic Brewing Company's Root Beer and Blueberry Soda. If you haven't tried them, do. Made in Bar Harbor, they are both delicious. Just ask any local kid.

iii *Groundhog Day* is a 1993 Harold Ramis film starring Bill Murray and Andie Mac-Dowell. Murray is self-absorbed newsman who keeps reliving the same day over and over until he finally learns humility and compassion.

09 March

i For an excellent article about the Great Auk, browse www.smithsonianmag.com/smithsonian-institution/with-crush-fisherman-boot-the-last-great-auks-died-180951982, accessed 09 March 2018.

ii In the natural world, counter-shading is a common form of camouflage. Think dolphins, any number of fish species, and a large array of birds, especially songbirds, where the upperparts are darker and the underparts whiter. This makes good sense when you think about it in terms of being preyed upon. When your upperparts are darker, predators looking down upon you see your dark back against a background that is varying degrees of dark—earth, forests, the inky depths. Likewise, when predators are below and looking up, white bellies tend to get lost in the white, or brightness, of the sky.

23 March

i Fun fact: Snow-mobiles are what people, mostly in the Lower 48, ride for recreation. In Alaska, they ride snow-machines, which are a mode of transportation. Same machine, different purpose.

ii Feng-Hsu, Lin, Laurie A. Graham, Robert L. Campbell, and Peter L. Davies. 2007. Structural modeling of snow flea antifreeze protein. *Biophysical Journal.* 92(5): 1717-1723. This article is available for free online at www.cell.com/biophysj/pdf/S0006-3495(07)70979-7.pdf, accessed 23 March 2018.

26 March

i The Downeast Chapter of Maine Audubon is also referred to as Downeast Audubon. They are the chapter focusing on Hancock County and offer a wonderful array of programs and field trips! Browse their website at www.downeastaudubon.org.

ii When naming hybrids, the usual nomenclature is to place an "x" between the two species, linking them, as in Mallard x American Black Duck.

30 March

i I have only found a few Killdeer nests in my life. When the adult is sitting on eggs, incubating them, their camouflage is so complete as to make them nearly invisible. The first Killdeer nest I ever found (and I have only found a handful in my life) was in the gravel of a parking space at my best friend's family KOA Campground. I saw the broken-wing act and knew a nest was nearby. So, Fred and I sat at a picnic table, as motionless as a pair of twelve-year-olds can be. Apparently, that was good enough. Soon enough, the adult's wing "healed," it flew off, describing a large arc, landing in the gravel not ten feet from us. It then wandered over to the merest depression in the rocks and settled down. It was on its nest! And we never saw it!

02 April

i Cornell Lab of Ornithology has useful information about American Kestrels, including plans for building your own nest box. For more information, browse www.nestwatch.org/learn/all-about-birdhouses/birds/american-kestrel.

You can also learn more about American Kestrels through the American Kestrel Partnership, a collaboration with the Peregrine Fund. In addition to their recommended plans for building nest boxes, they have detailed information on monitoring the development of your kestrel family and sharing the data through citizen science portals. For more information, browse kestrel.peregrinefund.org.

04 April

i As of March 2020, *Birds of North America* was replaced by *Birds of the World* (www.birdsoftheworld.org) All of the species originally listed in *Birds of North America* have robust content; whereas content is less thorough for species from more remote parts of the world, species that are newly discovered, rediscovered, or split from another species; or species that are lesser known. These accounts may have an editor's note stating "This is a shorter format account, originally published in [Handbook of Birds of the World] Alive. Please consider contributing your expertise to update and expand this account." This is a prime opportunity for a student of ornithology to contribute to our understanding of birds by authoring a species account.

10 April

i The anadromous Alewife (anadromous means they swim from the ocean, up freshwater rivers, to spawn) is a cold-water fish in the herring family. It was once an abundant and important food source for both wildlife and people. By some accounts, it was the most numerous of all the migratory fishes—in fact, it was so abundant that Native Americans used Alewives as fertilizer. Here in New England, their numbers were drastically reduced over the centuries by a combination of overfishing, damming of nearly every one of their spawning rivers and streams, and pollution.

In Somesville, Somes Stream has been dammed since the 1700s, used to power a variety of grist mills, sawmills, and woolen (or carding) mills. According to the website of the Somes-Meynell Wildlife Sanctuary, "Runs did not entirely disappear, because some fish were caught below and released above the dams by citizens interested in preserving an alewife run." At some point in time, fishways, a type of artificial rapids (also called a fish ladder), were installed, enabling Alewives to return to their Somes Pond spawning grounds without further assistance. Alas, these eventually fell into a state of disrepair.

With the 2005 restoration of the fishway, spawning in Somes Pond resumed. In just ten years, the number of returning Alewives has gone from zero to over 35,000! Today, you can watch the Alewives make their age-old spawning runs from early May through early June.

For more information, browse www.downeastfisheriestrail.org/sites/somesville-mill-pond or www.somesmeynell.org/?page_id=125. You may also volunteer as an Alewife counter with Somes-Meynell Wildlife Sanctuary.

20 April

[i] In late winter or early spring, often mid- to late-April, when temperatures range above about 40° Fahrenheit and there is a big rain over night, conditions are just right for amphibians to venture forth in search of vernal pools in which to spawn: this is a Big Night. As the small, delicate vertebrates are in the process of crossing roads in their search, all-too-often they become flattened fauna. This is where conscientious citizens come in. Don a reflective vest, grab a good flashlight (make sure you have fresh batteries), and look for a likely spot where amphibians will cross the road. You can speed them along by picking them up and carrying them across this dangerous obstacle. Of course, be sure to watch out for cars yourself.

[ii] Robertson, Bruce A., Rich MacDonald, Jeffrey V. Wells, Peter J. Blancher, & Louis Bevier. 2011. Chapter 7: Boreal migrants in winter bird communities. In: *Birds of Boreal Forests: Linking Reproduction, Movements and Conservation in the Western Hemisphere* (ed. J. Wells), Studies in Avian Biology 41, University of California Press. Pp. 85-94.

[iii] We visited Chichicaxtle 07 October 2006. You can browse hawk-watch data for this site, as well as others across North America, at the website for Hawk Migration Association of North America at www.hmana.org. The 01 October 2009 issue of *BirdWatching* has a good article about bird-watching in general and hawk-watching specifically, available online at www.birdwatchingdaily.com/featured-stories/destinations/birding-veracruz.

Endnotes

24 April

[i] There is much debate over the use of audio playback to attract birds. The thinking goes something like this: Songbirds (primarily the males) sing to attract mates and to defend territory against encroaching males of the same species. When a bird hears another male singing in too close proximity, it goes off to "fight" with it by using its own song, something akin to dueling banjos. Eventually, one of the males will back down—usually the interloper—while the winner, reinforced in the knowledge that it has the better song, goes back to tend to its family.

Use of audio playback, when used without discretion, can cause resident males to be the ones to back down and leave their territory. This then places all of the burden of raising chicks solely on the female. Studies have shown that when female songbirds lose a mate, whether to predation or being chased away by another song, they have a much lower chance of fledging young. Alas, far too many people are unaware of the impact they can have by using audio playback indiscriminately.

Personally, on the infrequent occasion when I use audio playback, I use it quite sparingly. For nesting birds, I don't use it at all. For sensitive, threatened, or endangered species, I don't use it. Wherever it is prohibited (such as all Federal lands, including Acadia National Park), I don't use it. And I don't use audio playback in areas where there is an abundance of birder traffic. When I DO use audio playback, I will broadcast one or two iterations of a song. And that is it! Either I find the bird or not.

25 April

[i] H. Roy Ivor is attributed this quote in his correspondence to Wendell Taber. In short, the rabbit hole that is the backstory to this quote begins with Arthur Cleveland Bent. Bent (1866—1954) is best known to students of ornithology as the author of the encyclopedic twenty-one-volume *Life Histories of North American Birds*, published one volume at a time, beginning in 1919 and completed posthumously in 1968. Bent readily took on numerous collaborators to make this the best possible work that it could be.

Toward the end of his life, Bent realized he would not finish his opus and so approached the Nuttall Ornithological Club, based at Harvard University in Cambridge, Massachusetts, about seeing the work through completion. This was a responsibility they were only too happy to accept.

In his final years, Bent appointed his friend, Wendell Taber, as his literary executor. It was in correspondence with Taber that Ivor wrote of the courtship song of the male Rose-breasted Grosbeak as being "so entrancingly beautiful that words cannot describe it."

To read this quote in context, as well as Bent's complete account of the Rose-breasted Grosbeak, turn to: Bent, Arthur Cleveland and Austin, Oliver L., Jr. 1968. *Life Histories of North American Cardinals, Grosbeaks, Buntings, Towhees, Finches, Sparrows, and Allies* (three parts). Bulletin of the United States National Museum No. 237. (See page 38 in Part I for the quote.)

---

29 April

ⁱ eBird has many wonderful features. In addition to serving as an internet-based application to track your bird observations and share them with ornithologists to enhance our understanding of bird populations and distribution, there are Bird Alerts. These are tools to let you know when a species you have never seen—a life bird—or a rare bird, or a new bird for the year has been reported. This can be customized regionally, down to the level of a county, with the ability to set up alerts to come hourly or daily, and is a feature for which you have to opt in. For this year, of course, I opted in with the hourly option, wanting to know when a bird for my Hancock County year-list may turn up.

01 May

ⁱ The International Migratory Bird Treaty Act of 1918 has been a cornerstone of American environmental jurisprudence, affording protection to all species of birds that migrate. It came about in response to the unregulated millinery trade where market hunters shot birds indiscriminately for the fashion industry and for the market. The Act banned shooting any bird, or possessing any part of any bird, that migrates (subsequent laws established regulations for hunting species such as waterfowl). Thanks to this pioneering and forward-thinking law, many bird species have been saved from the brink of extinction. Unfortunately, in recent decades, it has been under attack by some Republican lawmakers seeking to weaken its protective restrictions.

02 May

ⁱ In the early days of North American settlement by Europeans—in fact, well into the 1800s—many species were named for their resemblance to their European counterpart. Among birds, examples abound.

The American Robin was originally named just the single word Robin as it shared a red breast with the Robin of Europe. Of course, the Robin of Europe is a flycatcher whereas the American namesake is a thrush; the American Robin is also a much larger bird, to boot.

Blackbirds are another example. In Europe, the Blackbird is a thrush in the Family Turdidae. Watch its behavior closely and, if you didn't know better, you could be forgiven for thinking it is an American Robin, albeit a highly melanistic one (melanism is the condition of having an over-abundance of pigment, resulting in a much darker appearance). The Blackbird and the American Robin are both in the Genus *Turdus*, both have yellow bills, and both often forage on the ground. Meanwhile, the North American blackbirds—which include Red-winged Blackbird, Brown-headed Cowbird, Rusty Blackbird, and Common Grackle—are much more recently evolved. They are in the Family Icteridae and are exclusively a New World family.

A final example is the confusing use of the term "warbler." European warblers are in a number of different families, all of which are essentially flycatchers, while, the warblers of the New World are more appropriately called wood-warblers and are all in the single family Parulidae. And yes, the former Black-and-white Treecreeper (now Black-and-white Warbler) is from one of the more recently evolved families of birds, the Parulidae.

03 May

[i] Pierre Dugua de Monts, Sieur de Monts, was granted exclusive rights to colonize French lands in North America by King Henry in 1603. King Henry also made Dugua Lieutenant General of Acadia (which took in the region that today is the Canadian Maritimes) and New France.

[ii] This was our version of today's smartphone loaded with birding apps. If you want to see what a vintage 1960s solid state, hand-crank, portable record player looked like, search the internet for "Macy's Supre-Macy Solid State Portable Record Player" to get an idea.

07 May

[i] Fusiform is the term applied to objects shaped like a spindle. An excellent example would be the shape of the hull of a racing sailboat when looking from above: the bow and stern are pointed with both widening toward the middle.

[ii] You can read Steven Latta's paper about this very subject: Steven C. Latta, Heather A. Gamper, and James R. Tietz. (2001.) "Revising the convergence hypothesis of avian use of honeydew: evidence from Dominican subtropical dry forest." Oikos. 93(2): 250-259. The paper is available online at http://0310fcb.netsolhost.com/cons/Latta/23_Oikos.pdf.

[iii] MacArthur, Robert H. (1958). 'Population ecology of some warblers of northeastern coniferous forests. *Ecology*. 39(4): 599-619.
[iv] Orb-weaver spiders are cosmopolitan, with over 3,000 species found worldwide. They are typically the spiders that build the ubiquitous wheel-shaped webs found around our homes, as well in nearby fields and forests. According to Wikipedia, "'orb' was previously used in English to mean 'circular'".

09 May

[i] Big Heath is a 420-acre plateau peatland located in Acadia National Park just north of Ship Harbor and Wonderland. For more information about Big Heath, refer to page 240 in *Bogs of the Northeast*, by Charles W. Johnson and published in

1985. This book is a good addition to the library of any student of natural history. It is also available online at Google Books (the URL is too long to list, so just do an internet search for the book).

10 May

i This is birding slang for the five smallest sandpipers—Baird's, Least, White-rumped, Semipalmated, and Western, all members of the genus *Calidris*—the "peeps."

12 May

i Although I have been unable to uncover when the name changed from Black and Yellow Warbler to Magnolia Warbler, anyone wishing to learn more about some history of bird names may wish to read: Trotter, Spencer. (1909). 'An inquiry into the history of the current English names of North American land birds.' *Auk*. 26(4): 346-363. (Available online at sora.unm.edu/node/8978, accessed 12 May 2018.)

13 May

i In September, seven months after the Hamilton Pond dam failed, it was rebuilt. Once again, the Bar Harbor Fire Department has a water source for fire-fighting in the Hamilton Station area of Bar Harbor. And winter sports enthusiasts regained a favorite ice-skating and fishing pond. Although I will miss the shorebird surplus, rebuilding the dam was a good thing for the Bar Harbor community.

15 May

i According to their website (www.birdercertification.org), "Birder Certification Online is a project of the Cofrin Center for Biodiversity at the University of Wisconsin-Green Bay, with funding and collaboration from the Wisconsin Department of Natural Resources, the Wisconsin Bird Conservation Initiative, the National Park Service, and the U.S. Fish & Wildlife Service." This is a rigorous assessment of your bird identification skills that is based on "bird conservation regions." The tests are based on biogeographic regions. Within a region—the region encompassing Maine also spans most of New Hampshire, Vermont, and the Adirondack and Tug Hill regions of northern New York—tests require you to identify all the birds within an audio landscape. This test is hard, REALLY hard! The first time I took the test, I scored 82%. As you might imagine, that was a blow to my ego.

Endnotes

17 May

[i] Carroll Tyson and James Bond, in their 1941 *Birds of Mt. Desert Island, Acadia National Park, Maine*, noted that Cape May Warbler were known to breed in Hancock County, writing: "Summer resident: some years not uncommon in the extreme southern part of Mt. Desert Island, but rare elsewhere: also breeds on the mainland (e.g., Oak Point and near Bucksport): nest and eggs, taken June 15 [1936], now in collection of Museum of Acadia National Park."

Ralph Long, writing in his 1987 *Native Birds of Mount Desert Island and Acadia National Park*, noted that on "June 7, 1981 a nest containing six eggs was found forty-five feet above the ground in a Balsam Fir. The nest was about two feet below the crown, typical for a Cape May. Look for this warbler in tall "cathedral" shaped spruce not far from the ocean."

Tyson and Bond's reference to the "extreme southern part of Mt. Desert Island" makes sense. Of the entirety of Mount Desert Island, this section has some of the best remaining examples of primeval boreal forest today. And that would have been the case in their day, too. Long's record of breeding is the last for which I have knowledge. Between conversion of habitat and the warming climate, the Cape May Warbler's range has most certainly shifted considerably north.

[ii] Bond, James. (1937), 'The Cape May Warbler in Maine.' *Auk*. 54(3): 306-308. This article is available on-line for free at sora.unm.edu/node/17390.

22 May

[i] I once asked Glen Mittelhauser, executive director of the Maine Natural History Observatory, for a definition of a wetland; he said to take your shoes off and walk into the area in question: "If your socks get wet, it is a wetland."

04 June

[i] Today's Road Scholar was founded in 1975 as Elderhostel and has followed a mission of continuing education through travel for people over fifty years of age ever since. In the early 1990s, I led my first Elderhostel trip, a five-day canoeing venture through the wilderness of the St. Regis Canoe Area in the Adirondack Mountains of northern New York. More recently, I started working with Road Scholar, occasionally leading or lecturing tours to numerous regions, including along the Downeast Maine, New England and Canadian Maritime coast; Great Lakes; and Norway. Today's Road Scholar leads tours to every continent, on every ocean, and to over 150 countries. For more information on Road Scholar, browse their website at www.roadscholar.org.

[ii] Counter-shading is a form of camouflage found in many species of animals. Among birds, it is particularly prevalent in seabirds; among them, especially auks

and penguins. It is also found in species that have to worry about being seen from both above and below. Raptorial predators are often white below so that they blend in with the clouded sky when prey looks up and dark above such that they do not prominently stand out when living food looks to the trees or the ground. This rule of color patterning—dark above, light below—also applies to many birds that spend significant time flying, species such as swallows.

iii For more information about Blue-winged Warblers, including their vocalizations, browse www.allaboutbirds.org/guide/Blue-winged_Warbler.

10 June

i Great Pond Mountain Wildlands is a 4,700-acre preserve surrounding Great Pond Mountain and managed by the not-for-profit Great Pond Mountain Conservation Trust. This wonderful preserve is open to the public for all manner of outdoor recreation: birding, hiking, bicycling, cross-country skiing, and more. For more information, browse their website at www.greatpondtrust.org.

ii For more information on the Cape May Bird Observatory's and New Jersey Audubon's biggest fundraising event—the World Series of Birding—held annually since 1984, browse www.worldseriesofbirding.org.

iii Nightjars and goatsuckers are one and the same. Nightjars, or goatsuckers, are the family of birds that include local breeders such as Common Nighthawk and Eastern Whip-poor-will. It also includes non-local species such as Chuck-will's-widow. When nightjars were first described by science, the genus was *Caprimulgus*, which comes from the Latin—*Caper* = goat and *Mulego* = to milk—that translates to goatsucker.

So, where did "goatsucker" come from? Nightjars feed on insects at night, often resting on the ground between feedings. Over time, nightjars learned that insects are drawn to livestock and so go to perch near where their insectivorous food can is concentrated: at the feet of cows and goats. Whether some poor herdsman saw a nightjar fly up from near one of his goats, or maybe even saw one snatch an insect off a goat's teat, the myth that this wide-mouthed bird drinks milk from goats and sheep long persisted and eventually translated into their scientific and common names.

03 July

i Egevang, Carsten, Iain J. Stenhouse, Richard A. Phillips, Aevar Petersen, James W. Fox, and Janet R.D. Silk. (2010). 'Tracking of Arctic Terns *Sterna paradisaea* reveals longest animal migration.' *Proceedings of the National Academy of Sciences*. 107(5): 2078-2081.

Endnotes

---

09 July

[i] Aldo Leopold. (1949). *A Sand County Almanac and Sketches Here and There*. Oxford University Press. See p. 137.

[ii] See www.allaboutbirds.org/guide/Evening_Grosbeak, accessed 01 September 2018.

10 July

[i] Search for this title online and you should be able to find a site where you can watch it.

13 July

[i] The reality is that Carrion Crows can readily be visually differentiated from Hooded Crows. In the case of my exchange with Garrison, the humor would not have played out so well if I had not taken some license with the facts. As for "pinion feathers," those are the outermost of the primary flight feathers. (Some people use "pinion" to refer to all of the primary flight feathers—depending on the species, these number between nine and sixteen.)

19 July

[i] Mariners employ units such as knots and fathoms and nautical miles and a whole host of other salty nomenclature. In the case of distance, 1 nautical mile = 1.15 statute miles (the mileage we employ when we drive our cars). Partly out of tradition, and partly because of practicality, these units actually make sense when you learn about the latitudinal and longitudinal coordinate system segmenting the globe—on a chart or map, one nautical mile is equal to one minute of longitude.

[ii] Sooty Shearwaters nest in burrows on Oceanian islands. The chicks are fed and fed until they have consumed so much that they are too big to leave their subterranean confines. At this point, the parents abandon them to their own devices. For the chicks, this means living off their fat until they can make an exit. An advantage of this means of parenting is that while the chicks are living off their fat reserves, they are also growing and molting into their adult plumage. By the time they leave the burrow, they are ready for a life flying at sea.

30 July

[i] Located near Cape Neddick in southern Maine, the 133-foot Boon Island Light is the tallest in Maine. The height of lights is generally measured as the elevation of the focal plane of the light beacon above sea level at mean high tide. While Sequin Light is higher (180 feet), it is located in a tower atop a bluff, whereas Boon Island Light and Petit Manan Light both rise from near sea level.

27 August

[i] Depending on how you count (for instance, whether you are taking your number at high tide or low), estimates for the number of islands along the coast of Maine range from 3,166 to over 4,600; although that higher number likely includes every emergent rocky ledge. In either case, not bad for a coastline that measures 223 miles in a straight-line distance from Kittery in the southwest to Lubec in the northeast. Of course, if you take in every fractal curve of the coast, it suddenly stretches to nearly 3,500 miles; and over 5,000 miles when factoring in the shore-line of all the islands, too.

[ii] As a guide, my number one priority is the safety of my guests. During our initial contact, I always make it clear that no matter our plan, it is only tentative—the weather has the final say in where we go paddling.

[iii] See www.allaboutbirds.org/guide/Little_Gull, accessed 05 October 2018.

01 September

[i] The acronym for "radar"—Radio Detection And Ranging—has come into such common usage it is no longer capitalized. As an interesting, and tangentially related aside, early "sonar" (SOund Navigation And Ranging—a technique using propagation of sound underwater to detect objects—is another acronym to have entered common usage) technicians reported unearthly sounds that eventually were found to be the song of whales.

[ii] There is an excellent scientific article introducing the topic of nocturnal flight calls, blending some background history with contemporary technology: Evans, William R. (2005). 'Monitoring avian night flight calls—the new century ahead. *Passenger Pigeon.* 67(1): 15-24.

[iii] A good starting point to learn more about nocturnal flight calls is www.oldbird.org. There is also a listserv—www.northeastbird-ing.com/NFC_RULES.htm—providing a superb (if esoteric) forum for further discussions on this topic.

Endnotes

14 September

[i] When the sun is below the horizon, it can still cast visible light. Mariners have long used this in estimating time; meanwhile, astronomers have assigned more precision. Nautical twilight is when the sun is between 6° and 12° below the horizon. Civil twilight is that brief time between nautical twilight and when the sun crests the horizon. (These same conditions apply to the evening, too, just in reverse.) For more information, browse www.timeanddate.com/astronomy/different-types-twilight.html.

[ii] While the numbers of South Polar Skua is not known with any great precision, worldwide population estimates range between 10,000 and 20,000 individuals.

11 October

[i] Leaving the mainland across the causeway, you first come to Acadia National Park's Thompson Island. As a result of the manner in which the road was laid out long ago, Thompson Island melds seamlessly into Mount Desert Island. Locals (me included) tend to conflate Thompson Island with Mount Desert Island.

[ii] Ruddy Duck eggs look pretty much like those of most any other species of duck except for their pebbly texture. Perhaps that is why Phillips claimed they were "unique in appearance".

[iii] Phillips, J.C. (1926). *A Natural History of the Ducks*. Four volumes. Mineola, NY: Houghton Mifflin Co., Boston and New York. (Reprinted 1986 as two volumes, Dove Publications.)

[iv] Ruddy Ducks are divers. The fuller quote, helping to explain the taste, is that Ruddies are "known eaters of clams, fish, and other animal bits—all of which make them taste like low tide on a hot day".

[v] Hank Shaw. (06 December 2010). 'Ruddy Ducks: The original butterball turkey.' *The Atlantic*. Available online at www.theatlantic.com/health/archive/2010/12/ruddy-ducks-the-original-butterball-turkey/67472, accessed 11 October 2018.

17 October

[i] William "Bill" Evans is an expert in night flight calls. For more information on Bill, refer to my discussion on him and Old Bird, his not-for-profit organization, written 01 September.

[ii] www.xeno-canto.org is a website for sharing avian audio recordings. This is an excellent resource for the student of bird songs and calls.

---

24 October

[i] See the 04 June endnote for a reminder of Road Scholar, the organization and its mission.

[ii] In many natural communities, fire is a part of the order of things. In some cases, it is a means for cycling nutrients. Fire can propagate seeds. It can eliminate non-native species, giving a boost to better-adapted native species. Wildfire can also be devastating. All too often, fires trace their origins to us, whether intentional or accidental, larcenous or part of a landscape management plan. In the case of the Great Fire of '47, much has been written, both from the societal impacts and the manner in which it greatly affected local ecology.

12 November

[i] Population estimate per Dr. Sean Todd, Steven K. Katona Chair in Marine Sciences, College of the Atlantic, Bar Harbor, Maine.

[ii] In recent decades, we have learned that Basque fishermen long plied their trade seasonally in the northwest Atlantic, especially off the coast of Labrador. A number of French historians have claimed that Basque, as well as Breton and Norman, fishermen and whalers were in Labrador by the late 1300s! (For instance, see J.-P. Proulx. (1993). 'Basque whaling in Labrador in the 16th century.' *Newfoundland Studies.* 10: 260-286.)

Checklist

[i] Back on 18 February, when I observed my first Canada Jay of the year, its official name was still Gray Jay. A few months later, in May, the American Ornithological Society's Committee on Classification and Nomenclature of North and Middle American Birds accepted a proposal from Canadian ornithologists to restore the name to Canada Jay. This reflected a name that had been used for over 100 years until 1957. This decision was made official with publication of the annual supplement published in *The Auk*: Chesser, R. Terry, Kevin J. Burns, Carla Cicero, Jon L. Dunn, Andrew W. Kratter, Irby J. Lovette, Pamela C. Rasmussen, J.V. Remsen, Jr., Douglas F. Stotz, Benjamin M. Winter, and Kevin Winker. (2018). 'Fifty-ninth supplement to the American Ornithological Society's *Check-list of North American Birds.*' *The Auk.* 135(3): 798-813.

You can download a PDF of the complete article at https://academic.oup.com/auk/article/135/3/798/5148958 (accessed 06 May 2020). Navigate to page 807 to read the bit on the jay's name change.

CPSIA information can be obtained
at www.ICGtesting.com
Printed in the USA
LVHW020834251121
704426LV00002B/297